BASIC Programming

AN INSTRUCTIONAL MANUAL

B. J. HOLMES, B.Sc., M.Sc., Cert.Ed.

Barry Holmes *is a Senior Lecturer in Computer Studies at Oxford Polytechnic. He has taught computer programming for a number of different examinations, and has used the BASIC language extensively with a wide range of computers, applications and college courses.*

D.P. PUBLICATIONS
12 Romsey Road, Eastleigh,
Hants. SO5 4AL
1982

ACKNOWLEDGEMENTS.

The author wishes to express his thanks to the following:

Mr. C.S. French of Hatfield Polytechnic and Mr. P. Harrison of Hendon College of Further Education both of whom read and checked the manuscript and offered numerous helpful comments and suggestions.

International Computers Limited for permission to use photographs in chapter one. Commodore Business Machines Ltd. for permission to use a photograph in chapter one.

M. Fisher, Training Manager; International Computers Limited for permission to use flowchart examples in chapter two.

Messrs. E.C. Oliver and R.J. Chapman for their permission to use material from their book Data Processing.

The European Computer Manufacturers Association for permission to reproduce Standard ECMA—55, free copies of which are available from:

ECMA, 114 Rue du Rhone, CH—1204 Geneva, Switzerland.

Associated Examining Board [A.E.B.]
The British Computer Society.
City and Guilds of London Institute.
East Anglian Examinations Board.
Oxford and Cambridge Schools Examination Board.
Oxford Delegacy of Local Examinations.
University of Cambridge Local Examinations Syndicate for permission to reproduce past paper examination questions.

ISBN 0 905435 25 7

Copyright B.J. HOLMES © 1982

Reprinted with corrections 1983

Printed in Great Britain by
Spottiswoode Ballantyne Ltd,
Colchester, Essex.

Preface

AIMS OF THE MANUAL.

1. The primary aim of the manual is to teach the BASIC programming language to a depth sufficient to give confidence to any student requiring a knowledge of programming for:

    a. G.C.E. Computer Studies — 'O', 'O/A' and 'A' level examinations.

    b. City and Guilds programming examinations including 746 and 747.

    c. BEC/TEC National and Higher National Awards.

    d. First year undergraduate level.

    e. British Computer Society Part I examinations in programming.

    f. Anybody faced with programming computers for the first time ie. Accountants, Business Studies Students and 'home computer' enthusiasts.

NEED.

2. The need, as seen by the author, was for a book which:

    a. Taught good programming habits, through "top-down" design and "structured" coding.

    b. Included the documentation of programs.

    c. Familiarised the reader with the fundamentals of the methodology quickly and used that as a foundation to develop the more complex programming ideas and skills.

    d. Was packed with well tried and tested exercises with answers, taken from a wide variety of applications.

    e. Used a Standard for BASIC so that the reader was not confused by trying to deal with dialects of the language within the text.

    f. Assumed that the reader had **no** prior knowledge of programming.

APPROACH.

3.   a. The manual has been written as part of the tried and tested Instructional Manual Series in which introductions to each chapter tell the reader what they will find within that chapter. New material is introduced in manageable quantities with fully worked examples. Self testing is made easy through exercises at the end of chapters; answers to which are found in appendix I.

    b. The manual is well suited as a course text book with answers to selected questions (prefixed by *) provided in a separate lecturers supplement. A selection of project questions designed to test the readers knowledge and skills of programming are to be found at the end of Part One and Part Two of the manual. The project questions vary considerably in their complexity and could be used for the coursework component of many examinations.

c. The manual has deliberately **not** been written for a specific computer. However, readers are recommended to have access to a computer that uses BASIC in order to test their answers to many of the programming questions.

d. The manual teaches the reader how to write computer programs using the BASIC language independently of any make of computer. However, since there are minor variations in the language from one computer to the next the reader is constantly reminded throughout the book to consult the computer manual for their computer if a difference in a BASIC statement is likely to exist.

APPENDICES.

4. Use has been made of appendices and the reader should note carefully the purpose of each.

a. Appendix I. Contains answers to questions set at the end of chapters.

b. Appendix II. Contains examination questions covering the programming requirements for the G.C.E. in Computer Studies/Science at 'O', 'O/A' and 'A' level; City and Guilds 746 and 747 and British Computer Society part I examinations. The material required to answer these questions is covered in depth in the text.

c. Appendix III. Part One of the book has been written around the ECMA Standard for Minimal BASIC. The ECMA standard is contained in this appendix and made reference to throughout the book.

d. Appendix IV. The specification of COMAL—80 is included in this appendix as an example of extended BASIC specifically designed to enhance structured programming.

e. Appendices V and VI cover a subset of the British Standard Flow-charting symbols and the ASCII and EBCDIC codes respectively.

HOW TO USE THE MANUAL.

5. a. You are advised to read the manual chapter by chapter since subsequent work often builds on topics covered earlier.

b. In order to build a firm foundation of knowledge you are advised to answer all the questions that appear at the end of a chapter. The use of a computer to aid your learning is desirable but **not** absolutely necessary. Answers are provided to questions that are the basis of key learning material.

c. For readers studying to C.S.E. and 'O' level Part One of the book should provide sufficient programming knowledge. Those readers who plan to study for examinations beyond 'O' level are recommended to read the whole book and be able to answer fluently the majority of the questions and projects.

d. For those readers who are not taking any examination, the contents of this book is sufficient for you to competently tackle many programming applications.

Notes on the First Reprint

6. a. The opportunity has been taken to correct typographical errors found in the First Edition.

b. Minor amendments to the First Edition have been made. The only significant amendment relates to testing the exit condition from a loop. Flowcharts and coding have been changed in this respect.

c. Appendix VII has been inserted and contains suggested Schemes of Work for the readers studying for one of the examinations mentioned in the aims of the manual.

B.J.H.
Feb. 1983

Contents

Part One

A progressive study of programming techniques using the European Computer Manufacturers Association [E.C.M.A.] standard for Minimal BASIC.

1 Basic in Context

INTRODUCTION.

1. a. The aim of this chapter is to give the reader an insight into the relationship between the various parts of a computer system and show how the BASIC language fits into the system as a whole.

b. The details found in this chapter are necessarily brief, and serve merely as an introduction to the subject of computing. The reader who has a particular interest in this material can pursue it further in other books in this series eg. Data Processing and Computer Science. The reader who is only interested in learning the BASIC language should try to gain familiarity with the computer terminology which this chapter explains. Progress in BASIC will be swifter with this knowledge but hindered without it.

WHAT ARE PROGRAMS AND DATA?

2. a. A program is a sequence of coded instructions for the computer to obey, and represents a logical solution to a problem.

b. Data is the name given to *facts* about activities eg. hours worked by employees, materials used on a job, number of items of stock, etc. Data is input to a computer, processed under the direction of a program into information that is output in the form of payroll, reports, etc.

WHAT IS A DIGITAL COMPUTER?

3. a. A digital computer is a machine capable of storing and obeying a program at a very high speed. An instruction is obeyed in one hundred millionth of one second. The term *digital* implies the manner in which data and programs are represented and handled within a machine.

b. The heart of a digital computer is the *central processing unit* (C.P.U.), which is divided into three areas.

    i. **Main Memory** — used to temporarily store programs and data. A computer can only obey programs that are stored in the main memory.

    ii. **Arithmetic & Logic Unit (A.L.U.)** — performs the processes of arithmetic and logical operations on data.

    iii. **Control Unit** — fetches the instructions from main memory, interprets and obeys them and co-ordinates the flow of data about the computer system.

c. The C.P.U. is connected to three other units — *Input, output and Secondary Storage.* (Fig. 1.1)

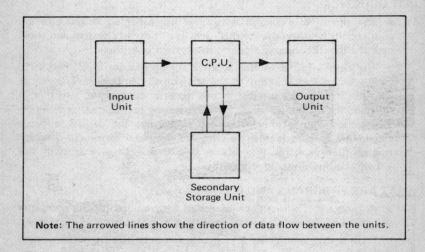

Note: The arrowed lines show the direction of data flow between the units.

Figure 1.1

d. The *peripheral* units to the C.P.U. have the following functions.

i.   **Input:** Data is prepared on an input medium, which is then read by the appropriate device and the data is transmitted to the C.P.U.

Examples of input devices.

Card reader (fig. 1.2) reads punched cards at the rate of up to 1000 cards per minute.

Paper tape reader (fig. 1.3) reads punched paper tape at the rate of up to 1000 characters per minute.

Visual display unit (V.D.U.) (fig. 1.4) allows information to be typed at the keyboard beneath the screen.

ii.   **Output:** Information is transmitted from the C.P.U. to the output device for printing or displaying.

Examples of output devices.

Lineprinter (fig. 1.5) prints characters simultaneously on a line at the rate of up to 2000 lines per minute.

Matrix printer (fig. 1.6) forms characters from dots on the page, prints at a slower speed than a lineprinter. Approximate rate of up to 120 characters per second.

Figure 1.2   Photograph by Courtesy of International Computers Limited.

Figure 1.3   Photograph by Courtesy of International Computers Limited.

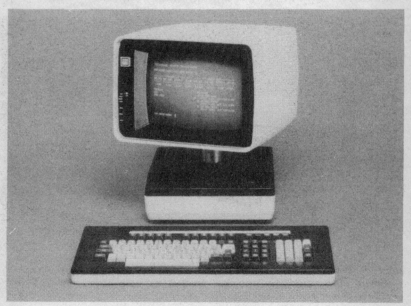

Figure 1.4   Photograph by Courtesy of International Computers Limited.

Figure 1.5   Photograph by Courtesy of International Computers Limited.

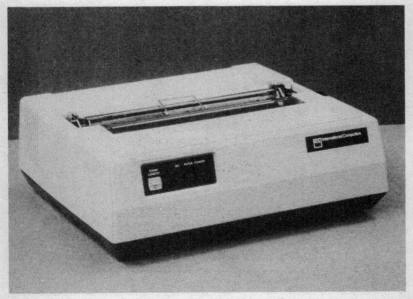

Figure 1.6   Photograph by Courtesy of International Computers Limited.

Figure 1.7   Photograph by Courtesy of International Computers Limited.

Figure 1.8   Photograph by Courtesy of International Computers Limited.

Figure 1.9   Photograph by Courtesy of Commodore Business Machines Ltd.

Visual display unit (fig. 1.4) displays information on a screen. A fast rate of display would be 960 characters per second.

iii.   **Secondary Storage:** Allows large quantities of information to be stored permanently on a secondary storage medium. The information can be input to or output from the C.P.U. thus in effect providing another input/output unit that can store a large quantity of information and transmit it very quickly.

Examples of secondary storage devices.

Magnetic tape unit (fig. 1.7) stores up to 40 million characters on one standard reel of tape and can transmit data at 160,000 characters per second.

Magnetic disc unit (fig. 1.8) stores up to 300 million characters on a multiple platter disc pack, and can transmit data at 312,000 characters per second.

Floppy disc unit (fig. 1.9) stores up to 800 thousand characters and can transmit data at 24,000 characters per second.

A typical microcomputer could have the following peripheral devices. (fig. 1.9).

Input: visual display unit
Output: matrix printer and visual display unit
Secondary storage: floppy disc unit.

iv. **Note.** When a *peripheral* device is connected directly to the C.P.U. it is said to be ON-LINE.

Input devices such as visual display units, teleprinters, paper tape punches and card punches can be used to prepare data on appropriate input media away from the computer. When used in this way the *peripheral* devices are said to be OFF-LINE.

HOW ARE PROGRAMS AND DATA STORED IN A COMPUTER?

4. Programs and data, are represented using binary codes. These are codes composed from the binary digits 0 and 1.

a. Within the main memory of the computer binary codes are physically represented by voltage levels eg. +5V represents binary digit 1, +1V represents binary digit 0.

Thus the binary code 10011101 would be represented by the waveform (fig. 1.10).

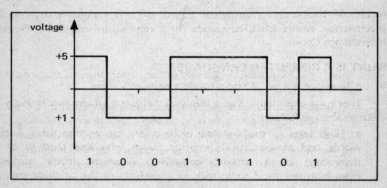

Figure 1.10

b. The physical representation of binary codes on peripheral devices depends upon the peripheral medium being used.

i. Paper tape and cards use the presence and absence of punched holes to represent binary digits.

ii. Magnetic tape and disc use the direction of magnetisation over very small areas of the medium to represent binary digits.

Example: Clockwise direction   represents 0.
Anticlockwise direction   represents 1.

iii. Programs and data are composed of *characters.* A character can be a letter of the alphabet, a digit or a special character such as < or ! Every character is assigned a unique binary code from either the EBCDIC (8 digit code) or ASCII (7 digit code) coding conventions (see Appendix VI). Computer manufacturers choose one coding convention for representing characters in their computers.

Figure 1.11 illustrates several characters and their representations in the two different codes.

CHARACTER	ASCII	EBCDIC
A	1000001	11000001
B	1000010	11000010
3	0110011	11110011
4	0110100	11110100
<	0111100	01001100
!	0100001	01011010

Figure 1.11

Note: ASCII stands for American Standard Corporation for Information Interchange, whilst EBCDIC stands for Extended Binary Coded Decimal Interchange Code.

WHAT IS A COMPUTER LANGUAGE?

5.   A language is a set of codes used to write programs.

There are essentially three levels of language which can broadly be distinguished as follows:

a. **High level** — the statements or codes are written using English words and mathematical notation. Such languages tend to be independent of a specific computer, however, many computer manufacturers tend to introduce a *dialect* of the language peculiar to their machine.

This example shows several BASIC statements in a program:—

```
10 READ X, Y
20 IF X > 10 THEN STOP
30 LET Z = X↑2 + Y↑2
```

b. **Low level** — the statements are written using mnemonic codes (ie. codes suggesting their meaning and thus easier to remember) to represent operations and addresses that relate to the main memory of a computer. Each low level language has instructions which correspond closely to the inbuilt operations of a specific computer. Hence, different computer models use a different low level language. Despite the many low level languages in existence they all adhere to the same broad principles of language structure.

Example of statements from a typical low level language.

> **LDA 5000**
> **ADD 6000**
> **STA 5000**

Where the language statements have the following meaning:

LDA 5000 Load a temporary storage area of the computer (accumulator) with the datum (data item) contained in memory address 5000.

ADD 6000 Add to the contents of the accumulator the contents of memory address 6000.

STA 5000 Store the contents of the accumulator at memory address 5000.

c. **Machine level** — program statements are coded into a binary format ready to be loaded directly into the main memory of a computer.

Example of machine level program.

> 11011101
> 10110011
> 01001100

Clearly this last form of computer language is quite incomprehensible without the aid of a reference manual describing what each code means.

DOES THE COMPUTER UNDERSTAND HIGH AND LOW LEVEL LANGUAGES?

6. Since the computer stores and uses information in a binary format the answer is no!

a. Program code written in either a high or low level language must be translated into a binary machine code that the computer recognises.

Translation is possible by using a computer manufacturer supplied program to translate high or low level language statements into binary machine code.

Translation to binary machine code from a high level language is by **compiler,** and from a low level language by **assembler.**

b. The translator (compiler or assembler) is stored in the main memory of the computer and uses the high or low level program as input data; the output data is the translated program in machine code format.

The resultant machine code must then be loaded into the main memory of the computer by a separate supplied program known as a **loader** before the computer can obey the program instructions.

c. An **interpreter** is a different type of translator. It does not convert the program language statements to a machine code format, but directs the C.P.U. to obey each program statement.

Whilst there are disadvantages associated with interpreting programs notably, slower execution speed and less program protection, it does offer the following advantages over compiled programs.

i.　There is no loading of a machine code program into memory, with the exception of the interpreter itself.

ii.　A high/low level program is stored in the main memory in a binary coded character format (not machine code) and can be obeyed immediately by the interpreter without having to be converted into machine code.

iii.　Many interpreters will inform of program errors during the process of obeying the program. This can be helpful during the initial stages of understanding how to program a computer and also at an advanced stage for speeding up the development time of a program.

iv.　Program statements can be changed and their effects noted without having to re-compile and load the program, thus again saving development time.

HOW ARE PROGRAMS PROCESSED?

7.　a. There are essentially three methods of using a computer to obey program instructions. However, the choice of method is dictated by such factors as:

i.　The nature of the application the program has been written for.

ii.　The configuration of the computer system being used.

b. **Interactive processing.** This allows a two-way communication between the user and the computer. If a program is being developed under such a system, changes can be made to the program and the effects immediately noted. This system of processing is common to all microcomputers.

c. **Batch processing.** Programs are put into a queue and processed one after another. The programmer cannot intervene during the processing to perform amendments to the program as was possible during interactive processing. In batch processing the program has to wait its turn before processing a batch of data. This necessarily means that there will be delay in obtaining the program's results, and consequently batch processing cannot be used when results are needed immediately for the purpose of controlling further actions of the computer system or its users.

A suitable application for batch processing would be running a payroll program, where for example details of hours worked by employees could be collected one week and processed as a batch to provide payslips the next week.

d. **Real-time processing.** Programs are processed in this manner when input data is changing continuously and the outcome of the process will affect the current situation the system is modelled on. A suitable application is an air-line reservation system where the number of seats bookable on a flight is changing constantly. Thus an enquiry about booking a seat on a flight must reflect the up to date vacancies on that flight.

WHAT ARE THE STAGES IN SOLVING A PROBLEM BY COMPUTER?

8. a. **Analysis** — this involves producing a documentary solution to a problem and includes such areas as feasibility study, system description and design and program specification.

b. **Programming** — this is the next step after analysis and involves implementing in program form the systems specification that the analyst has produced.

c. **Computer** — when a program has been tested and is error free to the satisfaction of the analyst, programmer and user it can then be implemented on the computer using data related to the problem. The solution to a problem will take the form of the output of information or results.

WHAT ARE THE TASKS OF A PROGRAMMER?

9. a. **Planning** — having either received or written a detailed specification of the solution to a problem the programmer should develop detailed program-level flow charts of the procedures to be carried out.

b. **Coding** — the programmer codes each stage of the flowchart using a suitable language and thus develops a computer program. The logic behind the solution to a problem having already been expressed in the flowchart.

c. **Testing** — once the program is coded it must be transferred to the computer through an input medium and tested using suitably exhaustive data. If errors are found in the program they must be corrected and the program re-tested until it is error-free.

WHY USE BASIC?

10. a. BASIC stands for **B**eginners **A**llpurpose **S**ymbolic **I**nstruction **C**ode. It was developed in 1964 as a means of teaching students how to program a computer quickly.

b. BASIC is a high level language that uses a very simple grammar, it is not only easy to write programs but also easy to understand what they are intended to do.

c. The language can be used to solve problems covering a wide range of applications.

d. Many small and inexpensive computers on the market use BASIC, therefore, one does not require a large expensive computer to study the principles of programming.

e. BASIC is an interpreted language which offers many benefits to the beginner. (BASIC is however sometimes handled by a compiler.)

f. BASIC is a language well suited to interactive processing.

g. Program development can be achieved in the minimum time and with the minimum effort.

2 Concepts of Flowcharting

INTRODUCTION.

1.   a. It is important that the reader is introduced to flowcharting before knowing about a computer language since the reader should:

     i.   Start to develop a specialised variety of mental effort and discipline that programming demands.

     ii.   Become fully conversant with the solution to a problem by charting the procedures.

     iii.   Provide a concise description of a solution without having to resort to a lengthy narrative.

    b. This chapter is concerned with the flowcharting of common every-day events since it is through these that the correct procedures of flowcharting can be achieved *without* the reader having a detailed knowledge of commercial/scientific applications, or a knowledge of a computer language.

DEFINITION OF A FLOWCHART.

2.   A flowchart is a diagram showing a sequence of events that describes the activities necessary in the solution to a problem. It is drawn using a set of conventional symbols, see appendix V, that represent various operations. The symbols are connected by arrowed lines to indicate the order in which activities will occur.

WORKED EXAMPLE.

3.   a. **Problem.** A man leaves work at the end of a day. If the time is 6.00 p.m. or earlier he travels home by bus. If the time is later than 6.00 p.m. he has a meal in a cafe before travelling home, by bus. Draw a flowchart of the man's activities.

    For the solution see figure 2.1.

Notes:

     i.   The flowchart is constructed from the **start** *terminal* symbol by representing each activity as stated in the problem.

     ii.   When two different activities; have a meal, not have a meal; are dependent upon the answer to a question *is the time later than 6.00 p.m.?* then the question is represented by a *decision* symbol, and the answer by one of the two flowlines leaving the symbol.

     iii.   Each symbol has been annotated in **English** describing the operation at that stage of the flowchart.

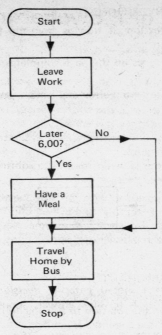

Figure 2.1

FLOWCHARTING SYMBOLS.

4. The following is a small selection of the symbols shown in appendix V but will be sufficient to demonstrate the fundamentals of flowcharting.

a.

A *terminal* symbol is used to denote the beginning and end of a flowchart. The symbol is annotated with the verbs START, STOP, END as appropriate.

b.

A *process* symbol is used to define the execution of an operation or event. The meaning of the operation or event is annotated within the symbol.

c.

A *decision* symbol is used to ask a specific question, the answer to which should be *yes* or *no*, corresponding to *true* or *false* respectively.

FLOWCHARTING CONVENTIONS.

5. a. The general direction of flow is from **top to bottom** and from **left to right** on the page.

    b. A flowline that goes **up** the page completes a *loop* or repetition of process.

    c. Only **one** flowline should enter and leave a *process* symbol.

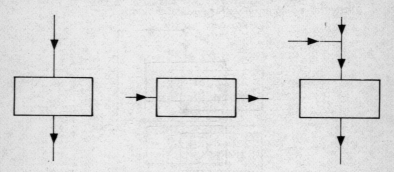

d. Only **one** flowline should enter a *decision* symbol; but **two** flowlines, one for each possible answer, should leave a *decision* symbol.

The exit flowlines are annotated with yes or no, to indicate which path is to be taken.

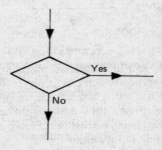

e. Only **one** flowline is used in conjunction with *terminal* symbols. Furthermore it is good practice to have only two *terminal* symbols in a flowchart, marking the beginning and the end.

CONSTRUCTS IN FLOWCHARTING.

6. Three *building blocks* can be identified in the construction of flow-charts. The *building blocks,* often referred to as constructs, are *sequencing, selection* and *repetition.* A flowchart will contain at least one of the constructs, possibly repeated several times in a chart.

a. **Sequencing.** This is a linear sequence of activities that involve a progression from one activity to the next in sequence. Figure 2.2 is a schematic diagram illustrating sequencing.

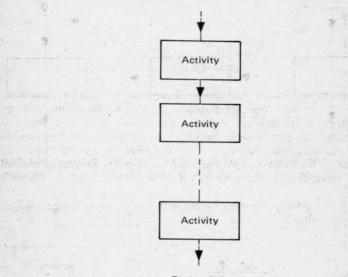

Figure 2.2

b. **Selection.** This is also known as conditional branching and relies upon testing a condition which can be either *true or false.* (eg. asking a question which has either a *yes* or a *no* answer.) Depending upon the outcome one of two flow paths is followed which leads to the appropriate activity being carried out. Figure 2.3 represents schematic diagrams of selection in its various forms.

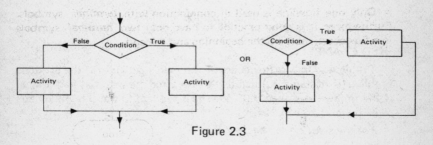

Figure 2.3

17

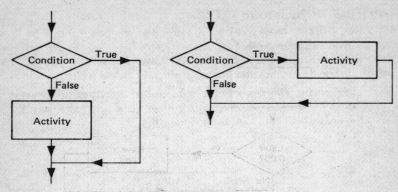

Figure 2.3 (Cont.)

c. **Repetition.** This is also known as iteration or looping. Repetitive sequences of activities occur often in programming and such an occurence is known as a *loop*. Repetition must not continue indefinitely, so a mechanism needs to be provided to break out of the loop and to allow continuation to the next set of activities. The control of the break out (or exit) can be at the beginning or the end of the loop as illustrated in figure 2.4.

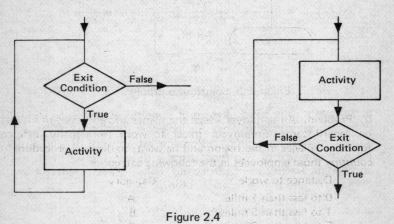

Figure 2.4

WORKED EXAMPLES.

7. a. **Problem.** Draw a flowchart of the man's activities if the previous problem is re-stated to include − − − after the man has had a meal if the time is later than 7.00 p.m. he is too late to travel home by bus so he travels home by taxi.

   For the solution see figure 2.5.

18

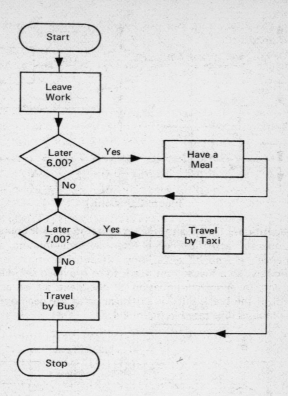

Figure 2.5. Solution to problem 7a.

b. **Problem.** An employer keeps the names and addresses of his staff on record cards. Employees travel to work from many different towns or villages in the region and he wants to devise a procedure for *counting* those employees in the following categories.

Distance to work	Category
0 to less than 1 mile	A
1 to less than 5 miles	B
5 to less than 20 miles	C
20 miles or further	D

The employer has for reference a map of the region with circles drawn from the place of work, having radii representing 1 mile, 5 miles and 20 miles.

From the record card he knows the town or village where an employee lives, therefore, the distance from work can be referenced using the map.

19

Flowchart the required procedure for categorising the employees by distance.

For the solution see figure 2.6.

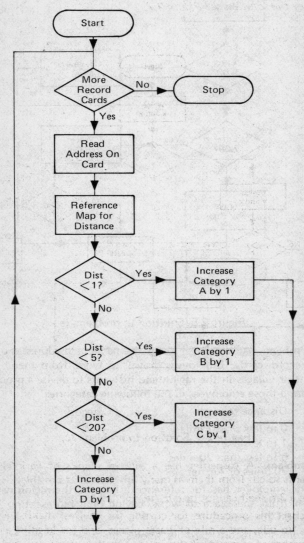

Figure 2.6. Solution to problem 7b.

c. **Problem.** Three coins of the same value are labelled X, Y and Z. Either X or Y is counterfeit since it is not the required weight. Coin Z is known to be genuine. A simple balance is used to weigh one coin against the other. Flowchart a procedure to detect the counterfeit coin, and state whether it is heavier or lighter than the genuine one.

For the solution see Figure 2.7.

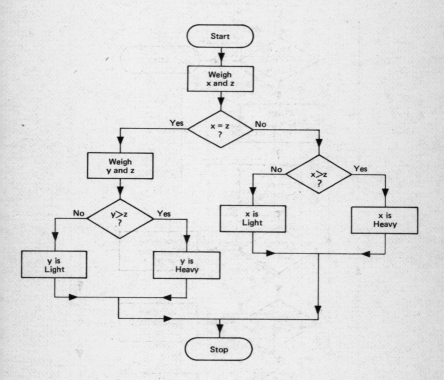

Figure 2.7. Solution to problem 7c.

d. **Problem.** A carpenter has a pile of planks of various lengths. He wants to cut from them as many 3m shelves as possible.

Where a 3m shelf cannot be cut, he will cut 1m ones.

Flowchart his procedure for cutting the shelves, making a 3m pile and a 1m pile, and a pile of waste pieces, and for keeping a count of the number of complete shelves placed in each of the two main piles.

For the solution see figure 2.8.

21

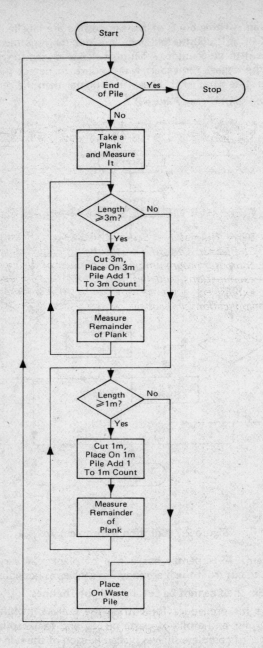

Figure 2.8. Solution to problem 7d.

Notes:

    i.   The flowchart is used repeatedly for processing all the planks in the pile. This is achieved by drawing a flowline **up** the page to complete a *loop.*

    ii.   The *end of pile?* question serves as a means of branching *out* of the *loop* when there are no more planks to be processed.

    iii.   **Beware** whenever a *loop* is drawn on a flowchart; have a method of branching *out* of it, otherwise the path becomes an *infinite* loop.

    The flowchart contains three loops, each containing a *decision* symbol to allow branching out of the loop.

EXERCISE.

1.   When you get in from school or college you have to plan your evening. This flowchart represents a simplified version of what you might do. Re-draw the flowchart and label the blank symbols with the instructions in the correct sequence.

[East Anglian Examinations Board]

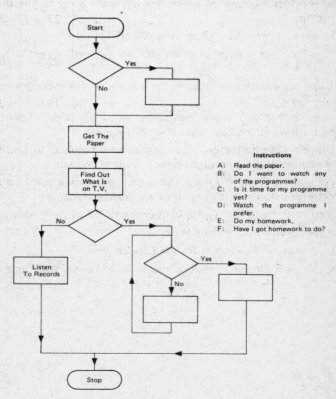

Instructions

A: Read the paper.
B: Do I want to watch any of the programmes?
C: Is it time for my programme yet?
D: Watch the programme I prefer.
E: Do my homework.
F: Have I got homework to do?

2. A butcher has recently received joints of meat. He wishes to calculate the total number of joints in each of the following weight-classes:

Those weighing up to 1kg (inclusive) TOTAL A; those weighing more than 1 kg and up to 2kg TOTAL B; those weighing more than 2kg and up to 4kg TOTAL C; those weighing more than 4kg TOTAL D.

Most of the joints are large, and likely to weigh more than 4 kg.

Each joint is to be weighed individually.

Flowchart a procedure that the butcher might follow in order to perform the minimum number of weighings.

[ICL Education and Training]

* 3. A survey is being made of passengers using a particular train route.

On each train using the route during the survey period, each passenger is asked his/her ticket type: first or second class; single, day or period return. This data is encoded for input to a computer.

Draw a flowchart for the analysis of the above data to give:

a. the total number of passengers using the route during the survey period.

b. the number of passengers with each ticket type.

c. the average number of passengers, per day, with day return tickets.
   [A.E.B.]

* 4. Draw a flowchart to indicate the procedures for making a telephone call at a 'Pay Phone'.

Assume that you know the number you wish to dial; have the right money for the call and have just lifted the receiver.

5. Draw a flowchart showing the procedures required to find the telephone number of John Smith who lives in Inner London.

All you know about John Smith is that he lives in a street named after a famous person, which is situated near a railway station.

You have the following aids in your search for the telephone number.

a. A street map of Inner London.

b. A telephone directory for the London area.

c. You are allowed to make a maximum of twenty telephone calls.

3 Program Flowcharts

INTRODUCTION.

1. a. The primary object of drawing flowcharts is to help the programmer to construct a logical and accurate program when he comes to write program instructions.

b. A flowchart is a valuable aid to developing and documenting the logic behind a computer program.

c. Flowcharting is first and foremost a means to an end, and that end is the coded computer program.

2. FURTHER FLOWCHARTING SYMBOLS DEFINED.

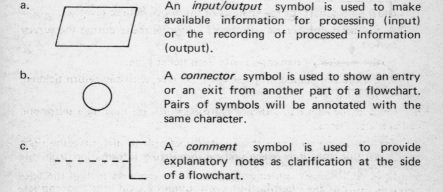

a. An *input/output* symbol is used to make available information for processing (input) or the recording of processed information (output).

b. A *connector* symbol is used to show an entry or an exit from another part of a flowchart. Pairs of symbols will be annotated with the same character.

c. A *comment* symbol is used to provide explanatory notes as clarification at the side of a flowchart.

WORKED EXAMPLES.

3. a. **Problem.** Part of an employee's time sheet contains the hourly pay rate and the number of hours worked per week on the job.

Draw a flowchart to read these details from the time sheet, calculate the gross wage, and write the gross wage on the time sheet. (See figure 3.1).

Notes:

i. If a computer is used to solve this problem then the flowchart must reflect that reading an hourly rate and number of hours worked will involve **inputting** this information to the computer.

25

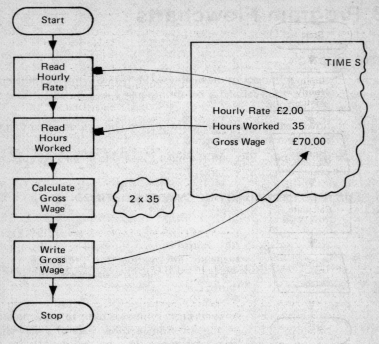

Figure 3.1

Writing the gross wage will be **outputting** information from the computer.

Thus the *input/output* symbol will be used at the appropriate stages of the flowchart.

ii. If a visual display unit is used as a means of communicating with the computer, then the input of information will be through the keyboard, and the output of information will be to the screen.

The previous solution can now be expressed as a program flowchart (figure 3.2).

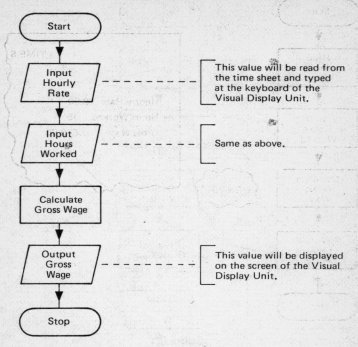

Figure 3.2

b. **Problem.** Convert the previous flowchart (figure 3.2) so that it will cater for calculating the gross wages of ten employees.

Notes:

i.   This will involve repeating the operations of the flowchart ten times by introducing a loop.

ii.   To control the number of times the loop is executed a counter representing the number of employees will be introduced.

iii. If the hourly rate is the same for all ten employees then it need only be input once.

The solution is figure 3.3.

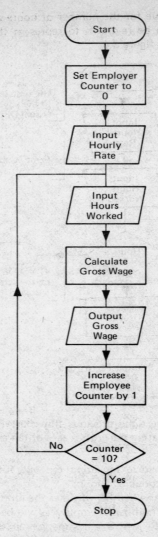

Figure 3.3. Solution to 3b.

c. **Problem.** When processing data it is not always possible to know how many data items there are in advance. In the previous problem the loop was controlled by a counter, but it is also possible to control the loop from data being input to the system. If the number of employees was not known in advance then a terminator value could be used to indicate the end of the data and thus exit from the loop. If

28

the terminator value for the number of hours worked was zero, then the flowchart can be re-drawn to represent the new situation. The solution is given in figure 3.4.

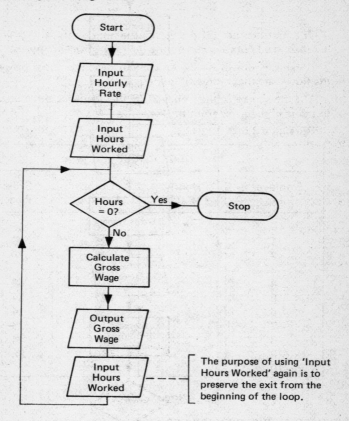

Figure 3.4. Solution to 3c.

DESK CHECKING A FLOWCHART.

4. a. In order to verify that the flowchart represents a correct solution to a problem it is important to work through and obey each operation of the flowchart with suitable test data.

When choosing test data the following points should be kept in mind:

  i.   The type and nature of the data is representative of the situation.

  ii. Numerical data should be chosen for ease of calculation.

  iii. Data is meaningful and within defined ranges.

b. The following list of numbers represent data by which the previous flowchart (figure 3.3) is checked.

2   20   25   35   30   40   27   32   18   22   40

The first number (2) represents the hourly rate, and the remaining numbers the hours worked by the ten respective employees.

A table is drawn having as column headings those parameters of the flowchart that represent numerical values.

The flowchart is then obeyed in the sequence directed, selecting test data in sequence from the list.

See figure 3.5.

DESK CHECK			
Employee Counter	Hourly Rate	Hours Worked	Gross Wage
0	2	20	40
1		25	50
2		35	70
3		30	60
4		40	80
5		27	54
6		32	64
7		18	36
8		22	44
9		40	80
10			

Figure 3.5

FURTHER WORKED EXAMPLES.

5. a. **Problem.** The lengths of the four sides of a quadrilateral, and one internal angle are input to a computer. Draw a flowchart to categorise the shape of the quadrilateral as a square, rhombus, rectangle, parallelogram or irregular quadrilateral.

Include a loop in the flowchart so that the shape of more than one quadrilateral can be determined.

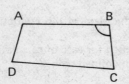

Lengths of sides
AB, BC, CD, DA known.
Angle B known.

To help the reader the following table summarises the shapes.

Name	Shape	All Sides Equal	Opposite Sides Equal	Angle 90°
Square		Yes	Yes	Yes
Rectangle		No	Yes	Yes
Rhombus		Yes	Yes	No
Parallelogram		No	Yes	No
Irreg. Quad		No	No	No

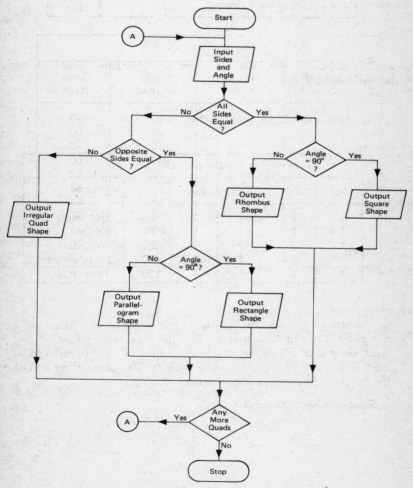

Figure 3.6. Solution to 5a.

i. Test data for solution to 5a.

Test data				
AB	BC	CD	DA	B
1	2	1	2	90
1	1	1	1	90
1	3	2	2½	80
1	2	1	2	80
1	1	1	1	120

Note: The choice of test data caters for every different shape of the categorised quadrilaterals.

ii. Desk check on solution to 5a.

Desk check					
AB	BC	CD	DA	B	SHAPE
1	2	1	2	90	Rectangle
1	1	1	1	90	Square
1	3	2	2½	80	Irregular
1	2	1	2	80	Parallelogram
1	1	1	1	120	Rhombus

b. **Problem.** The weights of newly born babies are input to a computer. Draw a flowchart to find the maximum, minimum and mean weights of all the weights of the babies. A value of zero can be used at the end of the list of baby weights. This denotes the end of the list and is known as a 'rogue' value.

Solution given is figure 3.7.

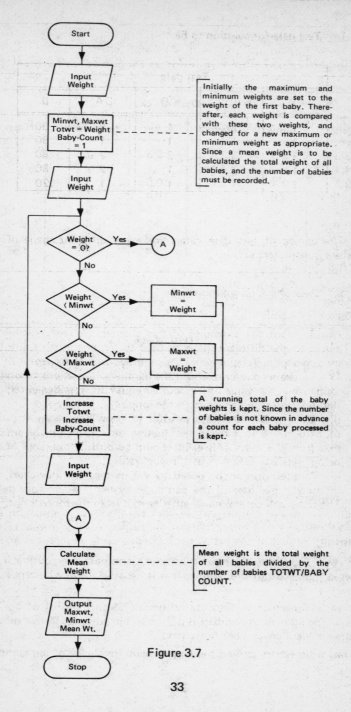

Figure 3.7

33

Test data (weights in kg)								
3.3	4.1	3.1	2.9	3.7	3.6	4.2	3.5	0

Desk check					
Weight	**Minwt**	**Maxwt**	**Totwt**	**baby-count**	**Mean**
3.3	3.3	3.3	3.3	1	
4.1		4.1	7.4	2	
3.1	3.1		10.5	3	
2.9	2.9		13.4	4	
3.7			17.1	5	
3.6			20.7	6	
4.2		4.2	24.9	7	
3.5			28.4	8	3.55
0					
Maxwt 4.2					
Minwt 2.9					
Mean 3.55					

c. **Notes.** From the examples of this chapter the reader should be aware of the different methods used to terminate procedure flow around a loop. To summarise the methods used so far are:

i. To use a counter to count the number of iterations around the loop. When the value of the counter equals the number of required iterations an exit is made from the loop.

ii. Since it is not always possible to know how many iterations of a loop are required a terminating data value can be used to exit from the loop. This value should be outside the range of data being used, and is known as a 'rogue' value.

iii. A question can be posed to the user of the flowchart, and ultimately the user of the computer system; "Any more data?" The reply will determine whether to exit from the loop or not.

EXERCISE.

1. Draw a flowchart to input a number, terminate the routine if the number is zero, output the number if it is negative, otherwise repeat the routine.

2. Draw a flowchart to find the arithmetic mean of a list of positive numbers. The number of numbers is not known in advance. Derive suitable test data and desk check your flowchart.

3. Draw a flowchart to find the largest value from a list of ten numbers.

Desk check your flowchart using the following numbers as test data.

      7   3   19   41   26 - 5   17   8   0   23

4. Draw a flowchart to perform the following task.

Input an amount of money to a computer as a whole number of Pounds Sterling. Produce a break-down of the notes required to make up the sum of money, using the minimum number of notes.

Only £10, £5 and £1 notes are used.

5. In a game for two players, each player throws two dice in turn and scores 3 points for each of the following occurrences:

Either dice shows a 6,

both dice show the same number,

the total of the two dice adds up to 9.

(**n.b.** It is possible to score more than 3 points on one throw).

The winner is the first person to score a total of 51 points exactly.

The players are identified as 1 and 2 and the total score of any player is shown as s(n), where n equals the player's number.

Draw a flowchart for the above procedure. Using two dice desk check your flowchart.

[A.E.B.]

6. Consider the following rules for calculating income tax in Utopia.

Personal allowances are £1200 for a single person and £2300 for a married man.

A child allowance is £100 per child.

Taxable Income is the amount remaining after deducting the personal allowance and total child allowance from the Gross Income.

Income Tax is calculated from Taxable Income according to the following table.

Taxable Income on	Percentage tax on Taxable Income
First £1000	no tax
Next £1000	20%
Next £2000	30%
Above £4000	40%

If gross salary, personal status (married or single) and number of children are input to a computer draw a flowchart to determine the tax paid on that income.

* **7.** 120 students take an examination. Four pass grades are awarded:—

   P1 for marks between 100 and 85 inclusive
   P2 for marks between 84 and 68 inclusive
   P3 for marks between 67 and 49 inclusive
   P4 for marks between 48 and 35 inclusive

   Two fall grades are awarded:—

   F1 for marks between 34 and 20 inclusive
   F2 for marks less than 20

   Each student is identified by a code number. Draw a flowchart to input the student's code and percentage mark gained by each student and to output each student's mark as a grade along with the student's code, and also the totals in each grade of pass or fail.

   [A.E.B.]

* **8.** The lengths of three sides of a triangle are input to a computer.

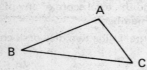

Sides AB BC and CA
are of known length.

Draw a flowchart to determine whether the triangle is isosceles, equilateral, right-angled or scalene, and output the shape of the triangle.

Derive suitable test data and desk check your flowchart.

Note: Scalene implies that the lengths of the three sides are *not* equal.

4 Elements of Basic

INTRODUCTION.

1. This chapter provides the reader with an insight into the relationship between data, storage of data, computer arithmetic and the BASIC language.

The chapter covers the following topics:

a. Types of data.

b. Data storage and its restrictions.

c. Naming conventions for data.

d. Computer arithmetic.

DATA TYPES.

2. Data can be classified into two types *numeric* and *string.*

a. Numeric data will be composed of integers and real numbers both signed or unsigned.
Examples.
  i.   176 −13 +2471 (integers)
  ii. −41.96 +0.2113 −31.87 (real numbers);

b. String data is a sequence of characters taken from the ASCII character set (see appendix VI).
Examples.
  i.   "TAX PAID"
  ii. "134 ST. CLEMENTS VIEW"

From the second example it can be seen that a string can consist of a combination of digits, letters and other characters.

Strings should be delimited by the use of double quotes or apostrophes.

Refer to your computer manual to see which delimeter your computer uses.

Throughout this book double quotes will be used to delimit strings.

The reason for using delimiters around a string is so that the computer can detect the beginning and the end of a string. The delimiters themselves do *not* form part of the string.

A NULL string contains no characters and can be represented by two delimiters together (ie.   " ").

Reference to appendix VI will show that the NULL character has been given the ASCII code of zero.

4 Elements of BASIC

DATA STORAGE.

3. The main memory of a computer is composed of thousands of memory cells. With most computers each cell is called a *byte* and can store a fixed quantity of information.

a. Numeric data are represented within a fixed number of bytes, hence there is a limitation as to:
  i. The range of numbers that can be stored.
  ii. The accuracy to which decimal fractions can be stored.

b. String data are represented as one character per byte of memory and there is usually a restriction on the maximum number of characters allowed in a string.

c. The restrictions on the amount of memory used to store either numeric or string data are inherent in the dialect of BASIC being used and cannot be changed by the programmer.

The following table figure 4.1 compares the restrictions on data storage between four different dialects of BASIC.

Dialect	Smallest Positive Number	Largest Positive Number	Accuracy	Max String Length
CBM PET	2.93×10^{-39}	$1.7 \times 10^{+38}$	9 sig. fig.	255
MSI	1.0×10^{-99}	$9.99\cdots \times 10^{+99}$	9 sig. fig.	128
PRIME	1.0×10^{-99}	$9.99\cdots \times 10^{+99}$	13 sig. fig.	160
APPLESOFT II	1.0×10^{-37}	$9.99\cdots \times 10^{37}$	9 sig. fig.	255

Figure 4.1

Example. Consider storing the following numbers using, say, the PET dialect of BASIC.
  i. $0.01369 \times 10^{-38} = 1.369 \times 10^{-40}$

  The smallest number that can be represented is 2.93×10^{-39}, thus the number cannot be represented since UNDERFLOW has occurred.

  ii. 0.947368291687

  The accuracy of representation is to 9 significant figures, thus the number is TRUNCATED to

  0.947368291

  iii. $29754.732 \times 10^{+36} = 2.9754732 \times 10^{+40}$

  The largest number that can be represented is $1.7 \times 10^{+38}$, thus the number cannot be represented since OVERFLOW has occurred.

d. Regardless of the computer being used:

   i. The **range** of numbers that can be stored is **finite**.
   ii. Decimal fractions can be represented to a limited **accuracy**.
   iii. The maximum allowable **length** of a string is **finite**.

VARIABLES

4. a. To access data stored in memory, from a computer program, it will be necessary to identify those areas of memory that contain the data.

Clearly a convention for naming areas of memory that contain particular items of data is required.

In Chapter 3 such a symbolism as

was used to reference numerical values. TOTWT and BABY-COUNT were names given to numerical values that *changed* continuously in the procedure specified by the flowchart. Such values are known as **variables,** and apply to string data as well as numeric data.

b. The BASIC language has rules for the construction of variable names.

   i. A numeric variable name can be:
   a single upper-case (capital) letter of the alphabet
   OR
   a single upper-case (capital) letter of the alphabet followed by a single decimal digit.

Note: This is an ECMA standard and rules of composition vary between dialects of BASIC.

Example: A, B, C0, D3, X9, Z1, etc are legal numeric scalar variable names.

   ii. A string variable name is a single (upper case) letter of the alphabet postfixed with a $ character.

Example: A$, B$, C$ etc are legal string variable names.

Note: Since both numeric and string variables refer to single items of data they can be known as *Scalar* variables.

c. The meaningful names given to items of data in a flowchart must be converted to legal variable names in BASIC.

To this end, the reader should adopt a habit of defining a glossary with every flowchart and ultimately program that is written.

Example.

Flowchart names	BASIC NAMES
MINWT	M1
MAXWT	M2
TOTWT	T
MEANWT	M3
BABY-COUNT	B

LITERALS

5. When a numeric or string value is used *literally,* and *not* referred to by a scalar variable name, then its value cannot be changed and is therefore known as a constant or literal.

Examples.

In the expression $Y = 2*X + 0.5$; X and Y are scalar variables and 2 and 0.5 are numeric literals.

In the expression **PRINT "ADDRESS"; A\$ ADDRESS** is a string literal and A\$ is a string variable.

ARITHMETIC EXPRESSIONS.

6. Arithmetic expressions in BASIC are formed according to the same rules of algebra as used in mathematics.

    a. The following symbols are used to denote arithmetic operations.

      ↑   exponentration (raising a number to a power)
      /   division
      *   multiplication
      −   subtraction
      +   addition

Examples.

algebraic expression	BASIC expression
a.b	A * B
$\dfrac{a}{b}$	A / B
a.b + c.d	A * B + C * D
b^a	B ↑ A

    b. Parenthesis can be introduced into a BASIC expression to clarify the meaning of the expression. **Warning** — ensure that there are the **same** number of left-hand parenthesis as right-hand parenthesis.

4 Elements of BASIC

Examples.

algebraic expression	BASIC expression
$\dfrac{a.b}{c.d}$	(A * B) / (C * D)
$(B^2 - 4.a.c)^{1/2}$	((B ↑ 2) − (4 * A * C)) ↑ 0.5

c. The BASIC language evaluates arithmetic expressions according to a hierarchy between the operators.

Operator	Priority
single + or −	highest
↑	
* /	
+ −	lowest

Operators having the same priority are evaluated from left to right.

Expressions contained within parenthesis are evaluated first.

Examples.

BASIC expression	algebraic equivalent
A + B/C	$(\dfrac{b}{c}) + a$
A + B/C/D	$(\dfrac{b}{c.d}) + a$
(A + B) ↑ C ↑ D	$((a + b)^c)^d$

Notes.

7. a. When using an *interpreter* to run BASIC programs it is usual for the interpreter to initialise all the variables of a program. Hence, numeric variables are set to zero, and string variables are set to the null character. If you get into a habit of **not** initialising variables, then it is a **BAD HABIT**, since some computers using BASIC compilers will **not** initialise the variables for you.

b. A string literal can be composed of any character from the ASCII character set. But **beware**, BASIC uses the comma character as a delimiter, try to avoid using embedded commas in string literals.

41

EXERCISE.

1. Identify the following data types and write a suitable variable name for each one.

a. 21.49   b. – 13   c. – 437.23   d. U.S.A.

e. NEW ZEALAND   f. O   g. 198   h. U.K.   i. + 987

j. – 1E.6

2. If a computer can store integers in the range + 32767 to – 32768 and real numbers in the range $\pm$ 0.1 x 10^{-49} to $\pm$ 0.9999 x 10^{+49} with an accuracy of 4 significant figures, then comment upon the representation of the following numbers.

a. 6195847   b. – 156   c. 376.4   d. 0.259376

e. 0.4378 x 10^{79} f. + 16973   g. – 3794.0 x 10^{-47}

h. 234785.69 x 10^{43} i. 0   j. – 0.9999999

3. Which of the following are legal variable names in BASIC? If not legal state the reason why.

a. A   b. AB   c. K33   d. 10F   e. E2   f. P$ g. B$3

h. x – 3   i. 17   j. REM   k. T6$ i. I

4. State which of the following are legal constants in BASIC. If not legal state the reason why.

a. 329   b. – 147.23   c. "ACCOUNT NUMBER"

d. "TAX TO DATE"   e. X5   f. "39, ST. GEORGE AVE"

g. + 137   h. "Y"   i. "734.96"   j. 50%

5. Refer to appendix VI to answer the following questions.

a. If a null character has a code zero, what ASCII code does a zero character have?

b. State the ASCII codes for the following characters.

i. A   ii. B   iii. ;   iv. 3   v. 9   vi. !

6. How are the following expressions written in the BASIC language.

a. $\dfrac{A + B}{C}$ b. $\dfrac{X}{Y + Z}$ c. $\dfrac{U.V.}{W.X}$ d. A^B

e. $\dfrac{D - B}{2.A}$ f. $\frac{1}{2}(A^2 + B^2)$ g. $(A - B)(C + D)^2$

h. $B^2 - 4AC$ i. $\dfrac{q_1\, q_2}{4\pi\, \mathrm{I}r^2}$ j. $2\pi\sqrt{\dfrac{a^2 + b^2}{2}}$

7. Find any errors in the following BASIC expressions.

    a. AB   b. X* − Y   c. (64 + B2) / − 6

    d. Z60 + D   e. ((A + B) / (C + D) ↑ 4   f. P ↑ .5

    g. (A − B) (A + B)   h. − 2 / A + − 6   i. $\dfrac{Q1}{X + Y}$

    j. r + s / t

8. Re-write the following BASIC expressions as mathematical expressions.

    a. X + Y ↑ 3   b. X + 2 / Y + 4   c. A * B / (C + 2)

    d. (X / Y) ↑ N − !   e. A / B + C * D / (F * G * H)

    f. − 1 / (2 * P) + Q ↑ 2 / (4 * R ↑ 2)

    g. (A ↑ 2 + B ↑ 2) ↑ (1 / 2)   h. 1 / (X + Y) ↑ 2

    i. A / B + C / D + E / F   j. U3 / U2 * U1 / U0

5 Eight Statement Basic

INTRODUCTION.

1.   In this chapter the reader is introduced to a small selection of statements from the BASIC language. The purpose of each statement is explained and worked examples are used to show how the statements are put together in the form of a computer program.

INPUT/OUTPUT

2.   The flowchart symbol is used to indicate the

input/output of data to or from a computer.

   BASIC has the corresponding verbs

INPUT and PRINT.

   If a visual display unit is used to communicate with a computer system then **INPUT** will allow data to be entered through the keyboard to the computer, and **PRINT** will display information from the computer on to the screen.

   When flowcharting an input/output symbol it is annotated with the appropriate action to take.

Example.

   Where **HOURS WORKED** and **GROSS WAGE** are both numerical items that are used in the flowchart.

   The **INPUT** and **PRINT** statements must therefore have a defined format (syntax) that will allow for the input/output of variables respectively.

   If **HOURS WORKED** and **GROSS WAGE** are given the BASIC variable names **H** and **G** respectively then:

INPUT H will allow a value for **HOURS WORKED** to be typed at the keyboard of the V.D.U. and

PRINT G will display a value for **GROSS WAGE** on the screen of the V.D.U.

The simplest format or syntax of **INPUT** and **PRINT** is:

INPUT   variable name
PRINT   variable name

ASSIGNMENT

3.   In the flowcharting described in Chapter 3, whenever a value was to be assigned to a variable or calculation performed a process symbol would be used and annotated with the operation required.

Example.

The BASIC verb used in assignment and arithmetic is **LET**.

In calculating the **GROSS WAGE (G)** the **HOURS WORKED (H)** is multiplied by the **HOURLY RATE (R)**.

This would be expressed in BASIC as

LET G = H * R

The result of the product **(H * R)** is assigned to the variable **G**.

If **G** had a value from a previous calculation it would now be over-written (lost) by the value of the current calculation.

The syntax of a **LET** statement is:

LET variable name = { constant
variable name
arithmetic expression }

where { } indicates a choice between the items listed.

Examples.

LET A = 3
LET X$ = "APPLES"
LET Y = Z
LET B = (C + D) / 3
LET C = C + 1

Notes.

    i.   This last example **LET C = C + 1** would appear at first sight to be incorrect, however, it implies that the current value of **C** is increased by 1. For example if **C** was 9 then after obeying the statement **LET C = C + 1, C** becomes 10.

    ii.   The two sides to the equation **must** be of similar data types.

        LET X\$ = (C + D) / 3 would be incorrect since **X\$** is a string variable and **(C + D) / 3** is an arithmetic expression.

TERMINATION.

4.   Flowcharts must have a beginning and an end indicated by the use of suitably annotated terminal symbols.

    BASIC has **no** equivalent to 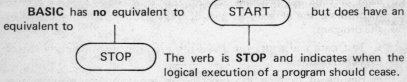 but does have an equivalent to

      The verb is **STOP** and indicates when the logical execution of a program should cease.

    BASIC also has the verb **END** and can be used in the same way as **STOP**. However, it is preferred by the author, that **END** should be used only to indicate the physical end of a program. The use of **END** in this way then becomes consistent with its use in other high level languages.

    STOP can appear anywhere in a **BASIC** program, however, **END** should be the **last** statement of a program.

PROGRAM STRUCTURE.

5.   A computer program is a sequence of instructions to be executed by the computer. The order in which instructions are written is of **paramount** importance since the computer will start executing a program from the first instruction, then progress to the second and so on, until redirected by a loop to repeat a sequence of instructions or a branch to change or avoid a sequence of instructions.

    The structure of a BASIC program is

a. One instruction or statement per line.

b. Each line must begin with a line number.

c. Line numbers are unsigned positive integers, the allowable range varies from machine to machine, however, 1 through 9999 is common.

d. Line numbers should increase in say steps of 10 to allow for the insertion of extra lines at a later stage of program development.

PROGRAM DOCUMENTATION.

6. The documentation of a computer program should reflect the stages in the development of a program and should contain:

a. A description of the problem to be solved.

b. A narrative based on a method of solving the problem.

c. A flowchart illustrating the various procedures in the solution of a problem.

d. A glossary of variable names used in the flowchart, cross-referenced against those variable names used in the program.

e. A listing of the program containing a detailed narrative as to what each part of the program is used for. It is often a good idea to incorporate the glossary as part of this narrative at the beginning of the program.

f. Test data and a dry-run table for the program showing a list of expected results.

g. Results of running the program on the computer with the test data used in (f).

YOUR FIRST PROGRAM.

7. Remember the flowchart for calculating a single employees wage given the number of hours worked and hourly rate?

The flowchart can now be coded into a computer program using the five BASIC statements already described.

A glossary is an essential part of documenting the development of a computer program. In this example the glossary gives the correspondance between the variable names used in the flowchart and their equivalent BASIC names.

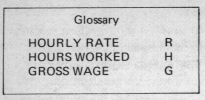

Glossary

HOURLY RATE	R
HOURS WORKED	H
GROSS WAGE	G

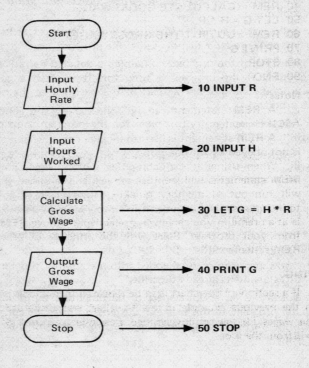

Start

Input
Hourly
Rate → **10 INPUT R**

Input
Hours
Worked → **20 INPUT H**

Calculate
Gross
Wage → **30 LET G = H * R**

Output
Gross
Wage → **40 PRINT G**

Stop → **50 STOP**

60 END

PROGRAM ANNOTATION.

8. a. The flowchart symbol – – – ⌐   allows extra information

to be written into the flowchart. The purpose being to provide a clear
and concise description of the solution. This is yet another ingredient
towards good standards of documentation and should also be reflected
in a computer program. The **REM** statement in **BASIC** will allow the
programmer to annotate a computer program.

The syntax of a **REM** statement is

REM string of characters.

b. **Example.** The previous program could be annotated as follows:

```
10  REM ·· INPUT HOURLY RATE AND HOURS WORKED
20  INPUT R
30  INPUT H
40  REM ·· CALCULATE GROSS WAGE
50  LET G = H * R
60  REM ·· OUTPUT THE GROSS WAGE
70  PRINT G
80  STOP
90  END
```

c. **Notes:**

i.   A **REM** statement can be followed by any combination of **ASCII** characters.

ii. A **REM** statement is used to include narrative in a program and is **not** obeyed by the computer.

iii. When using a microcomputer with a small main memory **REM** statements will soon use up valuable program space and you will run out of memory quickly. However, it is good practice to include as many comments in a program as necessary. If memory is at a premium you can always selectively remove **REM** statements from your program. Start with the principle of using plenty of **REM** statements.

LOOPING.

9. a. If a section of flowchart is to be repeated then a loop is introduced. In the previous example if the flowchart was to be used to process the wages for ten employees then a counter was used to control the exit from the loop.

Each time the section of chart to be repeated was processed, the counter would be increased

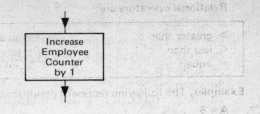

and then tested to see whether the wages for ten employees had been processed.

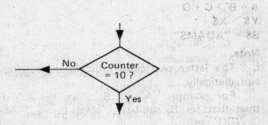

b. A conditional statement is used to make decisions in a program. BASIC provides the

IF · · THEN · · statement.

Example. If **EMPLOYEE COUNTER** is given the variable name **C**, then the decision symbol could be coded as:

IF C = 10 THEN STOP

The Syntax of a conditional statement is:

IF condition **THEN** instruction

The syntax of a condition is:

$$\left\{ \begin{array}{l} \text{constant} \\ \text{variable name} \\ \text{arithmetic expression} \end{array} \right\} \quad \begin{array}{l} \text{relational} \\ \text{operator} \end{array} \quad \left\{ \begin{array}{l} \text{constant} \\ \text{variable name} \\ \text{arithmetic expression} \end{array} \right\}$$

Relational operators are:

>	greater than	> =	greater than or equals
<	less than	< =	less than or equals
=	equals	< >	not equal

Examples. The following represent conditions:

A = 6
B > 15
X < Y
H > = I + J
A + B > C + D
Y$ > X$
B$ = "ADAMS"

Note.

i.   The latter two cases indicate that strings can be compared alphabetically.

For example "A" < "B" since the ASCII code for A is less than that for B, similarly, "APPLE" < "BANANA"; "GRAPE" > "FIG"; etc.

ii. Both sides of a condition **must** be of similar variable types.

iii. With a conditional statement if the condition is **true** (corresponding to a YES on a flowchart) the statement following THEN is obeyed.

However, if the condition is **false** (corresponding to a NO on a flowchart) the NEXT instruction in the program sequence is obeyed.

In the last program example if the condition C = 10 is false, then there is a requirement to loop back and repeat a section of flowchart, so the next instruction to be obeyed must be a loop instruction.

c. In BASIC this is **GOTO** but **GOTO** where?

The syntax is **GOTO** line number.

Thus to loop back to say line number 30 one would write **GOTO 30.**

Note: **Beware** never branch to a **REM** statement, since this is a bad habit, and is not consistent with other high-level languages.

A PROGRAM WITH A LOOP.

10. a. The flowchart to process the wages for ten employees can now be coded into a computer program.

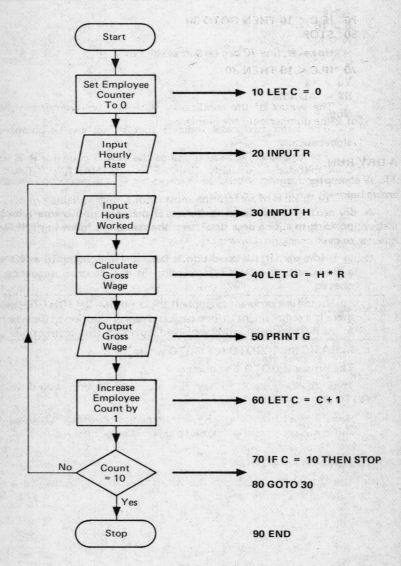

Glossary	
Employee Counter	C
Hourly Rate	R
Hours worked	H
Gross wage	G

Start

Set Employee Counter To 0 → 10 LET C = 0

Input Hourly Rate → 20 INPUT R

Input Hours Worked → 30 INPUT H

Calculate Gross Wage → 40 LET G = H * R

Output Gross Wage → 50 PRINT G

Increase Employee Count by 1 → 60 LET C = C + 1

No ← Count = 10 → 70 IF C = 10 THEN STOP

80 GOTO 30

Yes

Stop → 90 END

b. **Notes:**

i.   Line 60 would appear to be incorrect algebraically, however, the statement implies that the current value for **C** equals the previous value for **C** plus 1. Thus increasing the value of **C** by 1.

ii.   Lines 70 and 80 can be re-arranged if the condition was changed without altering the logic.

```
70   IF C < 10 THEN GOTO 30
80   STOP
```

However, line 70 can be abbreviated to

```
70   IF C < 10 THEN 30
```

The syntax of the conditional statement will permit the use of a line number only for branching.

A DRY-RUN.

11. A computer program should be checked for syntax errors and logical errors before it is run on a computer.

A dry-run of a computer program is achieved by obeying each instruction in turn, using test data, and constructing a table in a similar manner to desk checking a flowchart.

Using the same test data as chapter 3 for the previous flowchart.

```
test data:
  2   20   25   35   30   40   27   32   18   22   40
```

a dry run table can be constructed.

program line number(s)	C	R	H	G
10, 20, 30, 40, 50	0	2	20	40
60, 70, 80	1			
30, 40, 50			25	50
60, 70, 80	2			
30, 40, 50			35	70
60, 70, 80	3			
30, 40, 50			30	60
60, 70, 80	4			
30, 40, 50			40	80
60, 70, 80	5			
30, 40, 50			27	54
60, 70, 80	6			
30, 40, 50			32	64
60, 70, 80	7			
30, 40, 50			18	36
60, 70, 80	8			
30, 40, 50			22	44
60, 70, 80	9			
30, 40, 50			40	80
60, 70	10			

EXERCISE.

1. Detect the syntax errors in the following BASIC statements.

    a. **IMPUT H**   b. **OUTPUT Q**   c. **PR1NT Z3**

    d. **IF A $\neq$ B THEN 40**   e. **LET X $\uparrow$ 2 + Y $\uparrow$ 2 = Z**

    f. **LET H = I = J**   g. **LET X\$ = 36 + Y / Z**

    h. **IF A\$ $>$ B\$ THEN END**   i. **EXIT**   j. **IF P $>$ Q\$ THEN – 510**

2. The following program is written to detect and output negative integers only. Comment on the logical errors.

```
10    INPUT N
20    IF N < 0 THEN 10
30    PRINT N
40    GOTO 10
50    END
```

3. Give the following BASIC program a dry-run to determine the final values of A, B and C.

Note: No test data is required.

```
10    LET A = 1
20    LET B = 1
30    LET C = 2
40    PRINT A
50    PRINT B
60    IF C > 10 THEN STOP
70    LET A = A + B
80    LET B = B + A
90    LET C = C + 2
100   GOTO 40
110   END
```

4. Comment on the illegality of the arithmetic in the following program segment.

```
10    LET S = T
20    LET T = 0
30    LET A = S / T
40    LET B = 2.8 / T
```

5. Dry run the program with the following test data.

```
        5       7       3       8       4       3
10    INPUT X
20    LET C = 0
30    LET S = 0
40    INPUT Y
50    LET S = S + Y
60    LET C = C + 1
70    IF C < X THEN 40
80    LET A = S / X
90    PRINT A
100   STOP
110   END
```

6. The following program is written to INPUT a name of a town, find the population of that town and output the population.

Give the program a dry run with the test data provided and list the syntax and logical errors to be found.

Test data CANTERBURY, DOVER, HALIFAX.

```
10    INPUT T
20    IF T $ = DOVER THEN 60
30    IF T $ = "RAMSGATE" THEN PRINT "40090"
40    IF T $ = "CANTERBURY" THEN 50
50    PRINT 36290
60    PRINT "34160"
70    GOTO 10
80    END
```

* 7. Code a program from the following flowchart and glossary, and determine what the program does.

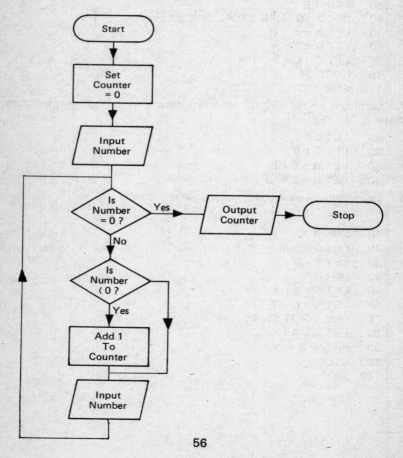

Glossary	
Flowchart name	BASIC name
COUNTER	C
NUMBER	N

* 8. Draw a flowchart, construct a glossary and code a program to:

    i.   Input two numbers and output their sum, difference, product and quotient.

        Modify the flowchart, glossary and program to:

    ii.   Repeat procedure i. for different pairs of numbers, and terminate the procedure when the second number is zero.

        Define suitable test data to

    iii. Desk check the flowcharts.

    iv. Dry run the programs.

6 Elementary Programming

INTRODUCTION.

1. By now the reader will have gained sufficient knowledge in the methodology required for writing a computer program.

This chapter deals with the problem of transferring the written program to a computer and the associated problems of running a computer program.

STORING A PROGRAM IN A COMPUTER.

2. There are three methods of preparing a written program for entry to a computer.

a. Typing the program statements line by line at the keyboard of an on-line input device such as a V.D.U., so that the program becomes directly resident in the main memory of the computer.

b. By preparing the program using an on-line data entry terminal and storing the program on magnetic disc or tape.

c. By preparing the program on an input medium such as punched cards or paper tape using an off-line key punch. The prepared program must then be read by an on-line input device such as a card or paper tape reader so that it can be transferred to the main memory of a computer.

The type of program entry system used will depend upon the way in which your computer system is configured. Most microcomputers will use a combination of methods (a) and (b).

Before a new program can be entered into the main memory of a computer the main memory should be cleared of any previously stored program. This is achieved by typing the BASIC command **NEW** at the keyboard of the on-line input terminal.

A computer program can then be typed at the terminal in the format in which it is written. At the end of typing each BASIC statement or command the carriage-return key must be pressed.

The program is stored in the main memory of the computer as it is entered at the keyboard of an on-line terminal (method a).

When the program has been entered it can be copied from the main memory on to either a magnetic tape or disc secondary storage medium.

The command for such copying of a program will differ between computers, however, **FILE** or **SAVE** are most common. *Refer to your computer manual.*

The format of the command being

FILE "filename"
or **SAVE** "filename"

where filename is a name given to the program so that it can be identified and recalled at a later time. Many dialects of BASIC use quotation marks around the filename.

The definition of legal filenames will vary between computers. *Refer to your computer manual.*

LOADING A PROGRAM FROM A SECONDARY STORAGE DEVICE.

3. A program that is stored on magnetic tape or disc is permanently recorded. Readers should develop the habit of storing their programs on tape or disc since the main memory of a computer is volatile. That is to say when you switch off the power from your computer the program stored in main memory will be destroyed!

The command for loading a program into the main memory will vary between computers, but **LOAD** or **OLD**, are common. *Refer to your computer manual.*

The format of the command being

LOAD "filename"
or **OLD** "filename"

The selected program is copied from the secondary storage medium into main memory.

When magnetic tape is used the computer will search serially through the tape until the correct program filename is matched and then the program will be loaded into main memory. The searching time can amount to several minutes especially if the program required is at the far end of the tape.

However, a program stored on magnetic disc will be located immediately then loaded into main memory.

RUNNING PROGRAMS.

4. When a computer program is in the main memory it can be *executed* or *run.* These terms mean the computer will obey each program statement in the order specified.

The command for a program to be executed is **RUN**

The computer will execute the program until one of the following occurs.

a. **STOP** statement is executed. This implies that program termination is a natural process as directed by the programmer.

b. **Syntax error.** The format of a statement in the program does not conform to the rules of the BASIC language.

c. **Execution error.** For example an arithmetic overflow error caused by, say, dividing a number by zero.

d. **Hardware error.** This is not the fault of the computer program but the machine itself.

LISTING A PROGRAM.

5. A computer generated copy of a program listing is important because:

a. It forms part of the documentation for a program being developed.

b. Is necessary when tracing the causes of errors in a program.

A program listing can be generated by using the command **LIST.**

If the computer terminal being used is a teletype then a printed (hardcopy) listing of the program stored in the main memory will be obtained. However, if the terminal is a V.D.U. then **LIST** will simply display a copy of the program on the screen. In the latter case *Refer to your computer manual* for the command to obtain a hardcopy of a program listing.

EDITING PROGRAMS.

6. When a program contains errors the process of finding the causes of the errors or *bugs* is called *de-bugging.*

De-bugging will inevitably mean changing or editing program statements.

Changes will involve:—

a. Insertion on new statements.

b. Amending existing statements.

c. Deleting statements.

Facilities for editing programs will vary between computers *refer to your computer manual,* however, (a) and (b) can be achieved by typing the line number and complete BASIC statement followed by return; (c) is achieved by typing the line number only followed by return.

Edited programs can be filed as before using the same or different filenames. Remember if a different filename is used then you will retain a copy of the file as it was before it was edited under the old name.

The techniques discussed for editing programs will only apply if the program has been loaded into the main memory of the computer.

PROGRAMMING EXAMPLES.

7. a. **Problem.** Devise and run a computer program to input a temperature in degrees Fahrenheit, convert the temperature to degrees centigrade and output the result. The formula for the temperature conversion is

$$\text{Centigrade} = (\text{Fahrenheit} - 32) \times 5 / 9$$

Flowchart

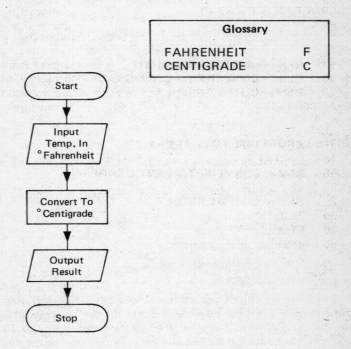

Glossary	
FAHRENHEIT	F
CENTIGRADE	C

Having written the program from the flowchart and given the program a dry-run the following is an example of a typical terminal session.

```
READY
NEW                                         clear memory
READY
10    INPUT F                               type program
20    LET C = (F — 32) * 5 / 9              line by line
30    PRINT C                               at terminal
40    STOP
50    END

RUN                                         command to execute
! 212                                       input value for F
100                                         output value for C

PROGRAM STOP AT 40                          computer informs
READY                                       user of line number
                                            that halted program


5     REM · · INPUT FAHRENHEIT             insert remarks in
15    REM · · CONVERT TO CENTIGRADE        program i.e. perform
25    REM · · OUTPUT RESULT                an edit of program
                                            in memory

LIST
5     REM · · INPUT FAHRENHEIT
10    INPUT F
15    REM · · CONVERT TO CENTIGRADE
20    LET C = (F — 32) * 5 / 9
25    REM · · OUTPUT RESULT
30    PRINT C
40    STOP
50    END

READY
RUN                                         Note the prompt ! is
! 32                                        computer generated
0                                           and varies between
                                            machines.

PROGRAM STOP AT 40
READY

FILE "TEMCON1"                              store the program on
READY                                       an appropriate
                                            secondary storage
                                            medium
```

Note: The prompt READY is output by the computer to signify that it is ready to receive BASIC statements or a command. Such a prompt will differ between, computers. *Refer to your computer manual.*

b. Problem. Modify the previous program so that it will allow more than one temperature to be input.

Clearly a loop will be introduced so that a section of the program can be used repeatedly. However, a method will have to be introduced to exit from the loop. In this example if a high temperature, say, 999 is input it will stop the program running.

Modified flowchart

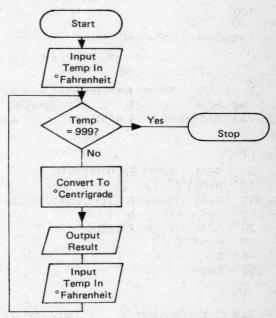

There will be **no** need to re-type the entire program since only a minor modification is necessary on the previous program.

The previous program can be re-loaded into the memory of the computer:

READY

```
OLD "TEMPCON1"
12    REM ·· TEST FOR EXIT FROM LOOP
13    IF F = 999 THEN STOP
32    INPUT F
35    GOTO 13
```

and by inserting four new lines (12), (13), (32) and (35) successfully edit the previous program.

```
LIST
5     REM · · INPUT FAHRENHEIT
10      INPUT F
12      REM · · TEST FOR EXIT FROM LOOP
13     IF  F = 999 THEN STOP
15        REM · · CONVERT TO CENTIGRADE
20        LET C = (F − 32) * 5 / 9
25        REM · · OUTPUT RESULTS
30        PRINT C
32        INPUT F
35     GOTO 13
40     STOP
50     END
READY
```

Upon inspecting the listing of the program it contains two **STOP** statements.

Clearly an edit is required by taking out line (40).

40 READY	by typing the line number only followed by return will remove that line.

```
RUN
! 106
41.11111111111
! 212
100
! 32
0
! 999
PROGRAM STOP AT 13
READY
```

FILE "TEMPCON2" READY	by changing the filename to TEMPCON2 the computer has also retained the original program TEMPCON1.

FURTHER PROGRAM WRITING.

8. a. **Problem.** Write a program to input the radii of circles and output their circumferences and areas. Terminate the routine by inputting a zero radius. Take mathematical π to be 3.14159 in the formula for circumference $C = 2 \pi R$ and Area $A = \pi R^2$, where R is the radius of a circle.

Flowchart

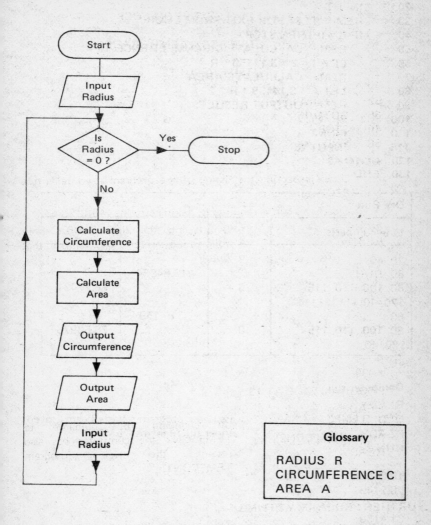

Glossary

RADIUS R
CIRCUMFERENCE C
AREA A

Program

```
10    REM ·· INPUT RADIUS
20       INPUT R
30       REM ·· TEST FOR EXIT FROM LOOP
40       IF R = 0 THEN STOP
50          REM ·· CALCULATE CIRCUMFERENCE
60          LET C = 2 * 3.14159 * R
70          REM ·· CALCULATE AREA
80          LET A = 3.14159 * R ↑ 2
90          REM ·· OUTPUT RESULTS
100         PRINT C
110         PRINT A
115         INPUT R
120      GOTO 40
130   END
```

Dry Run			
Line number(s)	R	C	A
20, 40	3		
60		18.84954	
80, 100, 110, 115	5		28.27431
120, 40			
60		31.4159	
80, 100, 110, 115	0		78.53975
120, 40			

Computer run

```
READY
OLD "TEMP"                       assume program has been saved
READY                            under the filename TEMP
RUN
! 3
18.84954
28.27431
! 5
31.4159
78.53975
! 0

PROGRAM STOP AT 40
READY
```

66

Notes:

i.   The accuracy to which a number is output from a calculation will vary between computers. The computer used to run this program gives an accuracy up to 13 significant figures, however, when calculating the results for (C) and (A) in the dry run 6 significant figures would have been more than adequate.

ii.   However, in reality the accuracy to which data should be output **must** reflect the accuracy to which the original data could be measured. In the previous example if the radius (R) was measured to an accuracy of 1 decimal place, then the values for circumference (C) and area (A) should be output to 1 decimal place.

Methods for outputting numbers to a required accuracy will be explained later in the text.

iii.   A further point to note is that if a negative value for a radius (R) had been input to the computer the value for the circumference (C) would be negative, and area (A) positive. This is clearly an undesirable result and the reader should be aware that inputting bad data to the computer will produce erroneous results or put another way *rubbish in will produce rubbish out!*

Methods for ensuring that only valid data are input to a computer will be explained later in the text.

b. **Problem.** Write a program to compute compound interest; input an amount, rate of interest and term; output the interest accumulated when the term has expired.

To help the reader who is not familiar with compound interest the following worked example will indicate how it can be calculated.

If the amount borrowed is £100 over a term of three years at a rate of interest of 10% then:

Interest after year 1 = 10% of £100 = £10
This interest is added to the amount, therefore,
Interest after year 2 = 10% of £110 = £11
Again this interest is added to the amount
Interest after year 3 = 10% of £121 = £12.10

Thus the interest over 3 years is **£33.10.**

The formula for compound interest will not be used in this problem.

Flowchart

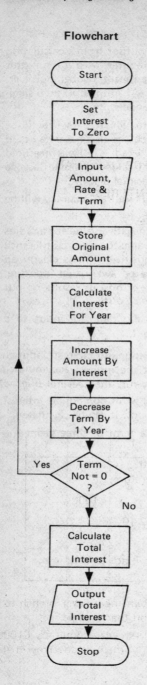

A first attempt at programming the solution could look like this:

```
10    REM ·· SET INTEREST TO ZERO
20    LET I = 0
30    REM ·· INPUT AMOUNT, RATE AND TERM
40    INPUT A
50    INPUT R
60    INPUT T
70    REM ·· STORE ORIGINAL AMOUNT
80    LET X = A
90      REM ·· CALCULATE INTEREST FOR ONE YEAR
100     LET I = A * R
110     REM ·· INCREASE AMOUNT BY INTEREST
120     LET A = A + I
130     REM ·· DECREASE TERM BY 1 YEAR
140     LET T = T − 1
150     REM ·· TEST FOR END OF TERM
160   IF T <> 0 THEN 90
170   REM ·· CALCULATE TOTAL INTEREST
180   LET Y = A − X
190   REM ·· OUTPUT TOTAL INTEREST
200   PRINT Y
210   STOP
220   END
```

However, if the program is given a dry-run then several *bugs* will appear.

Test data A = 100   R = 10   T = 3

Line number(s)	I	A	R	T	X	Y
20	0					
40, 50, 60		100	10	3		
80					100	
100	1000					
120	?	1000				
140		?		2		
160						
90 ?						

Bug 1. Line 90 is a **REM** statement. Remember **never** branch to a **REM** statement. (This is more of a bad habit than a bug).

Bug 2. The interest calculated for the first year comes to £1000, but the interest rate is only 10%, clearly there is an error in the equation on line 100.

The program will require the following amendments if it to run correctly.

```
100   LET I = A * R / 100
160   IF T < > 0 THEN 100
```

It is good practice to give the program in its amended form another dry run before going anywhere near the computer.

Using the same test data as before.

Line number(s)	I	A	R	T	X	Y
20	0					
40, 50, 60, 80		100	10	3	100	
100, 120, 140	10	110		2		
160						
100, 120, 140	11	121		1		
160						
100, 120, 140	12.1	133.1		0		
160						
180						33.1

computer run

READY
OLD "COMP"

READY
RUN
! 100   On each occasion a value is to be input,
! 10   the computer will output a prompt (!)
! 3   and *wait* for the user to input a value at
33.1   the keyboard of the terminal.
PROGRAM STOP AT 210
READY

EXERCISE

*1. Refer to your solution to the problem in chapter 5, question 8, part i.

a. Transfer the program to your computer.

b. LIST the program to ensure that it contains no typographical errors. If there are errors then edit them out.

c. RUN the program and if it contains no errors store the program on either magnetic tape or disc at your computer system.

d. If there are errors, during the RUN, in your program then give the program another dry-run in order to find the errors, correct the errors by performing an edit of your program, then return to part (b).

e. Repeat parts (a) to (d) for the program developed in part ii. of the problem.

The problems that follow require you to:

i.   Draw a flowchart.
ii. Construct a glossary
iii. Code a repetitive program. (Use a loop and exit condition).
iv. Invent test data where necessary and dry run the program.
v.   Proceed through steps (a) to (d) of question 1 in this exercise.

2. Devise a procedure to input a person's age in years, and name, if the age is between 18—25 years inclusive then output the name. Repeat the procedure for different names and ages, terminating the procedure when the age is 0 years.

3. Using the flowcharts developed in the exercise of chapter 3, write computer programs to:

a. Find the arithmetic mean of a set of numbers input to the computer and output the result (refer to question 2).

b. Input ten numbers to a computer and test which has the largest value, then output the result (refer to question 3).

4. A salesman earns a commission on the value of his sales. The following table shows the scale of the commission.

VALUE OF SALES (INCLUSIVE)	PERCENTAGE COMMISSION ON SALE VALUE
£1 — £999	1
£1000 — £9999	5
£10000 — £99999	10

Devise a procedure to input a figure for the value of his sales (in whole pounds only), and calculate and output his commission. Repeat the procedure to output different commissions from different sales figures. Terminate the routine when the sales figure is zero.

5. The difference in gas meter readings taken over two consecutive quarters of a year will give the amount of gas used in cubic feet.

Domestic gas is charged for on a sliding scale.

The first 50 therms 24p per therm.
Remainder 21p per therm.

If the difference in gas readings is multiplied by a factor of 1.040 this will give the number of therms used.

Devise a procedure to input meter readings from two consecutive quarters, calculate the cost (in pence) of gas used and output the result.

* **6.** A man is paid at the hourly rate of £8 per hour for the first 35 hours worked.

Thereafter overtime is paid at 1½ times the hourly rate for the next 25 hours and 2 times the hourly rate for a further 10 hours. He is not allowed to work more than 70 hours per week.

Devise a procedure to input the number of hours worked per week, calculate and output his gross weekly wage.

* **7.** A student studying Computer Science at a college is examined by coursework and written examination. Both components of the assessment carry a maximum of 50 marks.

The following rules are used by the examiners in order to pass or fail students.

     i.   A student must score a total of 40% or more in order to pass.

     ii.   A total mark of 39% is moderated to 40%.

However,

     iii. Each component must be passed with a minimum mark of 15.

     iv. If a student scores 40% or more but does not achieve the minimum mark in one component he is given a technical fail of 39% (This is **not** moderated to 40%).

Devise a procedure to input the marks for each component and output the final mark.

7 Further Input/Output

INTRODUCTION.

1. By now the reader may have realised the limitations of the statements **INPUT** and **PRINT** in the form they have been used.

a. The syntax of the **INPUT** statement has only allowed one variable per statement when clearly it might be more desirable to enter several values using only one **INPUT** statement.

b. When using the **INPUT** statement in a program it becomes both laborious and time consuming if the same data has to be entered through a keyboard each time the same computer program is run. Under such circumstances it would be far better to have the data written into the program.

c. The **PRINT** statement has only been used to output a single item of information. If the reader looks back at the output from programs there is little meaning attached to a few numbers and characters output from the programs. There is a need to improve the format of output from programs so that it becomes:
  i.   Descriptive of the data output.
  ii. Presented in a tidy and easily assimilated form.

MODIFIED INPUT STATEMENT.

2. a. The syntax of the **INPUT** statement can be expanded to include more than one variable name.

   INPUT variable name −1, variable name −2 · · · · · etc.

b. Therefore, there is no need to write three separate **INPUT** statements as illustrated in the last example of chapter 6.

```
40  INPUT A
50  INPUT R
60  INPUT T
```

The three statements can be combined into one statement:

```
40  INPUT A, R, T
```

However, when line 40 is executed the computer will expect three values separated by commas, corresponding to the variable names A, R, and T respectively, to be typed at the keyboard before the return key is pressed.

c. Thus if the last example of chapter 6 was edited such that line 40 was modified to that above, and lines 50 and 60 were deleted then the computer run would become.

```
READY
RUN
! 100, 10, 3
33.1
PROGRAM STOP AT 210
READY
```

READ/DATA.

3.   READ/DATA statements are used in a program when:

   a. The volume of data is large enough to preclude the use of **INPUT**.

   b. The data to be stored is of a permanent nature ie. a set of constants.

4.   a. The syntax of **READ/DATA** statements are:

   READ variable name -1, variable name $-2 \cdots\cdots$ etc.
   DATA literal -1, literal $-2 \cdots\cdots$ etc.

   i.   **Example**

   ```
   10   READ A, B, C
   20   DATA 5, 3, 2
   ```

   ii.   The variable names in the **READ** statement are associated with the literals in the **DATA** statement when both statements are scanned from left to right by the computer.

   iii.   In the example when the **READ** statement is executed the following assignments take place:

   $A = 5 \qquad B = 3 \qquad C = 2$

   iv.   **DATA** statements can be placed anywhere in a computer program since they are not executed by the computer, but only used by the **READ** statement.

   v.   However, it is advisable to group associated **READ** and **DATA** statements together since it will make dry running and de-bugging a program much easier, especially if the program contains a pro-liferation of **READ/DATA** statements.

   b. If there are fewer literals in a **DATA** statement than variable names in a **READ** statement then the next **DATA** statement in sequence will be scanned so that any outstanding variable names can be assigned literals.

   i.   Example.

   ```
   10   READ A, B, C, D
   20   DATA 10, 9
   30   READ E, F
   40   DATA 8, 7, 6
   50   DATA 5
   ```

ii. When the **READ** statements are executed the following assignments will take place.

A = 10   B = 9   C = 8   D = 7   E = 6   F = 5

iii. In this example the reader may wonder why one **READ/DATA** statement was not used. Well it could have been written as

```
10  READ A, B, C, D, E, F
20  DATA 10, 9, 8, 7, 6, 5
```

and the assignments would have been the same.

iv. However, there will come a time when data to be assigned to variable names will be physically too large to fit on to one BASIC line, and it will be necessary to divide the data into two or more **DATA** statements even though there might only be one **READ** statement.

c. It is worth noting that the length of a line in a BASIC program is governed by two factors.

i.   The type of input device/medium the programmer is using to input the program.

ii.   The implementation of BASIC being used. A line width of 80 characters is common.

d. The literals found in a **DATA** statement must be consistent with their associated variable names.

i.   **Example.**

```
10  READ A$, B$, C$
20  DATA "FORD", "B.L.", "VOLVO"
```

In this example string variables are used, however, it is possible to mix both string and numeric variables in the same **READ** statement provided they are respectively consistent with the literals in the **DATA** statement.

ii.   **Example.**

```
10  READ A$, S1, B$, S2
20  DATA "ENGLAND", 13, "WALES", 12
```

This would give the following assignments when the program segment was run.

A$ = ENGLAND   S1 = 13   B$ = WALES   S2 = 12

THE RESTORE STATEMENT.

5. a. If it is necessary to re-read part or all of the same set of data then a **RESTORE** statement should be used. This will alleviate the need to duplicate the same set of data in a program.

i. **Example.**

```
10   READ A, B, C, D
20   DATA 5, 7, 4, 2
30   RESTORE
40   READ E, F, G, H
```

ii. When the **READ** statements are executed the following assignments take place.

$A = 5$ $B = 7$ $C = 4$ $D = 2$ $E = 5$ $F = 7$ $G = 4$ $H = 2$

iii. Thus the **RESTORE** statement causes the computer to re-scan the **DATA** statement(s) starting at the lowest line-number.

iv. In the example if **RESTORE** had not been used the computer would inform the user that it was OUT OF DATA IN LINE 40 when the program segment was run, and the program would then stop running.

PRINTING STRING LITERALS.

6. a. Up to now the **PRINT** statement has only been used for printing values associated with variable names. However, there is a need to print descriptive output such as titles, headings and narrative.

This is achieved by writing the literal after the **PRINT** verb.

i. **Example.**

```
10   PRINT "TEMPERATURE CONVERSION"
20   PRINT "CENTIGRADE FAHRENHEIT"
```

When this program segment is run the resultant output would be.

```
TEMPERATURE CONVERSION
CENTIGRADE FAHRENHEIT
```

ii. Each **PRINT** statement above (line 10 and 20) will produce a separate line of output.

iii. A blank line can be output by writing **PRINT** only. In the example if **15 PRINT** is inserted into the program segment then the output would be:

```
TEMPERATURE CONVERSION

CENTIGRADE FAHRENHEIT
```

iv. Repeated use of **PRINT** on its own as separate BASIC statements will produce as many blank lines as there are **PRINT** statements.

ZONE PRINTING.

7. a. The output of information can be divided into zones across a screen or page by using commas between variable names and/or literals.

The width of each zone is the same across the screen or page, however, zone widths vary according to the dialect of BASIC being used. Between 10 and 21 character positions are common widths, giving between 4 and 5 print zones depending upon the width of the output medium being used.

Example.

i.   A BASIC dialect having a zone width of 10 characters using a screen of 40 character width will give 4 print zones, whereas a BASIC dialect having a zone width of 15 characters using a printer width of 80 characters will give 5 print zones.

Note.

Refer to your computer manual to determine the number of print zones applicable to the computer system you are using.

b. The syntax for zone printing is:

PRINX $\left\{ \begin{array}{l} \text{literal} -1 \\ \text{variable} -1 \end{array} \right\}$, $\left\{ \begin{array}{l} \text{literal} -2 \\ \text{variable} -2 \end{array} \right\}$, $\left\{ \begin{array}{l} \text{literal} -3 \\ \text{variable} -3 \end{array} \right\}$ · · · · · etc.

i.   **Example.**

```
10  READ A, B, C
20  DATA 4.6, -8.1, 7.9
30  PRINT A, B, C
```

If we assume a zone width of 14 characters then on running the program segment the following output is achieved.

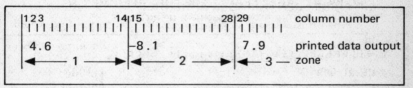

Note.

The **ECMA** standard stipulates that printed numbers have a leading space if the number is positive, a leading minus sign if the number is negative, and both have a trailing space. *Refer to your manual since this differs from BASIC dialect to dialect.*

ii.   **Example.**

```
10  READ A$, B$
20  DATA "SALARY", "TAX"
30  PRINT A$, B$
```

Output from program segment being run.

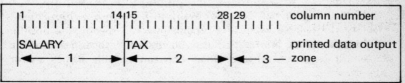

iii. **Example.**

```
10   READ R
20   DATA 10
30   LET C = 2 * 3.14 * R
40   LET A = 3.14 * R *R
50   PRINT "CIRCUMFERENCE", C
60   PRINT "AREA", A
```
Output from program segment being run.

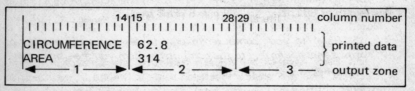

c. Suppression of zone printing. If a comma used for zone separation in a **PRINT** statement is **replaced** by a semi-colon (;) then the variables and/or literals listed in a **PRINT** statement will be printed one after another.

i. **Example.**

```
10   READ N$, A, H
20   DATA "JONES", 26,177.8
30   PRINT "NAME "; N$
40   PRINT "AGE (YEARS) "; A. "HEIGHT (CM) "; H
```
Output from program segment being run.

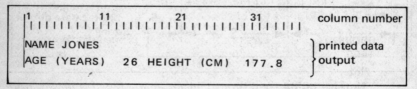

Note.

In line 30 if a space had not been deliberately introduced after NAME, ie. "NAME" then the printed result would be NAMEJONES. Although this technique has been used for printing AGE (YEARS) and HEIGHT (CM), whenever, a number is printed a leading space is output if the number is positive, or a hyphen is output (minus sign) if the number is negative.

TABULATION.

8. a. If the programmer does not want to use zoned output, then a facility is available where the programmer can specify the position and spacing of the printed output on the screen or page.

The use of **TAB (n)** will permit printing to start n columns from the left-hand margin of the screen or page;

n can be a numeric constant, variable or the result of an arithmetic expression.

In this text the range of n is $1 \leqslant n \leqslant$ line-width, however, some dialects of BASIC use $0 \leqslant n \leqslant$ line-width.

i.   The syntax for a combined **PRINT** and **TAB** statement is:

$$\textbf{PRINT } [\text{TAB } (n_1)] ; \begin{Bmatrix} \text{variable} -1 \\ \text{literal} -1 \end{Bmatrix} ; \quad [\text{TAB } (n_2)] ; \begin{Bmatrix} \text{variable} -2 \\ \text{literal} -2 \end{Bmatrix} \quad \dots$$

Note.

ii. Each item of the **PRINT** statement is separated by a semi-colon. This will ensure that each value is printed in the specified **TAB** position and departs from zone spacing. The square brackets [ ] denote that **TAB** is optional.

iii. **Example.**

```
10   PRINT TAB (3); "GROSS"; TAB (18); "NET"
20   READ A, B
30   DATA 1400, 1100
40   PRINT TAB (2); A; TAB (17); B
```
Output from program segment being run.

```
|1  3              14|  18
| | | | | | | | | | | | | | | | | | | | | |          column number

                                          }
     GROSS              NETT                  printed data output
     1400               1100
```

Note.

Since a leading space is printed with the values for **A** and **B**, they become lined up under the headings **GROSS** and **NETT**.

iv. **Example.**

```
10       READ F
20       DATA 5, 9, 15, 6, 1, 0
30       IF F = 0 THEN STOP
40           PRINT TAB (F); "*"
45           READ F
50       GOTO 30
60       END
```

Ouput from program being run.

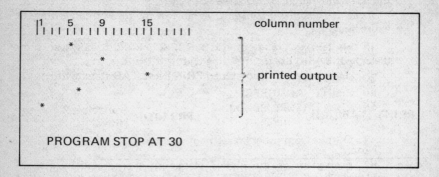

PROGRAM STOP AT 30

ZONE SPACING AND TABULATION.

9. a. Both zone spacing and tabulation can be mixed within a single **PRINT** statement.
    i.   **Example.**

    ```
    10   READ T, S
    20   DATA 1400, 6050
    30   PRINT TAB (5); "TAX", T; TAB (25); "SALARY", S
    ```
    Output from program segment being run.

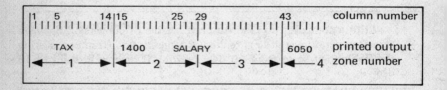

Note.
ii. If printed output continues across a zone then the next item to be printed will appear in the next zone if comma separation between the two items in the **PRINT** statement exists.

SUPPRESSION OF LINE FEEDS.

10. a. Generally the contents of each **PRINT** statement will be printed on a new line.

However, this can be overcome by using either comma or semi-colon punctuation at the end of the **PRINT** statement.

i. **Example.**

```
10  INPUT N$, R$, T$, P$
20  PRINT "NAME",
30  PRINT N$
40  PRINT "ADDRESS";
50  PRINT R$, T$, P$
```

Output from program segment when run.

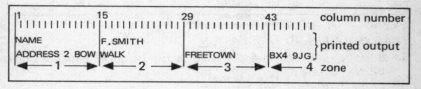

Assuming **N$** is input as "F. SMITH", **R$** as "2 BOW WALK", **T$** as "FREETOWN", and **P$** as "BX4 9JG".

WORKED EXAMPLES.

11. a. **Problem.**

Write a computer program to print a table of conversion between three temperature scales Fahrenheit, Centigrade and Reamur, covering the Fahrenheit scale from 20 degrees to 120 degrees in steps of 10 degrees.

Your table should include a title and headings for each temperature scale.

The conversion formulae are

Centigrade = (Fahrenheit—32) x (5 / 9)
Reamur = Centigrade x (4 / 5)

i. Flowchart

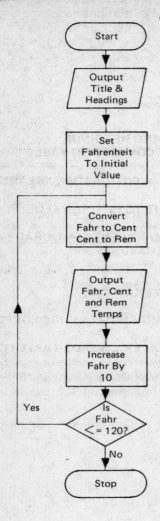

ii. **Glossary**

Fahrenheit	(fahr)	F
Centigrade	(cent)	C
Reamur	(rem)	R

iii. **Program.**

```
10    REM ·· OUTPUT TITLE AND HEADINGS
20    PRINT "TEMPERATURE CONVERSION TABLE"
30    PRINT
40    PRINT "FAHRENHEIT", "CENTIGRADE", "REAMUR"
50    PRINT
60    REM ·· SET FAHRENHEIT TO INITIAL VALUE
70    LET F = 20
80    REM ·· CALCULATE EQUIVALENT CENTIGRADE AND
90    REM ·· REAMUR TEMPERATURES
100      LET C = (F —32) * (5 / 9)
110      LET R = C * ( 4 / 5)
120      REM ·· OUTPUT TEMPERATURES
130      PRINT F, C, R
140      REM ·· INCREASE FAHRENHEIT BY 10 DEGREES
150      LET F = F + 10
160      REM ·· CHECK FOR UPPER LIMIT OF TABLE (120)
170   IF F < = 120 THEN 100
180   STOP
190   END
```

iv. Result of computer run.

```
TEMPERATURE CONVERSION TABLE

FAHRENHEIT              CENTIGRADE              REAMUR

20                     -6.6666666666667        -5.333333333334
30                     -1.1111111111111        -.8888888888889
40                      4.444444444444          3.555555555555
50                      10                      7.999999995999
60                      15.55555555556          12.4444444444444
70                      21.11111111111          16.88888888889
80                      26.66666666667          21.33333333333
90                      32.22222222222          25.77777777778
100                     37.77777777778          30.22222222222
110                     43.33333333333          34.66666666667
120                     48.88888888889          39.11111111111
STOP AT LINE 180
```

b. Problem.

Write a computer program to categorise the shape of a quadrilateral as either a square, rhombus, rectangle, parallelogram or irregular quadrilateral, having input the lengths of the four sides and one internal angle of the quadrilateral.

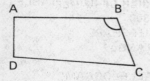

Reference chapter 3 paragraph 5a for the flowchart to the solution of this problem.

i.	Glossary.		
	Lengths of Sides	AB	A
		BC	B
		CD	C
		DA	D
	Angle at corner	B	X

ii.   Program.

```
10    REM ·· OUTPUT A PROMPT TO THE USER
20       PRINT "INPUT THE LENGTHS OF FOUR SIDES OF A QUAD"
30       REM ·· INPUT THE FOUR SIDES
40       INPUT A, B, C, D
50       PRINT
60       REM ·· OUTPUT A PROMPT TO THE USER
70       PRINT "INPUT ONE INTERNAL ANGLE"
80       REM ·· INPUT THE ANGLE
90       INPUT X
100      PRINT
110      REM ·· TEST FOR ALL SIDES EQUAL LENGTH
120      IF A <> B THEN 230
130        IF B <> C THEN 230
140          IF C <> D THEN 230
150            REM ·· TEST FOR SIZE OF ANGLE
160            IF X <> 90 THEN 200
170              REM ·· OUTPUT SHAPE
180              PRINT "SQUARE"
190            GOTO 350
200              PRINT "RHOMBUS"
210            GOTO 350
220          REM ·· TEST FOR OPPOSITE SIDES OF EQUAL LENGTH
230      IF A <> C THEN 320
240        IF B <> D THEN 320
250          REM ·· TEST FOR SIZE OF ANGLE
260          IF X <> 90 THEN 300
270            REM ·· OUTPUT SHAPE
280            PRINT "RECTANGLE"
290          GOTO 350
300            PRINT "PARALLELOGRAM"
310          GOTO 350
320      PRINT "IRREGULAR QUADRILATERAL"
330      REM ·· ASK USER IF MORE QUADRILATERALS ARE TO
340      REM ·· BE PROCESSED
350      PRINT
360      PRINT "CONTINUE? ANSWER Y (YES) N (NO)"
370      INPUT R$
380      REM ·· CHECK USER REPLY
390   IF R$ = "Y" THEN 20
400   STOP
410   END
```

iii. Result of computer run.

```
INPUT THE LENGTHS OF FOUR SIDES OF A QUADRILATERAL
!2,2,2,2

INPUT ONE INTERNAL ANGLE
!90

SQUARE

CONTINUE? ANSWER Y (YES) N (NO)
!Y
INPUT THE LENGTHS OF FOUR SIDES OF A QUADRILATERAL
!2,3,2,3

INPUT ONE INTERNAL ANGLE
!90

RECTANGLE

CONTINUE? ANSWER Y (YES) N (NO)
!Y
INPUT THE LENGTHS OF FOUR SIDES OF A QUADRILATERAL
!3,3,3,3

INPUT ONE INTERNAL ANGLE
!120

RHOMBUS

CONTINUE? ANSWER Y (YES) N (NO)
!Y

INPUT THE LENGTHS OF FOUR SIDES OF A QUADRILATERAL
!2,3,2,3

INPUT ONE INTERNAL ANGLE
!120

PARALLELOGRAM

CONTINUE? ANSWER Y (YES) N (NO)
!Y
INPUT THE LENGTHS OF FOUR SIDES OF A QUADRILATERAL
!4,5,5,6

INPUT ONE INTERNAL ANGLE
!80

IRREGULAR QUADRILATERAL

CONTINUE? ANSWER Y (YES) N (NO)
!N
STOP AT LINE 400
```

Notes.

i. When an **INPUT** statement is executed a prompt, either ! or ? depending upon the system, is output by the computer so that the user knows when to type information at the keyboard. The prompt, however, does not convey to the user what information to type or the quantity of information expected by the computer. In the last program **PRINT** statements at lines 20, 70 and 360 have been used to give instructions to the user about what information to type at the keyboard. These instructions will appear as printed output before the respective **INPUT** statements are executed.

ii. Notice from the events of the computer run through the last program that the prompt ! is printed after the various instructions to the user. Many dialects of BASIC will permit the programmer to replace the computer prompt by instructions to the user. The syntax of the modified **INPUT** statement being:

INPUT string literal, variable name —1, variable name —2 . . . .
or **INPUT** string literal; variable name —1, variable name —2 . . . .

However, beware this is not an ECMA standard. Refer to the BASIC manual for your computer to determine whether it is legal in your dialect of BASIC.

iii. In the last problem when testing whether the lengths of the sides of the quadrilateral are equal one of several possible methods has been used.

Line 120 to 140 could have been coded as:

```
120   IF A = B THEN 130
125   GOTO 230
130   IF B = C THEN 140
135   GOTO 230
140   IF C = D THEN 160
145   GOTO 230
160   IF X < > 90 THEN 200
```

I think the reader will agree that this program segment is undesirable since it not only requires more statements but involves extra branching.

Many dialects of BASIC permit the use of logical operators **(AND, OR, NOT)**, again this is not an ECMA standard. However, the use of logical operators does simplify the coding of multiple decisions.

Lines 120 to 140 could have been coded as:

IF A < > B OR B < > C OR C < > D THEN 230

The use of logical operators is explained to a greater depth in a later chapter.

iv. When the amount of data to be processed is dependent upon the user, the programmer cannot pre-define the number of times a loop in a program will be used.

Lines 330 to 390 show how the user is invited to reply whether there is more data to be processed or not.

c. **Problem.**

Write a computer program to find the maximum, minimum and mean weights of newly born babies, and output the results in a tabulated format.

The weights of the babies will not be input to the computer via a keyboard but read during program execution using **READ/DATA** statements.

Reference chapter 3 paragraph 5b for the flowchart to the solution of this problem.

The question in the flowchart "weight = 0?" can be programmed by including a weight of zero at the end of the **DATA** list, and testing for a zero weight as a means of making an exit from the loop.

i.   **Glossary** — reference flowchart.

WEIGHT	W
MINWT	M1
MAXWT	M2
TOTWT	T
MEANWT	M3
BABY-COUNT	B

ii.   **Program.**

```
10    REM ·· READ WEIGHT OF FIRST BABY
20    READ W
30    DATA 3.3, 4.1, 3.1, 2.9, 3.7, 3.6, 4.2, 3.5, 0
40    REM ·· SET MINWT MAXWT TOTWT TO WEIGHT OF BABY
50    LET M1 = W
60    LET M2 = W
70    LET T = W
80    REM ·· SET BABY-COUNT TO 1
90    LET B = 1
100   REM ·· READ WEIGHT OF NEXT BABY
110     READ W
130     REM ·· TEST FOR END OF DATA
140     IF W = 0 THEN 250
150       REM ·· COMPARE WEIGHT WITH MINWT
160       IF W < M1 THEN 190
170       REM ·· COMPARE WEIGHT WITH MAXWT
180       IF W > M2 THEN LET M2 = W
185       GOTO 210
190       LET MI = W
200       REM ·· INCREASE BABY-COUNT
210       LET B = B + 1
215       REM ·· INCREASE TOTWT BY WEIGHT
220       LET T = T + W
225       REM ·· READ WEIGHT OF NEXT BABY
230         READ W
235   GOTO 140
240   REM ·· CALCULATE MEANWT
250   LET M3 = T/B
260   REM ·· OUTPUT RESULTS IN TABULATED FORMAT
270   PRINT "MAX. WEIGHT ="; M2;
280   PRINT TAB (20); "MIN. WEIGHT ="; M1;
```

```
290   PRINT TAB (40); "MEAN WEIGHT ="; M3
300   STOP
310   END
```

iii. **Result of computer run.**

```
MAX.WEIGHT = 4.2    MIN.WEIGHT = 2.9    MEAN WEIGHT = 3.55
STOP AT LINE 300
```

d. **Problem.** Write a computer program to print an electricity bill. The layout of the bill is as follows.

```
                         ELECTRICITY BILL
                         -----------  ----

MR. P.L.SMITH                       REF.NO. 1793 8462 1961
16 CORN STREET                      DATE 21 AUG 1981
WATFORD

PREVIOUS    PRESENT    TARIFF       UNITS    PRICE        AMOUNT
READING     READING                          PER UNIT     (PENCE)

 681         1165      DOMESTIC      484      4.5          2178

QUARTERLY CHARGE                                           600

                                             TOTAL         2778
```

Note: Input the following details to the program.

Price per unit of electricity and the quarterly standing charge; and today's date.

The name, address, reference number, previous and present meter readings of a customer.

Hint: From this problem it is clearly a good idea to design computer output on squared paper before attempting to code the output segment of the program.

i. **Flowchart.**

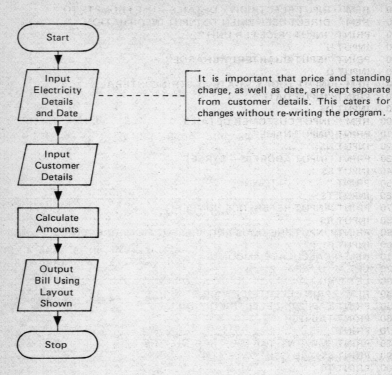

It is important that price and standing charge, as well as date, are kept separate from customer details. This caters for changes without re-writing the program.

ii.

Glossary	
Price per unit of electricity	U
Quarterly charge	Q
Today's date	D$
Name of customer	N$
Address — Street	S$
Town	T$
Reference number	R$
Previous meter reading	P1
Present meter reading	P2
Amount	A
Total	T

iii. Program.

```
10    REM ·· INPUT ELECTRICITY DETAILS — USE PROMPTS TO
20    REM ·· DIRECT USER WHEN TO INPUT INFORMATION
30    PRINT "INPUT PRICE PER UNIT"
40    INPUT U
50    PRINT "INPUT QUARTERLY CHARGE"
60    INPUT Q
70    REM ·· INPUT TODAY'S DATE AS STRING LITERAL
80    PRINT "INPUT DATE"
90    INPUT D$
100   REM ·· INPUT CUSTOMER DETAILS
110   PRINT "INPUT NAME"
120   INPUT N$
130   PRINT "INPUT ADDRESS — STREET"
140   INPUT S$
150   PRINT "        — TOWN"
160   INPUT T$
170   PRINT "INPUT REFERENCE NUMBER"
180   INPUT R$
190   PRINT "INPUT PREVIOUS AND PRESENT METER READINGS"
200   INPUT P1, P2
210   REM ·· CALCULATE AMOUNTS
220   LET A = U * (P2 — P1)
230   LET T = Q + A
240   REM ·· PRINT ELECTRICITY BILL
250   PRINT TAB (20); "ELECTRICITY  BILL"
260   PRINT TAB (20); "------------  ---- "
270   PRINT
280   PRINT "MR."; N$; TAB (35); "REF. NO."; R$
290   PRINT S$; TAB (35); "DATE"; D$
300   PRINT TS
310   PRINT
320   PRINT "PREVIOUS  PRESENT  TARIFF  UNITS  PRICE     AMOUNT"
330   PRINT "READING   READING                  PER UNIT  (PENCE)"
340   PRINT
350   PRINT P1; TAB (11); P2; TAB (20); "DOMESTIC"; TAB (30); P2 — P1;
360   PRINT TAB (38); U; TAB (49); A
370   PRINT
380   PRINT "QUARTERLY CHARGE"; TAB (50); Q
390   PRINT
400   PRINT TAB (39); "TOTAL"; TAB (49); T
410   STOP
420   END
```

```
INPUT PRICE PER UNIT
!4.5
INPUT QUARTERLY CHARGE
!600
INPUT DATE
!21 AUG 1981
INPUT NAME
!P.L.SMITH
INPUT ADDRESS - STREET
!16 CORN STREET
             - TOWN
!WATFORD
INPUT REFERENCE NUMBER
!1793 8462 1961
INPUT PREVIOUS AND PRESENT METER READINGS
!681
!1165
                    ELECTRICITY BILL
                    ----------- ----
```

MR. P.L.SMITH				REF.NO.1793 8462 1961	
16 CORN STREET				DATE 21 AUG 1981	
WATFORD					

PREVIOUS	PRESENT	TARIFF	UNITS	PRICE	AMOUNT
READING	READING			PER UNIT	(PENCE)
681	1165	DOMESTIC	484	4.5	2178
QUARTERLY CHARGE					600
				TOTAL	2778

```
STOP AT LINE 410
```

v. **Note:** *The reader should observe that the computer used to run this program does not print one space in front of a number, as stated in the ECMA standard.*

EXERCISE.

1. Comment upon the syntax errors in the following BASIC statements.

    a. **INPUT A; B; C**

    b. **INPUT A, B, C!**

    c. **READ X; Y, Z**

    d. **DATA −6 : 14, 32;**

    e. **RESTORE DATA**

    f. **PRINT "FLIGHT NUMBER;**

    g. **PRINT "NAME OF ACCOUNT" N$**

    h. **PRINT TAB (32); X; TAB (16); Y**

    i. **PRINT; PRINT; PRINT**

    j. **PRINT X / TAB (18); Y; TAB (36): Z**

2. Dry-run the following program segment with the data provided.

```
10      READ A, B, C
20      DATA 8, 16, 32, "EIGHT", "SIXTEEN", "THIRTY-TWO"
30      READ D$, E$, F$
40      RESTORE
50      READ X, Y, Z
```

3. Give the following program segment a dry-run and comment upon the errors.

```
10      READ A, B
20      DATA "SALARY", "TAX"
30      RESTORE
40      READ X$, Y$, Z$
```

4. Comment upon the figure that will be output when the following program segment is run.

```
10      LET R = 1
20        PRINT TAB (20); "I"
30        LET R = R + 1
40      IF R < 4 THEN 20
50      LET C = 17
60        PRINT TAB (C); "-";
70        LET C = C + 1
80      IF C < 24 THEN 60
90      PRINT "  "
100     PRINT TAB (20); "I"
110       LET R = R + 1
120     IF R < 7 THEN 100
130     STOP
140     END
```

5. Draw a flowchart, construct a glossary and write a computer program to print a currency conversion table from Pounds Sterling to French Francs, German Marks and Italian Lire.

   The table should contain a title and each column should have the name of the currency printed.

   Use as data a value for Pounds Sterling in the range from £5 to £50 in steps of £5.

   You can obtain the current conversion rates from your local bank.

* 6. Draw a flowchart, construct a glossary and write a computer program to print a simple telephone bill. Your program should input:

   a. Name of customer.

   b. Address.

   c. Telephone number.

d. Previous meter reading.

e. Current meter reading.

The number of units used in a quarter year is the difference between the current and previous meter readings. Assume the cost of a unit is 5p. The program should calculate the cost of using the telephone and include a fixed rental charge of 1200p per quarter to give a sub-total. Value added tax is charged at 15% on the sub-total. The sum of the sub-total and value added tax gives the total amount due.

The bill should be printed or displayed in the following format.

```
                    TELEPHONE  BILL
                    ---------  ---

NAME:  MR. F. SMYTHE                  ADDRESS:  28  FIELD  WAY
                                                OXFORD
TELEPHONE  NUMBER:  OXFORD  715                 OX1  6QT

PREVIOUS  METER  READING:  21794
CURRENT  METER  READING:    21936

CHARGES
-------

CALLS @ 5p  PER  UNIT  ON  142  UNITS             710
RENTAL                                           1200

SUB-TOTAL                                        1910
VAT @  15%                                        286·5

TOTAL  AMOUNT  DUE                               2196·5
```

* 7. Using the flowcharts developed in the exercise in chapter 3 construct glossaries, invent test data and write computer programs to:

a. Input the lengths of three sides of a triangle and output the shape of the triangle i.e. isosceles, equilateral, right-angled or scalene. (reference question 8).

b. Using the rules for calculating income tax in Utopia (reference question 6) input to the computer

  i.   Gross salary.

  ii. Personal status (married or single).

  iii. Number of children.

and output information under the following headings:

PERSONAL ALLOWANCE:

CHILD ALLOWANCE:

TAXABLE INCOME:

INCOME TAX:

8 Loops, Subroutines and Multiple Branching

INTRODUCTION.

1. This chapter deals with:

   a. **FOR/NEXT** statements.

   b. **GOSUB/RETURN** statements.

   c. **ON · · GOTO · ·** statement.

LOOPS.

2. Consider the problem of controlling the number of times a program segment is executed by introducing a loop. The coding would involve:

   a. Setting a loop counter to an initial value.

   b. Increasing the value of the loop counter each time a program segment within the loop has been executed.

   c. Testing the loop counter to determine whether its value has reached the number of loops of the program segment.

3. This situation is evident in a previous example (chapter 5, para 9) in which a loop counter was used to process the wages of ten employees.

   The three areas required for loop control are shown in both flowchart and coded form (Fig. 8.1).

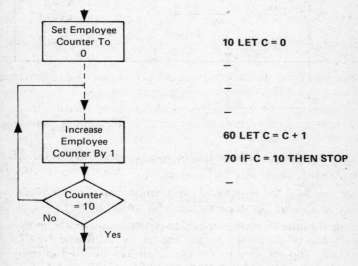

Figure 8.1.

4. a. The process of representing the control for a loop on a flowchart can be combined into one flowchart symbol.

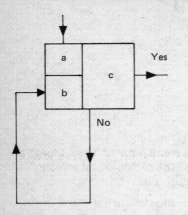

a — initialising the loop counter.
b — increasing the counter.
c — testing the value of the counter.

Hence the segment of flowchart above can be reduced to:

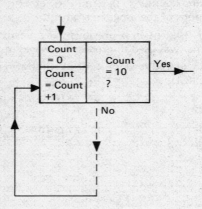

This symbol is **NOT** part of the British Standards Institution Flowchart symbols, it is used for convenience only in this text.

If you are preparing for an external examination then check with the Examinations Board about their acceptance of this "loop" symbol.

b. i. The process of coding the loop control into a computer program can be simplified by the use of the **FOR** and **NEXT** statements. The solution to the example taken from (chapter 5 para 9) could be re-stated as the flowchart shown in figure 8.2.

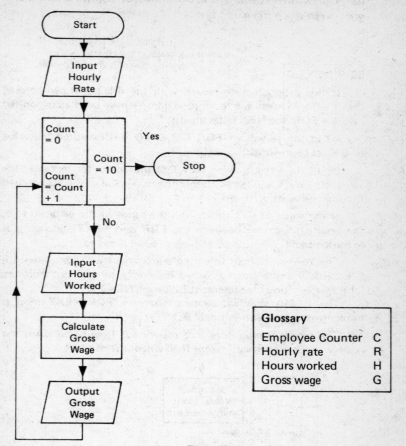

Glossary

Employee Counter	C
Hourly rate	R
Hours worked	H
Gross wage	G

Figure 8.2.

```
10      INPUT R
20      FOR C = 0 TO 9
30         INPUT H
40         LET G = H * R
50         PRINT G
60      NEXT C
70      STOP
80      END
```

97

ii.   The two statements that provide the loop control are:

20   FOR C = 0 TO 9

—

—

—

60   NEXT C

If this program is compared with the original it can be seen that the three areas a, b, c for loop control have been incorporated into the **FOR** and **NEXT** statements.

When the statement **FOR C = 0 TO 9** is executed the value of C is set to the initial value 0.

Upon the execution of **NEXT C** the computer increases the value of C by 1 and tests whether the new value of C has exceeded the final value of 9. (C = 10 ?)

If the value of C is still within the range of the values 0 to 9, the program segment between the **FOR** and **NEXT** statements is executed again.

The re-execution of this program segment will continue until C exceeds the final value 9, when the computer will exit from the loop by executing the statement following **NEXT C**.

iii. The ECMA standard suggests that the **FOR/NEXT** loop is implemented as shown in figure 8.3.

The reader should note that the loop is terminated when the counter limit is exceeded rather than when it is reached.

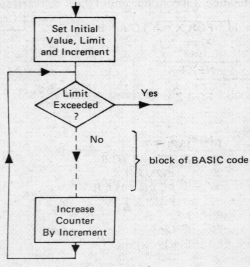

Figure 8.3.

5. The syntax of the **FOR/NEXT** statement is:

FOR numeric variable = initial   **TO** final   [**STEP** incremental value]
     name   value   value

NEXT numeric variable
     name

Note: STEP is optional, when omitted an Incremental value of +1 is assumed.

     Initial value, final value and incremental value can be numeric literals, numeric variable names or arithmetic expressions.

Examples.

     i.   **FOR K = 1 TO 9 STEP 2**
           —
           —
           NEXT K

K will be assigned the values 1, 3, 5, 7, 9 respectively, for each iteration of the program segment.

     ii.   **FOR L = I TO J STEP K**
           —
           —
           NEXT L

L will be assigned the values I, I + K, I + 2K, I + 3K, $\cdots\cdots$ J respectively, for each iteration. If I + nK will never become equal to J, then iteration will continue until I + nK is greater than the final value J.

     iii.   **FOR X = A TO A * B**
           —
           —
           NEXT X

     iv.   **FOR Z = 16 TO 4 STEP —4**
           —
           —
           NEXT Z

     If the incremental value is negative then initial value should be numerically higher than the final value.

RULES FOR USING FOR/NEXT LOOPS.

6.   a. Loops may be nested (embedded one inside the other).

```
10      PRINT "I", "VALUES OF J"
20        FOR I = 1 TO 2
30          PRINT I,
40            FOR J = 1 TO 3
50              PRINT J,
60            NEXT J
70          PRINT
80        NEXT I
90      STOP
100     END
```

The reader should dry-run this program to verify that the output is as follows:

I	VALUES OF J		
1	1	2	3
2	1	2	3

Note: The depth to which loops may be nested depends upon the computer system being used. However, in practise nesting rarely exceeds 3 or 4 loops in depth.

b. Loops must **never** cross, this program segment is **wrong**.

```
10      FOR I = 1 TO N
20      FOR J = 1 TO M
30      FOR K = 1 TO P
—
—
100     NEXT K
110     NEXT I
120     NEXT J
```

A method of trying to avoid this situation occurring is for the programmer to indent pairs of **FOR/NEXT** statements at different positions across the page or screen. Some computers will list **FOR/NEXT** statements using this *indented* format. This technique shows the starting and ending positions of loops in a program.

```
10      FOR I = 1 TO N
20        FOR J = 1 TO M
30          FOR K = 1 TO P
—
—
100         NEXT K
110       NEXT J
120     NEXT I
```

c. The numeric variable name given to a loop should **never** be reassigned within the loop.

```
┌─10      FOR I = 1 TO N
│ 20      LET I = I + 1
│ ─
│ ─
│ ─
└─60      NEXT I
```

d. It is permissible to branch outside of a **FOR/NEXT** range, provided the parameters of the loop are not changed, and transfer is back into the loop.

```
    ┌─10      FOR I = 1 TO N
 ┌──┼─20          GOTO 100
 │  └→30
 │   │
 │   │
 │   │
 │  ┌─60      NEXT I
 │  │
 │  │
 │  │
 └──→100         LET X = I * I
    │110     PRINT X
    └─120         GOTO 30
```

Branching out of a loop using **GOTO** is a BAD HABIT and should be avoided.

e. The following diagrams illustrate the ranges of several **FOR/NEXT** loops. Diagram i. shows branches that are permissible and diagram ii. shows those that are not.

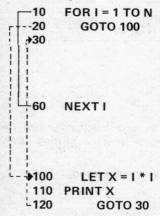

i. LEGAL BRANCHING   ii. ILLEGAL BRANCHING

101

f. Avoid fractional **STEP** values, since these could lead to rounding problems. ie. in long loops the values generated may not be exact representations of the values intended.

WORKED EXAMPLES.

7. a. **Problem.** Write a computer program to find the sum of the odd integers in the range 1 to 21 inclusive.

Flowchart

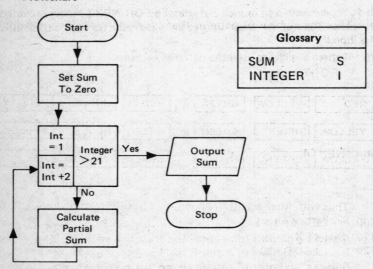

Glossary	
SUM	S
INTEGER	I

Program.

```
10    REM ·· SET SUM TO ZERO
20    LET S = 0
30    REM ·· SET UP LOOP TO GENERATE ODD INTEGERS
40    REM ·· IN THE RANGE 1 TO 21
50    FOR I = 1 TO 21 STEP 2
60       REM ·· CALCULATE PARTIAL SUM
70       LET S = S + I
80       REM ·· END OF LOOP
90    NEXT I
100   REM ·· OUTPUT SUM
110   PRINT "SUM OF ODD INTEGERS FROM 1 – 21 =";S
120   STOP
130   END
```

output

SUM OF ODD INTEGERS FROM 1 – 21 = 121

PROGRAM STOP AT 120

b. **Problem.** Consider having a number of childrens' wooden building bricks each of a different colour.

If two bricks are placed side by side they will form a pattern, change the position of one brick and another pattern is formed.

eg.

| RED | YELLOW | | YELLOW | RED |

Thus the number of patterns that can be formed using two bricks is 2 or 1 x 2.

If three bricks are used the patterns become:

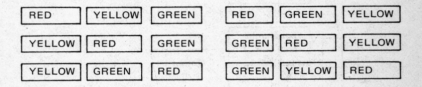

RED	YELLOW	GREEN		RED	GREEN	YELLOW
YELLOW	RED	GREEN		GREEN	RED	YELLOW
YELLOW	GREEN	RED		GREEN	YELLOW	RED

Thus with three bricks the number of patterns is 6 or 1 x 2 x 3.
Similarly with:

4 bricks   number of patterns is   1 x 2 x 3 x 4
5 bricks   number of patterns is   1 x 2 x 3 x 4 x 5
6 bricks   number of patterns is   1 x 2 x 3 x 4 x 5 x 6
etc.

From these results the reader should deduce that the number of patterns is always the product of the integers from 1 to the number of bricks.

Write a computer program to output a table of the number of patterns formed as the number of different coloured building bricks increases from 3 to 9.

i. **Flowchart.**

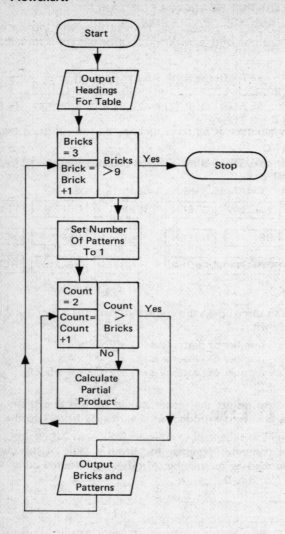

ii. **Glossary.**

Number of Bricks	B
Number of patterns	P
Counter	C

iii. **Program.**

```
10    REM ·· OUTPUT HEADINGS FOR TABLE
20    PRINT "BRICKS", "PATTERNS"
30    REM ·· SET UP LOOP TO GENERATE THE NUMBER
40    REM ·· OF BRICKS FROM 3 TO 9
50    FOR B = 3 TO 9
60       REM ·· SET NUMBER OF PATTERNS TO 1
70       LET P = 1
80       REM ·· SET UP LOOP TO CALCULATE NUMBER OF PATTERNS
90       FOR C = 2 TO B
100         LET P = P * C
110      NEXT C
120      REM ·· OUTPUT NUMBER OF BRICKS AND PATTERNS
130      PRINT B, P
140      REM ·· CHANGE THE NUMBER OF BRICKS
150   NEXT B
160   STOP
170   END
```

iv. **Result of computer run.**

BRICKS	PATTERNS
3	6
4	24
5	120
6	720
7	5040
8	40320
9	362880

STOP AT LINE 160

c. **Problem.** The table below shows the seasonal trends in the sales of one product taken over a period of 6 years. Write a computer program to calculate the average sales for each quarter.

Year	Quarters			
	1	2	3	4
1976	46	57	60	55
1977	45	56	62	54
1978	51	58	65	54
1979	49	59	61	55
1980	52	60	59	53
1981	53	59	64	54

i. **Flowchart.**

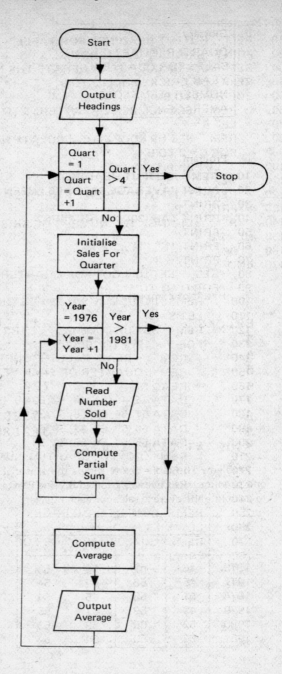

ii. **Glossary.**

QUARTER (QUART)	Q
SALES FOR QUARTER	S
YEAR	Y
NUMBER ITEMS SOLD	N
AVERAGE	A

iii. **Program.**

```
10     REM · · OUTPUT HEADINGS
20     PRINT "AVERAGE SALES BETWEEN 1976 — 1981"
30     PRINT
40     PRINT TAB (30); "QUARTERS"
50     PRINT
60     PRINT "1", "2", "3", "4"
70     PRINT
80     REM · · SET UP LOOP FOR QUARTER YEAR
90     FOR Q = 1 TO 4
100      REM · · INITIALISE SALES FOR QUARTER
110      LET S = 0
120      REM · · SET UP LOOP FOR YEARS
130      FOR Y = 1976 TO 1981
140        REM · · READ SALES FIGURE FOR THE SAME
150        REM · · QUARTER OF EACH YEAR
160        READ N
170        DATA 46, 45, 51, 49, 52, 53
180        DATA 57, 56, 58, 59, 60, 59
190        DATA 60, 62, 65, 61, 59, 64
200        DATA 55, 54, 54, 55, 53, 54
210        REM · · COMPUTE PARTIAL SUM
220        LET S = S + N
230        REM · · MOVE TO NEXT YEAR
240      NEXT Y
250      REM · · COMPUTE AVERAGE
260      LET A = S / 6
270      REM · · OUTPUT AVERAGE FOR QUARTER
280      PRINT A,
290      REM · · MOVE TO NEXT QUARTER
300    NEXT Q
310    STOP
320    END
```

iv. **Result of computer run.**

```
AVERAGE SALES BETWEEN 1976-1981
                           QUARTERS
1                  2                    3                  4
45.3333333333      58.16666666667       61.83333333333     54.16666666667
STOP AT LINE 310
```

v. **Note:** Each **DATA** statement contains the sales figures for the same quarter over a period of 6 years.

SUBROUTINES.

8. a. There is often a need when writing a computer program to write a program segment to perform a specific task, and use that segment at difference places within the program. The program segment should be written once, and branched to from different parts of a program. Such a program segment should provide the facility of returning the computer to the next executable statement after the one which caused the branch to the program segment. The use of **GOTO** to effect branching would mean that the program segment could only be referenced from one place in a program, hence, it is not general enough.

Such a program segment is known as a **Subroutine.**

b. Subroutines have the following advantages in program construction:

   i.   The same subroutine can be used anywhere in the program without re-writing it.
   ii. Subroutines can be written to perform specific tasks which are needed in a number of places in a program.
   iii. The de-bugging of a program is faster since it is easier to trace through subroutines than it is through one large program.
   iv. Altering parts of a program would be confined to inserting, deleting or amending subroutines.
   v.   The documentation of a large program is much simplified by the documentation of individual subroutines.

c. The creation of subroutines is possible by the use of the verbs **GOSUB** and **RETURN**. The following illustration shows that the statement **GOSUB 500** causes a branch to line 500, followed by the sequential execution of statements until the **RETURN** is executed. **RETURN** will cause a branch back to the next executable statement after **GOSUB 500**.

108

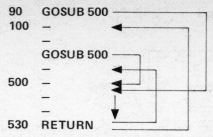

d. It is possible to *nest* subroutines, that is to have one subroutine branching to or *calling* another subroutine. The called subroutine then calls another subroutine, and so on. There is a limitation to the depth of nesting subroutines, however, this is sufficiently large as not to be a problem to the reader.

The following illustration shows three subroutines nested.

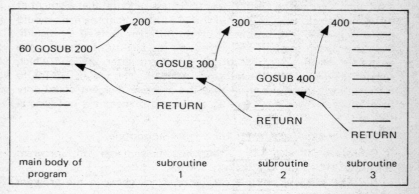

WORKED EXAMPLES.

9. a. **Problem.** Write a computer program to use the computer as a teaching machine for computer aided learning. The subject is the dates of historical events.

The strategy used in this program is as follows.

Ten questions will be asked relating to events in history. The student is invited to type at the keyboard of a terminal a date associated with an event.

If the date is wrong, the question is repeated and the student is given a second chance to give the correct answer.

If the date is wrong after the second attempt the student is given the right answer.

For every correct answer the student scores 1 point.

In the flowchart the symbol

is used to represent a call to a subroutine. Since the subroutine is only a segment of program the terminal symbols of the flowchart representing the subroutine are labelled with ENTER and EXIT.

i. **Flowchart.**

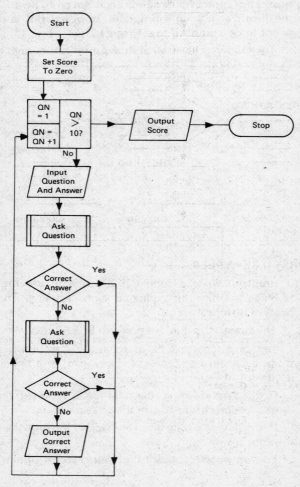

ii. Flowchart of Subroutine to "ASK QUESTION"

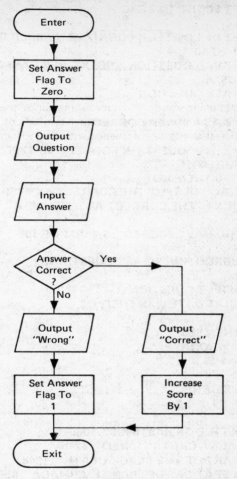

Note: *A correct answer is shown by assigning zero to the variable F; in the event of a wrong answer one would be assigned to the variable F.*

iii. **Glossary.**	
Score	S
QN (Question Number)	N
Question	Q$
Correct Answer	A
Student's answer	X
Answer Flag	F

iv. **Program.**

```
10    REM ·· SET SCORE TO ZERO
20    LET S = 0
30    REM ·· SET UP LOOP FOR COUNTING NUMBER OF QUESTIONS
40    FOR N = 1 TO 10
50        REM ·· READ QUESTION AND CORRECT ANSWER
60        READ Q$, A
70        REM ·· ASK QUESTION
80        GOSUB 500
90        REM ·· WAS ANSWER CORRECT?
100       IF F = 0 THEN 160
110           REM ·· ASK QUESTION FOR SECOND TIME
120           GOSUB 500
130           IF F = 0 THEN 160
140               REM ·· OUTPUT THE CORRECT ANSWER
150               PRINT "THE CORRECT ANSWER IS"; A
160   NEXT N
165   PRINT "YOU HAVE SCORED"; S; "OUT OF 10"
170   STOP
499   REM ·· SUBROUTINE TO ASK QUESTIONS
500   LET F = 0
510   REM ·· OUTPUT QUESTION
520   PRINT "WHAT DATE WAS THE": Q$
530   INPUT X
540   IF A = X THEN 580
550       PRINT "WRONG"
560       LET F = 1
570   GOTO 600
580       PRINT "CORRECT"
590       LET S = S + 1
600   RETURN
610   DATA "BATTLE OF HASTINGS", 1066
620   DATA "MAGNA CARTA SIGNED", 1215
630   DATA "START OF THE BLACK DEATH", 1348
640   DATA "DEFEAT OF THE SPANISH ARMADA", 1588
650   DATA "CIVIL WAR IN BRITAIN", 1642
660   DATA "GREAT FIRE OF LONDON", 1666
670   DATA "START OF THE FRENCH REVOLUTION", 1789
680   DATA "START OF THE BOER WAR", 1899
690   DATA "ACCESSION OF QUEEN ELIZABETH II", 1952
700   DATA "FIRST MAN SENT INTO SPACE", 1961
710   END
```

iv. **Results of computer run.**

```
WHAT DATE WAS THE BATTLE OF HASTINGS
!1066
CORRECT
WHAT DATE WAS THE MAGNA CARTA SIGNED
!1214
WRONG
WHAT DATE WAS THE MAGNA CARTA SIGNED
!1215
CORRECT
WHAT DATE WAS THE START OF THE BLACK DEATH
!1565
WRONG
WHAT DATE WAS THE START OF THE BLACK DEATH
!1564
WRONG
THE CORRECT ANSWER IS 1348
WHAT DATE WAS THE DEFEAT OF THE SPANISH ARMADA
!1588
CORRECT
WHAT DATE WAS THE CIVIL WAR IN BRITAIN
!1642
CORRECT
WHAT DATE WAS THE GREAT FIRE OF LONDON
!1666
CORRECT
WHAT DATE WAS THE START OF THE FRENCH REVOLUTION
!1700
WRONG
WHAT DATE WAS THE START OF THE FRENCH REVOLUTION
!1788
WRONG
THE CORRECT ANSWER IS 1789
WHAT DATE WAS THE START OF THE BOER WAR
!1899
CORRECT
WHAT DATE WAS THE ACCESSION OF QUEEN ELIZABETH II
!1952
CORRECT
WHAT DATE WAS THE FIRST MAN SENT INTO SPACE
!1961
CORRECT
YOU HAVE SCORED 8 OUT OF 10
STOP AT LINE 170
```

b. **Problem.** This example is designed for those readers who are students of mathematics or statistics.

Write a program to calculate the number of ways of selecting a team of R players from N players, and output the result.

The mathematical solution to this problem is found by using the expression.

$N ! / (R ! * (N - R) !)$! means factorial

Since three factorial values for N, R and N − R have to be calculated **one** subroutine for calculating the factorial value of a number should be incorporated into the program.

In this example the subroutine will have two variables X and P; where X represents a value for either N, R or (N − R) and P represents a value for N !, R ! or (N − R) !.

Both X and P are known as *parameters* of the subroutine and their respective values must be passed from and to the main program.

113

i. **Flowchart.**

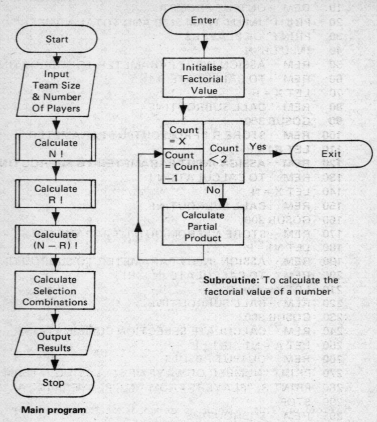

Main program

Subroutine: To calculate the factorial value of a number

ii. | **Glossary.** |

Main Program

Size of team	R
Number of players to choose from	N
N !	N1
R !	R1
Result N ! / (R ! * (N − R) !)	A

Subroutine

Partial factorial value and final value on return	P
Number whose factorial value is to be calculated	X
Counter	I

iii. **Program.**

```
10    REM ·· OUTPUT PROMPT
20    PRINT "INPUT TEAM SIZE AND TOTAL NUMBER";
30    PRINT "OF PLAYERS"
40    INPUT R, N
50    REM ·· ASSIGN INPUT PARAMETER TO SUBROUTINE
60    REM ·· TO CALCULATE R !
70    LET X = R
80    REM ·· CALL SUBROUTINE
90    GOSUB 300
100   REM ·· STORE R ! FROM OUTPUT PARAMETER
110   LET R1 = P
120   REM ·· ASSIGN INPUT PARAMETER TO SUBROUTINE
130   REM ·· TO CALCULATE N !
140   LET X = N
150   REM .. CALL SUBROUTINE
160   GOSUB 300
170   REM ·· STORE N! FROM OUTPUT PARAMETER
180   LET N1 = P
190   REM ·· ASSIGN INPUT PARAMETER TO SUBROUTINE
200   REM ·· TO CALCULATE (N − R) !
210   LET X = N − R
220   REM ·· CALL SUBROUTINE
230   GOSUB 300
240   REM ·· CALCULATE SELECTION COMBINATIONS
250   LET A = N1 / (R1 * P)
260   REM ·· OUTPUT RESULT
270   PRINT "NUMBER OF WAYS OF SELECTING A TEAM OF";
280   PRINT R; "PLAYERS FROM"; N; "PLAYERS IS"; A
290   STOP
295   REM ·· SUBROUTINE
300      LET P = 1
310      FOR I = X TO 2 STEP − 1
320         LET P = P * I
330      NEXT I
340   RETURN
350   END
```

Note: Ensure that the computer cannot continue sequentially executing instructions from the main program to the subroutine.

The statement **STOP** at line 290 will ensure this.

Remember the execution of Subroutine statements must only be made through a call to a subroutine using **GOSUB**.

iv. **Results of computer run.**

```
INPUT TEAM SIZE AND TOTAL NUMBER OF PLAYERS
!5,8
NUMBER OF WAYS OF SELECTING A TEAM OF5 PLAYERS FROM 8 PLAYERS IS 56
STOP AT LINE 290
```

MULTIPLE BRANCHING.

10. a. The techniques of branching dealt with so far fall into two categories.

    i.   unconditional branching **GOTO**

    ii.   conditional branching **IF ·· THEN ··**

The second category relies upon the answer to a question being *yes* or *no*. But what if the outcome of a decision has more than two answers?

b. Consider the problem of writing a program to test a person's knowledge of air-distances between cities in which the user is given a choice of answers. The correct answer to a question scores 20, whereas answers close to the correct answer score 10, but grossly wrong answers do not score marks.

The output from such a program could look like this:

```
WHAT IS THE DISTANCE IN MILES BETWEEN
LONDON AND NEW YORK?

IS IT:

1  —  3800
2  —  3400
3  —  3700
4  —  3500
5  —  3600

GIVE YOUR ANSWER BY TYPING THE CORRESPONDING
CODE BETWEEN 1 — 5.
!
```

The correct answer is choice 4, whereas choices 2 and 5 are close to the correct answer.

c. The program segment to interpret the reply and compute the score could be written as follows.

```
Glossary.

Reply (code 1 — 5)        A
Score                     S
```

```
        —
        —
150     INPUT A
160     IF A = 1 THEN 400
170     IF A = 2 THEN 350
180     IF A = 3 THEN 400
190     IF A = 4 THEN 300
200     IF A = 5 THEN 350
210     PRINT "WRONG CODE"
220     GOTO 150
300     PRINT "CORRECT ANSWER"
310     LET S = S + 20
320     GOTO 410
350     PRINT "CLOSE — THE ANSWER IS 3500 MILES"
360     LET S = S + 10
370     GOTO 410
400     PRINT "WRONG — THE ANSWER IS 3500 MILES"
410     —
        —
        —
```

d. Clearly there is a need to provide a mechanism in the language to allow for multiple branching.

Lines 160 through to 200 could be coded as:

160 ON A GOTO 400, 350, 400, 300, 350

which implies that if A = 1 branch to line 400, A = 2 branch to line 350, A = 3 branch to line 400, etc.

Hence the control structure of lines 160 to 200 remains the same.

11. a. The syntax of the **ON** statement is:

ON $\left\{ \begin{array}{l} \text{numeric variable name} \\ \text{arithmetic expression} \end{array} \right\}$ **GOTO** line-number —1,

line-number —2, line-number —3, · · · · ·

b. **Notes:**

i.   The numeric variable name or evaluated arithmetic expression should represent a positive integer.

ii. The value of the integer must not exceed the number of line numbers present after the **GOTO** verb.

iii. If the value of the integer lies outside of the permissible range then depending upon the BASIC system being used one of two actions will take place. The computer will notify the user of the error or the computer will execute the next statement in sequence after the **ON**.

Refer to your computer manual regarding this last note.

WORKED EXAMPLE.

12. Problem. Write a program to use the computer as a simple calculator having the four functions addition, subtraction, multiplication and division. Allow the user to input two numbers and choose the operation to be performed on them, then output the result. The program will terminate when the second number of the pair input is zero, thus avoiding the problem of dividing by zero.

i.   **Flowchart.**

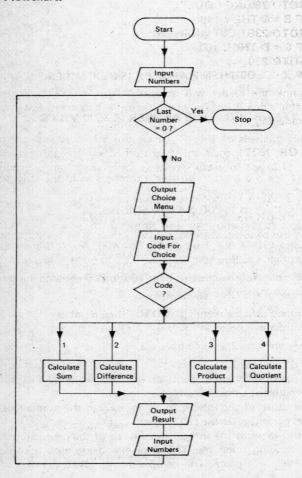

ii.

Glossary.	
Numbers to be calculated	A
	B
Menu code	X
Result of calculation	C

iii. **Program.**

```
10    REM · · PROMPT
20       PRINT "INPUT TWO NUMBERS A AND B, USE B = 0 TO EXIT"
30       INPUT A, B
40    REM · · TEST FOR END OF ROUTINE
50    IF B = 0 THEN STOP
60       REM · · OUTPUT CHOICE IN THE FORM OF A MENU
70       PRINT "DO YOU WANT THE NUMBERS"
80       PRINT "1 — ADDED"
90       PRINT "2 — SUBTRACTED"
100      PRINT "3 — MULTIPLIED"
110      PRINT "4 — DIVIDED"
120      PRINT "INPUT A CODE FROM 1 TO 4"
130      INPUT X
140      REM · · BRANCH TO APPROPRIATE SEGMENT OF CODE
150      REM · · DEPENDING UPON THE VALUE OF X
160      ON X GOTO 180, 210, 240, 270
170         REM · · CALCULATE SUM
180         LET C = A + B
190      GOTO 290
200         REM · · CALCULATE DIFFERENCE
210         LET C = A — B
220      GOTO 290
230         REM · · CALCULATE PRODUCT
240         LET C = A * B
250      GOTO 290
260         REM · · CALCULATE QUOTIENT
270         LET C = A / B
280      REM . . OUTPUT RESULT
290      PRINT "ANSWER"; C
292      PRINT "INPUT TWO NUMBERS A AND B, USE B = 0 TO EXIT"
294         INPUT A, B
300   GOTO 50
310   END
```

iv.   **Result of computer run.**

```
INPUT TWC NUMBERS A AND B, USE B=0 TO EXIT
!5,2
DO YOU WANT THE NUMBERS
1 - ADDED
2 - SUBTRACTED
3 - MULTIPLIED
4 - DIVIDED
INPUT A CODE FROM 1 TO 4
!1
ANSWER 7
INPUT TWO NUMBERS A AND B, USE B=0 TO EXIT
!4,8
DO YOU WANT THE NUMBERS
1 - ADDED
2 - SUBTRACTED
3 - MULTIPLIED
4 - DIVIDED
INPUT A CODE FROM 1 TO 4
!2
ANSWER -4
INPUT TWO NUMBERS A AND B, USE B=0 TO EXIT
!8,3
DC YOU WANT THE NUMBERS
1 - ADDED
2 - SUBTRACTED
3 - MULTIPLIED
4 - DIVIDED
INPUT A CODE FROM 1 TO 4
!3
ANSWER 24
INPUT TWO NUMBERS A AND B, USE B=0 TO EXIT
!57,25
DO YOU WANT THE NUMBERS
1 - ADDED
2 - SUBTRACTED
3 - MULTIPLIED
4 - DIVIDED
INPUT A CODE FROM 1 TO 4
!4
ANSWER 2.28
INPUT TWC NUMBERS A AND B, USE B=0 TO EXIT
!1,0
STOP AT LINE 50
```

EXERCISE

1.   Comment upon the errors in the following segments of code.

```
a. 10    FOR I = 10 TO 1
   20    —
   30    —
   40    NEXT
```

120

```
b. 10    FOR I = 1, 3
   20       FOR J = 1, 4
   30    —
   40    —
   50      NEXT I
   60    NEXT J
c. 10    FOR I = 1 TO 5
   20    LET I = 3 * I ↑ 2 + 4 * I — 7
   30    —
   40    —
   50    NEXT I
```

* 2. Test the following program on your computer and determine what happens if X is not equal to 1, 2 or 3.

```
10    INPUT X
20    ON X GOTO 40, 60, 80
30       PRINT "X IS NOT 1, 2 OR 3"
35    STOP
40       PRINT "X = 1"
50    GOTO 10
60       PRINT "X = 2"
70    GOTO 10
80       PRINT "X = 3"
90    GOTO 10
100   END
```

3. Comment upon the subroutine structure used in the following program.

```
10    GOSUB 500
20    —
30    —
      —
      —
500   GOSUB 600
      —
      —
570   RETURN
600   GOTO 10
610   —
      —
      —
650   RETURN
```

4. Write a program to output.

    a. The odd integers between 1 and 49.

    b. The squares of even integers between 2 and 50.

    c. The sum of the cubes of odd integers between 11 and 19.

5. Write a program to calculate and output the overtime pay for ten employees. Overtime is paid at £12.00 per hour for every hour worked over 40 hours per week. Assume that employees **do not** work for fractional parts of an hour.

6. The following table represents the number of cars sold at a garage over a period of 6 months.

Month	Cars Sold
1	5
2	4
3	7
4	9
5	8
6	6

Write a computer program to read the table month by month, and output the following bar chart. Each * represents one car sold.

```
    0 _ _ _ _ 5 _ _ _ _ 10 SALES
  1 | *  *  *  *  *
  2 | *  *  *  *
  3 | *  *  *  *  *  *  *
  4 | *  *  *  *  *  *  *  *  *
  5 | *  *  *  *  *  *  *  *
  6 | *  *  *  *  *  *
```

MONTHS

* 7. Using the strategies in the examples of (9a) and (10b) of this chapter write a program to represent a teaching machine that uses multiple choice answers to questions. Select a topic of your choice.

* 8. The following table shows that the product code of an article indicates the percentage commission a salesman can earn from the value of a sale.

Product Code	Commission %
1	0.5
2	1
3	2
4	2.5
5	3.5

Write a program to input

a. The product code $(1-5)$.

b. The value of a sale.

and output the commission on that product.

If a salesman sells more than one type of product calculate and output his total commission.

9. Write a program to output the first twenty terms of the Fibonacci series $(1\ 1\ 2\ 3\ 5\ 8\cdots)$.

Note: The next value in the series is the sum of the previous two values.

* **10.** Write a program using three **FOR/NEXT** loops to identify and output the integer values of X, Y and Z that satisfy the equation

$$Z^2 = X^2 + Y^2 \quad \text{ie. } X = 3, Y = 4, Z = 5$$

Terminate the procedure when $Z > 25$.

Note: *To avoid problems with rounding errors your solution should calculate squares by using * instead of ↑. (Eg. X^2 should be found using X * X not X ↑ 2.)*

9 Arrays

INTRODUCTION.

1. This chapter deals with:

a. The limitations of data storage techniques explained so far, and the need for structuring data.

b. The concepts of one and two dimensional arrays.

c. The declaration of arrays and methods used to input and manipulate data within arrays.

d. Programming examples illustrating the use of arrays.

LIMITATIONS OF METHODS LEARNED SO FAR.

2. Consider the problem of writing a program to input and store examination marks for a class of forty school pupils studying eight subjects, and calculate the average mark for each subject.

In trying to solve the problem with the techniques already taught:

a. Each mark would be stored using a unique scalar variable name for reference. However, there are 320 marks to store and BASIC will only allow a maximum of 286 variable names.

Clearly in attempting to write such a program we shall soon exhaust the list of legal variable names.

b. If it was possible to assign a unique scalar variable name to each mark then the coding required to input the data would also be very cumbersome.

Indeed it would result in either a proliferation of **READ/DATA** or **INPUT** statements, such as:

```
10     INPUT A0, A1, A2, A3, A4 · · · · · A9
20     INPUT B0, B1, B2, · · · · B9
30     · · · · ·
40     · · · · ·
```

c. In calculating the average mark for each subject the amount of coding would be lengthy. The variable name associated with each pupils mark for a subject would need to be known in advance of writing the program.

To calculate the average mark for a subject the coding would appear as say:

```
110    LET M1 = (A0 + B0 +C0 +D0 + · · · · · Z0 + · · · · .) / 40
```

d. Should it be necessary to change any of the pupils marks then a reference would be made to a specific data name. For example we would need to know that the variable name for pupil number 21 in examination subject 5 was say W4, in order to change the mark.

This in itself would involve a substantial amount of coding.

e. Thus we see that unique scalar variable names are cumbersome when processing sets of related data items because:—

i. Each data item needs individual treatment.

ii. The data set is not structured and therefore cannot be manipulated.

iii. Program coding or changes to coding are lengthy and laborious.

DATA STRUCTURING REQUIREMENTS.

3. In attempting to solve this problem it is evident that there is a requirement to structure data within a program such that:

a. Access to data for either input, processing or output can be made through a common variable name.

b. Data within a structure can be manipulated.

c. Coding within a program is reduced to a minimum.

The average marks problem will be solved later in the chapter (problem D) using the techniques that follow.

A ONE-DIMENSIONAL ARRAY (also known as a LIST or a VECTOR).

4. a. The smallest component of an array is called a *cell* or *element* and contains either a number or a string literal.

Fig. 9.1 | 143 | a *cell* containing an item of data.

b. The cells are grouped together to form a one-dimensional array.

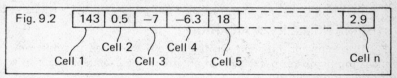

Fig. 9.2

Note: The maximum number of cells is dependent upon the BASIC system being used. In practice it can range from a few cells to several thousand cells.

c. An array can be given **one** variable name, depending upon the type of data to be stored in the array, using the same rules of composition as for scalar variable names.

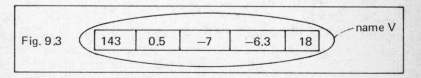

Fig. 9.3

d. Each cell is given an address called a **subscript**, that defines the position of a cell within an array.

Fig. 9.4

Contents of cells	143	0.5	−7	−6.3	18
Subscripts	1	2	3	4	5

e. The **contents** of each cell is accessed by the **name** given to the array, followed in parenthesis by the **subscript** of the cell.

Thus the notation V (1) = 143 implies that V is the name of the array, 1 is the subscript denoting the position of the cell, and 143 is the contents of the cell.

From Figure 9.4 it is clear that

V (2) = 0.5, V (3) = −7, V (4) = −6.3, V (5) = 18

THE DECLARATION OF A ONE-DIMENSIONAL ARRAY.

5. a. Before an array can be used in a program the name and number of cells that the structure contains must be declared at the **beginning** of a program, in order that the computer knows how much space to allocate for storing data.

b. The declaration of the name and size of the array is made using a **DIM** statement (short for DIMension).

The declaration of array V would be:

10 DIM   V (5)

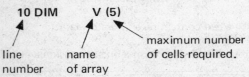

line   name   maximum number
number   of array   of cells required.

STORING NUMBERS IN AN ARRAY.

6. The following program segments show the three possible ways of allocating numbers to the cells of an array. The examples relate to array V previously described.

a. **READ/DATA.**

```
10    DIM V (5)
20    REM ·· THE VALUE OF I REPRESENTS THE SUBSCRIPT
30    REM ·· WHICH CHANGES AFTER EACH DATUM
40    REM ·· HAS BEEN READ INTO ITS APPROPRIATE CELL
50    FOR I = 1 TO 5
60       READ V (I)
70    NEXT I
80    DATA 143, 0.5, −7, −6.3, 18
```

Line number	I	V (I)
50	1	0
60	1	143
70	1	143
50	2	0
60	2	0.5
70	2	0.5
50	3	0
60	3	−7
70	3	−7
50	4	0
60	4	−6.3
70	4	−6.3
50	5	0
60	5	18
70	5	18

Dry run of program segment (a).

Notes: i.   The zeros in the column headed V (I) indicate that BASIC initialises the contents of each cell to zero after the declaration of the array.

ii.   After running the program I has changed from 1 to 5 and the contents of each cell is shown in figure 9.4.

b. INPUT.

```
10    REM · · THIS IS A SIMILAR TECHNIQUE TO PROGRAM
20    REM · · SEGMENT (a)
30    DIM V (5)
40    FOR I = 1 TO 5
50        REM · · DATA IS ENTERED AT A KEYBOARD DURING
60        REM · · RUN TIME, AND IS STORED IN THE
70        REM · · RESPECTIVE CELLS OF THE ARRAY
80        INPUT V (I)
90    NEXT I
```

c. LET

```
10    REM · · THIS TECHNIQUE WOULD NORMALLY BE
20    REM · · CONFINED TO ASSIGNING SMALL QUANTITIES
30    REM · · OF DATA AND IS APPLICABLE IF THE
40    REM · · ARRAY IS TO CONTAIN THE RESULTS OF
50    REM · · ARITHMETIC ASSIGNMENTS
60    DIM V (5)
70    REM · · NOTE THE SUBSCRIPTS ARE NUMERIC LITERALS
80    REM · · AND NOT DATA NAMES
90    LET V (1) = 143
100   LET V (2) = 0.5
110   LET V (3) = −7
120   LET V (4) = −6.3
130   LET V (5) = 18
```

127

STORING ALPHANUMERIC STRINGS IN AN ARRAY.

7. a. The techniques of **READ/DATA**, **INPUT** and **LET** previously described for storing numbers also apply to storing alphanumeric strings in an array. **String arrays are not defined in the ECMA Standard.**

b. However, the names of arrays must conform to string variable names. (Use of $ postscript).

c. The contents of the array must be alphanumeric.

d. The maximum size of a string in each cell will depend upon the BASIC system being used.

e. BASIC will initialise the contents of a string array with a **null** character in each cell ie. empty

f. **Example:** To store the names of six motor car manufacturers in an array such as:

FORD	B.L.	VAUXHALL	VOLVO	SAAB	AUDI

the coding would be:

```
10    REM · · DECLARE THE NAME AND SIZE OF THE ARRAY
20    DIM C$ (6)
30    REM · · USE THE TECHNIQUE OF 6 (A) TO READ
40    REM · · AND STORE THE DATA
50    FOR I = 1 TO 6
60       READ C$ (I)
70    NEXT I
80    REM · · NOTE THE STRINGS USED AS DATA ARE
90    REM · · ENCLOSED BETWEEN QUOTATION MARKS
100   DATA "FORD", "B.L.", "VAUXHALL"
110   DATA "VOLVO", "SAAB", "AUDI"
```

WORKED EXAMPLES USING A ONE-DIMENSIONAL ARRAY.

8. **Problem.**

a. The prices of five different articles are stored in a one-dimensional array as shown.

PRICE	20	15	16	18	14
PRODUCT-CODE	1	2	3	4	5

Each article is given a product-code from 1 to 5. To reference a price for an article the product code is used as a subscript to the array.

  i.   Draw a flowchart,
  ii. Construct a glossary and

iii. Code a program to input from a keyboard device the product code and quantity sold for an article and calculate and print the cost of a sale. Terminate the procedure when the product code is out of range.

SOLUTION.

i. **Flowchart.**

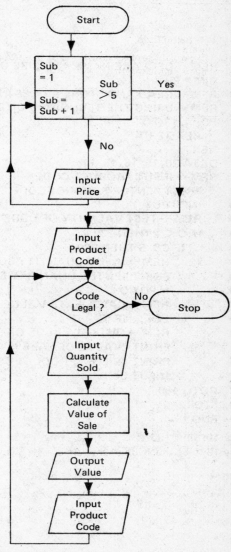

ii.

Glossary.	
Subscript	I
Price	P (I)
Product Code	C
Quantity Sold	Q
Value of Sale	S

iii. **Program.**

```
10    REM ·· DECLARE NAME AND SIZE OF ARRAY
20    DIM P (5)
30    REM ·· READ AND STORE PRICES IN ARRAY
40    REM ·· USING THE TECHNIQUE OF 6a
50    FOR I = 1 TO 5
60       READ P (I)
70    NEXT I
80    DATA 20, 15, 16, 18, 14
90    REM ·· INPUT PRODUCT CODE
100      PRINT "ENTER PRODUCT CODE"
110      INPUT C
120      REM ·· TEST VALIDITY OF CODE IF ILLEGAL STOP
130      IF C < 1 THEN 230
140         IF C > 5 THEN 230
150            REM ·· INPUT QUANTITY SOLD
160            PRINT "ENTER QUANTITY SOLD"
170            INPUT Q
180            REM ·· CALCULATE VALUE OF SALE
190            LET S = P (C) * Q
200            REM ·· OUTPUT VALUE OF SALE
210            PRINT "VALUE OF SALE IS"; S
211            PRINT "ENTER PRODUCT CODE"
212            INPUT C
220      GOTO 130
230      STOP
240      END
```

Note: In line 190 if C = 3, say, then P (3) from the array is the price 16, thus the value of the sale S = 16 * Q.

iv. **Result of computer run.**

```
ENTER PRODUCT CODE
!3
ENTER QUANTITY SOLD
!200
VALUE OF SALE IS 3200
ENTER PRODUCT CODE
!2
ENTER QUANTITY SOLD
!589
VALUE OF SALE IS 8835
ENTER PRODUCT CODE
!5
ENTER QUANTITY SOLD
!200
VALUE OF SALE IS 2800
ENTER PRODUCT CODE
!6
STOP AT LINE 230
```

Problem.

b. i.   Draw a flowchart.
   ii. Construct a glossary and
   iii. Code a program to input at the keyboard of a terminal each letter of a single word in spelling order, and store each letter in a separate cell of an array.

Test whether the word is a *palindrome* (ie. spelled the same backward as forward). Assume that a word has a maximum of twenty letters.

Repeat the procedure so that many single words can be tested.

Terminate each word by a colon, and the procedure by a full-stop.

Having tested a word if it is a palindrome then output the message "WORD IS A PALINDROME" otherwise input the next word.

i. Flowchart.

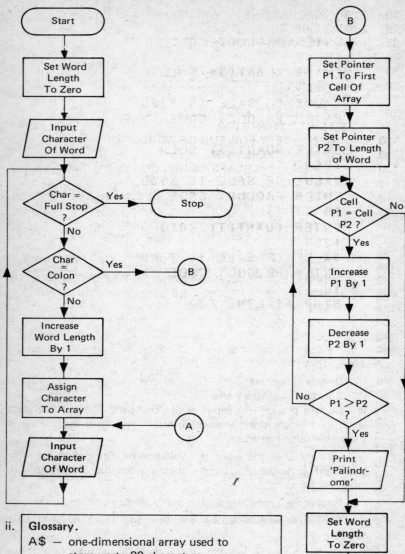

ii.
Glossary.
A\$ — one-dimensional array used to store up to 20 characters.
L — length of word.
T\$ — temporary storage for input character.
P1 — Pointer to L.H. end of array.
P2 — Pointer to R.H. end of array.

132

iii. Program.

```
10    REM · · DECLARE NAME AND SIZE OF ARRAY
20    DIM A$ (20)
30    REM · · SET WORD LENGTH TO ZERO
40       LET L = 0
50       REM · · INPUT A CHARACTER FROM KEYBOARD
60       PRINT "ENTER ONE CHARACTER"
70       INPUT T$
80       REM · · TEST TO END PROCEDURE
90    IF T$ = "." THEN STOP
100      REM · · TEST FOR END OF WORD
110      IF T$ = ":" THEN 200
120         REM · · INCREASE WORD LENGTH BY ONE
130         LET L = L + 1
140         REM · · ASSIGN CHARACTER TO ARRAY
150         LET A$ (L) = T$
160         REM · · INPUT THE NEXT CHARACTER
165         PRINT "ENTER ONE CHARACTER"
166         INPUT T$
170      GOTO 90
180      REM · · SET POINTERS P1 AND P2 TO FIRST AND
182      REM · · LAST CELL RESPECTIVELY OF ARRAY USED
184      REM · · TO STORE WORD
200      LET P1 = I
210      LET P2 = L
220      REM · · COMPARE THE CONTENTS OF CELLS POINTED
230      REM · · AT BY P1 AND P2
240      IF A$ (P1) < > A$ (P2) THEN 350
250         REM · · MOVE CELL POINTERS TOGETHER BY
260         REM · · ONE CELL EACH AND TEST FOR POINTERS
270         REM · · CROSSING OVER
280         LET P1 = P1 + 1
290         LET P2 = P2 − 1
300      IF P1 < = P2 THEN 240
310         REM · · IF THE EXECUTION OF THE PROGRAM
320         REM · · REACHES THIS FAR THE WORD IS A
330         REM · · PALINDROME
340         PRINT "WORD IS A PALINDROME"
345         REM . . SET WORD LENGTH TO ZERO
350         LET L = 0
355   GOTO 165
360   END
```

iv. Result of computer run.

```
ENTER ONE CHARACTER
!R
ENTER ONE CHARACTER
!A
ENTER ONE CHARACTER
!D
ENTER ONE CHARACTER
!A
ENTER ONE CHARACTER
!R
ENTER ONE CHARACTER
!:
WORD IS A PALINDROME
ENTER ONE CHARACTER
!P
ENTER ONE CHARACTER
!O
ENTER ONE CHARACTER
!O
ENTER ONE CHARACTER
!P
ENTER ONE CHARACTER
!:
WORD IS A PALINDROME
ENTER ONE CHARACTER
!S
ENTER ONE CHARACTER
!I
ENTER ONE CHARACTER
!G
ENTER ONE CHARACTER
!N
ENTER ONE CHARACTER
!:
ENTER ONE CHARACTER
!.
STOP AT LINE 90
```

A TWO-DIMENSIONAL ARRAY (ALSO KNOWN AS A TABLE OR A MATRIX).

9. a. A two-dimensional array is formed by placing one-dimensional arrays together in **rows**, and allowing the respective cells of each one-dimensional array to form **columns**.

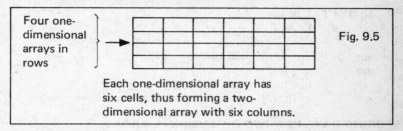

Four one-dimensional arrays in rows

Each one-dimensional array has six cells, thus forming a two-dimensional array with six columns.

Fig. 9.5

b. The smallest element of the structure is still a **cell**, and can contain either a number or an alphabetic string as before.

c. A two-dimensional array is given a name in the same way as a one-dimensional array is named.

d. Each **row** and **column** are given subscripts to denote the unique position of a cell.

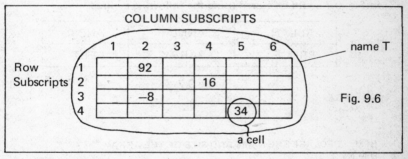

COLUMN SUBSCRIPTS

Fig. 9.6

e. Access to any cell of the array will be through
  i.   The name of the two-dimensional array.
  ii. The **row** subscript that the cell is found in.
  iii. The **column** subscript that the cell is found in.
The subscripts follow the name of the array and are parenthesised.

The row subscript is written **before** the column subscript and separated by a comma.

Thus with reference to Fig. 9.6 the notation $T(1, 2) = 92$ implies that T is the name of the array, 1 is the ROW value for the cell, 2 is the COLUMN value for the cell, and 92 is the contents of the cell.

From Fig. 9.6 it is clear that

$T(2, 4) = 16$, $T(3, 2) = -8$ and $T(4, 5) = 34$.

135

THE DECLARATION OF A TWO-DIMENSIONAL ARRAY.

10. Two-dimensional arrays are declared in a similar manner to one-dimensional arrays.

The declaration of array T would be:

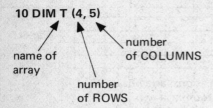

10 DIM T (4, 5)

name of array — number of ROWS — number of COLUMNS

STORING DATA IN A TWO-DIMENSIONAL ARRAY.

11. a. The techniques of using **READ/DATA**, **INPUT** and **LET** for storing numbers and strings as described in paras 6 and 7, apply also to two-dimensional arrays.

A double loop is used to accommodate the two subscripts when either **reading** or **inputting** data.

b. **Example.** The data found in the two-dimensional array illustrated in Fig. 9.7 could be stored using the following coding.

ALLAN	ANNE	ANDY
BRUCE	BARRY	BERT

Figure 9.7

```
10     REM · · DECLARE THE NAME AND SIZE OF THE ARRAY
20     DIM N$ (2, 3)
30     REM · · SET UP AN OUTER LOOP TO CONTROL THE ROW SUBSCRIPT
40     FOR I = 1 TO 2
50       REM · · SET UP AN INNER LOOP AT CONTROL THE COLUMN SUBSCRIPT
60       FOR J = 1 TO 3
70         REM · · USE A READ/DATA STATEMENT TO INPUT DATA
80         REM · · SHOWN IN FIG. 9.9
90         READ N$ (I, J)
100      NEXT J
110    NEXT I
120    DATA "ALLAN", "ANNE", "ANDY"
130    DATA "BRUCE", "BARRY", "BERT"
```

c. **Dry run.**

Line number(s)	I	J	N$ (I, J)
40	1	0	—
60	1	1	null
90, 100	1	1	ALLAN
60	1	2	null
90, 100	1	2	ANNE
60	1	3	null
90, 100, 110	1	3	ANDY
40	2	3	null
60	2	1	null
90, 100	2	1	BRUCE
60	2	2	null
90, 100	2	2	BARRY
60	2	3	null
90, 100, 110	2	3	BERT

WORKED EXAMPLES USING TWO-DIMENSIONAL ARRAYS.

12. Problem.

a. Problem a, para 8a is re-stated such that the sale price of the five articles decreases for quantities sold in excess of 100, and decreased further for quantities sold in excess of 500.

The prices are stored in a two-dimensional array (figure 9.8).

SALES PRICE < = 100	20	15	16	18	14
SALES PRICE > 100	18	14	13	17	13
SALES PRICE > 500	15	11	10	12	9

Figure 9.8.

The product code and quantity sold is input at the keyboard as before.

i.   Draw a flowchart,
ii. Construct a glossary and
iii. Code a program to calculate and print the value of a sale.

Terminate the procedure as stated in problem A.

9 Arrays

i. Flowchart.

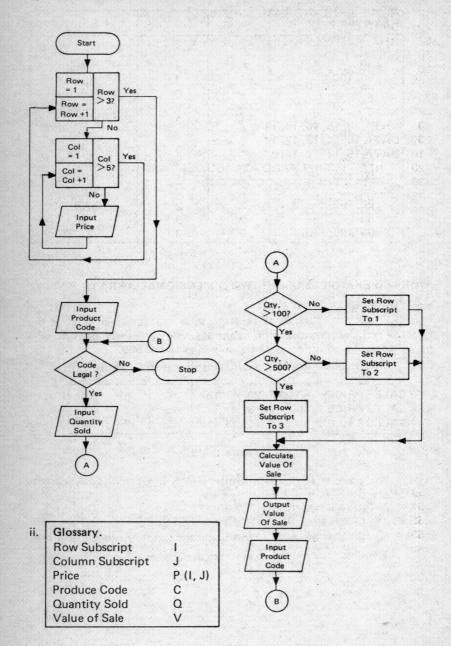

iii. **Program.**

```
10    REM ·· DECLARE NAME AND SIZE OF ARRAY
20    DIM P (3, 5)
30    REM ·· STORE PRICES IN ARRAY P
40    FOR I = 1 TO 3
50       FOR J = 1 TO 5
60          READ P (I, J)
70       NEXT J
80    NEXT I
90    DATA 20, 15, 16, 18, 14
100   DATA 18, 14, 13, 17, 13
110   DATA 15, 11, 10, 12, 9
120      REM ·· INPUT PRODUCT CODE
130      PRINT "ENTER PRODUCT CODE"
140      INPUT C
150      REM ·· TEST VALIDITY OF CODE IF ILLEGAL STOP
160      IF C < 1 THEN 370
170         IF C > 5 THEN 370
180            REM ·· INPUT QUANTITY SOLD
190            PRINT "ENTER QUANTITY SOLD"
200            INPUT Q
210            REM ·· DETERMINE WHICH PRICE ROW IS USED
220            REM ·· IN ARRAY P
230            IF Q < = 100 THEN 270
240               IF Q < = 500 THEN 290
250                  LET I = 3
260               GOTO 330
270                  LET I = 1
280               GOTO 330
290                  LET I = 2
300               REM ·· CALCULATE THE VALUE OF THE SALE
310               REM ·· USING I AS THE ROW SUBSCRIPT AND
320               REM ·· C AS THE COLUMN SUBSCRIPT
330               LET S = P (I, C) * Q
340               REM ·· OUTPUT VALUE OF SALE
350               PRINT "VALUE OF SALE IS"; S
351               REM ·· INPUT PRODUCT CODE
352               PRINT "ENTER PRODUCT CODE"
353               INPUT C
360      GOTO 160
370   STOP
380   END
```

iv. **Result of computer run.**

```
ENTER PRODUCT CODE
!2
ENTER QUANTITY SOLD
!36
VALUE OF SALE IS 540
ENTER PRODUCT CODE
!3
ENTER QUANTITY SOLD
!350
VALUE OF SALE IS 4550
ENTER PRODUCT CODE
!4
ENTER QUANTITY SOLD
!2123
VALUE OF SALE IS 25476
ENTER PRODUCT CODE
!1
ENTER QUANTITY SOLD
!100
VALUE OF SALE IS 2000
ENTER PRODUCT CODE
!6
STOP AT LINE 370
```

Problem.

b. i. Draw a flowchart,
   ii. Construct a glossary and
   iii. Code a program to input and store the examination marks for a class of forty school pupils studying eight subjects, calculate and output the average mark in each subject.

i.   **Flowchart**.

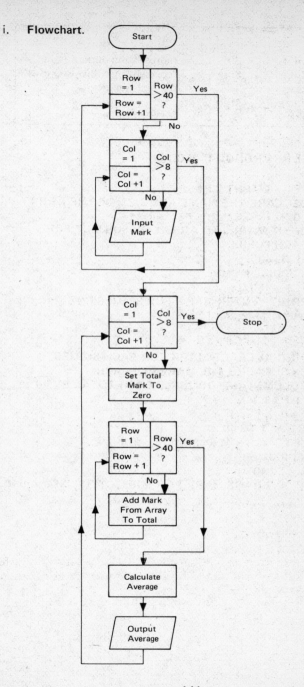

ii. | **Glossary.**

Row Subscript	P	representing pupil number
Col Subscript	S	representing subject number
Total of marks	T	for each subject.
Individual mark	M (P, S)	
Average mark	A	for each subject.

iii. **Program.**

```
10    REM · · DECLARE THE NAME AND SIZE OF THE ARRAY
20    DIM M (40, 8)
30    REM · · INPUT MARKS TO ARRAY BY SUBJECT FOR
40    REM · · EACH PUPIL
50    FOR P = 1 TO 40
60       PRINT "PUPIL NUMBER"; P
70          FOR S = 1 TO 8
80             PRINT "ENTER MARK FOR SUBJECT"; S
90             INPUT M (P, S)
100         NEXT S
110   NEXT P
120   REM · · FIND AVERAGE MARK FOR EACH SUBJECT
130   REM · · BY SUMMING THE MARKS IN EACH
140   REM · · COLUMN, AND DIVIDING EACH TOTAL BY 40
150   FOR S = 1 TO 8
160      LET T = 0
170         FOR P = 1 TO 40
180            LET T = T + M (P, S)
190         NEXT P
200      LET A = T / 40
210      PRINT "AVERAGE MARK FOR SUBJECT"; S; "IS"; A
220   NEXT S
230   STOP
240   END
```

iv. **Result of program run.**

```
PUPIL NUMBER 1
ENTER MARK FOR SUBJECT 1
!56
ENTER MARK FOR SUBJECT 2
!45
ENTER MARK FOR SUBJECT 3
!67
ENTER MARK FOR SUBJECT 4
!34
ENTER MARK FOR SUBJECT 5
!78
ENTER MARK FOR SUBJECT 6
!23
ENTER MARK FOR SUBJECT 7
!43
ENTER MARK FOR SUBJECT 8
!78
PUPIL NUMBER 2
ENTER MARK FOR SUBJECT 1
!56
ENTER MARK FOR SUBJECT 2
!75
ENTER MARK FOR SUBJECT 3
!45
ENTER MARK FOR SUBJECT 4
!56
ENTER MARK FOR SUBJECT 5
!46
ENTER MARK FOR SUBJECT 6
!66
ENTER MARK FOR SUBJECT 7
!87
ENTER MARK FOR SUBJECT 8
!6
 |
 |
etc.
 |
 |
 |
AVERAGE MARK FOR SUBJECT 1 IS 56
AVERAGE MARK FOR SUBJECT 2 IS 60
AVERAGE MARK FOR SUBJECT 3 IS 56
AVERAGE MARK FOR SUBJECT 4 IS 45
AVERAGE MARK FOR SUBJECT 5 IS 62
AVERAGE MARK FOR SUBJECT 6 IS 44.5
AVERAGE MARK FOR SUBJECT 7 IS 65
AVERAGE MARK FOR SUBJECT 8 IS 42
STOP AT LINE 230
```

SUMMARY

13. a. Use should be made of arrays when storing sets of related data because access and manipulation of data within a program is simplified and program coding is reduced to a minimum.

b. The name and size of an array is declared at the beginning of a program using a **DIM** statement.

c. Reference to the contents of an array is through the name of an array and a subscript(s).

d. A one-dimensional array uses one subscript to identify the position of a data cell, whereas, a two-dimensional array uses two subscripts, the first identifies the **row** and the second identifies the **column** for the position of the data cell.

e. BASIC initialises the contents of arrays to zero for numeric arrays, and with null characters for string arrays.

POINTS TO NOTE.

14. a. Subscripts by definition must be **positive integers**. However, BASIC will allow a subscript of zero.

b. If an array is **not** declared using a DIM statement then a default value is often assumed by the BASIC system. This value will vary from system to system but a default of eleven cells is common, which implies that a **DIM** statement need not be used for arrays of eleven or less cells. However, it is bad practice to omit a **DIM** statement.

c. The programmer is given a choice of whether to use a subscript of zero or a subscript of 1 as the lowest subscript. A choice can be made by using the statement:

OPTION BASE 0
                    1

Such a statement must precede the **DIM** statement. If **OPTION BASE** is **not** specified then the minimum value for a subscript is taken to be zero.

EXERCISE.

1. Comment upon the possible errors in the following program segments.

```
a. 10    DIM A (12)
   20    FOR I = 1 TO 50
   30       INPUT A (I)
   40    NEXT I
b. 10    DIM X (I)
   20    LET X1 = 3.14
   30    LET X2 = 14
   40    LET X3 = −73.4
```

144

```
c. 10    DIM B (20, 30)
   20    INPUT M, N
   30    FOR I = 1 TO N
   40      FOR J = 1 TO M
   50        LET A (I, J) = 2 * B (I + N, J + M)
   60      NEXT J
   70    NEXT I

d. 10    DIM V10
   20    FOR I = 1 TO N
   30      READ V (I)
   40    NEXT I
   50    DATA BLUE, RED, WHITE, BLACK, YELLOW.

e. 10    DIM T (5, 2)
   20    FOR I = 1 TO 2
   30      FOR J = 1 TO 5
   40        READ T (I, J)
   50        DATA FORK, SPADE, SHEARS, TROWEL, RAKE
   60        DATA 26, 91, 108, 42, 11
   70      NEXT J
   80    NEXT I
```

Draw a flowchart, construct a glossary, write a program and prepare suitable test data for the following.

2. A two-dimensional array T, has 6 rows and 9 columns. Devise a procedure to set the contents of every cell to 100.

3. A one-dimensional array X contains 8 numbers sorted into ascending order. Devise a procedure which moves the items in X to another one-dimensional array Y, so that Y contains the 8 numbers sorted into descending order.

4. Devise a procedure to input numbers to two one-dimensional arrays A and B having 10 cells each and output:

a. Those numbers that are common between the two arrays. The numbers within **each** array are **not** duplicated.

b. The sums of the corresponding elements between A and B.

c. The smallest of the corresponding elements between A and B.

5. Devise a procedure to input letters from a word and store each letter in a cell of a one-dimensional array V, count the number of vowels in the word, and output the value of the count.

6. The median of a set of numbers is that number which has the same number of values above and below it. In the set

0   3   9   18   7   5   4   the median is 5 since three numbers are larger and three numbers are smaller than 5.

Devise a program to compute the median of a set of numbers input to the computer.

    a. For an **odd** number of values (easy).

  * b. For an **even** number of values (more difficult).

Note: Clearly for an odd number of values the median will be the central value of an ordered set of numbers. An even number of values will not have one central value, but two central values. The median is taken to be the average of the two central values.

7. Devise a routine to store numbers in a two-dimensional array M having 4 rows and 5 columns and output the highest and lowest values in:

    a. Each row.

    b. Each column.

* 8. The following diagram represents the names of frozen foods stored in the one-dimensional array F$, and the corresponding quantity of stock for each food in the one-dimensional array S.

	F$		S
1	FISH FINGERS	1	32
2	HADDOCK SLICES	2	86
3	BEEFBURGERS	3	94
4	HAMBURGERS	4	128
5	SAUSAGE ROLLS	5	67
6	PEAS	6	142
7	BEANS	7	27
8	CARROTS	8	56
9	SPROUTS	9	17
10	CHIPS	10	46

Devise a procedure to represent the two arrays F$ and S with the information shown. Input the name of an item of stock and search the array F$, by comparing the value input with the contents of each cell of F$. When a match is found for the item of stock use the corresponding subscript to output the quantity of stock from array S.

* 9. The following frequency table was obtained in a test of distances to take-off of 100 aeroplanes of the same type.

Frequency F	2	4	9	14	19	19	15	10	5	3
Distance X	325	335	345	355	365	375	385	395	405	415

Devise a procedure to store the contents of the table in a two-dimensional array A having 2 rows and 10 columns.

Calculate the arithmetic mean distance to take-off of the data stored in array A by using the expression $\dfrac{\Sigma f x}{\Sigma f}$.

output the arithmetic mean distance.

10 Mathematics

INTRODUCTION.

1. Programs can be written for mathematical applications using BASIC since the language features:

    a. An exponential format for representing real numbers.

    b. Standard mathematical functions.

    c. User defined functions.

These features are explained, with examples, in this chapter.

EXPONENTIAL FORMAT.

2.   a. A real number can be represented in one of two-ways.

      i.   As an unscaled literal eg. 474.981.

      ii.   In a standard form notation that requires the use of a scaling factor.

      eg. 4.74981×10^2

         In the BASIC language the number in the last example would be represented as

      4.74981E2

    where 4.74981 is known as the mantissa, 2 is the exponent and the base 10 has been replaced by the letter E.

        This notation is known as an exponential format or scientific notation.

    b. The syntax of a number written in exponential format is:

    $\pm$ mantissa E $\mp$ exponent

      i.   The + sign is optional for both the mantissa and the exponent.

      ii.   The exponent must be an integer.

      iii. The type of computer and dialect of BASIC being used will determine the accuracy to which the mantissa is represented and the largest positive and negative values of the exponent.

    Note: *Check the BASIC manual for your computer to determine the permissible sizes of numbers represented in exponential format.*

    c. Consider the following representations of numbers in a computer that will store a mantissa to an accuracy of 9 significant figures, and a signed 2 digit exponent in the range 0 to 38.

	Number	BASIC representation
i.	3.7948×10^{16}	3.7948E+16
ii.	−0.00037948	−3.7948 E − 4
iii.	26394782	26394782
iv.	−2.6394782	−2.6394782

Note: In iii. and iv. the numbers can be represented within 9 significant figures, therefore, BASIC would not convert the numbers to exponential format.

v.   739.4621348   7.39462134E+2

Note: In v. the last digit cannot be represented and is therefore truncated from the mantissa.

vi. $-17694.327 \times 10^{35}$ overflow

Note: In vi. when the number is adjusted to standard form notation the exponent becomes 39; the largest exponent permissible is 38; the number is too large to be represented and is said to have overflowed.

vii. $0.000000471 \times 10^{-34}$ underflow

Note: In vii. when the number is adjusted to standard form notation the exponent becomes -41; the largest negative exponent permissible is -38; the number is too small to be represented and is said to have underflowed.

SUPPLIED FUNCTIONS.

3.   The BASIC language will allow the following functions to be used within arithmetic expressions.

The argument of the function has been denoted by the letter X.

Arguments can be: numeric literals ie. constants.
                                numeric variables.
                                arithmetic expressions.

a. **ABS (X)**   returns the absolute value or   modulus   X.
   eg. ABS $(-3.7) = 3.7$

b. **ATN (X)**   returns the arctangent of X in radians $-$ ie. the angle whose tangent is X. The range of the function is
                    $-\pi / 2 < ATN (X) < \pi / 2$
   eg. ATN $(1) = 0.7854 \cdots$
       since the tangent of $\pi / 4$ $(0.7854 \cdots)$
       $= 1$.

c. **COS (X)**   returns the cosine of X, where X is in radians.
   eg. COS $(1.0472) = 0.5$

Note. $\pi / 3 \doteqdot 1.0472$ radians.

d. **EXP (X)**   returns the exponential of X.
   ie. The value of the base of natural logarithms raised to the power X. (e^X).
   eg. EXP $(1) = 2.71828 \cdots$

e. **INT (X)**   returns the largest integer not greater than X.
   eg. INT $(1.3) = 1$
       INT $(-1.3) = -2$

f. **LOG (X)** returns the natural logarithm of X; **X must be greater than zero.**
  eg. LOG (2.71828) = 1
     LOG (1) = 0

g. **RND** returns the next pseudo-random number in a uniformly distributed set of numbers in the range.
     $0 <= RND (X) < 1$.

i. **Note:** Many dialects of BASIC permit the function RND (X), the parameter X determining the sequence of random numbers to be generated. The following table shows some of the inconsistencies of RND (X) between several different dialects of BASIC.

BASIC dialect	value of X	meaning
PRIME	X > 0	X initialises random number generator, and returns X as function value.
	X = 0	Returns a random number in the range 0 to < 1.
	X < 0	X initialises random number generator, and returns a value in range 0 to 1.
APPLESOFT II	X > 0	Returns a different random number in range 0 to < 1 each time used.
	X = 0	Returns the last random number again.
	X < 0	A different fixed number is returned for each different negative argument. After which **RND** with positive argument will follow a fixed sequence.
MSI	X <> 0	Returns a specific random number each time used.
	X = 0	Returns a random number in the range 0 to < 1.
CBM P.E.T.	X > 0	Returns a different random number in range 0 to < 1 each time used.
	X = 0	Returns the last random number again.
	X < 0	Returns a new sequence of random numbers. Same value of X gives same sequence.

ii. The BASIC statement **RANDOMIZE** when executed will allow the **RND** function to produce different sequences of random numbers.

h. **SGN (X)**   returns 1 if the argument is positive, 0 if the argument is zero, and −1 if the argument is negative.

   eg. SGN (+4.79) = 1
      SGN (0) = 0
      SGN (−79) = −1

i. **SIN (X)**   returns the sine of X, where X is in radians.
   eg. SIN (0.5236) = 0.5

Note $\pi / 6 \stackrel{\wedge}{=} 0.5236$ radians.

j. **SQR (X)**   returns the square-root of X; **X must not be negative.**
   eg. SQR (5) = 2.236 · · · ·

k. **TAN (X)**   returns the tangent of X, where X is in radians.
   eg. TAN (0.7854) = 1

Note $\pi / 4 = 0.7854$ radians.

WORKED EXAMPLES.

4. a. **Problem.** Write a program to print a table showing the values of EXP (X) and LOG (X) for X varying between 1 and 10 in steps of 0.5.

i. **Flowchart.**

ii. | **Glossary.** | |
| --- | --- |
| X function argument | X |
| Calculated EXP (X) | Y |
| Calculated LOG (X) | Z |

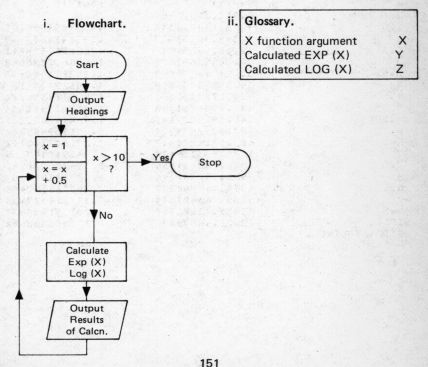

iii. **Program.**

```
10    REM · · OUTPUT HEADINGS
20    PRINT "X", "EXP (X)", "LOG (X)"
30    REM · · SET UP LOOP
40    FOR X = 1 TO 10 STEP 0.5
50       REM · · CALCULATE EXP (X) & LOG (X)
60       LET Y = EXP (X)
70       LET Z = LOG (X)
80       REM · · OUTPUT CALCULATED RESULTS
90       PRINT X, Y, Z
100   NEXT X
110   STOP
120   END
```

iv. **Result of computer run.**

X	EXP(X)	LOG(X)
1	2.718281828459	0
1.5	4.481689070338	.4054651081081
2	7.389056098929	.6931471805599
2.5	12.18249396007	.9162907318741
3	20.08553692319	1.098612288668
3.5	33.11545195869	1.252762968495
4	54.59815003313	1.38629436112
4.5	90.01713130051	1.504077396776
5	148.4131591026	1.609437912434
5.5	244.6919322642	1.704748092238
6	403.4287934927	1.791759469228
6.5	665.1416330442	1.871802176902
7	1096.633158428	1.945910149055
7.5	1808.042414455	2.014903020542
8	2980.957987041	2.07944154168
8.5	4914.768840297	2.140066163496
9	8103.083927574	2.197224577336
9.5	13359.72682966	2.251291798607
10	22026.4657948	2.302585092994

STOP AT LINE 110

b. **Problem.** Test the accuracy of your computer by writing a program to evaluate.

$$\sin^2 x + \cos^2 x - 1$$
and $$\tan^2 x - \sec^2 x + 1$$

for values of x between 0 and 1 in steps of 0.1 radians.

i. **Flowchart.**

ii. **Glossary.**

X function argument	X
$\sin^2 x + \cos^2 x - 1$	Y
$\tan^2 x - \sec^2 x + 1$	Z

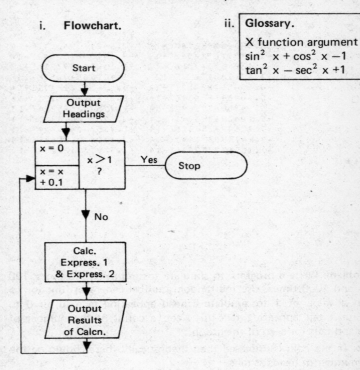

iii. **Program**

```
10   REM ·· OUTPUT HEADINGS
20   PRINT "X", "Y", "Z"
30   REM ·· SET UP LOOP
40   FOR X = 0 TO 1 STEP 0.1
50      REM ·· CALCULATE Y & Z
60      LET Y = SIN (X) ↑ 2 + COS (X) ↑ 2 −1
70      LET Z = TAN (X) ↑ 2 − (1 / (COS (X) ↑ 2)) + 1
80      REM ·· OUTPUT CALCULATED RESULTS
90      PRINT X, Y, Z
100  NEXT X
110  STOP
120  END
```

153

iv. **Results of computer run.**

X	Y	Z
0	-5.6843418860181E-14	-2.8421709430041E-14
.1	-1.2789769243680E-13	-9.9475983316642E-14
.2	-1.1368683772160E-13	-1.1368683772160E-13
.3	-1.4210854715300E-13	-1.4210854715300E-13
.4	-8.5265128291210E-14	-8.5265128291210E-14
.5	-5.6843418860810E-14	-8.5265128291210E-14
.6	-9.9475983000642E-14	-1.7053025658240E-13
.7	-5.6843418860810E-14	-8.5265128291210E-14
.8	-7.1054273576010E-14	-1.7053025658240E-13
.9	-9.9475983000642E-14	-3.4106051316490E-13
1	-7.1054273576010E-14	-3.9790393202570E-13

STOP AT LINE 110

c. Problem. Write a program to simulate tossing a coin 10 times; 100 times and 1000 times. Use the random number generator function to return a value of 1 to simulate a head appearing face-up, or 0 to simulate a tail appearing face-up. Keep a count of the number of heads and tails for each of the groups.

Notes: If the coin is unbiased then theoretically there should be the same number of heads as tails.

If the RND (0) function returns a value X, say, in the range:

$0 <= X < 1$ then for

$X = 0.47135$ $R = INT (0.47135 + 0.5)$
$= INT (0.97135)$
$= 0$

$X = 0.73195$ $R = INT (0.73195 + 0.5)$
$= INT (1.23195)$
$= 1$

Without the + 0.5 in the expression for R, R would always be 0.

i. **Flowchart.**

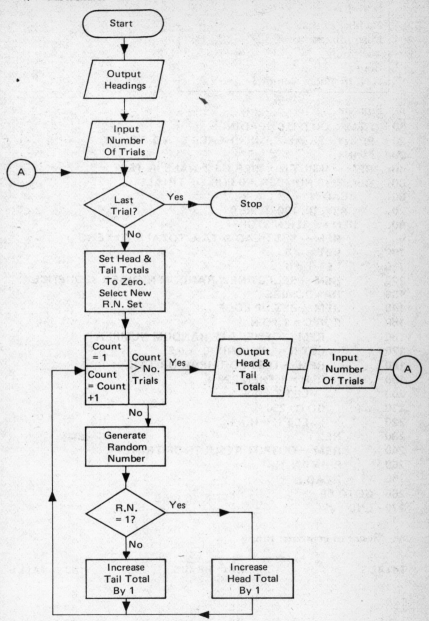

ii.

Glossary.	
Number of trails	N
Head total	H
Tail total	T
Count	C
R.N. (Random Number)	R

iii. **Program.**

```
10    REM ·· OUTPUT HEADINGS
20    PRINT "TRIALS", "NO. HEADS", "NO. TAILS"
30    PRINT
40    REM ·· INPUT NUMBER OF TRIALS IN TEST
50    REM ·· IF NUMBER = 0 END OF TRIALS
60      READ N
70      DATA 10, 100, 1000, 0
80      IF N = 0 THEN STOP
90        REM ·· SET HEAD & TAIL TOTALS TO ZERO
100       LET H = 0
110       LET T = 0
120       REM ·· SELECT NEW RANDOM NUMBER SEQUENCE
130       RANDOMIZE
140       REM ·· SET UP LOOP
150       FOR C = 1 TO N
160          REM ·· GENERATE RANDOM NUMBER
170          LET R = INT (RND (0) + 0.5)
180          REM ·· TEST FOR HEAD OR TAIL
190          IF R = 1 THEN 220
200             LET T = T + 1
210          GOTO 230
220             LET H = H + 1
230       NEXT C
240       REM ·· OUTPUT RESULTS OF TRIALS
250       PRINT N, H, T
255       READ N
260    GOTO 80
270    END
```

iv. **Result of computer run.**

TRIALS	NO. HEADS	NO. TAILS
10	4	6
100	56	44
1000	507	493
STOP AT LINE 80		

USER DEFINED FUNCTIONS.

5. a. In addition to the supplied functions the programmer can define new functions within a program.

   The syntax of a user defined function would be:

   DEF FNα = arithmetic expression.
   or **DEF FN**α (β) = arithmetic expression.

   where α is a single letter A $-$ Z, and β is a numeric variable that is also used in the arithmetic expression.

   Examples.
   i.   **DEF   FNF (X)** = X $\uparrow$ 4 $-$ 1
   ii. **DEF   FNA (X)** = A * X + B
   iii. **DEF   FNP** = 3.14159

   b. The following rules apply to defined functions.
   i.   A function is defined as a program statement at the beginning of a program before it is used.
   ii. The definition of a function is limited to one program line.
   iii. The definition of a function can use supplied functions and other defined functions.
   iv. The definition is not recursive ie. it must not appear on both sides of the equation.
   v.   A function is used by making reference to its name in context within a program.

   c. **Example.** If a value is to represent a financial amount then its decimal fraction should be represented to no more than two places. However, BASIC will return a number to the accuracy of the machine, therefore, there is a need for a function to truncate a number to two decimal places and another to round to two decimal places.

   If **FNT (X) = INT (100 * ABS (X)) / 100**
   then for X = 36.9713467   FNT (X) = 36.97
   Since   100 * ABS (X) = 3697.13467
                    INT (100 * ABS (X)) = 3697
             INT (100 * ABS (X)) / 100 = 36.97

   The function defined as **FNT (X)** can be used to truncate a number to two decimal places.

   If **FNR (X) = INT (100 * ABS (X) + 0.5) / 100**
   then for X = 4279.74581   FNR (X) = 4279.75
   Since   100 * ABS (X) = 427974.581
                100 * ABS (X) + 0.5 = 427975.081
          INT (100 * ABS (X) + 0.5) = 427975
       INT (100 * ABS (X) + 0.5) / 100 = 4279.75

   Thus the function **FNR (X)** can be used to round a number to two decimal places.

The function **FNT (X)** is used in the following program to calculate and print the compound interest on a principal (P) borrowed over (N) years at a rate of (R) %.

The amount (A) owing at the end of the term is given by:

$$A = P \left(1 + \frac{R}{100}\right)^N$$

```
10    REM · · DEFINE FUNCTION TO TRUNCATE NUMBER
20    DEF FNT (X) = INT (100 * ABS (X)) / 100
30    REM · · INPUT VALUES FOR P, R and N.
40    PRINT "ENTER VALUES FOR PRINCIPAL, RATE AND TERM"
50    INPUT P, R, N
60    REM · · CALCULATE AMOUNT (A) OWING
70    LET A = P * (1 + R / 100) ↑ N
80    REM · · CALCULATE INTEREST
90    LET I = A − P
100   REM · · PRINT INTEREST
110   PRINT "COMPOUND INTEREST = £"; FNT (I)
120   STOP
130   END
```

(handwritten annotations:) line 110 `PRINT`; line 120 `PAUSE 100` and `FNS()`; line 130 `GO TO 20.`

Results of computer run.

```
ENTER VALUES FOR PRINCIPAL, RATE AND TERM
!2000,5,6
COMPOUND INTEREST = £680.19
STOP AT LINE 120
```

FURTHER WORKED EXAMPLES.

6. a. Write a computer program to plot the value of sine X and cosine X for $15° \leqslant X \leqslant 360°$ in intervals of $15°$.

The program should display a horizontal axis to represent the angle X, and a vertical axis to represent the sine and cosine of the angle.

A scale should also be displayed for each axis.

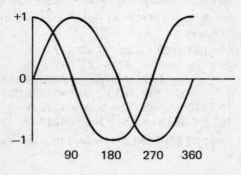

Fig. 10.1

158

The graph, see fig. 10.1, should be stored in a two-dimensional array having 21 rows and 51 columns. Each cell of the array being used to store a single character.

Before the plotted points for sine X and cosine X can be stored in the array each cell must be initialised with a space character, then the vertical axis with scale and horizontal axis can be stored.

Using the functions SIN(X) and COS(X) the co-ordinates of the graph can be used as subscripts to the array and an "*" character can be stored to represent the plot of sin (X) and a "+" character stored to represent the plot of cos (X).

When the plotting of characters is completed the contents of the array can be printed row by row, and finally the horizontal scale can be printed at the bottom of the graph.

Since the functions SIN (X) and COS (X) will only produce values in the range −1 to +1 inclusive it is necessary to convert the values to suitable ordinates for plotting. The ordinate values must correspond to row values (1 to 21) inclusive of the array. Thus the ordinate (+1) is transformed to row 1, and the ordinate (−1) is transformed to row 21. Intermediate ordinates must also be transformed to row values. To achieve this transformation it is necessary to define two functions:

FNS (X) = 11 − INT (10 * SIN (X))

When X = 0°, 180°, 360°   FNX (X) = 11 (horizontal axis)
         X = 90°   FNS (X) =   1 (first row)
         X = 270°   FNS (X) = 21 (last row)

Similarly
FNC (X) = 11 − INT (10 * COS (X))
will transform the ordinates to row values of the array.

i.   Flowchart of procedures necessary in solution of problem.

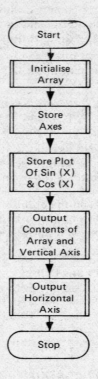

Flowcharts for subroutines to initialise array, store axes and output horizontal axis are too trivial to be included. The reader should have enough programming experience to code these without the need for a flowchart.

ii. **Flowchart of subroutine to store plot of sin (X) and cos (X).**

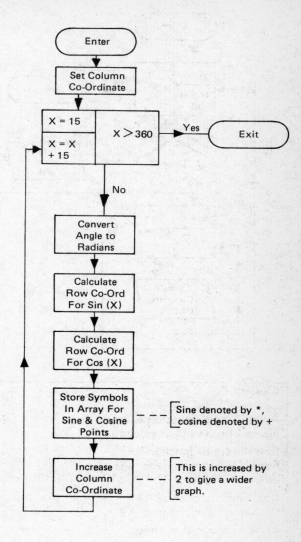

iii. **Flowchart of subroutine to output contents of array and vertical axis.**

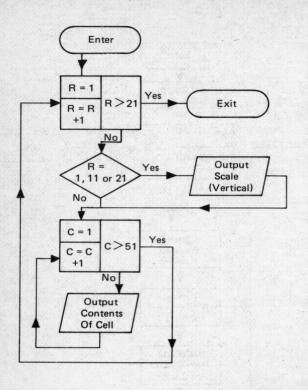

---

iv. | **Glossary.**

Array to store characters of graph, having 21 rows and 51 columns.	A$ (21, 51)
Sine and cosine functions, respectively, that represent the ordinate value for a cell.	FNS FNC
Row subscript of array A$	R
Column subscript of array A$	C
Angle represented in degrees	X
Angle represented in radians	X1
Row co-ordinate for sine X	R1
Row co-ordinate for cosine X	R2

v. Program.

```
10      REM ·· DECLARE ARRAY AND FUNCTIONS
20      DIM A$ (21, 51)
30      DEF FNS (X) = 11 — INT (10 * SIN (X))
40      DEF FNC (X) = 11 — INT (10 * COS (X))
50      REM ··
60      REM ·· INITIALISE ARRAY WITH SPACES
70      GOSUB 1005
80      REM ·· STORE AXES
90      GOSUB 1100
100     REM ·· STORE PLOT OF SIN (X) AND COS (X) IN ARRAY
110     GOSUB 1190
120     REM ·· OUTPUT CONTENTS OF ARRAY
130     GOSUB 1500
140     REM ·· OUTPUT HORIZONTAL AXIS WITH VERTICAL SCALE
150     GOSUB 1700
160     STOP
1000    REM ··
1005       FOR R = 1 TO 21
1010          FOR C = 1 TO 51
1020             LET A$ (R, C) = "   "
1030          NEXT C
1040       NEXT R
1050    RETURN
1060    REM ··
1100       FOR R = 1 TO 21
1110          LET A$ (R, 1) = "I"
1120       NEXT R
1130       FOR C = 2 TO 51
1140          LET A$ (11, C) = "—"
1150       NEXT C
1160    RETURN
1170    REM ·· SET COLUMN CO-ORDINATE FOR PLOTTING FIRST
1180    REM ·· SET OF POINTS — START IN THIRD COLUMN OF ARRAY
1190       LET C = 3
1200       REM ·· CALCULATE SINE AND COSINE OF ANGLE FOR
1210       REM ·· 15 < = X < = 360 DEGREES
1220       FOR X = 15 TO 360 STEP 15
1230          REM ·· CONVERT ANGLE X TO RADIANS
1240          LET X1 = X * 3.14159 / 180
1250          LET R1 = FNS (X1)
1260          LET R2 = FNC (X1)
1270          REM ·· REPRESENT POINTS ON GRAPH BY CHARACTERS
1280          REM ·· STORED IN ARRAY
1290          LET A$ (R1, C) = "*"
```

```
1300        LET A$ (R2, C) = "+"
1310        REM ·· INCREASE COLUMN CO-ORDINATE
1320        LET C = C + 2
1330     NEXT X
1340   RETURN
1350   REM ··
1500     FOR R = 1 TO 21
1510        IF R = 1 THEN 1560
1520        IF R = 11 THEN 1580
1530        IF R = 21 THEN 1600
1540        PRINT "   " ;
1550        GOTO 1610
1560        PRINT "+1";
1570        GOTO 1610
1580        PRINT " 0";
1590        GOTO 1610
1600        PRINT "−1";
1610        FOR C = 1 TO 51
1620           PRINT A$ (R, C);
1630        NEXT C
1640        PRINT "   "
1650     NEXT R
1660     PRINT
1670   RETURN
1700     PRINT TAB (14); "90"; TAB (25); "180"; TAB (37); "270";
1710     PRINT TAB (49); "360"
1720   RETURN
1730   END
```

vi. Result of program run.

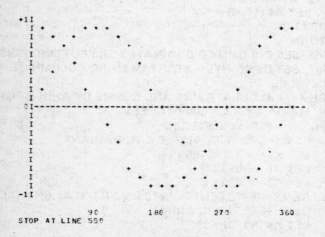

STOP AT LINE 550

164

vii. **Note:**

Sine $75° = 0.9613 \cdots$

Sine $90° = 1.0000$ (however, the computer has represented sine $90° = 0.9999 \cdots$)

Thus FNS $(75°) = 11 - \text{INT} (9.613 \cdots) = 2$

and FNS $(90°) = 11 - \text{INT} (9.999 \cdots) = 2$

A similar problem also exists for SINE X at $270°$, and COSINE X at $180°$ and $360°$.

b. **Problem.** Write a program to simulate playing a fruit-machine.

The player is invited to gamble an amount of money between 10p and 50p, in multiples of 10p.

For each 10p stake the player is allowed two pulls on the arm of the fruit-machine.

The machine contains three wheels, each engraved with the name of a fruit or the word JACKPOT.

The machine pays 30p on any line of three fruits that have the same names, or 100p on a line of three JACKPOT symbols.

The player is allowed to hold up to two wheels before a second pull on the arm of the machine.

Note: The names of the fruits are stored in a one-dimensional array.

ORANGE	LEMON	APPLE	BANANA	PLUM	JACKPOT
1	2	3	4	5	6

The position of each fruit on a wheel is given a number 1 to 6 inclusive. To simulate a wheel spinning and stopping showing the name of a fruit, a random number between 1 and 6 is generated. This random number is then a subscript to the array that contains the name of the fruits.

A second one-dimensional array is used to simulate the three wheels of a fruit machine.

6	3	4
1	2	3

The contents of the array represents the numerical value of a fruit on each of three wheels. The diagram can be interpreted as meaning wheel 1 shows a JACKPOT, wheel 2 an APPLE and wheel 3 a BANANA.

When the contents of the array are inspected, three numbers of the same value will give a winning line. If the value of the numbers is 6, then this is a JACKPOT.

To hold any wheel is simply a matter of specifying a subscript of the array. When a new set of random numbers are generated to simulate the second pull, only numbers will be generated for those wheels whose subscripts have **not** been indicated for a hold. When there are no holds on the wheels three random numbers must be generated, one for each wheel.

If this game is to be displayed on the screen of a visual display unit it is important that the player is given time to read the details and results of the game. To this end a timed delay should be introduced after every two pulls. In practice the timed delay is a loop having a large number of iterations.

i. **Outline flowchart showing a breakdown of the procedures necessary in the solution to the problem.**

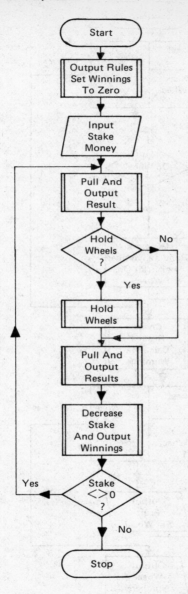

167

Subroutine to pull handle and output result.

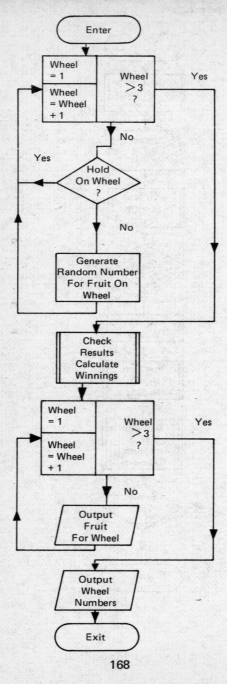

Flowchart of subroutine to check results, and calculate winnings.

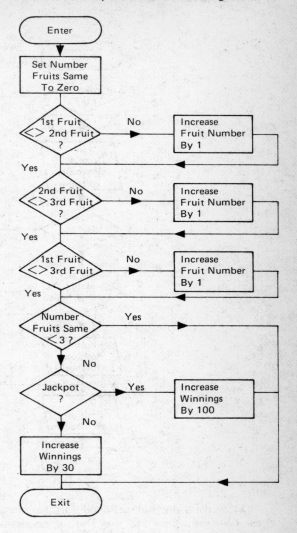

Subroutine to hold wheels.

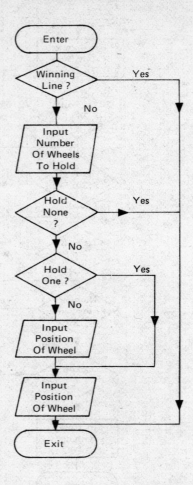

Flowcharts are not provided for the subroutines to output the rules and set winnings to zero, and decrease stake and output winnings since they both involve only a simple sequence of instructions.

The reader should by now be developing sufficient confidence in problem solving and subsequently program coding to realise **when** flowcharts are useful in analysing the solution to a problem.

ii. **Glossary**

Vector used to store the names of six fruits	F$ (6)
Vector used to store the results of generating random numbers.	R (3)
Vector subscript	I
Stake money	S
Number of holds	H
Position of wheels to be held	P1
	P2
Number of fruits the same	X
Winnings	W
Player's reply	A$

iii. **Program.**

```
10    REM ·· DECLARE ARRAYS AND STORE NAMES OF FRUITS
20    DIM F$ (6), R (3)
30    FOR I = 1 TO 6
40       READ F$ (I)
50    NEXT I
60    DATA "ORANGE", "LEMON", "APPLE", "BANANA", "PLUM", "JACKPOT"
70    REM ·· DISPLAY RULES OF GAME
80    GOSUB 1000
90    REM ·· INPUT STAKE MONEY
100   PRINT "WHAT IS YOUR STAKE"
110   PRINT "INPUT 10P TO 50P IN MULTIPLES OF 10P"
120   INPUT S
130   REM ·· PULL FRUIT MACHINE HANDLE AND OUTPUT RESULT
140      GOSUB 1300
150      REM ·· ASK PLAYER IF HE/SHE WANTS TO HOLD
160      PRINT "DO YOU WANT TO HOLD ANSWER Y (YES) N (NO)"
170      INPUT A$
180      IF A$ = "Y" THEN GOSUB 1500
190      REM ·· SECOND PULL
200      GOSUB 1300
210      REM ·· DECREASE STAKE MONEY AND OUTPUT WINNINGS SO FAR
220      GOSUB 1700
230      REM ·· TEST VALUE OF REMAINING STAKE
240   IF S <> 0 THEN 140
250   STOP
```

```
 999    REM · · SUBROUTINE TO DISPLAY RULES
1000       PRINT "RULES FOR PLAYING THE FRUIT MACHINE"
1010       PRINT
1020       PRINT "AT THE START OF THE GAME YOU STAKE AN AMOUNT"
1030       PRINT "OF MONEY YOU WISH TO GAMBLE, MINIMUM STAKE"
1040       PRINT "10P, MAXIMUM STAKE 50P IN MULTIPLES OF 10P"
1050       PRINT
1060       PRINT "YOU GET TWO PULLS FOR 10P"
1070       PRINT
1080       PRINT "BEFORE THE SECOND PULL YOU CAN HOLD ONE"
1090       PRINT "OR TWO WHEELS"
1100       PRINT
1110       PRINT "PAYOUT IS 30P ON ANY LINE OF FRUITS THAT"
1120       PRINT "ARE THE SAME"
1130       PRINT
1140       PRINT "PAYOUT IS 100P ON THREE JACKPOT SYMBOLS
1150       PRINT
1160       PRINT "GOOD LUCK · · · · ·"
1170       REM · · SET WINNINGS TO ZERO
1180       LET W = 0
1190       REM · · REMOVE HOLD ON WHEELS
1200       LET P1 = 0
1210       LET P2 = 0
1220    RETURN

1298    REM · · SUBROUTINE TO PULL HANDLE AND OUTPUT RESULTS
1299       REM · · SELECT NEW RANDOM NUMBER SEQUENCE
1300       RANDOMIZE
1310       FOR I = 1 TO 3
1320          REM · · TEST FOR HOLD ON WHEELS
1330          IF P1 = I THEN 1370
1340          IF P2 = I THEN 1370
1350          REM · · GENERATE RANDOM NUMBER IN RANGE 1 — 6
1360       LET R(I) = INT (6*RND(0) + 1)
1370       NEXT I
1380       REM · · CHECK RESULTS AND CALCULATE WINNINGS
1390       GOSUB 1400
1391       REM · · OUTPUT RESULTS
1392       PRINT
1393       FOR I = 1 TO 3
1394          PRINT F$ (R (I)),
1395       NEXT I
1396       PRINT
1397       PRINT "1", "2", "3"
1398    RETURN
```

```
1398  REM · · SUBROUTINE TO CHECK RESULTS AND CALCULATE WINNINGS
1399    REM · · SET NUMBER OF FRUITS THE SAME TO ZERO
1400    LET X = 0
1405    IF R (1) <> R (2) THEN 1415
1410      LET X = X + 1
1415    IF R (2) <> R (3) THEN 1425
1420      LET X = X + 1
1425    IF R (1) <> R (3) THEN 1435
1430      LET X = X + 1
1435    IF X < 3 THEN RETURN
1440      REM · · TEST FOR JACKPOT
1445      IF R (1) = 6 THEN 1460
1450        LET W = W + 30
1455      GOTO 1470
1460        LET W = W + 100
1470  RETURN

1498  REM · · SUBROUTINE TO HOLD WHEELS
1499    REM · · TEST FOR WINNING LINE
1500    IF X = 3 THEN RETURN
1510      PRINT "HOW MANY WHEELS DO YOU WISH TO HOLD?"
1520      PRINT "MAXIMUM OF TWO"
1530      INPUT H
1540      IF H = 0 THEN RETURN
1550        PRINT "INPUT THE POSITION OF THE WHEEL(S) TO BE HELD"
1560        PRINT "POSITIONS ARE 1, 2 OR 3"
1570        IF H = 1 THEN 1590
1580          INPUT P1
1590        INPUT P2
1600  RETURN

1698  REM · · SUBROUTINE TO DECREASE STAKE AND OUTPUT WINNINGS
1699    REM · · DECREASE STAKE
1700    LET S = S − 10
1710    REM · · OUTPUT WINNINGS
1720    PRINT "YOU HAVE WON A TOTAL OF"; W; "P"
1730    REM · · GENERATE A TIMED DELAY SO THAT PLAYER
1740    REM · · HAS TIME TO READ WHAT IS PRINTED
1750    FOR I = 1 TO 5000
1760    NEXT I
1770    REM · · RESET ANY HOLDS
1780    LET P1 = 0
1790    LET P2 = 0
1800  RETURN
1810  END
```

iv. Results of computer run.

```
RULES FOR PLAYING THE FRUIT MACHINE

AT THE START OF THE GAME YOU STAKE AN AMOUNT
OF MONEY YOU WISH TO GAMBLE, MINIMUM STAKE
10P, MAXIMUM STAKE 50P IN MULTIPLES OF 10P

YOU GET TWO PULLS FOR 10P

BEFORE THE SECOND PULL YOU CAN HOLD ONE
OR TWO WHEELS

PAYOUT IS 30P ON ANY LINE OF FRUITS THAT
ARE THE SAME

PAYOUT IS 100P ON THREE JACKPOT SYMBOLS

GOOD LUCK.....
WHAT IS YOUR STAKE
INPUT 10P TO 50P IN MULTIPLES OF 10P
!50

LEMON                BANANA               ORANGE
1                    2                    3
DO YOU WANT TO HOLD ANSWER Y (YES) N (NO)
!N

JACKPOT              LEMON                BANANA
1                    2                    3
YOU HAVE WON A TOTAL OF 0P

JACKPOT              ORANGE               LEMON
1                    2                    3
DO YOU WANT TO HOLD ANSWER Y (YES) N (NO)
!N

PLUM                 APPLE                ORANGE
1                    2                    3
YOU HAVE WON A TOTAL OF 0P

BANANA               APPLE                BANANA
1                    2                    3
DO YOU WANT TO HOLD ANSWER Y (YES) N (NO)
!Y
HOW MANY WHEELS DO YOU WISH TO HOLD ?
MAXIMUM OF TWO
!2
INPUT THE POSITION OF THE WHEEL(S) TO BE HELD
POSITIONS ARE 1, 2, OR 3
!1
!3

BANANA               LEMON                BANANA
1                    2                    3
YOU HAVE WON A TOTAL OF 0P

APPLE                ORANGE               LEMON
1                    2                    3
DO YOU WANT TO HOLD ANSWER Y (YES) N (NO)
!N

BANANA               LEMON                APPLE
1                    2                    3
YOU HAVE WON A TOTAL OF 0P

APPLE                LEMON                JACKPOT
1                    2                    3
DO YOU WANT TO HOLD ANSWER Y (YES) N (NO)
!Y
HOW MANY WHEELS DO YOU WISH TO HOLD ?
MAXIMUM OF TWO
!1
INPUT THE POSITION OF THE WHEEL(S) TO BE HELD
POSITIONS ARE 1, 2, OR 3
!3

JACKPOT              JACKPOT              JACKPOT
1                    2                    3
YOU HAVE WON A TOTAL OF 100P
STOP AT LINE 250
```

EXERCISE.

1. Show how the following numbers would be expressed in the BASIC language if a computer represents numbers to an accuracy of 9 significant figures and a signed exponent in the range 0 to 38.

a. 4817.395

b. -0.0001942

c. 178431.8×10^{32}

d. $+129.74$

e. 183796219

f. -0.0000002684715

g. 14937.86×10^{-19}

h. $274647941.3768 \times 10^{26}$

i. 938.24×10^{37}

j. $+79.27194 \times 10^{-38}$

2. What are the values of the following functions?

a. ABS (-4.29)

b. INT (-4.29)

c. SGN (-4.29)

d. ATN (3.7321)

e. TAN $(30°)$

f. LOG (5.0)

g. EXP (2)

h. SQR (-49)

i. SIN $(-270°)$

j. SGN (0.001)

Note: To obtain the answers to these questions if your computer can be used in an interactive mode then type PRINT followed by the function. The computer will return an answer to you. This is known as using BASIC in a *calculator mode* or direct mode.

eg. **PRINT ABS (-4.29)**

The calculator mode will apply to all arithmetic expressions.

eg. **PRINT 3 ↑ 2 + 4 ↑ 2**

3. If $\text{Log}_b x = \dfrac{\text{Log}_a x}{\log_a b}$ then derive a user defined function to calculate the logarithm of a number of any valid given base.

Use this function in writing a computer program to find the logarithms of the numbers from 2 to 10 in steps of 0.5 to the bases 2 to 10 in steps of 2.

Your output should be presented in the form of a table having the numbers down the page and the bases across the page.

*4. Write a program to calculate the roots of a quadratic equation $ax^2 + bx + c = 0$ from the formula $x = \dfrac{-b \pm \sqrt{b^2 - 4ac}}{2a}$.

The values of a, b and c being input at the beginning of the program. Consider the implications within your program of $b^2 < 4ac$.

*5. Write programs to print graphs for:

a. $y = \tan(x)$ $0° \leqslant x \leqslant 360°$

b. $y = \log_{10}(x)$ $0 < x \leqslant 5$

c. $y = \ell^x$ $-10 \leqslant x \leqslant 10$

6. Write programs to test the accuracy of your computer by evaluating:

    a. $(x^{1/2})^2 - x$ $0 \leqslant x \leqslant 1$ step of 0.05

    b. $\varrho^{\log(x)} - x$ $1 \leqslant x \leqslant 10$ step of 1

    c. $\tan(\arctan(x)) - x$ $-100 \leqslant x \leqslant +100$ step 10

* 7. Write a program to convert kilometres to miles, yards, feet and inches. Print a table of conversion for the range 1 to 51 kilometres in steps of 5 kilometres.

8. The line $Y = 2X + 3$ divides the X, Y plane into two regions. Write a program to input ordered pairs of numbers that represent co-ordinates in the X, Y plane. Compute whether the point indicated by the co-ordinates lies above, below or on the line. Print the the co-ordinates indicating the position of the point relative to the line.

* 9. Write a program to simulate the rolling of two dice and determine the number of doubles that appear for the digits 1 to 6 inclusive, when the dice are rolled.

    a. 10 times,   b. 100 times,   c. 1000 times.

10. Write a program to simulate the game of dice for two players described in the exercise of chapter 3 question 5.

11 Sorting and Searching Techniques

INTRODUCTION.

1. a. The reader should be well aware of the need to present information in a usable form. Consider the organisation of a telephone directory: entries are ordered into strict alphabetical sequence by name. To find a telephone number knowing the name of the person you wish to call is simply a matter of locating the appropriate section of the directory from the first few letters of the surname, and then **searching** several pages until a match is found for the surname. The address and telephone number of the person will be listed against the surname.

b. Another example of the organisation of information is that of a bus timetable from a central station. The destinations of buses are ordered alphabetically by town or village, and for each destination a chronological listing of bus departure times from the central station, with arrival times at places on route are given. If the time of departure of a bus from the station is to be found the page containing the destination can quickly be found because of the alphabetical ordering of towns on respective pages of the timetable. Departure times are also listed in a defined sequence (chronologically) making reference to a specific part of a day simple. Bus departure and arrival times can then be selected from that part of the timetable.

c. Both examples require the information to be ordered or **sorted** on a part of the information. Telephone directories sorted on names, bus timetables on destinations and times of day. Such information is said to have been sorted on a **key**. Names of people, town or village destination names and times of the day being examples of keys to information.

d. Computers are capable of storing very large amounts of information, and it is of paramount importance that the information is kept in an ordered format for the following reasons.
   i. To provide fast access to the information given an appropriate key.
   ii. To allow for an orderly presentation of information when producing reports.
   iii. To simplify changes to the information — insertions, amendments and deletions — without destroying the key order of the remaining information.

e. The purpose of this chapter is to provide an insight into methods used to organise information. Such methods must provide for:

i. A means of sorting information using a defined key, so that information is represented in an ordered format.

ii. A means of searching through the information efficiently using a particular key such that the access time to information is fast.

CLASSIFICATION OF SORTING METHODS.

2. a. Sorting methods used in computing can be classified into two areas:

i.   **Internal Sorting** — which involves the storage in main memory of all information to be sorted.

ii. **External Sorting** — when the information is too large to be stored and sorted in main memory it is stored on an external storage medium and successive parts of the data are sorted in the main memory.

b. The type of sorting method used will depend upon at least one of the following factors.

i.   The amount of information to be sorted. Clearly it would be very time consuming to use a relatively inefficient sorting method on a large quantity of information.

ii. The computer configuration being used — the size of main memory, number of tape and/or disc units.

iii. The nature of the application and mode under which the application runs eg. real time or batch.

THE ROLE OF BASIC IN SORTING.

3. At this stage it is important not to lose sight of why BASIC was introduced as a high-level language.

a. Essentially BASIC was designed as a language with easy to use facilities for input, output, evaluation and branching so that beginners could write programs quickly. BASIC lacks the sophistication of a commercial programming language such as COBOL that provides a verb to sort information.

b. To improve program development BASIC is often implemented using an interpreter. A BASIC interpreter is good for interactive computing but is slow when sorting large volumes of data.

c. Because of its simplicity BASIC has grown in popularity with the new generation of micro-computers. However, such computers often lack the storage facilities for sorting large volumes of information.

d. For these reasons the reader is recommended to investigate the availability of a sorting package for their computer system if large volume information sorting is contemplated.

INTERNAL SORTING METHODS.

4. The following illustrates two methods for internal sorting. The first the *Shuttlesort* (also known as *Sifting* or *Linear Insertion with Exchange*) is suitable when the speed of the sorting method is not important or where the number of keys to be sorted is small ie. less than 100.

The second method the *Shell Sort* (also known as *Merge Exchange*) after D.L. Shell is an extension of the *Shuttlesort* yet it sorts far faster than the *Shuttlesort* and as a consequence can be used for sorting larger numbers of key ie. less than a 1000.

a. **Shuttlesort.** Figure 11.1 illustrates the position of 8 keys and their respective values.

Key Position	Key Value
1	7
2	3
3	18
4	2
5	6
6	5
7	11
8	4

Figure 11.1

We shall assume that the keys are to be sorted into ascending order, such that key position 1 will contain the lowest key (2) and key position 8 will contain the highest key (18) when the sort is completed.

i.   The list of keys (key values) is examined only **once,** ie. only one pass is made through the list of keys.

ii.   Adjacent pairs of keys are compared, if the first key is greater than the second key of the pair, the keys swap (exchange) positions.

iii.   If a swap is made, the smaller key of the pair is then compared with its adjacent predecessor in the list. If the predecessor is larger then the keys swap positions. This process of comparison and swapping continues **up** the list until either a smaller predecessor is encountered or the top of the list is reached. This process is known as *sifting*.

iv.   Comparison of keys resumes from the position at which the initial swap was made. The method is repeated until the bottom of the list is reached.

Figure 11.2 illustrates the movement of the keys in the list as

KEY POSITION		KEY VALUE																				
1	(TOP)	7	7	3↑	3	3	3	2↑	2	2	2	2	2	2	2	2	2	2	2	2	2	2
2		3	3	7↓	7	7	2↑	3↓	3	3	3	3	3	3	3	3	3	3	3	3	3	3
3		18		18	18	2↑	7↓	7	7	6↑	6	6	6	5↑	5	5	5	5	5	5	5	4↑
4		2			2	18↓	18	18	6↑	7↓	7	7	5↑	6↓	6	6	6	6	6	6	4↑	5↓
5		6						6	18↓	18	18	5↑	7↓	7	7	7	7	7	7	4↑	6↓	6
6		5									5	18↓	18	18	18	11↑	11	11	4↑	7↓	7	7
7		11													11	18↓	18	4↑	11↓	11	11	11
8	(BOTTOM)	4															4	18↓	18	18	18	18

Figure 11.2

the sort progresses. A comparison is shown as], and a swap is shown as ↑ for a key moving up the list, and ↓ for a key moving down the list.

v.   In using a computer to implement this method the list of keys to be sorted would be stored in a one-dimensional array. The position of each key being denoted by the subscript of the array.

b. The implementation of the *Shuttlesort* follows. Since the routine can be used as a general sorting package for, say, less than 100 keys it has been expressed as a subroutine.

i.   **Flowchart of Subroutine to Sort Keys.**

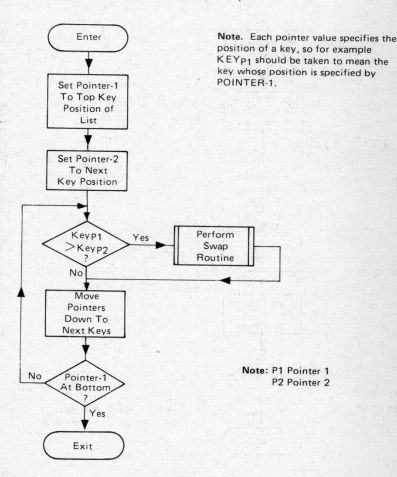

Note. Each pointer value specifies the position of a key, so for example KEY_{P1} should be taken to mean the key whose position is specified by POINTER-1.

Note: P1 Pointer 1
P2 Pointer 2

ii. **Flowchart of Subroutine to Swap Keys** — *Swap routine.*

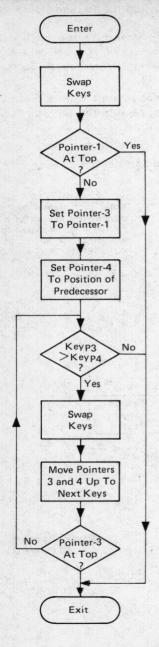

Note: P3 Pointer 3
P4 Pointer 4

iii.

Glossary.		
Pointer—1	P1	
Pointer—2	P2	
Pointer—3	P3	
Pointer—4	P4	
List of Keys	V	one-dimensional array.
Number of keys	N	
Temporary Store	T	used in swapping numbers.

iv. **Subroutine to Sort Keys Using a Shuttlesort.**

```
1000    REM ·· SET POINTERS
1010    LET P1 = 1
1020    LET P2 = 2
1030    REM ·· COMPARE KEYS V(P1) AND V(P2) ARE ADJACENT KEYS
1040    IF V(P1) > V(P2) THEN GOSUB 2000
1050       REM ·· MOVE POINTERS DOWN LIST OF KEYS
1060       LET P1 = P1 + 1
1070       LET P2 = P2 + 1
1080    REM ·· TEST FOR BOTTOM OF LIST
1090    IF P1 < N THEN 1040
1100    RETURN

1999    REM ·· SUBROUTINE TO SWAP KEYS
2000    LET T = V(P1)
2010    LET V(P1) = V(P2)
2020    LET V(P2) = T
2030    REM ·· TEST POINTER—1 FOR TOP OF LIST
2040    IF P1 = 1 THEN RETURN
2050       REM ·· SET POINTERS
2060       LET P3 = P1
2070       LET P4 = P3 − 1
2080       REM ·· COMPARE KEYS
2090       IF V(P4) < = V(P3) THEN RETURN
2100          LET T = V(P3)
2110          LET V(P3) = V(P4)
2120          LET V(P4) = T
2130          REM ·· MOVE POINTERS UP LIST TO NEXT KEYS
2140          LET P3 = P3 − 1
2150          LET P4 = P4 − 1
2160       REM ·· TEST FOR TOP OF LIST
2170       IF P3 > 1 THEN 2090
2180    RETURN
```

Notes.

i.   When swapping the position of two keys it is necessary to include a temporary storage area for one of the keys, since a direct assignment

LET V(P3) = V(P4)

would overwrite the value contained in **V(P3)**.

ii.   The routine requires the number **N** of keys to be known in advance. If this is not possible then an *out of range* key could be used to indicate the bottom of the list. If such a value was chosen to be **999** in the example then line **1090** would be modified to:

1090 IF V(P1) < 999 THEN 1040.

iii. The routine can be easily modified to sort keys that are alphabetic. The only modification being to **V** and **T**, so that they become **V$** and **T$**.

c. Shell Sort. Figure 11.3 illustrates the position of 11 keys and their respective values.

Key Position	Key Value
1	3
2	11
3	6
4	4
5	9
6	5
7	7
8	8
9	10
10	2
11	1

Figure 11.3

To sort the keys into ascending order the following method is applied.

i.   The list of keys is divided into groups containing pairs of keys. However, if the number of keys in the list is odd then one group will contain three keys. The **distance** between keys in a group is initially half the size of the list (N/2) where N is the number of keys in the list. If the list contains an odd number of keys then the initial distance is (N−1) / 2.

From Figure 11.3 there are five groups of keys at the following key positions.

(1, 6, 11)
(2, 7)
(3, 8)
(4, 9)
(5, 10)

ii.   On the first pass through the list, pairs of keys in each group are compared, if the first key of the pair is greater than the second key of the pair then a swap is made. With the exception of the group containing three keys, the keys of the other groups will be in ascending order for each pair only.

To order the group containing three keys the process of sifting is applied to the keys.

iii.   The **distance** between the keys of a group is then **halved**. This effectively changes the keys in each group. A pass is then made through the list of keys comparing keys from each group and swapping where necessary. This will **not** ensure that the keys of each group are in ascending order, therefore, it is necessary to apply the process of sifting during the progression through the list.

iv.   Process iii is repeated until the distance between the keys is **one**. The final pass through the list then becomes a simple sift.

v.   Thus the idea of the Shell sort is that in the early stages far-apart keys are compared, instead of adjacent ones. This tends to eliminate large amounts of disorder quickly, so later stages have less work to do.

Figure 11.4 illustrates the shell sort applied to the keys in the list of figure 11.3 the nomenclature used is identical to that used to illustrate the Shuttlesort.

d. The implementation of the Shell Sort follows, again for the sake of generality this is expressed as a subroutine.

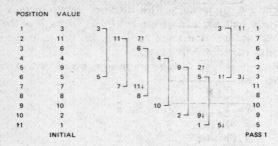

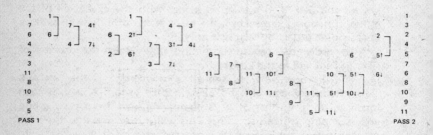

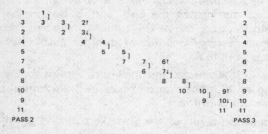

Figure 11.4

186

i. **Flowchart of Subroutine to Sort Keys Using a Shell Sort**

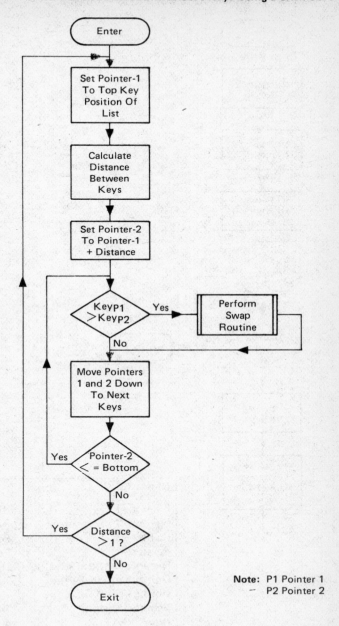

Note: P1 Pointer 1
 — P2 Pointer 2

187

ii.   **Flowchart of Subroutine to Swap Keys — (Shell Sort).**

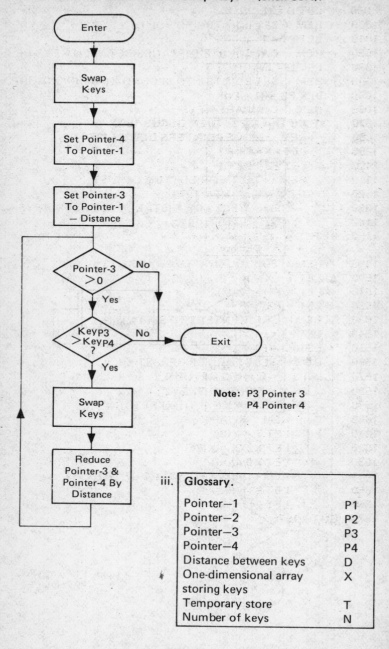

Note: P3 Pointer 3
       P4 Pointer 4

iii.

Glossary.	
Pointer—1	P1
Pointer—2	P2
Pointer—3	P3
Pointer—4	P4
Distance between keys	D
One-dimensional array storing keys	X
Temporary store	T
Number of keys	N

188

iv.   **Program.**

```
 999       LET D = N
1000       REM · · SET POINTER TO TOP OF LIST
1010       LET P1 = 1
1020       REM · · CALCULATE DISTANCE BETWEEN KEYS OF A GROUP
1030       LET D = INT (D/2)
1040       REM · · SET POINTER TO SECOND KEY OF A GROUP
1050       LET P2 = P1 + D
1060       REM · · COMPARE KEYS
1070       IF X(P1) > X(P2) THEN GOSUB 1500
1080          REM · · MOVE POINTERS DOWN LIST
1090          LET P1 = P1 + 1
1100          LET P2 = P2 + 1
1110          REM · · TEST FOR BOTTOM OF LIST
1120          IF P2 < = N THEN 1070
1030             REM · · TEST FOR DISTANCE BETWEEN KEYS
1140                IF D > 1 THEN 1010
1150    RETURN

1499       REM · · SUBROUTINE TO SWAP KEYS
1500       LET T = X(P1)
1510       LET X(P1) = X(P2)
1520       LET X(P2) = T
1530       REM · · SET POINTERS TO SIFT LIST
1540       LET P4 = P1
1550       LET P3 = P1 − D
1560       REM · · TEST FOR TOP OF LIST
1570       IF P3 < = 0 THEN RETURN
1580          REM · · COMPARE KEYS
1590          IF X(P3) < = X(P4) THEN RETURN
1600             REM · · SWAP KEYS
1610             LET T = X(P3)
1620             LET X(P3) = X(P4)
1630             LET X(P4) = T
1640             REM · · MOVE POINTERS UP THE LIST
1650             LET P3 = P3 − D
1660             LET P4 = P4 − D
1670    GOTO 1570
```

MERGING

5. a. Merging is the process of interleaving keys from sorted lists of keys to provide a single list of sorted keys. Figure 11.5 shows two input lists A and B and the result of a *two-way* merge on the lists to produce list C.

INPUT LISTS				OUTPUT LIST	
LIST A		LIST B		LIST C	
Key position	Key value	Key position	Key value	Key position	Key value
1	1	1	3	1	1
2	4	2	6	2	3
3	5	3	7	3	4
4	9	4	10	4	5
5	12	5	13	5	6
				6	7
				7	9
				8	10
				9	12
				10	13

Fig. 11.5 An illustration of a two-way merge.

b. The method of merging two lists consists of comparing individual keys between the lists, the smaller key of the two is written to the output list. The larger key is then compared with the next key from the list whose predecessor was output. The process is repeated until one input list becomes empty in which case the remaining keys of the other input list are output.

Figure 11.6 illustrates this method.

Key position	List	Key values	output list C
1	A]	1]	1
1	B	3	
2	A]	4]	3
1	B	3	
2	A]	4]	4
2	B	6	
3	A]	5]	5
2	B	6	
4	A]	9]	6
2	B	6	
4	A]	9]	7
3	B	7	
4	A]	9]	9
4	B	10	
5	A]	12]	10
4	B	10	
5	A]	12]	12
5	B	13	
	A]	empty	13
5	B	13	

Figure 11.6.

c. An implementation of a two-way merge follows. The procedure has been expressed as a subroutine for the sake of generality. However, it is assumed that the keys are stored in two, one-dimensional arrays that represent lists A and B respectively. The result of merging the two lists is stored in a third one-dimensional array and represents list C.

i.   **Flowchart of subroutine to merge two lists of keys.**

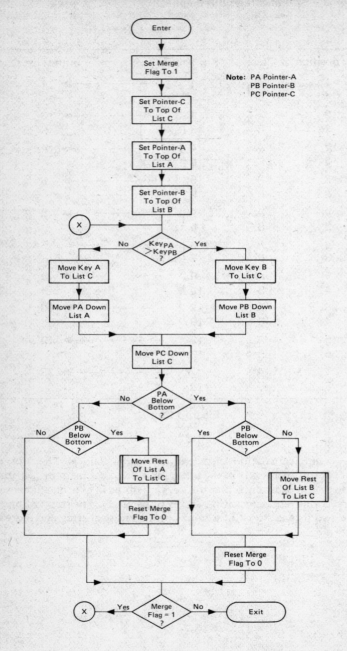

192

ii. **Flowchart of Subroutine to empty a List of Keys.**

The flowchart is specifically related to moving the remainder of list B to list C, however, the logic of the chart can be extended to emptying list A onto list C.

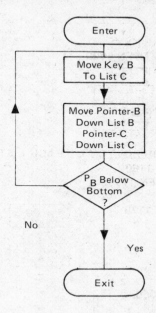

iii. | **Glossary.** | |
|---|---|
| Merge Flag | F |
| Pointer—A | P1 |
| Pointer—B | P2 |
| Pointer—C | P3 |
| List A | A | one-dimensional arrays. |
| List B | B |
| List C | C |
| Length of List A | N | number of keys in |
| Length of List B | M | each list. |

Note: The pointers are used as subscripts in each one dimensional array.
ie. A(P1); B(P2); C(P3).

iv. **Program.**

```
 999     REM · · SET MERGE FLAG TO 1
1000     LET F = 1
1005     REM · · SET POINTERS TO TOP OF EACH LIST
1010     LET P1 = 1
1020     LET P2 = 1
1030     LET P3 = 1
1040     REM · · COMPARE KEYS
1050     IF A(P1) > B(P2) THEN 1090
1060        LET C(P3) = A(P1)
1070        LET P1 = P1 + 1
1080     GOTO 1120
1090        LET C(P3) = B(P2)
1100        LET P2 = P2 + 1
1120        LET P3 = P3 + 1
1125     REM · · TEST FOR BOTTOM OF EACH LIST
1130     IF P1 > N THEN 1160
1140        IF P2 > M THEN 1190
1150     GOTO 1210
1160     IF P2 > M THEN 1175
1170        GOSUB 2000
1175        LET F = 0
1177        GOTO 1210
1190        GOSUB 2100
1200        LET F = 0
1210     IF F = 1 THEN 1050
1220   RETURN

1999     REM · · MOVE REMAINDER OF LIST B TO LIST C
2000     LET C(P3) = B(P2)
2010     LET P2 = P2 + 1
2020     LET P3 = P3 + 1
2030     REM · · TEST FOR BOTTOM OF LIST B
2040     IF P2 < = M THEN 2000
2050   RETURN

2099     REM · · MOVE REMAINDER OF LIST A TO LIST C
2100     LET C(P3) = A(P1)
2110     LET P1 = P1 + 1
2120     LET P3 = P3 + 1
2130     REM · · TEST FOR BOTTOM OF LIST A
2140     IF P1 < = N THEN 2100
2150   RETURN
```

SEARCHING LISTS.

6. a. **Serial Search.** There is a requirement to be able to search through a list of keys and be able to match a key in that list. Having matched a key it is a very simple matter to obtain the information associated with that key.

i. For example, consider the names of personnel to be stored in one array and their switchboard telephone extensions in another array (see fig. 11.7).

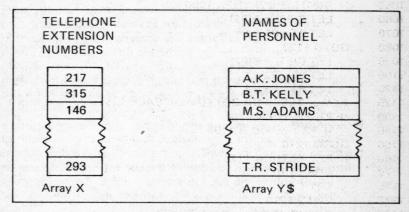

Figure 11.7.

If the extension numbers are stored in array X, and the names of respective personnel in Y$ and the maximum number of entries in both arrays is N. Then if K represents an extension number and we want to find the name of the person at that extension the following program segment can be used to search array X. P represents the position of a key in both arrays.

ii. **Program.**

```
999     REM · · SUBROUTINE TO DEMONSTRATE SERIAL SEARCH
1000    REM · · SET POINTER AT TOP OF LIST
1010    LET P = 1
1020    REM · · INSPECT KEYS
1030    IF K = X(P) THEN 1120
1040      REM · · MOVE POINTER DOWN LIST OF EXTENSIONS
1050      LET P = P + 1
1060      REM · · CHECK FOR BOTTOM OF LIST
1070      IF P < = N THEN 1030
1080        REM · · KEY NOT MATCHED
1090        PRINT "KEY MATCH NOT FOUND"
1100    RETURN
1110    REM · · OUTPUT INFORMATION RELATING TO KEY
1120    PRINT "NAME OF PERSON"; Y$(P)
1130  RETURN
```

iii. This method of searching a list has the advantage that the keys in the list do not have to be sorted. The method is suitable for searching a list containing a small number of unordered keys. However, if the number of keys was large, say, 1000 extension numbers in a factory then the average number of key comparisons necessary before a match was found would be 500. Clearly this is unacceptable owing to the increased time factor involved.

iv. If however, the keys were sorted into a list and a serial search was used to find a key match there would be seldom any need to compare every key in the list if the key was in fact not contained in the list. When the value of the key being compared with a key in the list is **smaller** than the key in the list then clearly a key match cannot be found. This assumes that the keys are arranged in ascending order, if they are in descending order then a key match cannot be found when the key being compared is **larger** than a key in the list.

b. **Binary Search.** This method requires that keys are sorted into a list. The key to be matched is compared with keys at the extremities of the list to ensure that it does lie in the list. The list is then divided into two, and the relative position of the key with regard to one of the two lists is found. This sub-list is again divided into two lists and the relative position of the key with regard to one of the two new lists is found. The method continues until:

i. A key match is obtained.

ii. The size of a sublist is reduced to two keys and neither key matches.

Figure 11.8 illustrates the subdividing of a list until a key match is obtained. When a sublist contains an even number of keys the mid-value is taken to be the next lowest key from centre. The key to be matched in this illustration is 54. Notice that only **three** comparisons are necessary compared with **ten** in the serial search.

INITIAL LIST	SUB-LIST 1	SUB-LIST 2
2		
5		
8		
14		
21		
25 → key (ie. 54) > mid-value	25	
27	27	
39	39	
53	53 → key (ie. 54) > mid-value	53
54	54	54 → key (ie. 54)
60	60	60 = mid-value

Figure 11.8.

196

c. An implementation of the binary search follows.

For the purpose of generality a marker or flag is set to 0 if a key match is found and to 1 if it is not.

The list of keys will be assumed to have been stored in a one-dimensional array. On return from the subroutine if the flag is set to 0 then the subscript of the matching key in the array is used to access the remaining information pertaining to that key. The remaining information being stored in another array similar to Y$ in figure 11.7.

i. **Flowchart.**

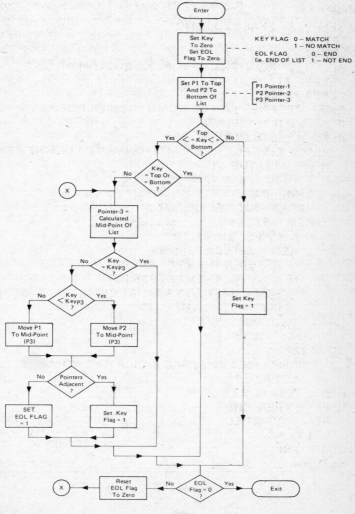

ii.

> **Glossary.**
>
> | End of List Flag | F1 | |
> |---|---|---|
> | Flag | F2 | |
> | Pointer—1 | P1 | |
> | Pointer—2 | P2 | |
> | Pointer—3 | P3 | (mid-point of list) |
> | Key | K | |
> | Array used to store keys | V | |
> | Number of keys in list | N | |

iii. **Program.**

```
1000   REM ·· SET FLAGS TO ZERO
1010   LET F1 = 0
1020   LET F2 = 0
1030   REM ·· SET POINTERS TO TOP AND BOTTOM OF LIST
1040   LET P1 = 1
1050   LET P2 = N
1060   REM ·· TEST KEY FOR BEING OUTSIDE LIST OF KEYS
1070   IF K < V(P1) THEN 1250
1080   IF K > V(P2) THEN 1250
1090     REM ·· TEST FOR KEY-MATCH ON KEYS AT EITHER END
1100     IF K = V(P1) THEN 1270
1110     IF K = V(P2) THEN 1270
1120       REM ·· CALCULATE MID-POINT OF LIST
1130       LET P3 = INT ((P1 + P2) /2)
1140       REM ·· TEST FOR KEY MATCH
1150       IF K = V(P3) THEN 1270
1160         REM ·· SELECT SUBLIST
1170         IF K < V(P3) THEN LET P2 = P3
1180         IF K > V(P3) THEN LET P1 = P3
1190           REM ·· TEST FOR SUBLIST REDUCED TO TWO KEYS
1200           IF P2 − P1 = 1 THEN 1250
1210             REM ·· SET EOL FLAG
1220             LET F1 = 1
1230   GOTO 1270
1240             REM ·· SET KEY FLAG INDICATING NO MATCH
1250           LET F2 = 1
1260   REM ·· TEST FOR EOL
1270   IF F1 = 0 THEN 1310
1280     REM ·· RESET EOL FLAG
1290     LET F1 = 0
1300   GOTO 1130
1310   RETURN
```

EXERCISE.

* 1. Write a program to store ten names of people in a one-dimensional array V$, and adapt the *shuttlesort* subroutine of 4 b iv to sort the names into ascending alphabetic sequence.

Output the list of sorted names.

2. Write a program to store the sex of a person, the year that person was born and the name of the person. Store these details in a two-dimensional array for twenty people.

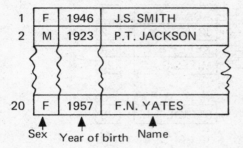

Sex   Year of birth   Name

The sex and year of birth entries must **not** be ordered when the details are initially stored.

The sex is to be taken as the *primary* key, and the year of birth as the *secondary* key.

Pass through the twenty rows of the array sorting the information into **descending** order on the *primary* key. Then pass through the twenty rows of the array again, this time sorting the information into **ascending** order on the *secondary key,* within each primary key group.

The array will then contain information sorted into two groups: males and females. Within each group the people will be ordered by year of birth, hence the oldest people will appear at the top of the group and the youngest at the bottom of the group.

Output the contents of the array.

* 3. Write a program to store the names and addresses of twenty people in a two-dimensional array. The names **must** be stored in alphabetical order. If the names are input in alphabetical order there will be **no** need to sort the array on the name.

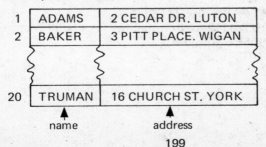

name   address

Extend the program to input the name of person; and modify the binary search of 6c iii to search the first column of the array to match a key with the name that was input. If a key match is found output the address of the person, otherwise output the name not found.

* **4.** Modify the *telephone extension number* example of 6 a i such that both number and name are stored in strict ordered sequence in two, one-dimensional arrays. Associated with each array is a second one-array used to store pointers to the details in the other array.

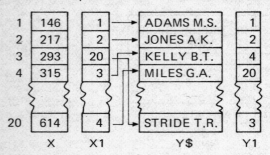

Thus given an extension number (293) say X can be searched until a match is found. The subscript of X (3) can be used to access X1 that contains a pointer (20) to the name of the person in array Y$. The pointer is used as a subscript to Y$.

Alternatively, given the name of a person KELLY B.T. Y$ is searched until a match is found. The subscript of Y$ (3) can be used to access Y1 that contains a pointer (4) to the extension number in array X. The pointer is used as a subscript to X.

Write a program to store twenty extension numbers and names with their respective pointers in arrays X, X1, Y$ and Y1. Use a binary search to locate a name given an extension number and vice versa.

5. Figure 11.9 illustrates a method of sorting five numbers. Draw a flowchart to illustrate this method and write a computer program to implement the sorting method described.

Extend the program to cater for a list of up to 100 keys, and refine the program in such a way that:

a. There will be no need to perform 99 passes through the list if the keys are sorted on less than 99 passes.

b. Keys that have been already ordered need not be re-examined on subsequent passes through the list.

KEY POSITION	KEY VALUE	PASS 1				PASS 2				PASS 3			PASS 4	
1 (TOP)	17	17⌉	13↑	13↑	13	13⌉	9↑	9⌉	5↑	5⌉	1↑	5	5⌉	1↑	1
2	13	13⌉	17↑	9↑	9⌉	9	13⌉	5↑	9⌉	1↑	5	1	1⌉	5↑	5
3	9	9	17↑	5↑	5⌉	5⌉	1↑	13⌉	1↑	9	9	9	9	9	9
4	5	5	17↑	1	1	1	13↓	13	13	13⌉	13	13⌉	13	13⌉	13
5 (BOTTOM)	1	1	17↑	17↓	17	17	17	17	17	17	17	17	17	17	17

Note: The keys are required to be sorted into **ascending** order. Since the values of the keys appear initially in descending order it is necessary to pass through the list of keys (N − 1) times. In this example N = 5 (number of keys) and therefore a maximum of 4 passes through the list of keys is necessary before the keys are sorted into ascending order.

Figure 11.9

12 Projects

INTRODUCTION.

The following problems are designed to test the knowledge and skills the reader has gained from studying the past eleven chapters.

Each solution to a problem should contain:

a. Analysis of the problem.

b. Flowchart.

c. Glossary of terms.

d. Annotated computer program.

e. Test data.

f. Dry-run of either the flowchart or the program.

g. The results from the program being run on a computer.

QUESTIONS.

1. Write a program to produce estimates for turfing and fencing a rectangular or square garden plot.

The length and width of a plot in metres (m) is input to a computer and an itemised estimate containing

a. Total cost of turfing the plot.

b. Total cost of fencing three sides of the plot.

c. Total cost of labour for turfing and fencing.

d. Sub-total for items (a), (b) and (c).

e. Value added tax on item (d) at the rate of 15%.

f. Grand total for items (d) and (e).

is output from a computer.

The cost of turf is £0.50 m^2.

The cost of fencing is £2.00 m.

Labour cost £7.50 per hour.

The labour cost is calculated from the fact that it takes one man one hour to lay 3 m^2 of turf, and one hour to erect 6 m of fencing.

The computer system developed should cater for more than one estimate each time the package is run.

2. Write a program to represent a *Currency Exchange Bureau* that converts up to ten foreign currencies into sterling.

A commission is charged on each transaction according to the following scale of charges.

Amount customer receives in sterling	Commission
< £10	fixed charge 50p
£10 to < £100	fixed charge £1
£100 to < £1000	½% of exchange
£1000 to < £10000	1% of exchange
£10000 or above	1¼% of exchange

The system developed should allow for

a. New exchange rates to be input each day (obtainable from a bank or newspaper).

b. A *menu* driven system to allow the user to select a currency and input an amount to be exchanged.

c. The total transactions for each currency to be output at the close of trading.

d. The total commission to be output at the close of trading.

e. The amount to be exchanged, exchange rate, sterling equivalent, commission and nett sterling amount (sterling equivalent less commission) to be output for each transaction.

3. The following rules enable an insurance company to determine the type of motor-insurance to issue, and the cost of the premium with any excesses to its clients.

If the age of the driver is 25 years or more, the car is manufactured in the U.K. and the accident record is good, the premium charged is 6% of the declared value of the car and a comprehensive policy is issued. If the accident record is not good, the premium is raised to 7%, the policy holder pays the first £10 of a claim and a comprehensive policy is issued.

If the age of the driver is 25 years or more, the car is **not** of U.K. manufacture and the accident record is good, the policy holder pays the first £10 of any claim and a comprehensive policy of 6% is issued. If the above conditions apply except that the accident record is **not** good, the premium is raised to 7% and a third party only policy is issued.

If the age of the driver is **less** than 25 years, the car is manufactured in the U.K. and the accident record is good the premium charged is 6% and a comprehensive policy is issued with the holder paying the first £10 of a claim.

If the age of the driver is less than 25 years, the car is **not** manufactured in the U.K. and the accident record is good, the premium charged is 8%, the policy holder pays the first £10 of any claim and a comprehensive policy is issued. If the accident record is not good and all other conditions apply then the risk is declined.

203

Assume that if a person has **not** had an accident within the last three years then the accident record is good.

Write a computer program to output

a. The type of motor insurance policy.

b. The amount of the premium.

c. Excess payable on any claim if applicable.

when the following information is input to the system.

  i. Age of driver.

  ii. U.K. or foreign car.

  iii. Number of years since last accident.

  iv. Insured value of car.

4. The modulus 11 check digit for a code number is calculated as follows.

Using the code number 57632 as an example: multiply each digit by its associated weight; here we have the weights 6, 5, 4, 3, 2

 ie. $(5 \times 6) + (7 \times 5) + (6 \times 4) + (3 \times 3) + (2 \times 2) = 102$

The sum is then divided by 11 and the remainder 3 is the calculated modulus 11 check digit. The code number becomes 576323.

If the check digit is 10, substitute this value with the character X.

Write a program to input a five digit code number, calculate the modulus—11 check digit and output the six character modified code number.

5. Write a program that will input an amount in sterling (maximum £99.99) and analyse the note and coinage breakdown as follows.

  i. The minimum number of bank notes should be used from £10, £5 and £1 notes.

  ii. The minimum number of decimal coins should be used from 50p, 10p, 5p and 1p coins.

6. A hotel is to be used for a convention for delegates from five different computer companies. The hotel management propose to use their computer to record the number of delegates arriving from each company.

Each delegate will be required to type at the terminal his name and a code number (1—5) representing his company.

Write a program to store the names of those delegates who come from the same company and output a list of the companies together with the personnel attending the convention.

Assume that each company has sent no more than ten delegates.

Hint: The following data structures should be used.

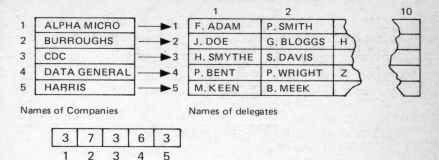

Names of Companies   Names of delegates

A one dimensional array used to store the subscript of the next free column in the array used to store the delegates names.

For example the next free column for the ALPHA MICRO delegates is column 3, for the BURROUGHS delegates is column 7, etc.

7. A small airline that operates flights to **one** destination uses a computer system to:

a. Provide an enquiry system regarding the number and type of seats available for a flight on a specified day.

b. Issue a single ticket to a passenger containing the following information.
    i.   Name of destination.
    ii.   Type of seat booked ie. first class or tourist class.
    iii. Departure, arrival times and date.
    iv. Cost of ticket.
    v.   Name of the passenger.

c. Output a passenger list for each flight.

Assume the following:

a. There is only **one** flight per day at different times over a period of five days. The airline operates from Monday to Friday only. The duration of the flight is 2 hours.

b. Every aeroplane used has a maximum of fifty seats, the distribution of first class seats to tourist class seats being 10 to 40 respectively.

c. A seat is bookable up to one week in advance but **not** on the day of the flight.

d. The cost of a first class seat is £50, whilst that of a tourist class seat is £30.

Write a computer program to implement the airline reservation system. Use the following data structures in your solution.

	Seats Available		Departure Time		Names of Passengers Booked								
	First	Tourist											
(MON)	1	3	19	900	1	S. MAY	J.			P. THOMAS	N.K.		
(TUE)	2	9	3	1200	2	P. BROWN	S.			F. TIBBS	P. GRE		
(WED)	3	0	2	1400	3	T. JONES	V.	HOSKINS		B. HULME	J. WR		
(THU)	4	5	23	1900	4	L. WYNN	B.			S. FLINT	M. WIL		
(FRI)	5	1	7	1600	5	P. SMITH	T.			P. GAYLE	T. JO		

DAYS OF WEEK

1   10   11   12   50

← FIRST → ← TOURIST →

First Tourist

	First	Tourist
1	8	32
2	2	48
3	0	49
4	6	28
5	10	44

The contents of this array gives the subscript of the next free column in the array used to store the names of passengers.

8. Write a program to plot three histograms for the following frequency distributions that relate to marks scored in I.Q. tests by pupils at three different schools.

I.Q. Marks	Number of Pupils		
	School A	School B	School C
75–84	19	13	30
85–94	34	68	121
95–104	89	140	98
105–114	135	73	27
115–124	45	11	6
125–134	8	3	0
135 and over	2	0	0

The histograms should be printed vertically.

FREQUENCY

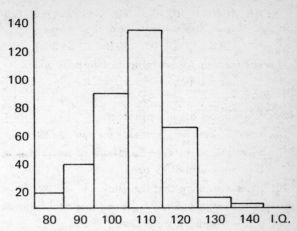

An appropriate distance should be chosen to represent the vertical scale for frequency and horizontal scale for I.Q. Both scales should be printed as shown in the diagram.

9. Write subroutines to calculate the arithmetic mean and standard deviation of a series of n discrete values.

Note. The mean, denoted by $\bar{x}$ (or $\bar{y}$) is calculated from the formula

$$\bar{x} = \frac{\Sigma x}{n} \qquad (\text{or } \bar{y} = \frac{\Sigma y}{n})$$

where Σx means the sum of all x values.

The standard deviation, denoted by S_x (or S_y) is calculated from the formula.

$$S_x = \sqrt{\frac{\Sigma (x - \bar{x})^2}{n}} \qquad (\text{or } S_y = \sqrt{\frac{\Sigma (y - \bar{y})^2}{n}} \qquad)$$

Examples. For these three x values: 9, 10, 14.

$$n = 3, \quad \Sigma x = 9 + 10 + 14 = 33 \quad \text{so } \bar{x} = \frac{33}{3} = 11$$

$$\Sigma (x - \bar{x})^2 = (9 - 11)^2 + (10 - 11)^2 + (14 - 11)^2 = 14$$

$$S_x = \sqrt{\frac{14}{3}} \, \hat{=} \, 2.160$$

Use the subroutines to calculate the coefficient of correlation for the following bivariate distribution, in which x represents the number of vehicles per kilometre of road in Great Britain, and y the maintenance cost (million pounds) for the roads between 1948 and 1957.

YEAR	1948	1949	1950	1951	1952	1953	1954	1955	1956	1957
x	20.3	22.3	24	25	26.4	28.4	30.9	34.1	36.6	39.9
y	20.6	23.5	27	26.3	32.6	35.7	36.5	39.8	42.4	43.2

The formula for coefficient of correlation is:

$$r = \frac{\Sigma (x.y) - n.x.y}{n.S_x.S_y}$$

n — number of pairs of values.

$\bar{x}$ and $\bar{y}$ — arithmetic means for each series of figures.

S_x and S_y — standard deviations of each series.

$\Sigma (x.y)$ — sum of xy pairs.

10. Write a program that will allow:

    a. the lengths of two sides and one internal angle

or b. the lengths of three sides

or c. the length of one side and the two internal angles at the extremities of a line

to be input as the minimum information to construct a triangle. (The program should **not** draw the triangle).

Calculate the sizes of the remaining angles and/or sides, the area of the triangle and the radius of both the inscribed circle and the circumcircle.

The reader may wish to make reference to the following information.

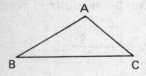

A,B, C — sizes of internal angles.

a, b, c — lengths of the three sides.

s — semi perimeter $= \dfrac{a + b + c}{2}$

$$\frac{a}{SinA} = \frac{b}{SinB} = \frac{c}{SinC} = 2R$$

$$a^2 = b^2 + c^2 - 2\,b\,c\,\cos A$$

Area of triangle $\triangle = \sqrt{s\,(s - a)\,(s - b)\,(s - c)}$

Radius of circumcircle $R = \dfrac{a\,b\,c}{4\,\triangle}$

Radius of inscribed circle $r = \dfrac{\triangle}{s}$

11. A simple method for evaluating an integral $\int_a^b f(x)\,dx$ by computer is to find the area between the plotted function $y = f(x)$, the x axis and the limits x = a, x = b, using Simpson's rule.

An approximation to the area becomes

$$\tfrac{1}{3} h \left(y_0 + 4y_1, + y_2 \right)$$

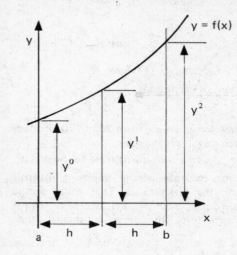 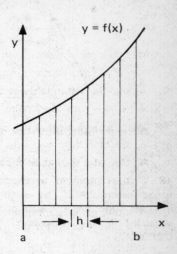

If the area under the curve is divided into strips, and Simpson's rule is applied to each strip between the limits x = a and x = b then clearly the more strips there are the more accurate will be the estimation of the area. Also the more strips there are the smaller h becomes.

Write a program to evaluate the area under a curve using Simpson's rule, and apply the program to find:

a. $\int_1^4 x^2 \, dx$ b. $\int_0^\pi \sin(x) \, dx$ c. $\int_1^3 \log(x) \, dx$

Run the program using different values for h, and compare the results with the theoretical values.

12. Write a program to plot the trajectory of a missile fired at an angle θ to the horizontal ground, with an initial velocity of $u \text{ ms}^{-1}$.

The equation of the trajectory is:

$$y = x\tan\theta - \frac{gx^2}{2u^2 \cos^2\theta}$$

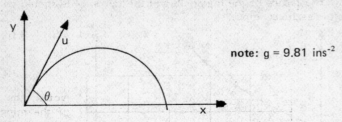

note: g = 9.81 ins^{-2}

Different plots should be made for θ varying from 20° to 70° in steps of 5°.

A value of u should be chosen to give a convenient scale to the graph.

13. Write a program to check the accuracy of the following intrinsic functions in BASIC by summing the given series. The reader should evaluate functions by setting up a loop in which each successive term is obtained from the previous term until the term is smaller than 0.00000005.

a. SIN (x) = $\dfrac{x}{1!} - \dfrac{x^3}{3!} + \dfrac{x^5}{5!} - \dfrac{x^7}{7!} + \dots$

b. COS (x) = $1 - \dfrac{x^2}{2!} + \dfrac{x^4}{4!} - \dfrac{x^6}{6!} + \dots$

c. $e^x = 1 + \dfrac{x}{1!} + \dfrac{x^2}{2!} + \dfrac{x^3}{3!} + \dots$

NB. These formulae are merely given for practise in programming and should not be treated as a practical alternative to the intrinsic functions in BASIC.

14. A minefield has been divided into a lattice having 5 rows facing North/South and 5 rows facing East/West.

A mine is buried at random at each of **three** squares of the lattice.

A remote controlled tank has to cross the minefield from North to South, moving one square at a time in either a North/South, South/North, East/West or West/East direction.

The result of moving to a square containing a buried mine is the total destruction of the tank.

Write a computer program to simulate the situation.

The computer should be used to generate the random position of the mines.

A remote operator instructs the computer where he wants the tank to move by specifying the co-ordinates of the square he wants it to move into.

The lattice of the minefield and the tanks route should be displayed before each new move.

NORTH

	1	2	3	4	5
1		*			
2	*	*			
3	*				
4	*	*	*	*	
5				*	

SOUTH

Note: The positions of the mines are **not** shown on the lattice, the '*' indicates the path the tank has taken. The tank can start from **any** square in the North.

Part Two

The second part of the book is devoted to those features of the BASIC language that are common to many dialects, yet are not included in the E.C.M.A. standard.

The aim of Part Two is not only to give an insight into more advanced BASIC statements but to equip the reader with the necessary skills to tackle with confidence many applications in data processing.

Part Two

13 String Processing

INTRODUCTION.

1. a. The reader will already be familiar with the definition of a string chapter 4 para 2 and the use of string variables and literals in programming. The purpose of this chapter is to define and demonstrate the string functions and statements that are implemented on the majority of computers using BASIC.

    b. There is a need to be able to manipulate string data used in:
    i. the processing of text, and
    ii. records in a file.

    c. String functions are **not** part of the ECMA standard for minimal BASIC, therefore, you are advised to consult your computer manual to see if they are implemented on your computer and whether their format is different to that described.

STRING FUNCTIONS.

2. a. **ASC (X$)** Returns the numeric decimal value of the ASCII code of a single character within the argument or, in the case of a string, the ASCII value of the first character of the string.

    i. Example.
    ```
    10    LET X$ = "A"
    20    PRINT ASC (X$)
    ```
    The ASCII code for character A is 65, so when the program segment is run the value 65 is printed.

    ii.
    ```
    10    PRINT ASC ("CABLE-CAR")
    ```
    The ASCII code for the first character C is printed, this will result in the value 67 being printed.

    b. **CHR$ (Y)** Returns a single character whose ASCII value is Y. Y is a numeric constant, variable or expression that has a value between the limits of the ASCII code $0 \leqslant Y \leqslant 127$. The function **CHR $** serves the opposite purpose to **ASC,** and is useful in outputting ASCII control characters as part of a **PRINT** statement.

    i. Examples.
    ```
    10    PRINT CHR$ (81)
    ```
    This would result in the character Q being printed since the ASCII code for Q is 81.

ii.

```
10    PRINT CHR$ (7)
```

This would result in the warning BELL of the terminal sounding, since the ASCII code for activating the BELL is 7. On some visual display units a *beep* sound is used.

c. **LEFT$ (X$, Y)**   Returns the leftmost Y characters from the string X$.

i. **Examples.**

```
10    LET X$ = "ABCDEFGHIJ"
20    PRINT LEFT$ (X$, 4)
```

This segment when run will output the first four characters of X$; ABCD.

ii.

```
10    LET Y = 3
20    PRINT LEFT$ ("ABCDEFGHIJ", Y)
```

The output would be; ABC.

d. **RIGHT$ (X$, Y)**   Returns the rightmost Y characters from the string X$.

i. **Example.**

```
10    LET X$ = "PQRSTUVWXYZ"
20    LET Y = 5
30    PRINT RIGHT$ (X$, Y)
```

Since the last five characters of X$ are VWXYZ these will be printed.

e. **MID$ (X$, Y, Z)**   Returns a sub-string of X$, starting at character position Y and containing Z characters.

i. **Example.**

```
10    LET X$ = "PQRSTUVWXYZ"
20    LET Y = 4
30    LET Z = 5
40    PRINT MID$ (X$, Y, Z)
```

The fourth character of X$ is S, this is the beginning of the substring which contains five characters, hence the string that is output will be STUVW.

Note: The parameters Y and Z used in the last three functions can be numeric constants, variables or expressions.

f. **VAL (X$)**   Return a numeric constant equivalent to the value of the number represented by the string X$. The string X$ should consist of all digits, if it does not the consequences will depend on the version of BASIC being used, so consult your manual on this matter.

216

i. **Example.**
10   LET X$ = "12345"
20   LET Y = VAL (X$)
30   PRINT Y

The numeric constant 12345 would be output from this program segment. The value of Y can be used in an arithmetic expression since the function **VAL** has essentially converted the data type from string to numeric.

g. **STR$ (Y)**   This is the reverse operation of **VAL**, the value of Y is converted into a string literal. Y can be either a numeric constant, variable or expression.

i. **Example.**
10   LET Y = 7384
20   LET X$ = STR$ (Y)
30   PRINT X$

The result of running the program segment would be to print the string literal 7384.

h. **LEN (X$)**   Return the number of characters that are contained within the string X$.

i. **Example.**
10   LET X$ = "ABCDEFGHIJ"
20   PRINT LEN (X$)

Since there are ten characters in the string X$, the numeric constant 10 will be printed.

i. **Notes.**

i. The parameter X$ used to define some of the functions can be either a string literal or a string variable.

ii. Those string functions that return a numeric value can be used as part of an arithmetic expression.

iii. Some dialects will output an error message if the argument is the null string.

iv. Error conditions arising from the misuse of the string functions can vary between different manufacturers computers.

STRING STATEMENTS.

3. a. **Single character input.** Although the **INPUT** statement can be used to enter a single character at the keyboard of a terminal it has the following disadvantages.

i. A prompt is displayed or printed at the terminal. The system prompt can be replaced by a user prompt in many dialects of BASIC, however, an application may be such that any kind of prompt is undesirable.

ii. The return key must always be pressed to signal to the computer that input is complete.

iii. The depression of the return key only can often cause a program to be terminated, or the computer will not recognise the return character as data and require further data to be input.

b. The **GET** statement (or its equivalent) will allow **any** single ASCII character to be entered through a keyboard **without** having to use the return key to signal that input is complete.

The syntax of the GET statement is

> **GET**   string variable

i. **Example.**
The following program segment will allow any set of characters to be typed at the keyboard of a terminal, and only when a full-stop is entered will the program terminate.

```
10    GET A$
20    IF A$ <> "." THEN 10
30    STOP
```

c. The **CHANGE** statement converts a string literal into the decimal ASCII code for each character and stores these values in a one-dimensional array. The statement can also be used so that the converse is obeyed; the numeric contents of a one-dimensional array is converted to a string of ASCII characters.

The syntax of the **CHANGE** statement is

> **CHANGE**   string literal   **TO**   numeric array
>   numeric array   string literal

i. **Example.**
Convert the alphabet to twenty-six ASCII codes, and output each character of the alphabet with its respective code.

```
10    DIM A (26)
20    LET X$ = "ABCDEFGHIJKLMNOPQRSTUVWXYZ"
30    CHANGE X$ TO A
40    PRINT "CHARACTER", "ASCII CODE"
50    FOR I = 1 TO 26
60       PRINT MID$ (X$, I, 1), A (I)
70    NEXT I
80    STOP
```

STRING CONCATENATION.

4. a. **String Manipulation.** String literals and variables can be manipulated in the following ways.

i. Alphabetic comparison of strings through the comparison of their ASCII codes. "ALPHA" is less than "BETA" since the ASCII code for A (65) is less than that for B (66). Thus A$ < B$ is true if A$ = "ALPHA" and B$ = "BETA."

ii. Strings can be stored in arrays.

iii. Parts of a string can be made available through the use of string functions.

iv. Strings can be increased in size by *adding* other strings to the *end* of the previous string.

b. This last item (iv), is known as *string concatenation.* A plus sign + is used to denote that two strings are to be joined.

i. **Examples.**

```
10   LET A$ = "GRAPE"
20   LET B$ = "FRUIT"
30   LET C$ = A$ + B$
40   PRINT C$
50   LET C$ = B$ + A$
60   PRINT C$
70   STOP
```

If this segment of program was run it would result in two concatenated strings being output:—

GRAPEFRUIT
FRUITGRAPE

ii. The following program segment will allow any character to be typed at the keyboard of a terminal and saved as part of a concatenated string. The program terminates when a full-stop is typed.

```
10    REM · · INITIALISE STRING USED TO STORE
20    REM · · CHARACTERS WITH THE NULL CHARACTER
30    LET X$ = ""
40       REM · · INPUT ONE CHARACTER
50       GET A$
60       REM · · TEST FOR FULL-STOP
70       IF A$ = "." THEN 110
80          REM · · CONCATENATE STRING X$
90          LET X$ = X$ + A$
95          GET A$
100      GOTO 70
110   STOP
```

WORKED EXAMPLES.

5. a. **Problem.** Draw a flowchart, construct a glossary and code a program to input a sentence terminated by a full stop at the keyboard of a terminal; count the number of vowels in the sentence and output the results of the classified vowel count.

219

i.   Flowchart.

Main Program

```
          ┌──────────┐
          │  Start   │
          └──────────┘
               │
     ┌──────────────────┐
     │ Input &          │
     │ Store ASCII      │
     │ Codes For        │
     │ Vowels           │
     └──────────────────┘
               │
     ┌──────────────────┐          Set up a one-dimensional array of 5 cells
     │ Initialise       │ ─ ─ ─ ─  to store the frequency of occurrences of
     │ Array For        │          vowels.
     │ Vowel Count      │
     └──────────────────┘
               │
     ┌──────────────────┐
     │ Input            │
     │ One              │
     │ Character        │
     └──────────────────┘
               │
          ╱────────╲         Yes    ┌──────────┐        ┌──────────┐
         ╱  Char.   ╲ ─────────────▶│ Output   │ ─────▶ │  Stop    │
         ╲  = "."   ╱               │ Count of │        └──────────┘
          ╲────────╱                │ Vowels   │
               │ No                 └──────────┘
     ┌──────────────────┐
     │ Inspect          │
     │ Character        │
     │ For vowel        │
     └──────────────────┘
               │
     ┌──────────────────┐
     │ Input            │
     │ One              │
     │ Character        │
     └──────────────────┘
               │
               └──────▶ (back to decision)
```

Subroutine

```
          ┌──────────┐
          │  Enter   │
          └──────────┘
               │
     ┌──────────────────┐
     │ Obtain ASCII     │
     │ Code For         │
     │ Character        │
     └──────────────────┘
               │
     ┌──────┬───────────┐
     │ I = 1│           │  Yes
     ├──────┤  I > 5    │ ─────────────────────────┐
     │I = I+1│          │                           │
     └──────┴───────────┘                           │
               │ No                                 ▼
          ╱────────╲       Yes   ┌──────────┐   ┌──────────┐
         ╱  Char.   ╲ ──────────▶│ Increase │   │  Exit    │
         ╲ = Vowel  ╱            │Classified│──▶└──────────┘
          ╲    ?   ╱             │Vowel Count│
          ╲────────╱             │  By 1     │
               │ No              └──────────┘
```

Note: The ASCII codes for the input character and vowel are compared in the decision.
CHAR = VOWEL?

ii.

> **Glossary.**
>
> | | |
> |---|---:|
> | One dimensional array used to store the ASCII codes for the five vowels AEIOU. | V (5) |
> | One dimensional array used to store the frequency of occurences for each vowel. The first cell holds the number of A's, second cell the number of E's, etc. | C (5) |
> | String of vowels | S$ |
> | Subscript of arrays | I |
> | Single character of sentence | X$ |
> | ASCII code of character X$ | P |

iii. **Program.**

```
5     DIM V(5), C(5)
10    REM ·· INPUT AND STORE ASCII CODES FOR VOWELS
20    READ A$
30    DATA "AEIOU"
40    CHANGE A$ TO V
50    REM ·· INITIALISE ARRAY C
60    FOR I = 1 TO 5
70      LET C(I) = 0
80    NEXT I
90      REM ·· INPUT SINGLE CHARACTER AT KEYBOARD
100     GET X$
110     REM ·· TEST FOR END OF SENTENCE
120     IF X$ = "." THEN 190
130       REM ·· BRANCH TO SUBROUTINE THAT INSPECTS
140       REM ·· CHARACTER FOR VOWEL AND INCREASES
150       REM ·· VOWEL COUNT
160       GOSUB 500
165     GET X$
170     GOTO 120
180   REM ·· OUTPUT CLASSIFIED VOWEL COUNT
190   PRINT "VOWEL", "COUNT"
200   FOR I = 1 TO 5
210     PRINT MID$ (A$, I, 1), C(I)
220   NEXT I
230   STOP
```

(continued)

```
480   REM ··SUBROUTINE TO CHECK AND COUNT VOWELS
490     REM ··OBTAIN ASCII CODE FOR CHARACTER
500     LET P = ASC (X$)
510     REM ··INSPECT CHARACTER FOR VOWEL
520     FOR I = 1 TO 5
530       IF P = V(I) THEN 570
540     NEXT I
550     GOTO 580
560       REM ··INCREASE VOWEL COUNT
570       LET C(I) = C(I) + 1
580   RETURN
590   END
```

iv. Results of computer run.

THE QUICK BROWN FOX JUMPED OVER THE LAZY DOG.

VOWEL	COUNT
A	1
E	4
I	1
O	4
U	2

Note: This program serves to illustrate the use of CHANGE, GET, MID$ and ASC however, it is not necessary to convert to and from ASCII codes line 530 could have been represented by

530   IF X$ = V$(I) THEN 570

where V$ is an array containing the strings "A", "E", "I", "O", "U"

Further amendments then necessary for the program to run correctly would be

```
5     DIM V$(5), C(5)
10    FOR I = 1 TO 5
20      READ V$(I)
30    NEXT I
40    DATA "A", "E", "I", "O", "U"
160   GOSUB 520
210   PRINT V$(I), C(I)
490
500
```

b. Draw a flowchart, construct a glossary and write a program to input at the keyboard of a terminal an integer written in Roman Numerals, and output at the terminal the decimal value of this number.

Note: Assume a **maximum** of 20 Roman Numerals in the representation of a number.

The following table shows the Roman Numerals and their equivalent decimal values.

Roman Numeral	Decimal Value
I	1
V	5
X	10
L	50
C	100
D	500
M	1000

Legal representations of 3, 8, 13, 18 etc. are respectively III, VIII, XIII, XVIII and **not** IIV, IIX, XIIV, XIIX.

Similarly legal representations of 4, 9, 14, 19 etc. are respectively IV, IX, XIV, XIX and **not** IIII, VIIII, XIIII, XVIIII.

For the purpose of this exercise assume that only legal representations of numbers are input to the computer.

The data structures used are two arrays.

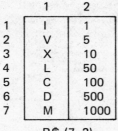

R$ (7, 2)

Note: In array R$ the decimal equivalents to the Roman Numerals **must** be stored as strings.

When a Roman number is input at the keyboard it is divided up into single characters, each character is translated into its decimal equivalent; and that decimal equivalent is stored in array S.

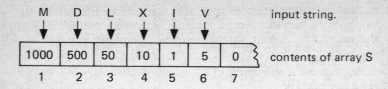

input string.

contents of array S

Since IV implies 4 and not 6 the contents of array S must be corrected to reflect this fact.

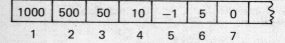

Hence the sum of S then becomes 1564.

i. **Flowchart.**

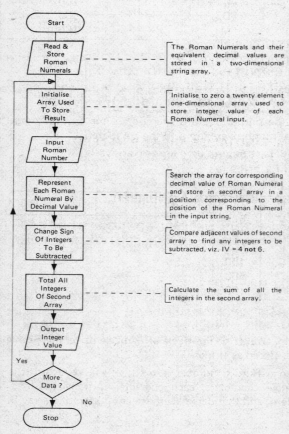

ii.

Glossary.	
Two-dimensional array to hold Roman Numerals and their equivalent decimal values.	R$ (7, 2)
One-dimensional array used to hold the decimal equivalent of each Roman Numeral from the number input at the keyboard.	S (20)
Array Subscripts.	I J
Roman Number.	N$
Total value of all integers stored in second array S	T
User reply to question	A$
Length of input string.	L

iii. **Program.**

```
10    DIM R$(7,2), S(20)
20    REM · ·
30    FOR I = 1 TO 7
40       READ R$(I, 1), R$(I, 2)
50       DATA "I", "1", "V", "5", "X", "10", "L", "50"
60       DATA "C", "100", "D", "500", "M", "1000"
70    NEXT I
80       REM · · INITIALISE ARRAY S TO ZERO
90       FOR I = 1 TO 20
100          LET S(I) = 0
110       NEXT I
120       REM · · INPUT ROMAN NUMBER
130       INPUT N$
140       REM · · STORE DECIMAL EQUIVALENT OF EACH ROMAN
150       REM · · NUMERAL IN CONSECUTIVE CELLS OF
160       REM · · ARRAY S
170       FOR I = 1 TO LEN (N$)
180          FOR J = 1 TO 7
190          REM · · SEARCH ARRAY FOR DECIMAL EQUIVALENT OF
200          REM · · ROMAN NUMERAL
210          IF MID $ (N$, I, 1) < > R$ (J, 1) THEN 240
230             REM · · STORE DECIMAL VALUE IN ARRAY S
230             LET S(I) = VAL (R$ (J, 2))
240          NEXT J
250       REM · · REPEAT PROCEDURE FOR EACH ROMAN NUMERAL
260       REM · · OF THE NUMBER INPUT
270       NEXT I
280       REM · · COMPARE ADJACENT CELLS OF ARRAY S
```

```
290     REM ·· THOSE VALUES TO BE SUBTRACTED ARE
300     REM ·· MULTIPLIED BY −1
310     LET L = LEN(N$) −1
320     FOR I = 1 TO L
330       IF S(I) > = S(I + 1) THEN 350
340       LET S(I) = −1 * S(I)
350     NEXT I
360     REM ·· FIND THE SUM OF THE CONTENTS OF ARRAY S
370     LET T = 0
380     FOR I = 1 TO LEN(N$)
390       LET T = T + S(I)
400     NEXT I
410     REM ·· OUTPUT DECIMAL EQUIVALENT OF ROMAN
420     REM ·· NUMBER
430     PRINT
440     PRINT "DECIMAL VALUE = "; T
450     REM ·· ASK USER IF ANY MORE DATA
460     PRINT "MORE DATA − INPUT Y(YES) N(NO)"
470     INPUT A$
480 IF A$ = "Y" THEN 90
490 STOP
500 END
```

iv. Results of computer run.

```
!MDCLXIV

DECIMAL VALUE = 1664
MORE DATA - INPUT Y(YES) N(NO)
!Y
!MMMDV

DECIMAL VALUE = 3505

MORE DATA - INPUT Y(YES) N(NO)
!Y
!IX


DECIMAL VALUE = 9
MORE DATA - INPUT Y(YES) N(NO)
!Y
!DCCCX
```

226

```
DECIMAL VALUE = 810
MORE DATA - INPUT Y(YES) N(NO)
!Y
!MVIII

DECIMAL VALUE = 1008
MORE DATA - INPUT Y(YES) N(NO)
!Y
!MDCVIII

DECIMAL VALUE = 1608
MORE DATA - INPUT Y(YES) N(NO)
!N
STOP AT LINE 490
```

c. Draw a flowchart, construct a glossary and code a program to translate an **integer** value input at the keyboard of a terminal to an amount stated in words. Output at the terminal the figurative amount.

This routine is used in part of a program to print bank cheques. You can assume that the largest figure input is less than one thousand million, and that cheques for a zero amount are not required.

Two arrays are used in the solution to this problem, the first to store the figurative equivalents of the digits, and the second to store the input number in a modified form.

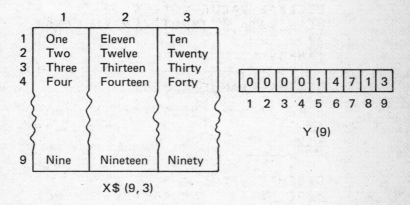

	1	2	3
1	One	Eleven	Ten
2	Two	Twelve	Twenty
3	Three	Thirteen	Thirty
4	Four	Fourteen	Forty
9	Nine	Nineteen	Ninety

X$ (9, 3)

0	0	0	0	1	4	7	1	3
1	2	3	4	5	6	7	8	9

Y (9)

A number would be input without any leading zeros, the purpose of array Y is to isolate the number into digits and introduce leading zeros.

i.   Flowchart Main Program.

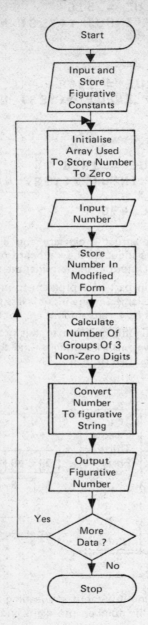

Subroutine to convert a number to a figurative string.

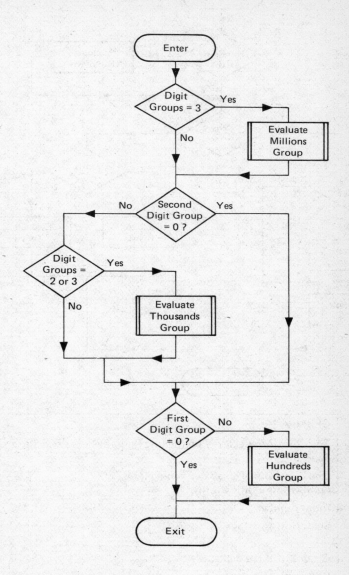

Subroutine to evaluate a group of three digits.

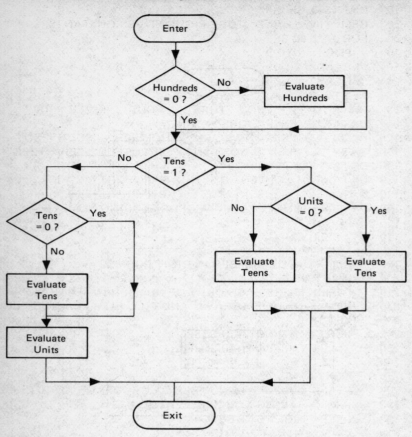

ii. | **Glossary.** | |
| --- | --- |
| Two dimensional array containing figurative constants. | X$ (9, 3) |
| One dimensional array containing input number in modified form. | Y (9) |
| Input number. | N$ |
| Subscripts to arrays. | I |
| | J |
| Groups of three digits. | G |
| Result stored as a string. | T$ |
| User reply to question. | A$ |

iii. **Program.**

```
10     DIM X$(9, 3), Y(9)
20     REM · · INPUT AND STORE FIGURATIVE CONSTANTS
30     FOR J = 1 TO 3
40        FOR I = 1 TO 9
50        READ X$(I, J)
60        NEXT I
70     NEXT J
80     DATA "ONE", "TWO", "THREE", "FOUR", "FIVE", "SIX"
90     DATA "SEVEN", "EIGHT", "NINE"
100    DATA "ELEVEN", "TWELVE", "THIRTEEN", "FOURTEEN"
110    DATA "FIFTEEN", "SIXTEEN", "SEVENTEEN", "EIGHTEEN"
120    DATA "NINETEEN"
130    DATA "TEN", "TWENTY", "THIRTY", "FORTY", "FIFTY"
140    DATA "SIXTY", "SEVENTY", "EIGHTY", "NINETY"
150       REM · · INITIALISE ARRAY FOR STORING NUMBER
160       FOR I = 1 TO 9
170          LET Y(I) = 0
180       NEXT I
190       REM · · INPUT NUMBER IN DIGIT FORM
200       INPUT N$
210       REM · · STORE EACH DIGIT OF NUMBER IN SEPARATE
220       REM · · CELL OF ARRAY Y AND FILL WITH LEADING ZERO
230       LET J = 9
240       FOR I = LEN(N$) TO 1 STEP −1
250          LET Y(J) = VAL (MID$ (N$, I, 1))
260          LET J = J − 1
270       NEXT I
280       REM · · CALCULATE NUMBER OF GROUPS OF 3 DIGITS
290       REM · · HAVING NON-ZERO VALUE
300       IF LEN (N$) > 6 THEN 360
310          IF LEN (N$) > 3 THEN 340
320             LET G = 1
330          GOTO 380
340             LET G = 2
350          GOTO 380
360             LET G = 3
370       REM · · PROCESS THE NUMBER ACCORDING TO ITS GROUP
380       LET T$ = ""
390       GOSUB 700
400       REM · · OUTPUT FIGURATIVE NUMBER
410       PRINT T$
420       PRINT
430       PRINT "MORE DATA ENTER Y(YES) N(NO)"
440       INPUT A$
```

```
450   IF A$ = "Y" THEN 160
460   STOP
470   REM
480   REM · · SUBROUTINE TO CONVERT A NUMBER TO A
490   REM · · FIGURATIVE STRING
700     ON G GOTO 790, 750, 710
710       LET I = 1
720       GOSUB 1000
730       LET T$ = T$ + "MILLION,"
740       IF MID$ (N$, 4, 3) = "000" THEN 780
750         LET I = 4
760         GOSUB 1000
770         LET T$ = T$ + "THOUSAND,"
780         IF RIGHT$ (N$, 3) = "000" THEN 810
790           LET I = 7
800           GOSUB 1000
810   RETURN
820   REM
830   REM · · SUBROUTINE TO EVALUATE A GROUP OF THREE DIGITS
840   REM · · HUNDREDS = 0 ?
1000    IF Y(I) = 0 THEN 1030
1010      REM · · BUILD HUNDREDS STRING
1020      LET T$ = T$ + X$ (Y(I), 1) + "HUNDRED"
1025      REM · · TENS = 1 ?
1030    IF Y(I + 1) = 1 THEN 1100
1040      REM · · TENS = 0 ?
1050      IF Y(I + 1) = 0 THEN 1080
1060        REM · · BUILD TENS STRING
1070        LET T$ = T$ + X$ (Y(I + 1), 3) + " "
1075        REM · · BUILD UNITS STRING
1080      LET T$ = T$ + X$ (Y(I + 2), 1)
1090      GOTO 1150
1095    REM · · UNITS = 0 ?
1100    IF Y(I + 2) = 0 THEN 1140
1110      REM · · BUILD TEENS STRING
1120      LET T$ = T$ + X$ (Y(I + 2), 2) + " "
1130    GOTO 1150
1140      LET T$ = T$ + X$ (Y(I + 1), 3)
1150  RETURN
1160  END
```

232

iv. **Results of computer run.**

```
!1234
ONE THOUSAND, TWO HUNDRED THIRTY FOUR

MORE DATA ENTER Y(YES) N(NO)
!Y
!45
FORTY FIVE

MORE DATA ENTER Y(YES) N(NO)
!Y
!156
ONE HUNDRED FIFTY SIX

MORE DATA ENTER Y(YES) N(NO)
!Y


!78653760
SEVENTY EIGHT MILLION, SIX HUNDRED FIFTY THREE THOUSAND, SEVEN HUNDRED SIXTY

MORE DATA ENTER Y(YES) N(NO)
!Y
!13
THIRTEEN

MORE DATA ENTER Y(YES) N(NO)
!Y
!4001
FOUR THOUSAND, ONE

MORE DATA ENTER Y(YES) N(NO)
!N
STOP AT LINE 460
```

EXERCISE.

1. Detect the errors in the following statements.

    a. LET K$ = ASC (X$)   b. LET K = CHR$ (X$)

    c. PRINT RIGHT $ (X$, 3, 4)   d. PRINT MID ("X$", 3, 1)

    e. LET Y$ = VAL (X)   f. PRINT VAL ("ABCD")

    g. PRINT LEN $ (X$)   h. GET Z

    i. CHANGE X$ TO Y$ j. Y$ = Y$ − X$

2. Write a program to READ from a DATA statement the alphabet. Your program should then print

    a. the entire alphabet

    b. the first six characters of the alphabet

    c. the last ten characters of the alphabet

    d. the tenth character of the alphabet

sections b, c and d require you to use the correct string function.

3. Write a program to create a string from every other letter in the alphabet starting at letter A (eg. ACEG . . . . .) and print

    a. the length of the string

    b. the position of the substring "QSU", as the number of the character positions from the beginning of the string.

4. Write a program to input a short poem and analyse the number of occurences of each letter. Output a table showing the frequency of use for each letter in the alphabet.

* **5.** Extend the program of paragraph 5 (c iii) to cater for decimal fractions. Eg. change 37.642 into words THIRTY SEVEN POINT SIX FOUR TWO.

6. Write a program to input a sentence, count the number of words in the sentence and output the result.

* **7.** Write a program to input a word (max. 20 letters) and output a list of possible anagrams. This could involve printing all the permutations of the letters in the word, however, this would result in many meaningless words. Therefore, only print those words that obey **one** of the following rules.

    a. Every other letter must be a vowel.

    b. Pairs of consonants are allowed.

    c. Groups of three consonants are allowed if they belong to the following set

      SPR   STR   THR   GHT   CHR   SHR   SPL   SCH   SCL

    or any group of three consonants containing the letter Y.

* **8.** Most dialects of BASIC will not store, say, a 20 digit integer without converting the number to a floating point form. Clearly this will lead to truncation errors and subsequent arithmetic calculations cannot be based on the original values of the integers.

    Write a program to store two twenty digit integers as characters of a string, and perform the operations of addition and subtraction on the two integers. Output the answer as a string of digits.

14 Data Validation

INTRODUCTION.

1. a. In chapter 6 para 8 it was stated that inputting bad data to the computer will produce erroneous results, or put another way **rubbish in will produce rubbish out!**

From previous worked examples there has been little or no attempt to inspect input data to ensure that it would not produce the wrong results in calculations and consequently lead to incorrect results being output.

If the reader looks back over a selection of worked examples it is clear that the programs will only function correctly if the user enters data that is of the correct nature.

b. It is left to the reader to consider, for example, how the following programs would have run if:

i. In the quadrilaterals problem (Ch. 7, 11.b) the data was negative.

ii. In selecting players for a team (Ch. 8, 9.b) the team size was greater than the number of players available.

iii. In the menu driven program (Ch. 8, 12) the selected value from the menus was not an integer.

iv. In the sales problem (Ch. 9, 8.a) the product code used as a subscript was fractional or negative or both.

v. In the cheque writing problem (Ch. 13, 5.c) the currency value was non-numeric.

c. The process of inspecting all data that is input to the computer and rejecting data that is unsuitable for use in a program is known as data validation.

A data validation program should ensure that:

i. All errors present in input data are detected.

ii. The type of error is notified to the user of the system.

iii. Only valid data is passed on for processing.

TYPES OF ERRORS.

2. Data that is input to a computer program could contain one or more of the following errors.

a. **Type Error.**

i.   The variable name to be assigned a datum is of a different type to the datum being input. For example if the datum "ABCD" was input to a program using the statement **INPUT N**, the BASIC system being used could return this as an error, since there is a conflict of data types. "ABCD" is a **string** literal; **INPUT N** expects a **numeric** literal.

ii.   Conflict between the use of real or integer numeric literals. If an input datum is to be used as, say, a subscript to an array an error will occur if the datum is real. For example, in a one-dimensional array X, X (3.75) has no meaning.

b. **Format Error.** The size and arrangement of the data is not that required by the program. Such an error can result from:

i.   An excessive number of characters in a string.

ii.   Areas within a data format are not correctly defined. For example, the format of a date within a program is described as DDMMYY yet input at the keyboard as MMDDYY.

Note. DD, MM and YY are three, two-digit integers describing the day, month and year respectively.

c. **Range Error.** A datum does not lie within pre-defined limits. For example, the numerical value of a month is recognised as being in the range 1 to 12, any value for a month outside these limits would be in error.

d. **Relationship Error.** If one item of data is related to another item of data, then a specific value for one item can dictate the range of values for a second item.

For example, when validating a date in a year, if the month is March then the maximum value permissible for the number of days would be 31. This maximum value would change for, say, the month September. However, the maximum value would not only be different for February but dependent upon whether the year was a Leap Year or not.

e. **Not Feasible Data Error.** Many data parameters cannot be given exact limits, therefore, in such cases a value that is thought to be **reasonable** would be chosen to validate such data. For example, in validating the weights of newly born babies, a **maximum** weight of 7.0 kg would be reasonable. Weights above this value are likely to be in error.

f. Data Absent Error. Checks should be made to ensure that all data requested by a program are in fact present. When using the **INPUT** statement if a datum is not entered at the keyboard the system will respond by asking the user to enter more data.

Conversely, if too many items of data are input as a response to an **INPUT** statement then the machine will ignore the extra data, and continue processing.

eg.10   **INPUT A,B,C**
      RUN
      ! 5, 7, 3, 2, 9
      EXTRA IGNORED

However, a situation could arise when an item of data contains a comma such as in an address. In such circumstances it would be undesirable for the *extra* data to be ignored.

eg.10   **INPUT N$**
      RUN
      ! 23, ST. GEORGE CLOSE

BASIC provides a version of **INPUT** that allows a single string of characters, including commas, to be input. The string is delimited by the *return* character. The alternative is known as **LINE INPUT** often abbreviated to **LINPUT**.

eg.10   **LINPUT N$**
      RUN
      ! 23, ST. GEORGE CLOSE

would store the entire string.

TYPE ERROR VALIDATION.

3.   a. **String Input.** To avoid the situation described in (2ai) it is advisable when using the **INPUT** statement to input **all** data, regardless of type (numeric or string) as string data. Thus numeric data can be input to a program by coding, say, **INPUT N$,** but the converse is **not** true as indicated in (2ai). When numeric data is input as a string it **must be converted to the numeric data type** using the **VAL** function before the value can be used in arithmetic expressions, numeric comparisons or subscripts.

237

Several BASIC systems cause program termination when only the *return* key is depressed as a response to inputting data. Since this is undesirable in an applications system the **INPUT** statement should be substituted by an input subroutine using the **GET** statement or its equivalent.

i.   **Example.** The following program subroutine will allow characters to be input via a terminal keyboard, stored as the string X$, and the routine terminated when the *return* key is depressed.

```
500   REM · · SET STRING TO NULL CHARACTER
510   LET X$ = ''''
520      GET Y$
530      REM · · TEST FOR RETURN CHARACTER
540      IF ASC (Y$) = 13 THEN RETURN
550         REM · · BUILD INPUT STRING
560         LET X$ = X$ + Y$
570   GOTO 520
```

BEWARE! When inputting a string of characters in this manner it is possible for the comma character to be stored as part of a string. For example, when inputting the number and street of an address.

However, the comma character is used in many BASIC systems as a delimiter between items of data. If a string containing a comma is stored it could lead to the string becoming corrupted.

To remedy this problem all commas can be removed from a string even though they may have been typed at a keyboard. A simple modification to the previous subroutine would be:

```
545   IF ASC (Y$) = 44 THEN 520
```

b. **Classification of data types in a string.** When processing data the following categories of data type are usually required.

i.   **Alphabetic.** All the characters of the string are letters of the alphabet **only**.

ii.   **Numeric.** The character string is composed from the digits 0 to 9, **one** decimal point (.) for real numbers, an optional plus sign (+) or an obligatory minus sign (−) preceding the magnitude of a number.

iii. **Alphanumeric.** The character string is composed from all the *printable* characters from the ASCII table of characters.

WORKED EXAMPLES OF TYPE ERROR VALIDATION.

4.   Examples of program routines used in the validation of data types.

    a. Alphabetic validation.

      i.   Flowchart.

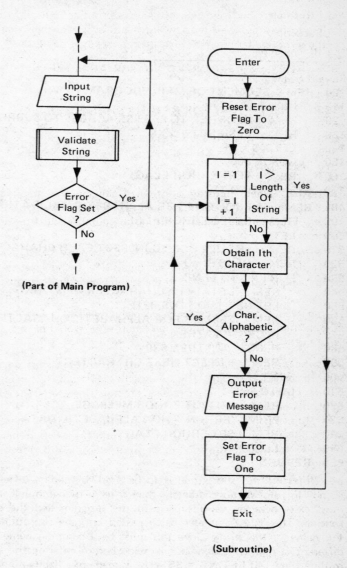

(Part of Main Program)

(Subroutine)

239

ii.

Glossary.	
Input string	S$
String to be validated	X$
Error flag	F
Subscript	I
Ith character	C$

iii. **Program.**

```
100   REM ·· SEGMENT OF MAIN PROGRAM
110     INPUT S$
120     REM ·· IN ORDER TO PASS S$ ACROSS TO SUBROUTINE
130     REM ·· ASSIGN IT TO X$
140     LET X$ = S$
150     GOSUB 500
160     REM ·· TEST ERROR FLAG
170   IF F = 1 THEN 110

498   REM ·· SUBROUTINE FOR ALPHABETIC VALIDATION
499     REM ·· RESET ERROR FLAG
500     LET F = 0
510     REM ·· SET UP LOOP TO INSPECT EACH CHARACTER
520     REM ·· OF STRING
530     FOR I = 1 TO LEN(X$)
540       REM ·· OBTAIN Ith CHARACTER OF STRING
550       LET C$ = MID$ (X$, I, 1)
560       REM ·· TEST C$ FOR ALPHABETIC CHARACTER
570       IF C$ < "A" THEN 630
580       IF C$ > "Z" THEN 630
590       REM ·· INSPECT NEXT CHARACTER
600     NEXT I
610·    GOTO 660
620       REM ·· OUTPUT ERROR MESSAGE
630       PRINT "ERROR — NON ALPHABETIC DATA"
640       REM ·· SET ERROR FLAG
650       LET F = 1
660   RETURN
```

iv. **Notes:** If this subroutine is to be used to validate different strings for alphabetic characters then a form of communication must exist between various parts of the program and the subroutine. The only parameter being passed into the subroutine is the name of the string, since this must be a common name for different strings an assignment is made before entering the subroutine (line 140 **LET** X$ = S$). Use is made of a flag (a numeric variable having one of two values 0 — RESET, 1 — SET) to communicate whether the string was in error. Notice the flag is tested (line 170 **IF F = 1 THEN 110**) to determine whether an error existed in the string. Since this subroutine is used to validate different strings the flag must be reset each time the subroutine is entered. An attempt has been made to explicitly define the nature of an error if it exists (line 630), this provides an invaluable guide to the user of the system.

b. **Numeric Validation.**

   i.   **Flowchart.**

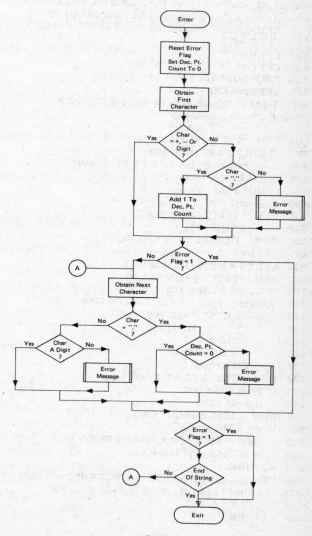

ii.
Glossary.	
String to be validated	X$
Any character from string	C$
Error flag	F
Subscript	I
Decimal point count	P

iii. **Program.**

```
498   REM ·· SUBROUTINE FOR NUMERIC VALIDATION
499   REM ·· RESET ERROR FLAG AND SET DECIMAL
500   REM ·· POINT COUNT TO ZERO AND SUBSCRIPT TO 1
510   LET F = 0
520   LET P = 0
525   LET I = 1
530   REM ·· OBTAIN FIRST CHARACTER
540   LET C$ = LEFT$ (X$, I)
550   REM ·· TEST C$ FOR + − OR DIGIT 0 TO 9
560   IF C$ = "+" THEN 650
570   IF C$ = "−" THEN 650
580     IF C$ < "0" THEN 630
590     IF C$ > "9" THEN 630
600       REM ·· ADD 1 TO DEC. PT. COUNT
610       LET P = P + 1
620     GOTO 650
630     GOSUB 1000
640   REM ·· TEST ERROR FLAG
650   IF F = 1 THEN 800
660   REM ·· OBTAIN NEXT CHARACTER
670   LET I = I + 1
680   LET C$ = MID$ (X$, I, 1)
690   REM ·· TEST C$ FOR DEC. PT.
700   IF C$ = "." THEN 780
710     REM ·· TEST C$ FOR DIGIT 0 TO 9
720     IF C$ < "0" THEN 750
730     IF C$ > "9" THEN 750
740       GOTO 800
750         GOSUB 1000
760       GOTO 800
770   REM ·· TEST DEC. PT. COUNT = 0
780   IF P = 0 THEN 800
790     GOSUB 1000
795   REM ·· TEST ERROR FLAG
800   IF F = 1 THEN 830
810     REM ·· TEST FOR END OF STRING
820     IF I < LEN(X$) THEN 670
830   RETURN
999   REM ·· SUBROUTINE TO OUTPUT ERROR MESSAGE
1000     PRINT "ERROR — NON NUMERIC DATA"
1010     LET F = 1
1020   RETURN
```

iv. **Notes:** If the input string is numeric and contains a leading sign and/or decimal point care must be exercised when using the **VAL** function. Some dialects demand that the first character should be a digit in the range 0—9, and that the string used as an argument in the **VAL** function must either consist of numeric characters or at least start with numeric characters. In the latter case only the numeric characters at the start of the string will be converted to a numeric value.

Other dialects state that if the first non-space character of the string is not a "+", "−", "." or digit then a zero will be returned when the **VAL** function is used. Refer to your computer manual.

The following test can be used to determine whether a numeric quantity is integer or real. X represents a numeric value.

DEF FNT(X) = X − INT(X)

If FNT(X) = 0 then X is **INTEGER**, otherwise X is **REAL**.

c. **Restricted Alphanumeric Validation.** Here are two methods of testing whether the individual characters of a string belong to a given restricted character set.

i. A direct comparison is made between characters of the string and the restricted characters. This method was used in the last example:

```
560   IF C$ = "+" THEN 650
570   IF C$ = "−" THEN 650
700   IF C$ = "." THEN 780
```

However, if the restricted character set contains many characters the second method is to be preferred since it reduces the amount of programming.

ii. The restricted character set is stored as individual characters in a one-dimensional array. When the characters of a string are to be validated, each character in turn is compared with the characters stored in the array. If a match between the characters exist then the next character in the string is processed, otherwise the string is declared as being invalid.

Example. A restricted character set is given as + − * / ↑ [ ]. Validate the string X$ as being composed of characters from the restricted character set or alphabetic characters.

```
10    DIM V$(7)
20    FOR I = 1 TO 7
30    READ V$(I)
40    NEXT I
50    DATA "+", "−", "*", "/", "↑", "[", "]"
      −
      −
      −
```

```
699   REM · · VALIDATION SUBROUTINE
700      LET F = 0
710      FOR I = 1 TO LEN(X$)
720         LET C$ = MID$ (X$, I, 1)
730         FOR J = 1 TO 7
740            IF C$ = V$(J) THEN 780
750         NEXT J
760         IF C$ < "A" THEN 800
770         IF C$ > "Z" THEN 800
780      NEXT I
790      GOTO 820
800      PRINT "ERROR — CHARACTER TYPE MISMATCH"
810      LET F = 1
820   RETURN
```

FORMAT AND DATA ABSENT VALIDATION.

5. a. **Format Validation.** If the length of a string representing data is restricted to a fixed number of characters a check can be made on the length of a string by using one of the following techniques.

   i. Use the **LEN** function to determine if the length of the input string is within a permissible limit. If the string is too long then truncate it using the **LEFT$** function, or report the error to the user and re-input the string.

   ii. Count the number of characters being input under a **GET** statement and terminate the input routine when either the *return* key is depressed or the number of characters exceeds the stated limit.

   b. When areas within a string representing different items of data are **not** input in an order specified validation can be difficult. For example if a date is input using the format DDMMYY and the user enters a date as 120122 we assume that the user did mean 12th January 1922, and did not intend the date to be 1st December 1922. A method of detecting the transposition of digits within a datum is possible by using a check digit validation (para 7a), however, the check digit is calculated in advance and is appended as part of the datum. Such a scheme would be impractical when inputting, say, dates of birth at a terminal.

   c. **Data absent validation.** If a **GET** statement is being used to input data, then should the user depress the *return* key only as a response to data being input, the length of the input string would be zero. Thus using the **LEN** function to check the length of the string will determine whether data has been entered or not. This function can also be used in determining whether areas within the input string are of the correct length. For example if a date was input as 12011922 using the format DDMMYY then a length check would reveal that the date consisted of too many digits and the user would be invited to re-enter the date.

RANGE VALIDATION

6.   a. Range validation has already been used when implementing other validation techniques. For example, to check whether a character is alphabetic in (4aiii).

> **570   IF C$ < "A" THEN 630**
> **580   IF C$ > "Z" THEN 630**

The validation technique simply involves testing whether a datum lies between or outside of pre-defined limits.

Program coding for range testing can be simplified if the dialect of BASIC that you are using incorporates the logical operations **AND** and **OR**.

If α and β are defined limits the coding used to determine whether **X** was valid would be:

> **IF (X = > α) AND (X < = β) THEN ·····**

for **X** to lie **inside** the range $\alpha - \beta$ or,

> **IF (X < α) OR (X > β) THEN ·····**

for **X** to lie **outside** the range $\alpha - \beta$.

b. **Feasible data validation.** The program coding technique is identical to that of range error validation, the only difference being in the manner in which the limits for the range are obtained.

If a programmer is required to code a date validation routine the ranges for the number of days in each month are fixed quantities that are well defined.

But what if the programmer is to code a validation routine to input a person's height, weight and age; what limits should be used then? Clearly the programmer should research what would be reasonable ranges for these three attributes, then data input to the computer could be checked as being feasible or not.

c. **Relationship validation.** When two or more data items are related, then the range of legal values for a datum is dependent upon the values of the related data items.

For example, February 29th is a Legal date if the year is a Leap year. A person whose height is only 1 m is **not** likely to weigh more than 50 kg, yet a person whose height is 1.7 m is quite likely to weigh more than 50 kg.

d. **Example of programming techniques used for relationship validation.**

The following subroutine is used to validate a date in the twentieth century. The date has been input using the format DDMMYY and has **already** been validated for format and data type and has been divided into day, month and year.

i. **Flowchart.**

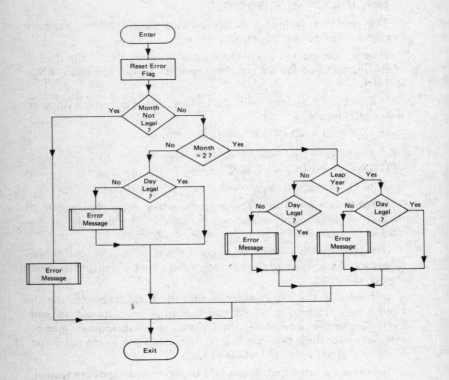

ii.	**Glossary.**	
	Day	D
	Month	M
	Year	Y
	Array containing number of days in each month	V
	Error Flag	F
	Leap Year Indicator	L

iii. **Program.**

```
10    REM ·· SET UP A ONE-DIMENSIONAL ARRAY IN
20    REM ·· THE MAIN PROGRAM TO CONTAIN THE
30    REM ·· MAXIMUM NUMBER OF DAYS IN EACH
40    REM ·· MONTH FOR A NON LEAP YEAR
50    DIM V(12)
60    FOR I = 1 TO 12
70       READ V(I)
80    NEXT I
90    DATA 31, 28, 31, 30, 31, 30, 31, 31, 30, 31, 30, 31
      —
      —
      —
500   REM ·· SUBROUTINE TO VALIDATE DATE
510      LET F = 0

530      IF M < 1 OR M > 12 THEN 640
540      IF M = 2 THEN 580
550         IF D > = 1 AND D < = V (M) THEN 650
560            GOSUB 800
570      GOTO 650
580      LET L = Y — 4 * INT(Y/4)
590      IF L = 0 THEN 630
600         IF (D > = 1) AND (D < = 28) THEN 650
610            GOSUB 800
620      GOTO 650
630         IF (D > = 1) AND (D < = 29) THEN 650
640            GOSUB 800
650      RETURN
799      REM ·· SUBROUTINE TO OUTPUT ERROR MESSAGE
800         PRINT "ERROR — INVALID DATE"
810         LET F = 1
820   RETURN
```

247

MODULUS −11 CHECK DIGIT.

7. a. Data that relates to, say, a code number for an item of stock could pass the valid format test despite having two digits transposed when the data was input. If the code number contains a check digit then the order in which digits have been input becomes self checking.

Question 4 of chapter 12 gives an explanation of how a check digit is calculated. If the calculation is repeated, but this time including the check digit with a weight of 1, then the remainder after division by 11 should be zero. If it is **not** zero an error has been made in transcribing the code number.

The check digit method will ensure a detection of all transcription and transposition errors and 91% of random errors.

b. **Example.** The following subroutine is used to check whether a code number using a modulus −11 check digit has been input to the computer without error. The code number contains six digits, the least significant digit being 0 to 9 or X (X represents a check digit of 10). The code number has already been validated for string size (format) and type.

i. Flowchart.

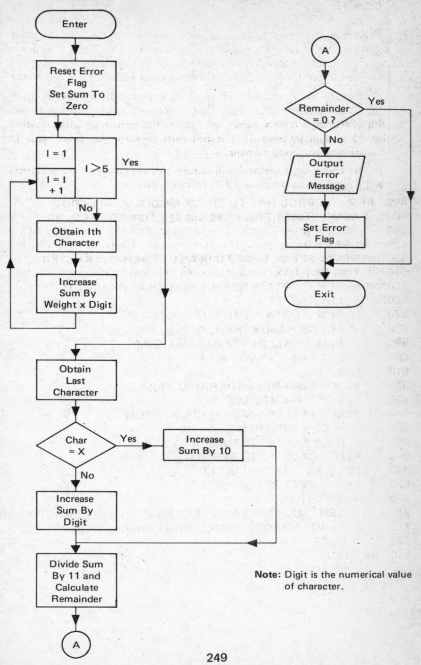

Note: Digit is the numerical value of character.

249

ii.

Glossary.	
Error Flag	F
Sum	S
Subscript	I
Weight	J
Remainder	R
Input string	X$
Single character of string	C$

iii. **Subroutine.**

```
499   REM ·· SUBROUTINE TO CHECK MODULUS −11 CODE
500     REM ·· RESET ERROR FLAG, SET SUM TO ZERO
510     LET F = 0
520     LET S = 0
530     REM ·· SET UP LOOP TO INSPECT EACH CHARACTER
540     FOR I = 1 TO 5
550       REM ·· OBTAIN WEIGHT FOR THAT CHARACTER
560       LET J = 7 − I
570       REM ·· OBTAIN I TH CHARACTER
580       LET C$ = MID$ (X$, I, 1)
590       REM ·· CALCULATE PARTIAL SUM
600       LET S = S + J * VAL (C$)
610     NEXT I
620     REM ·· INSPECT LAST CHARACTER
630     LET C$ = RIGHT$ (X$, 1)
640     REM ·· TEST C$ AND CALCULATE SUM
650       IF C$ = "X" THEN S = S + 10
660       IF C$ <> "X" THEN S = S + VAL (C$)
670     REM ·· CALCULATE REMAINDER
680     LET R = S − 11 * INT(S / 11)
690     REM ·· TEST REMAINDER
700     IF R = 0 THEN 740
710       REM ·· OUTPUT ERROR MESSAGE AND SET ERROR FLAG
720       PRINT "ERROR − CHECK DIGIT CALCULATION"
730       LET F = 1
740   RETURN
```

15 Concepts of File Processing

INTRODUCTION.

1. a. The only methods described up to now for inputting data to a computer program are through the verbs **INPUT, LINE INPUT, GET** and **READ/DATA**. These four forms, although useful, are **not** adequate for coping with large volumes of data. Their use has the following disadvantages.

    i.   **INPUT, LINE INPUT** or **GET** rely on the user entering data through a keyboard device such as a visual display unit. The advantage of using a high-speed computer to process work becomes redundant since the speed of the computer system becomes dependent upon the typing speed of the user at the terminal.

    ii. Data that is input via a keyboard to the main memory of a computer is **not** permanently stored. Switch the power off from the computer and the data stored in the main memory is destroyed. Switch the power on again and the user must re-load and run the program before entering all the data again!

    iii. Data that is represented in a program through a **READ/DATA** statement uses valuable memory space and causes the program to be larger than is necessary for its processing power. This is critical if you are using a microcomputer with a small memory.

    iv. Data that is represented in a program cannot be amended, increased in volume or deleted without having to change part of the program.

    b. To avoid these disadvantages data should be stored on magnetic tape of disc in the form of a data file. Such storage has the following advantages.

    i.   Peripheral devices such as magnetic tape and disc units can transfer data from the medium on which it is stored to the main memory of a computer at a very fast speed (hundreds of thousands of characters per second). Thus the speed of data input/output becomes more realistic in terms of the power of the computer.

    ii. Data can be permanently stored on both magnetic tape and disc. Switch the power off and the data remains on the magnetic medium. Magnetic tapes and disc packs are portable, so not only can data be moved from one computer to another but libraries of data can also be kept.

    iii. Data is no longer represented using READ/DATA statements in a program. Such statements would only be used to represent constants within a program.

iv. Data stored on magnetic tape or disc can be duplicated for security.

v. Changes to data held on peripheral media (magnetic tape or disc) will not involve changes to the program. In fact a program can and will bring about changes to the data, and not the reverse.

c. The purpose of this chapter is to provide the reader with the fundamental concepts of file processing without making any specific references to the BASIC language. The following areas are covered.

   i. The organisation of data files.

  ii. Methods of access to data held on file.

 iii. Types of data files.

 iv. Processing of data files.

ELEMENTS OF A COMPUTER FILE.

2.   a. A computer **file** is a collection of information stored on magnetic tape, magnetic disc, punched cards or punched paper tape.

The reader has already come across the concept of a file when storing a computer program on magnetic tape or disc, or if using a batch entry system preparing a program on punched paper tape or cards. The *program file* was composed of a line by line collection of BASIC statements stored under a name given to the program. See chapter 6 para 2.

b. Data files are similar in concept. Each line of data is known as a *logical* **record** and is subdivided into smaller areas of discrete information known as **fields**. Each **field** is composed of a series of **characters**. Figure 15.1 shows that a hierarchical relationship exists between characters, fields and records of a file.

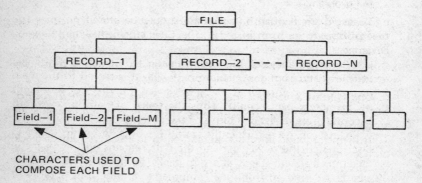

Figure 15.1

i.   The number of characters grouped into a field can vary from field to field in a record.

ii.   The records of a file can be of either **fixed** length or **variable** length. For example figure 15.2 illustrates the format of a fixed length record used to store the details of a factory employee.

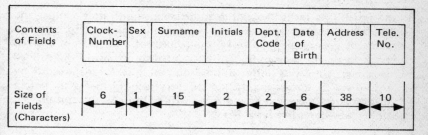

Figure 15.2

Each record in this example has a fixed length of 80 characters, however, although such fields as SURNAME, INITIALS and ADDRESS have fixed lengths of 15, 2 and 38 characters respectively, their contents will not always fill the size of the fields. Each field that is not completely filled will be *padded* with space characters. The result will be an accumulated waste of space between the records of the file. For this reason the fields of a record can be allowed to vary according to the size of the data contained in them. This in turn will bring about records of varying length throughout the file. The records of such a file are said to be of variable length.

c. Notice from figure 15.2 that the information contained in the file is related to specific details, in this example personnel in a factory. Different files are used to store different types of details, for example stock records, details of airline flight reservations, details of customer, etc. Different types of details are **not** mixed in one file.

d. One field of a record is specified as the *primary* key to that record. For example in figure 15.2 CLOCK-NUMBER is a **unique** value for an employee in the factory and could be used as the key to a record. Thus if one required information relating to an employee whose clock number was known in advance, the file would be searched comparing the clock number of each record with the known clock number. When a match was found the information for that record could be extracted.

e. A *physical* record is defined as one or more logical records read into or written from main memory as a *unit* of information. Records are not usually transferred to and from main memory as single *logical* records but grouped together and stored in an area of memory known

253

as a *buffer*. When information is transferred to the buffer it is transferred as a *block* of logical records; and again when information is
transferred from the buffer to the storage medium it is transferred
as a *block* of logical records.

FILE ORGANISATION.

3. a. **Serial**. The records of a file are positioned one after another and
    stored on an appropriate medium (magnetic tape or disc, punched
    cards or paper tape). However, the records of a file are **not** ordered
    on a key, and the position of adjacent records has no pre-defined
    meaning. To access information from the file a serial record by
    record search, comparing the key of every record is necessary before
    a key match is possibly found. Figure 15.3 illustrates the organisation
    of logical records in a serial file.

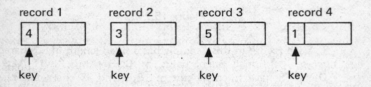

Figure 15.3. A series of records **not** placed in an ascending or descending
order by the key. Records organised in this manner form a serial file.

b. **Sequential**. The records of a file are stored in similar manner to a
serial file with **one** exception. The positions of records are ordered
on a specific key and, therefore, the position of adjacent records has
a meaning. For example in figure 15.2 if the employee records are
ordered by CLOCK-NUMBER the positions of adjacent records must
be such that the records are placed in numerical sequence by CLOCK-
NUMBER. If the *primary* key for the file had been SURNAME then
the records of the file would be positioned into alphabetical sequence
by SURNAME. Access to an individual record is still based on a
record-by-record search through the file until a key match is possibly
found, but in this case it will not be necessary to search the whole
file if the required record is not present.

Figure 15.4 illustrates a sequential file.

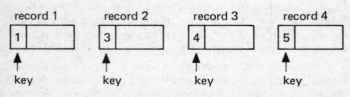

Figure 15.4.

The sequence of records are placed into ascending order of key value. Hence, the records are organised into a sequential file. If searching for a record with a key of 2, reaching key 3 would indicate that the record with key 2 was not in the file.

c. **Indexed Sequential.** Files organised in this manner are usually stored on magnetic disc. The file is represented by two areas on a disc. One area contains an **index** and the other area contains the stored records of the file. The operation of a magnetic disc unit is such that access to a record is possible **without** having to search through each record in turn on the file.

The index to the file contains a list of sorted record keys. Not every key to a record is stored in the index, but only those necessary to reference a physical record. Associated with each key in the index is a *pointer* to a position on the surface of the disc where the record belonging to that key is stored.

To access a record stored on the disc the index must first be read into the main memory of the computer. Knowing the key of the required record the index is searched until either a key match is found or the key is possibly between two adjacent keys of the index. This latter case would imply that the record may exist within the physical record, yet does not have a key stored in the index. In either event the *pointer* is used to retrieve a physical record from the surface of the disc. The required logical record can then be retrieved from the physical record.

If the records of the file are organised sequentially then it is possible to use the file as a sequential file and not refer to the index.

Note: In concept the records are stored in sequence, however, in practice implementations of indexed sequential files differ. Some have the records stored on the disc surface in sequence, others do not.

Figure 15.5 shows the organisation of indexed sequential file.

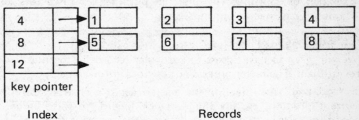

Figure 15.5

d. **Random.** Files organised in this manner are usually stored on magnetic disc. A key is used as a pointer to its appropriate record stored on a disc. Before the key can be used as a pointer it undergoes a mathematical translation to produce a unique numerical value that represents the position of a storage area on the disc surface.

Notes:

i. There are only a few dialects of BASIC that implement Indexed sequential file organisations.

ii. However, many dialects of BASIC that use a disc operating system (DOS) do implement a version of a Random file organisation known as a *Relative* file organisation. The key is numeric (1, 2, 3 . . . . .) and can easily be translated into a pointer to a storage area on the disc surface.

TYPES OF FILES.

4.   a. **Master file.** These are files of a fairly permanent nature eg. stock file, personnel file, customer file, etc. A feature to note is the regular *updating* of these files to show a current position. For example orders will be processed decreasing the amount of stock in the stock file. It is seen therefore that master records will contain both data of a static nature, eg. a stock number, description of stock, and minimum re-order level, and data which, by its nature will change each time a transaction occurs, eg. depletion of stock level.

b. **Movement file.** Also called Transaction file. This is made up of the various transactions created from source documents. In a stock control application the file will contain a list of stock items that have been sold. This file will be used to update the *master* file. As soon as it has been used for this purpose it is no longer required. It will therefore have a very short life, because it will be replaced by a file containing the next list of stock items that have been sold.

c. **Reference file.** A file with a reasonable amount of permanency. Examples of data used for reference purposes are price lists, tables of rates of pay, names and addresses.

PROCESSING ACTIVITIES.

5.   We will need to have access to particular records in the files in order to process them. The major processing activities are given below:

a. **Updating.** When data on the master record is changed to reflect a current position, eg. updating a stock record from the amount of stock sold. Note that the old data on the record is replaced by the new data.

b. **Referencing.** When access is made to a particular record to ascertain what is contained therein, eg. reference is made to a prices file during an invoicing run. Note that this does **not** involve any alteration to the record itself.

c. **File Maintenance.** New records must be added to a file and records need to be deleted. Prices change, and the file must be altered. Customer's addresses also change and new addresses have to be inserted to bring the file up to date. These particular activities come under the heading of maintaining the file. File maintenance can be carried out as a separate run but the insertion and deletion of records is sometimes combined with updating.

d. **File enquiry or interrogation.** This is similar in concept to referencing. It involves the need to ascertain a piece of information from, say, a master record. For example, a customer may query a statement sent to him. A file enquiry will get the data in dispute from the record so that the query may be settled.

SORTING FILES.

6. Records that are initially stored on a transaction file are not usually in key sequence. Before the transaction file can be processed against a sequential master file the records must be sorted into the same key order as the master file.

a. **Internal Sorting.** If the number of records on the transaction file is small enough to occupy the main memory of a computer then the file can be read, and records stored in an array. The records in the array can then be sorted by key; and when the sort is completed they can be stored as a sorted transaction file. If the number of records is too large to store in an internal array, the file can be divided into several smaller files, each file in turn being sorted internally, and finally the individually sorted files can be *merged* to produce one sorted transaction file.

b. **External Sorting.** The following method can be used to sort records of large files, and is known as a *Merge-Sort*. Figure 15.6 illustrates the Merge-Sort using only a small number of record keys.

i. This method is based on the fact that every unsequenced file will have sequences of keys which are in order (even if the sequence is of length one) scattered throughout the file. The sequences or strings of keys are merged to form longer strings of ordered keys. This process continues until eventually only one merged string is output. Note a string here refers to a sequence of keys.

ii. The method requires five serial files to be used, one input file and four work files. The four work files should be as long as the input file, in which case there will be no worry about successive strings being too long for a file.

iii. The input file is read and written onto one of the four work files (A initially) as long as each succeeding key is greater than the previous one. This provides a sequenced string on file A(S1).

This same procedure is used to produce a sorted string on the second file B(S2). The first file (A) written on again, after the first string, producing two strings (S1) (S3). Alternate files will be used for the output of strings until all the keys of the input file have been written onto these two files.

iv. Next, the two files (A and B) are used as input files, and the first string in each (S1 and S2) is **merged** and output to the third file (C). The second two strings (S3 and S4) are merged and output to the fourth file (D). The next two strings (S5 and S6) are output to the third file (C) again; and in a sort involving many more keys the files will be alternated until all the strings have been merged onto files C and D.

v. Files C and D are then used as input files and merged strings are written to files A and B. When all the strings from C and D have been merged the procedures described in iv and v are continued alternately until there is only one string remaining, in which case the file has been sorted.

vi. Note, the main memory is only used to compare two keys and store two records belonging to the keys being compared.

Input File (Keys Only)	Work Files A, B, C and D							Output File Sorted
	A	B	C	D	A	B	A
5	5 S1	9 S2	5	8 S8	5	7 S11	5 S12
15	15	14	9	10	8	11	7
9	10 S3	17 S7	14		9	13	8
14	7	8 S4	15		10 S10	21	9
17	11 S5	13 S6	17		14		10
10	21		7		15		11
8			11 S9		17		13
7			13				14
11			21				15
21							17
13							21

Figure 15.6

PROCESSING SEQUENTIAL FILES.

7. Insertion, amendment and deletion of records held on a master file requires the details of the records in the *update* to be stored in key order sequence on a transaction file. The records of the master file are also stored in the same key order sequence. The two files are processed together, and the result is a third file known as the *son* of the master file. The old master file is known as the *father*. Figure 15.7 shows a representation of the two files being processed to produce a new master file.

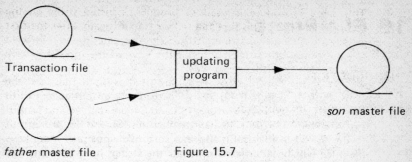

father master file   Figure 15.7

With this technique if the *son* master file was ever corrupted (data destroyed) then the file could be re-created from the original transaction and master file. These two files should be kept for the purposes of file security.

Figure 15.8 shows the contents of three files after the *father* master file has been updated to produce a *son* master file.

1	3	
8	2	Jones
9	2	Jenkins
15	1	Phelps
19	1	Hill

Transaction
File

1	Adams
3	Simons
4	Collins
10	Blake
11	Dawson
12	Rees
15	Wells
16	Rowe
19	Turner
20	Howe

Father master
file

3	Simons
4	Collins
8	Jones
9	Jenkins
10	Blake
11	Dawson
12	Rees
15	Phelps
16	Rowe
19	Hill
20	Howe

Son master
file

The transaction file contains three fields

first — key

second — transaction code   1 — amend

                                   2 — insert

                                   3 — delete

third — name.

Father and son master files contain records with two fields — key and name.

Figure 15.8

16 File Processing

INTRODUCTION.

1. a. This chapter deals with the following aspects related to file processing techniques.

    i.   Activities required for serial/sequential file processing.

    ii.   Creating a serial/sequential file.

    iii. Reading a file.

    iv. Amendment, insertion and deletion of records in a file.

    v.   Access to records in a relative file.

b. File processing verbs are **not** part of the ECMA standard for Minimal BASIC, yet the majority of BASIC dialects implement file processing. The verbs used are **not** consistent between dialects, and it is for this reason that the details of such verbs will not be considered in this chapter.

c. The file processing verbs used in the programs of this chapter have been printed in italics. The reader is advised to investigate the equivalent verbs for their particular computer and hence dialect of BASIC.

ACTIVITIES REQUIRED FOR SERIAL/SEQUENTIAL FILE PROCESSING.

2. a. **Opening a file.** Before a file can be used it **must** be opened. In opening a serial or sequential file a *record pointer* is automatically reset to point at the first record in the file. If the file is empty (contains no records) then the *record pointer* will point at a record created by the computer system marking the end of the file.

In some dialects of BASIC the action of opening a file will cause buffer areas to be created within the main memory and allocated to respective files. However, other dialects of BASIC use pre-defined buffers for all file input/output. Many dialects of BASIC require the mode under which a file is opened to be specified. A file is opened for *INPUT* if records are to be read, *OUTPUT* if records are to be written to the file or *APPEND* if records are to be written at the end of an existing file.

b. **Reading a file.** This is a similar process to reading from a **DATA** statement. However, a file replaces a series of **DATA** statements and fields of a record represent respective items of data. The first execution of a *READ* statement will cause the *input* buffer to be filled with a physical record. The first logical record in the buffer is then accessed. The execution of subsequent *READ* statements will cause successive records to be accessed in sequence from the buffer. When all the logical records from the buffer have been accessed, the buffer will be refilled by a physical record upon the execution of the next *READ* statement. Figure 16.1 is used to illustrate the relationship between records in the buffer area and the *READ* statement.

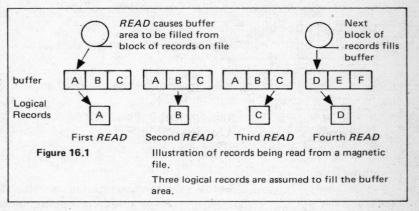

Figure 16.1   Illustration of records being read from a magnetic file.

Three logical records are assumed to fill the buffer area.

c. **Testing for the end of file.** The repeated execution of a *READ* file statement will eventually cause the *record pointer* to point to the end of the file indicating that all the records in the file have been read. For this reason it is important that a method for detecting the end of a file is incorporated into the file processing statements of the BASIC language. In the absence of a method a run-time error will occur when the *record pointer* is set beyond the last record of the file and an attempt is made to read a record.

There are three methods available for testing when the end of a file has been reached. The first is independent of the dialect of BASIC being used, while the last two methods are dependent upon the dialect of BASIC and computer being used. The methods are:

i.   Ensuring that the last record of the file contains a *rogue* value, and testing for this value after every *READ*. A similar technique was used earlier in the book with READ/DATA statements. (chapter 7 para. 11c.)

ii.   Using a BASIC statement to *trap* when the end of file has been reached, and executing this statement when such a condition is true. This method requires that the *trap* statement is placed before a *READ* statement, yet **cannot** be executed until **after a** *READ* statement has read **beyond** the end of the file.

Common statements used to trap the end of file in BASIC are:

ON END#1 GOTO 200
or   *ON ERR GOTO 200*

The second statement requires an error condition to arise (eg. read beyond end of file) before it is executed.

The flowchart representation for this method of testing for the end of a file is shown in figure 16.2 with the appropriate BASIC code.

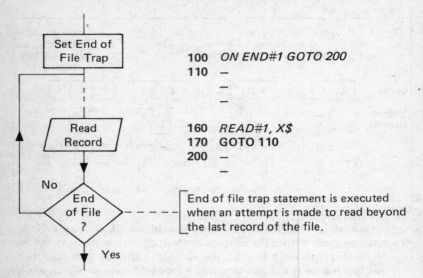

100	*ON END#1 GOTO 200*
110	*—*
	—
	—
160	*READ#1, X$*
170	**GOTO 110**
200	*—*
	—

End of file trap statement is executed when an attempt is made to read beyond the last record of the file.

Figure 16.2

iii. An end of file BASIC function is used in conjunction with a conditional statement. The function returns a value equivalent to true if the end of file is reached or false if the *record pointer* is not at the end of the file.

The implementation of this function varies between computers. Some computers test for the end of file before a read statement, yet others require reading beyond the file to set the function to the true state.

In this and subsequent chapters we will assume the second method for testing the end of file (ie. using a trap).

d. **Writing to a file.** This is the activity of storing a record on a file. The format of a logical record would be specified in a program, and the fields used to represent that format would be assigned values before writing a record. The use of successive *WRITE* statements will cause the *output* buffer to be filled, having one logical record placed after the next in sequence. When the buffer is full the computer system will store the contents of the buffer on the magnetic file. The buffer is then empty, and ready to receive more logical records. Figure 16.3 illustrates writing records to a file.

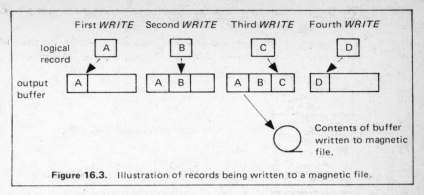

Figure 16.3. Illustration of records being written to a magnetic file.

e. **Appending records to a file.** Often it is desirable to attach records to the end of an existing file. The activity of appending allows records to be written to a file starting at a position after the last record of the file. Some BASIC dialects cater for this activity. However, the same result can be obtained if the file containing the additional records is *merged* with the existing file.

f. **Closing a file.** When all processing activities are completed on a file it must be closed. The activity of closing a file serves the following purposes.

    i.   The contents of a buffer (may be partially full) is written to the file if the mode is set to *OUTPUT*. An end of file marker is then appended to the file.

    ii.   File *housekeeping* activities such as recording the number of records for a particular file and the name of the file are stored in a file directory by the computer system.

    iii.   To allow the file to be re-opened for a different mode of processing. For example a file that is opened for *OUTPUT* could be closed, and re-opened in the *INPUT* mode ready for reading.

FILE CREATION.

3.   a. **Problem.** A college administrator wishes to keep a file of staff names, their respective departments and telephone extension numbers. The following program illustrates how variable length records can be created and stored as a file.

Figure 16.4. Shows how variable length records would be stored. Each line represents one record. In practice the beginning of one record follows the end of another record.

HOLMES, BJ, COMPUTING, 328

WASHINGTON, PM, EXAMINATIONS, 197

CLARK, R, MANAGEMENT, 415

EVANS, D, MATHS, 218

Figure 16.4

i. **Flowchart.**

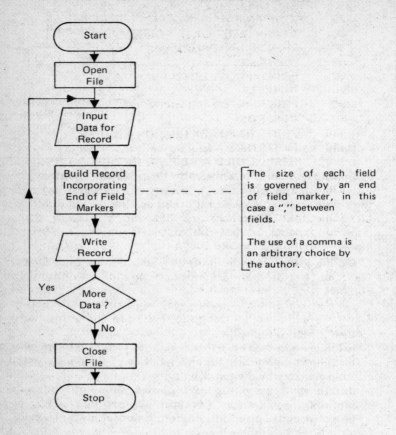

ii. **Glossary**

Surname	S$
Initials	I$
Department	D$
Extension Number	N$
Record String	X$
Reply	A$

iii. **Program.**

```
10   REM ·· OPEN FILE
20   DEFINE FILE#1 = "STAFF"
30      REM ·· INPUT DATA FOR RECORD
40      PRINT "INPUT SURNAME"
50      INPUT S$
60      PRINT "INPUT INITIALS"
70      INPUT I$
80      PRINT "INPUT DEPARTMENT"
90      INPUT D$
100     PRINT "INPUT EXTENSION NUMBER"
110     INPUT N$
120     REM ·· BUILD A RECORD INCORPORATING
125     REM ·· COMMAS AS FIELD SEPARATORS
130     LET X$ = S$ + "," + I$ + "," + D$ + "," + N$
140     REM ·· WRITE RECORD
150     WRITE#1, X$
160     REM ·· MORE DATA
170     PRINT "MORE DATA INPUT Y(YES) N(NO)"
180     INPUT A$
190  IF A$ = "Y" THEN 40
200  REM ·· CLOSE FILE
210  CLOSE#1
200  STOP
210  END
```

b. Consider the problem of introducing records having a fixed length. This will require the lengths of the four fields to be known in advance. If an entry to a field is smaller than the field it must be stored to the left of the field and filled with space characters to the right of the field. This is known as **left justifying** a datum within a field. Alternatively the datum may be too large to fit into the field and will have to be **truncated** in order to fit.

If the following diagram represents the respective field widths (in characters) for SURNAME, INITIALS, DEPARTMENT and EXTENSION NUMBER.

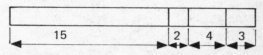

Then the records illustrated in figure 16.4 would be changed to those in figure 16.5.

HOLMES▽▽▽▽▽▽▽▽	BJ	COMP	328
WASHINGTON ▽▽▽▽▽	PM	EXAM	197
CLARK▽▽▽▽▽▽▽▽▽	R	MANA	415
EVANS▽▽▽▽▽▽▽▽▽	D	MATH	218

Note: ▽ indicates the introduction of a space character.

Figure 16.5

When designing fixed length records care should be taken to ensure that important information does not change its meaning through truncation. For example the loss of a digit in an extension number would render the number useless.

There are times when a datum should be stored in the right-hand end of a field. This is known as **right justification,** and has space filling to the left of the datum in the field. Quantities of money should be right justified in a field to give an alignment about a decimal point. Numeric values are normally filled with zeros to the left of the digits.

The following program illustrates how to create a file containing fixed length records as illustrated in figure 16.5.

  i.   **Flowchart.**

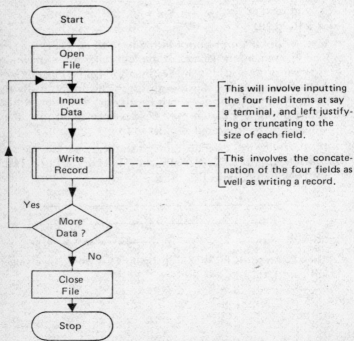

Start

Open File

Input Data —————— This will involve inputting the four field items at say a terminal, and left justifying or truncating to the size of each field.

Write Record —————— This involves the concatenation of the four fields as well as writing a record.

Yes

More Data ?

No

Close File

Stop

ii.   **Subroutine to input fields of a record.**

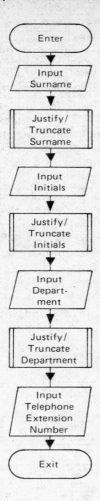

267

iii. **Subroutine to Left justify or truncate a datum.**

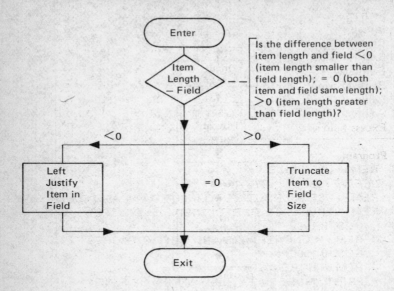

iv. **Subroutine to concatenate fields and write record.**

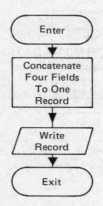

```
v.   Glossary.

     Surname                  S$
     Initials                 I$
     Department               D$
     Extension Number         N$
     Field Size               F
     Record String            X$
     Reply                    A$
     Common String            C$
     Excess field size        E
```

vi. **Program.**

```
10    REM · · OPEN FILE
20    DEFINE FILE#1 = "STAFF"
30    REM · · USE SUBROUTINE TO INPUT DATA AND JUSTIFY OR
40    REM · · TRUNCATE TO REQUIRED FIELD SIZES
50       GOSUB 1000
60       REM · · CONCATENATE AND WRITE RECORD
70       GOSUB 1500
80       REM · · MORE DATA
90       PRINT "MORE DATA INPUT Y(YES) OR N(NO)"
100      INPUT A$
110   IF A$ = "Y" THEN 50
120   REM · · CLOSE FILE
130   CLOSE#1
140   STOP
150   END

999      REM  · SUBROUTINE TO INPUT DATA
1000     PRINT "INPUT SURNAME"
1010     INPUT S$
1020     REM · · DECLARE FIELD LENGTH AND JUSTIFY/TRUNCATE ITEM
1030     LET F = 15
1040     LET C$ =  S$
1050     GOSUB 1400
1060     LET S$ = C$
1070     PRINT "INPUT INITIALS"
1080     INPUT I$
1090     LET F = 2
1100     LET C$ = I$
1110     GOSUB 1400
1120     LET I$ = C$
1130     PRINT "INPUT DEPARTMENT"
1140     INPUT D$
1150     LET F = 4
```

```
1160    LET C$ = D$
1170    GOSUB 1400
1180    LET D$ = C$
1190    PRINT "INPUT EXTENSION NUMBER"
1200    INPUT N$
1210 RETURN

1398    REM ·· SUBROUTINE TO JUSTIFY/TRUNCATE DATA
1399    REM ·· TEST DIFFERENCE BETWEEN SIZE OF DATUM AND FIEL
1400    LET E = LEN (C$) − F
1410      IF E = 0 THEN 1495
1420        IF E > 0 THEN 1490
1430        REM ·· LEFT JUSTIFY DATUM
1440          FOR I = 1 TO ABS(E)
1450            LET C$ = C$ + "   "
1460          NEXT I
1470        GOTO 1495
1480        REM ·· TRUNCATE DATUM TO FIT FIELD
1490        LET C$ = LEFT$ (C$, F)
1495 RETURN

1499    REM ·· SUBROUTINE TO WRITE RECORD
1500    LET X$ = S$ + I$ + D$ + N$
1510    REM ·· WRITE RECORD
1520    WRITE#1, X$
1530 RETURN
```

c. **Appending records to a file.** This is the activity of writing records having first moved the record pointer to the end of the file. This can be implemented in one of two ways.

   i.   By using three files master, transaction and *son* master. The contents of the master file is transferred to the *son* master and when the end of the master file is reached the records of the transaction file can be written to the *son* master file. The appended file is the *son* master file.

   ii.   Dialects of BASIC often have a verb to move the *record pointer* to the end of a file so that any writing to the file causes records to be appended to the end of the file.

d. **Sequential files.** The method of creating a file discussed so far, will produce a serial file. Standard file processing techniques, that will be discussed later in this chapter, use sequential files. The serial file must therefore be sorted on an appropriate key.

The key used for the records of the staff telephone extension numbers file could be surname and initials.

The method used to sort the file will depend upon:
   i.   The size of the file.

ii.   The number of secondary storage devices available. This really applies to tape-drive units in a tape-merge sort.

iii. The size of main memory available.

iv.   The speed at which the file should be sorted.

If an internal sort is contemplated then the records must first be read and stored in an array, then one of the sorting techniques described in chapter 11 should be used. Alternatively, if the file is too large to be stored in an array in the main memory then an external sort, described in chapter 15 paragraph 6b, should be used.

However, in either event the reader is recommend to investigate the availability of a sorting package for their computer system.

READING A SERIAL/SEQUENTIAL FILE

4.   a. **Variable Length records**. The file created in paragraph 3, illustrated in figure 16.4, will be used as an *INPUT* file in the following program and its contents displayed.

    i.   **Flowchart.**

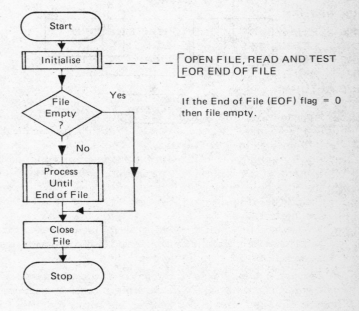

[OPEN FILE, READ AND TEST
FOR END OF FILE

If the End of File (EOF) flag = 0
then file empty.

ii. **Flowchart of subroutine for initialisation.**

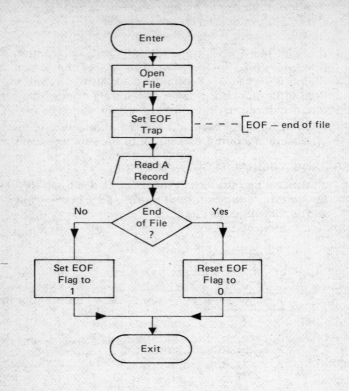

iii. **Flowchart of subroutine to process records.**

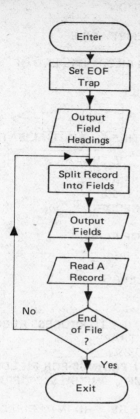

iv. **Glossary.**

Surname	S$	
Initials	I$	
Department	D$	
Extension Number	N$	
Record String	X$	
Position of a character in the record string	I	
Single character of record string	C$	
EOF flag	F	F = 0 file empty

273

v.   Program.

```
10    REM ·· INITIALISATION
20    GOSUB 1000
30    REM ·· TEST FOR EMPTY FILE
40    IF F = 0 THEN 80
50        REM ·· PROCESS FILE UNTIL END OF FILE
60        GOSUB 2000
70        REM ·· CLOSE FILE
80    CLOSE#1
90    STOP

999       REM ·· SUBROUTINE FOR INITIALISATION
999       REM ·· OPEN FILE
1000  DEFINE FILE#1 = "STAFF"
1010      REM ·· SET EOF TRAP
1020  ON END#1 GOTO 1080
1030      REM ·· READ A RECORD
1040  READ#1, X$
1050      REM ·· RESET EOF FLAG
1060      LET F = 1
1070      GOTO 1090
1075      REM ·· SET EOF FLAG
1080      LET F = 0
1090  RETURN

1998      REM ·· SUBROUTINE TO PROCESS RECORDS
1999      REM ·· SET EOF TRAP
2000  ON END#1 GOTO 2300
2010      REM ·· OUTPUT HEADINGS FOR FIELDS OF A RECORD
2020  PRINT "SURNAME", "INITIALS", "DEPARTMENT", "EXTENSIO
2030  PRINT
2040      REM ·· DIVIDE RECORD INTO FIELDS
2050      LET S$ = " "
2060      LET I = 1
2070      LET C$ = MIDS (X$, I, 1)
2080      IF C$ = "," THEN 2120
2090      LET S$ = S$ + C$
2100      LET I = I + 1
2110      GOTO 2070
2120      LET I$ = " "
2130      LET I = I + 1
2140      LET C$ = MID$ (X$, I, 1)
2150      IF C$ = "," THEN 2180
2160      LET I$ = I$ + C$
2170      GOTO 2130
2180      LET D$ = " "
2190      LET I = I + 1
```

```
2200      LET C$ = MID$ (X$, I, 1)
2210      IF C$ = "," THEN 2240
2220      LET D$ = D$ + C$
2230      GOTO 2190
2240      LET N$ = RIGHT$ (X$, LEN (X$) — I)
2250      REM ·· OUTPUT FIELDS
2260      PRINT S$, I$, D$, N$
2270      REM ·· READ A RECORD
2280      READ#1, X$
2290   GOTO 2050
2300 RETURN
2310 END
```

vi   Results.
Contents of file

HOLMES,BJ,COMPUTING,328
WASHINGTON,PM,EXAMINATIONS,197
CLARK,R,MANAGEMENT,415
EVANS,D,MATHS,218

Result of computer run.

SURNAME	INITIALS	DEPARTMENT	EXTENSION
HOLMES	BJ	COMPUTING	328
WASHINGTON	PM	EXAMINATIONS	197
CLARK	R	MANAGEMENT	415
EVANS	D	MATHS	218
STOP AT LINE 90			

vii. **Note:** Some dialects of BASIC use commas as data delimiters, in which case lines 1040 and 2280 should be replaced by a *READ LINE* statement. *READLINE* allows the reading of an entire record ignoring commas as data delimiters, thus a record containing commas is **not** broken up by *READLINE.*

viii. Alternatively some dialects of BASIC will allow the contents of record fields to be read, this convenience implies that it is **not** necessary to divide the record string into fields as illustrated in the last program. However, each field **must** be separated by a delimiter (in this example a comma).

The subroutine to process a record could then be re-written as:

```
1998      REM ·· SUBROUTINE TO PROCESS RECORDS
1999      REM ·· SET EOF TRAP
2000      ON END#1 GOTO 2100
2010      REM ·· OUTPUT HEADINGS FOR FIELDS OF A RECORD
2020      PRINT "SURNAME", "INITIALS", "DEPARTMENT", "EXTENSIO
2030      PRINT
2040      REM ·· OUTPUT FIELDS
2050      PRINT S$, I$, D$, N$
2060      REM ·· READ RECORD AND ASSOCIATE VARIABLE NAMES
2070      REM ·· GIVEN IN STATEMENT WITH FIELDS OF RECORD
2080      READ*#1, S$, I$, D$, N$
2090      GOTO 2050
2100 RETURN
```

Line 1040 of the subroutine for initialisation would also be changed to:

```
1040   READ*#1, S$, I$, D$, N$
```

The same results would be obtained as illustrated in 4. a. vi. if this modified program was run.

b. **Fixed Length Records.**

i.   The following subroutine would be suitable for reading a file containing fixed length records, illustrated in figure 16.5, and printing the contents of each field in each record.

The subroutine to process a record in 4. a. v. is modified.

```
1998      REM ·· SUBROUTINE TO PROCESS RECORDS
1999      REM ·· SET EOF TRAP
2000      ON END#1 GOTO 2140
2010      REM ·· OUTPUT HEADINGS FOR FIELDS OF A RECORD
2020      PRINT "SURNAME", "INITIALS", "DEPARTMENT", "EXTENSIO
2030      PRINT
2040      REM ·· DIVIDE RECORD INTO FIELDS
2050      LET S$ = LEFT$ (X$, 15)
2060      LET I$ = MID$ (X$, 16, 2)
2070      LET D$ = MID$ (X$, 18, 4)
2080      LET N$ = RIGHT$ (X$, 4)
2090      REM ·· OUTPUT FIELDS
2100      PRINT S$, I$, D$, N$
2110      REM ·· READ A RECORD
2120      READ#1 X$
2130      GOTO 2050
2140 RETURN
```

ii. **Results**
Contents of file

HOLMES   BJCOMP328
WASHINGTON   PMEXAM197
CLARK   R MANA415
EVANS   D MATH218

Result of computer run.

SURNAME	INITIALS	DEPARTMENT	EXTENSION
HOLMES	BJ	COMP	328
WASHINGTON	PM	EXAM	197
CLARK	R	MANA	415
EVANS	D	MATH	218
STOP AT LINE 90			

MERGING TWO SEQUENTIAL FILES.

5. a. **Problem.** If two sequential files exist containing the surname,
    initials, department and telephone extension number for staff based
    on two sites of a college, then write a program to merge the two files
    into a third file, knowing that the key is surname and initials, and
    records are of fixed length. The two existing files will be A and B
    respectively, the third will be C.

    i. **Flowchart.**

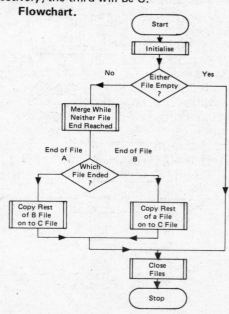

ii. **Flowchart for initialisation subroutine.**

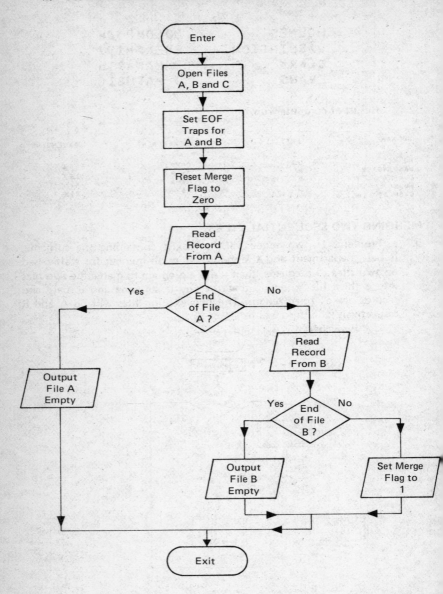

iii. **Flowchart for merging files while neither file is empty.**

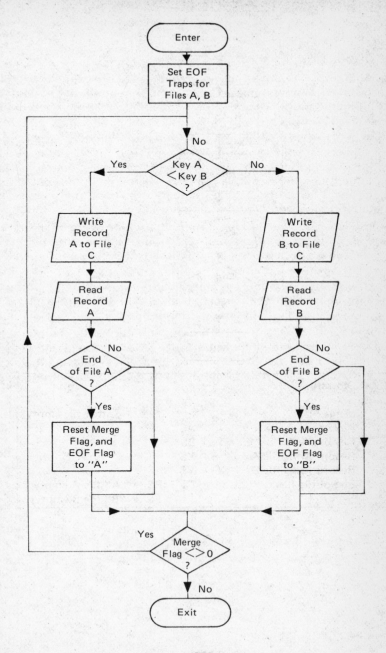

iv. **Flowchart for copying either file A or file B to file C.**

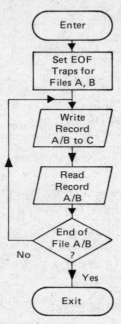

v. **Glossary.**

Merge Flag	F	(F = 1 neither file empty)
Key of file A	A$	
Key of file B	B$	
Record string file A	X$	
Record string file B	Y$	
End of file flag	F$	(F$ = "A" file A empty
		F$ = "B" file B empty)

280

vi. Program.

```
10    REM · · INITIALISATION PHASE
20    GOSUB 1000
30    REM · · TEST FOR FILE BEING EMPTY
40    IF F = 0  THEN 150
50       REM · · MERGE PHASE
60       GOSUB 1500
70       REM · · INSPECT WHICH FILE EMPTY
80       IF F$ = "A" THEN 130
90          REM · · COPY REST OF A TO C
100         GOSUB 1800
110         GOTO 150
120         REM · · COPY REST OF B TO C
130      GOSUB 1900
140      REM · · CLOSE FILES
150   GOSUB 2000
160   STOP

998          REM · · SUBROUTINE FOR INITIALISATION
999          REM · · OPEN FILES A, B AND C
1000         DEFINE FILE#1 = "A"
1010         DEFINE FILE#2 = "B"
1020         DEFINE FILE#3 = "C"
1030         REM · · SET EOF TRAPS FOR FILES A AND B
1040         ON END#1 GOTO 1150
1050         ON END#2 GOTO 1170
1060         REM · · RESET MERGE FLAG
1070         LET F = 0
1080         REM · · READ RECORD FROM FILE A
1090         READ#1, X$
1100         REM · · READ RECORD FROM FILE B
1110         READ#2, Y$
1120         REM · · SET MERGE FLAG
1130         LET F = 1
1140      GOTO 1180
1150         PRINT "FILE A IS EMPTY"
1160      GOTO 1180
1170      PRINT "FILE B IS EMPTY"
1180 RETURN
```

```
1498        REM · · SUBROUTINE TO MERGE FILES
1499        REM · · SET EOF TRAPS FOR FILES A AND B
1500        ON END#1 GOTO 1740
1510        ON END#2 GOTO 1650
1540        REM · · OBTAIN KEYS
1550        LET A$ = LEFT$ (X$, 17)
1560        LET B$ = LEFT$ (Y$, 17)
1570        REM · · COMPARE KEYS
1580        IF A$ < B$ THEN 1690
1590        REM · · WRITE RECORD B TO FILE C
1600        WRITE#3, Y$
1610        REM · · READ RECORD B
1620        READ#2, Y$
1630     GOTO 1770
1640        REM · · RESET MERGE FLAG, AND EOF FLAG
1650        LET F = 0
1660        LET F$ = "B"
1670     GOTO 1770
1680        REM · · WRITE RECORD A TO FILE C
1690        WRITE#3, X$
1700        REM · · READ RECORD A
1710        READ#1, X$
1720     GOTO 1770
1730        REM · · RESET MERGE FLAG, AND EOF FLAG
1740        LET F = 0
1750        LET F$ = "A"
1760     REM · · TEST FOR END OF MERGE
1770        IF F <> 0 THEN 1550
1780 RETURN

1795        REM · · SUBROUTINE TO COPY REST OF FILE A TO FILE C
1796        REM · · SET EOF TRAP FOR FILE A
1800        ON END#1 GOTO 1840
1810        WRITE#3, X$
1820        READ#1, X$
1830     GOTO 1810
1840 RETURN

1895        REM · · SUBROUTINE TO COPY REST OF FILE B TO FILE C
1896        REM · · SET EOF TRAP FOR FILE B
1900        ON END#2 GOTO 1940
1910        WRITE#3, Y$
1920        READ#2, Y$
1930     GOTO 1910
1940 RETURN
```

```
1999   REM·· SUBROUTINE TO CLOSE FILES
2000   CLOSE#1, 2, 3
2010   RETURN
2020 END
```

vii. **Results**

   File A

```
APPLETON            JNCPS 446
BAINBRIDGE          R EDUC210
BEAUMONT.           JECATR415
BUTLER              NJCOMP422
DAINDRIDGE          J LIB 552
DUNFORD             C ARCI512
```

   File B

```
AXFORD              B LPE 397
AYERS               CACOMP305
BARRETT             DACONS579
ELLIOTT             MJGPS 447
```

   Result of program run file C.

```
APPLETON            JNCPS 446
AXFORD              B LPE 397
AYERS               CACOMP305
BAINBRIDGE          R EDUC210
BARRETT             DACONS579
BEAUMONT            JECATR415
BUTLER              NJCOMP422
DAINDRIDGE          J LIB 552
DUNFORD             C ARCI512
ELLIOTT             MJGPS 447
```

Note: The program only merges the two files it does not print the contents of each file. These results were obtained after the program had run by listing the contents of the three files.

FILE MAINTENANCE.

6. Information that is contained in data files is not always static, it can be subject to changes. Such changes to the information will come about through *insertion, amendment* and *deletion* of records (refer to chapter 15 para. 5). The process of changing the information held on data files is known as *updating*.

283

a. **Insertion**. If **new** records are to be inserted into a master file from a transaction file then the process is identical to merging two files, provided the transaction file does not contain records that have duplicate keys. In the event that the transaction file used to insert new records into the master file does contain duplicate keys then the following modifications can be made.

    i.   The merge routine is modified to cope with the existence of duplicate keys on the transaction file.

    ii.   The transaction file is processed and all duplicate records are reported and removed from the file.

b. **Amendment**. This is the process of changing the contents of fields in a record (but **not** the key field) held on a master file. How fields change will depend upon the application, but the changes can be categorised into:

    i.   The original contents of fields in records held on a master file are not used but replaced by new field values.

    eg. In the file shown in figure 16.5 if a telephone extension number was to change the original extension number would be replaced by a new extension number.

    ii.   The original contents of fields in records held on a master file are used together with new values from a transaction file. The combination of the original field values and the transaction field values replace the original field values.

    eg. In a master file containing customer accounts a field used to indicate the balance outstanding is combined with balances from a transaction file to produce the new balance outstanding. This new value is then used to replace the original field value.

The amendment or transaction file contains the details of those fields that are to be changed. The number of fields in the transaction file record does not have to be the same as in a master file record.

The transaction file is processed against the master file to produce a *son* master file. (refer to chapter 15 para. 7).

The process of amendment can utilise some of the procedures used in merging two files. However, records will not be added to the *son* master file, instead the contents of records on the master file will be modified and then written to the *son* master file.

c. **Worked example**. Modify the previous merge program to allow amendments to be made to the master file. In this example amendments will be made to complete record with the exception of the key field.

If the procedure for merging files while neither file is empty (section 5. a. iii.) is replaced by the following procedure for amending records then the remaining procedures used in the merge routine can be adopted for the routine to amend records.

If, however, the end of the master file is reached before the end of the transaction file, the remaining records of the transaction file are not copied to the *son* master file but output as being in error.

In this procedure the transaction file is file A, the master file is file B and the *son* master file is file C.

If on comparison of keys record A is found to be before record B in position then clearly record A does **not** exist on the master file. The routine does not halt, but indicates the error, reads the next record on the transaction file and continues to process the two files.

The format of the records on both the transaction and master files are the same as described in the section 3b. (ie. fixed length records containing surname, initials, department and telephone extension number).

i.   **Flowchart of subroutine to amend records on the master file.**

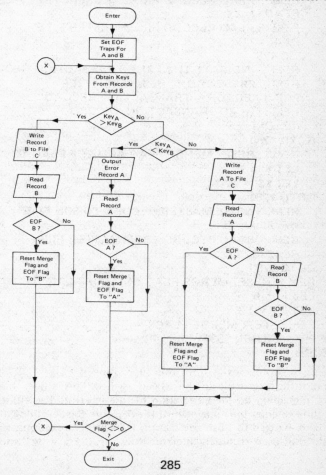

285

ii. The following subroutine is used to amend records on the master file. The glossary is the same as in 5. a. v.

```
1498    REM ·· SUBROUTINE TO AMEND RECORDS
1499    REM ·· SET EOF TRAPS FOR FILES A AND B
1500    ON END#1 GOTO 1700
1510    ON END#2 GOTO 1765
1520    REM ·· OBTAIN KEYS
1530       LET A$ = LEFT$ (X$, 17)
1540       LET B$ = LEFT$ (Y$, 17)
1550    REM ·· COMPARE KEYS
1560       IF A$ > B$ THEN 1740
1570       IF A$ < B$ THEN 1650
1580          REM ·· WRITE TRANSACTION RECORD TO SON FILE
1590          WRITE#3, X$
1595          REM ·· READ RECORD FROM TRANSACTION FILE
1600          READ#1, X$
1610          REM ·· READ RECORD FROM MASTER FILE
1620          READ#2, Y$
1630          GOTO 1780
1640          REM ·· INDICATE THAT THE TRANSACTION RECORD IS N
1645          REM ·· PRESENT ON THE MASTER FILE
1650          PRINT "ERROR — TRANSACTION RECORD"; X$
1660          REM ·· READ TRANSACTION RECORD
1670          READ#1, X$
1680          GOTO 1780
1690          REM ·· RESET MERGE FLAG AND EOF FLAG TO "A"
1700          LET F = 0
1710          LET F$ = "A"
1720          GOTO 1780
1730          REM ·· WRITE MASTER RECORD TO SON FILE
1740          WRITE#3, Y$
1745          REM ·· READ RECORD FROM MASTER FILE
1750          READ#2, Y$
1755          GOTO 1780
1760          REM ·· RESET MERGE FLAG AND EOF FLAG TO "B"
1765          LET F = 0
1770          LET F$ = "B"
1775          REM ·· TEST MERGE FLAG
1780       IF F <> 0 THEN 1530
1785 RETURN
```

When the computer exits from this subroutine if F$ = "B" then the end of the master file will have been reached. This implies that the records remaining on the transaction file are in error. Therefore, the subroutine to copy the remainder of file A to file C (subroutine 1800) must be re-written to flush the records from the transaction file and indicate that each record is in error. However, if F$ = "A" and the last record of B has been read then the system must branch to the close files routine.

```
1795       REM ·· SUBROUTINE TO FLUSH RECORDS FROM FILE A
1796       REM ·· SET EOF TRAP FOR FILE A
1800       ON END#1 GOTO 1860
1810       PRINT "ERROR — TRANSACTION RECORD"
1820       PRINT X$
1830       REM ·· READ TRANSACTION RECORD
1840       READ#1, X$
1850    GOTO 1820
1860 RETURN
```

iii. **Results of running the program.**

```
ERROR-TRANSACTION RECORDBARRETT           DACONS579
STOP AT LINE 160
```

Note: Key BARRETT does not appear on the master file, therefore, cannot be amended, and is output as an error in the transaction file.

Transaction file A

```
BAINBRIDGE          R MATH328
BARRETT             DACONS579
BUTLER              NJMATH317
DUNFORD             C COMP422
```

Master file B.

```
APPLETON            JNCPS 446
BAINBRIDGE          R EDUC210
BEAUMONT            JECATR415
BUTLER              NJCOMP422
DAINDRIDGE          J LIB 552
DUNFORD             C ARCI512
```

Son **master file C.**

```
APPLETON            JNCPS 446
BAINBRIDGE          R MATH328
BEAUMONT            JECATR415
BUTLER              NJMATH317
DAINDRIDGE          J LIB 552
DUNFORD             C COMP422
```

d. **Deletion.** This is the process of removing records from a master file. The keys of the records to be removed are stored on a transaction file. The two files are processed to produce a third file the *son* master file. This routine is very similar to that for the amendment of records, the only difference being that if there is a key match the record from the transaction file is **not** written to the *son* master file.

RANDOM FILE PROCESSING.

7. a. With sequential file processing a key to a record does **not** give the position of that record in relation to the storage medium (tape or disc) being used to store the file. Therefore, it is impossible given a key to a record to access that record directly, without having to inspect each key of each record that is stored before the record that is required.

However, with random files the key to each record is translated by the computer system into a position on the disc surface where the record is stored. Thus knowing the key to a record means that access to that record is direct without having to search through the keys of other records on the file.

The processing activities (insertion, deletion and amendment) that were described for sequential files also apply to random files. However, it is common practice to overwrite records on a master file and not produce a *son* master file as was indicated in sequential file processing. However, it is essential that a copy of the master file is made before overwriting records on the master file. If the master file became corrupted during a computer run it would then be possible to restore the master file to its original state from the copy that had been taken prior to processing the master file.

b. The only new activity associated with random file processing is to **position** the record pointer against the record to be processed having first specified the key to the record. Many dialects of BASIC that use a disc operating system will implement **Relative** files. Thus the key is a positive integer which denotes the position of a record relative to the beginning of a file. A record having a key of 1 would be at the beginning of a file, one with a relative key of 2 would be the second record on a file, and so on. A record key must therefore be converted to a relative file key. The following methods are suitable for such conversion.

    i.   Hashing. A mathematical function is used to translate a record key to a relative key. Such a technique is not considered in this book.

    ii.   Index. A table can be used to store record keys and their respective relative keys.

    iii.   Offset. If the record key is numeric then subtracting a constant will produce a relative key. (see next example).

WORKED EXAMPLE.

c. **Problem.** Devise an enquiry system such that the details of motor spares can be accessed directly using the stock number as a key to a stock record. The stock number is a four digit number having a lowest value of 1001. The format of a fixed length stock record is:

A	B	C

Field A. Description of stock item, length 25 chars.

Field B. Quantity in stock, length 3 chars.

Field C. Unit price, length 5 chars — last two characters represent a decimal fraction, and the decimal point is not stored.

Assume that the stock file is already created, and that the first record (relative key 1) has the stock number 1001.

Stock numbers are represented on the file in consecutive ascending order and do **not** contain *gaps* between numbers.

(ie. 1001, 1002, 1003, 1004 . . . . and not 1001, 1003, 1004).

i. **Flowchart of main program.**

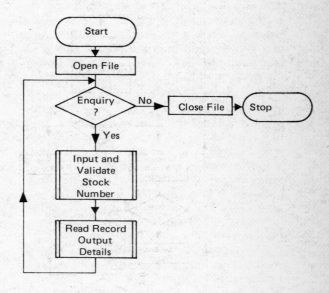

ii. **Flowchart of Subroutine to read record and output fields.**

iii. **Flowchart of Subroutine to input and validate stock number.**

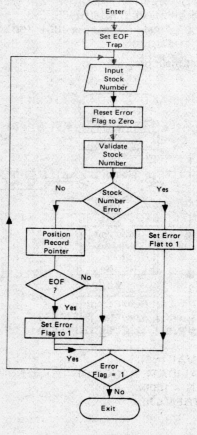

iv. **Glossary.**

User reply	R$
Stock number	N$ (input) N (validated)
Error flag	F
Description of stock	S$
Quantity	Q$
Unit price	P$
Relative key	K
Stock record	X$
Price as decimal value	E$

v. **Program.**

```
10    REM ·· OPEN RELATIVE FILE
20    DEFINE FILE#1 = "STOCK", ASCDA, 17
30    REM ·· IS THERE A STOCK ENQUIRY?
40       PRINT "DO YOU WANT TO ENQUIRE ABOUT AN ITEM OF STOCK?"
50       PRINT "ANSWER Y (YES) N (NO)"
60       INPUT R$
70       IF R$ = "Y" THEN 120
80          REM ·· CLOSE FILE
90          CLOSE#1
100         STOP
110         REM ·· INPUT AND VALIDATE STOCK NUMBER
120      GOSUB 500
130      REM ·· READ RECORD AND OUTPUT DETAILS
140      GOSUB 800
150   GOTO 40

494      REM ·· SUBROUTINE TO INPUT AND VALIDATE STOCK NUMBER
499      REM ·· SET EOF TRAP
500      ON END#1 GOTO 660
505         PRINT "ENTER STOCK NUMBER AS A FOUR DIGIT INTEGER"
510         INPUT N$
520         REM ·· RESET ERROR FLAG
530         LET F = 0
540         REM ·· CHECK IF NUMBER IS AN INTEGER
550         IF LEN (N$) <> 4 THEN 670
560         FOR I = 1 TO 4
570            IF MID$ (N$, I, 1) < "0" THEN 670
580            IF MID$ (N$, I, 1) > "9" THEN 670
590         NEXT I
600         LET N = VAL (N$)
610         REM ·· VALIDATE RANGE OF STOCK NUMBER
620         LET K = N − 1000
630         IF K < 1 THEN 670
```

```
640       REM ·· ATTEMPT TO LOCATE POSITION OF RECORD
650       POSITION#1 TO K
655       GOTO 680
660       LET F = 1
665       GOTO 680
670       LET F = 1
680    IF F = 1 THEN 505
690   RETURN
```

Note: The duplication of lines 655, 660 and 665, 670 are to preserve the structure of the program.

```
799       REM ·· SUBROUTINE TO READ RECORD AND OUTPUT FIELD
800       READ#1, X$
810       REM ·· DIVIDE RECORD INTO FIELDS
820       LET S$ = LEFT$ (X$, 25)
830       LET Q$ = MID$ (X$, 26, 3)
840       LET P$ = RIGHT$ (X$, 5)
850       LET E$ = LEFT$ (P$, 3) + "." + RIGHTS (P$, 2)
860       REM ·· OUTPUT FIELDS
870       PRINT "DESCRIPTION"; S$
880       PRINT "QUANTITY"; Q$
890       PRINT "UNIT PRICE £"; E$
900   RETURN
910   END
```

vi. **Results.**

Example of STOCK file, each line represents a record terminated by ",". Record 1 has key 1001 relative key 1, record 2 has key 1002 relative key 2, etc.

```
AIR FILTER              04500350,
OIL FILTER              09000275,
SPARK PLUGS             15000080,
CONTACT POINTS          17500240,
REAR BRAKE PADS         08600775,
FRONT BRAKE PADS        05101000,
SHOCK ABSORBER          02402395,
PISTON                  01401485,
CONNECTING ROD          01401745,
HEAD GASKET             02300600,
```

Example of program being run using the STOCK file illustrated.

```
DO YOU WANT TO ENQUIRE ABOUT AN ITEM OF STOCK ?
ANSWER Y (YES) N (NO)
!Y
ENTER STOCK NUMBER AS A FOUR DIGIT INTEGER
!1003
DESCRIPTION SPARK PLUGS
QUANTITY 150
UNIT PRICE £ 000.80
DO YOU WANT TO ENQUIRE ABOUT AN ITEM OF STOCK ?
ANSWER Y (YES) N (NO)
!Y
ENTER STOCK NUMBER AS A FOUR DIGIT INTEGER
!1001
DESCRIPTION AIR FILTER
QUANTITY 045
UNIT PRICE £ 003.50
DO YOU WANT TO ENQUIRE ABOUT AN ITEM OF STOCK ?
ANSWER Y (YES) N (NO)
!Y
ENTER STOCK NUMBER AS A FOUR DIGIT INTEGER
!1008
DESCRIPTION PISTON
QUANTITY 014
UNIT PRICE £ 014.85
DO YOU WANT TO ENQUIRE ABOUT AN ITEM OF STOCK ?
ANSWER Y (YES) N (NO)
!Y
ENTER STOCK NUMBER AS A FOUR DIGIT INTEGER
!1234
ENTER STOCK NUMBER AS A FOUR DIGIT INTEGER
!1002
DESCRIPTION OIL FILTER
QUANTITY 090
UNIT PRICE £ 002.75
DO YOU WANT TO ENQUIRE ABOUT AN ITEM OF STOCK ?
ANSWER Y (YES) N (NO)
!N
STOP AT LINE 100
```

EXERCISE.

*1. The reader is advised to consult the BASIC manual for their computer and write the equivalent file processing verbs for:

a. Opening and closing serial or sequential files.

b. Reading from and writing to both serial/sequential and random access files.

c. Appending records to a file.

d. Testing for the end of a file.

(a), (b) and (c) should be answered with respect to:
   i.   fixed length records.
   ii. variable length records.

*2. When the reader has established a repertoire of file processing verbs for their machine, by answering question 1, the following programs should be modified and run on their computer.

   a. The program to create a serial file containing variable length records (Refer to para. 3a.). Invent your own test data for this file.

   b. The program to create a serial file containing fixed length records (Refer to para. 3b.).

   c. The program to read a file containing variable length records (Refer to para. 4a.).

   d. The program to read a file containing fixed length records (Refer to para. 4b.).

*3. a. Create a transaction file and a master file containing fixed length records having the following format.

A	B	C

Field	Size of field	Description of contents
A	4 digits	Stock number
B	20 characters	Stock description (left justified)
C	5 digits	Cost of stock (right justified)

Both files should be organised so that the records are in ascending numerical sequence by stock number. The stock numbers on the transaction file should be numerically larger than those on the master file.

example of a record

   1210BEST ▽ BITTER ▽ BARREL ▽▽ 02960   ▽ — indicates
   1212BEST ▽ BITTER ▽ FIRKIN ▽▽ 00950   one space

Note. The cost of each stock item is £29.60 and £9.50 respectively, hence, the need for the value being right-justified in the field, with the left part of the field filled with zeros.

   b. Output the contents of both files.

*4. Using the files created in question 3 append the transaction file to the master file.

   a. Using the merge routine described in para. 5.

   b. Using an *APPEND* statement from your dialect of BASIC.

*5. a. In chapter 15 figure 15.8 was used to describe the amendment, insertion and deletion of records in a master file. Write a program to read only **once,** the transaction and master files described, and perform the update creating a *son* master file.

b. Output the contents of the three files.

Note. The reader is recommended to attempt the file processing projects described in chapter 20, in order to gain a greater familiarity and understanding of this subject.

17 Input and Output Design

INTRODUCTION.

1. a. This chapter is concerned with the design and layout for the input and output of data and information, and the storage of data on a file. The topics covered are classified into the following areas.

    i.   The design of information on the screen of a V.D.U. or page of a teleprinter.

    ii. The format of records on a file and the use of codes to represent data.

    iii. The layout of reports.

    b. The chapter also covers several non-standard verbs associated with output design which tend to be widely implemented in dialects of BASIC.

SCREEN AND PAGE DESIGN.

2. a. The only contact many computer users have with a computer is through, say, a visual display unit or teleprinter. When developing a computer system where the input/output phase is dominated by user interaction with the system it is important that the following points are kept in mind.

    i.   The information displayed on a screen or printed at a teleprinter *talks* the user through the input/output phase of the system.

    ii. Provides the user with adequate information so that the system can be operated without having to resort to reading a manual.

    iii. Data entry is clearly defined regarding the sequence in which data is *keyed-in* and the format of the data.

    iv. Error messages to the operator are informative and relate to the last operation, and the correction of data is made easy without having to re-type a lot of data.

    v.   The system developed is *user-friendly*.

    b. The programmer's job of coding an input/output phase of a program is made easier if every item of information that is conveyed to the user is drawn on a design document. Figure 17.1 illustrates the design of one screen or page of information that is output to a user. The design is taken from a *medical package* requiring data to be input on a person if they belong in an *at risk group* category.

    c. Many dialects of BASIC include program statements specifically for clearing the information displayed on the screen of a visual display unit and moving the cursor to its initial or home position.

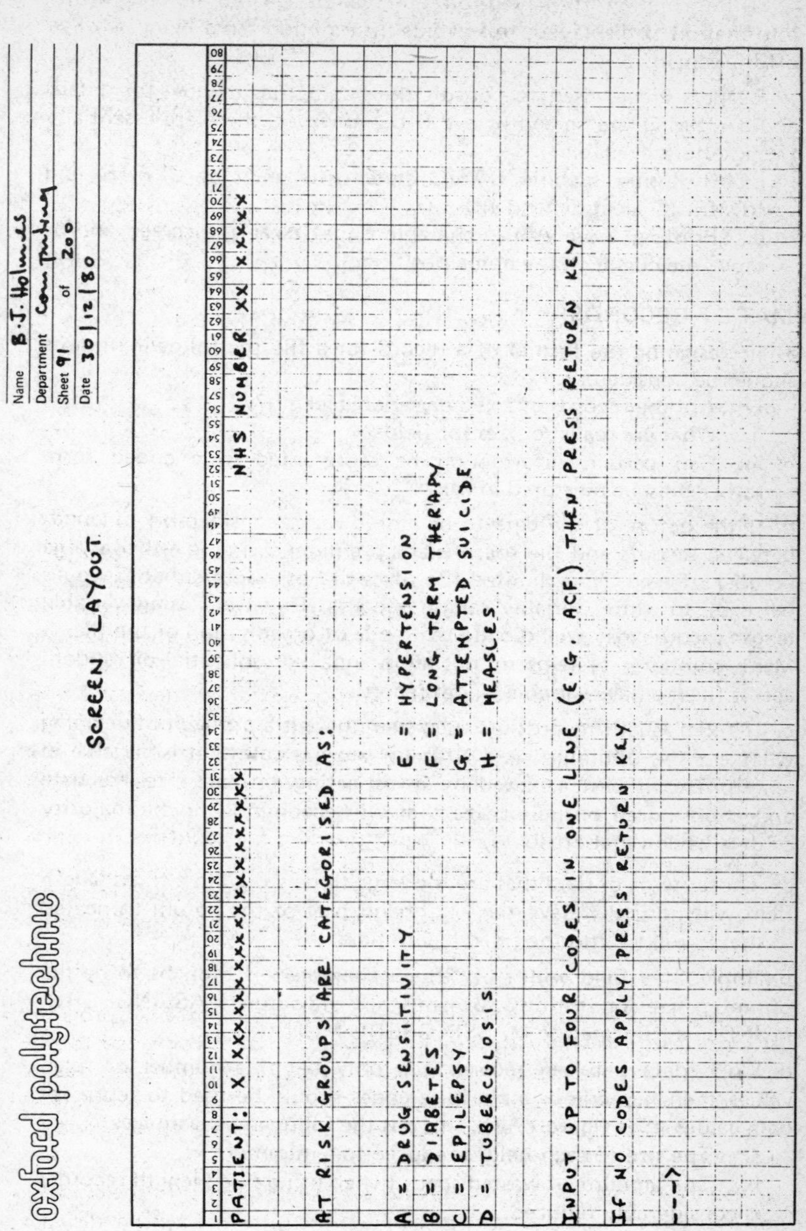
oxford polytechnic
Name B.J. Holmes
Department Computing
Sheet 91 of 200
Date 30/12/80
SCREEN LAYOUT
PATIENT: X XXXXXXXXXXXXXXXXXXXXXX NHS NUMBER XX XXXXX
AT RISK GROUPS ARE CATEGORISED AS:
A = DRUG SENSITIVITY
E = HYPERTENSION
B = DIABETES
F = LONG TERM THERAPY
C = EPILEPSY
G = ATTEMPTED SUICIDE
D = TUBERCULOSIS
H = MEASLES
INPUT UP TO FOUR CODES IN ONE LINE (E.G. ACF) THEN PRESS RETURN KEY
IF NO CODES APPLY PRESS RETURN KEY
--->

Figure 17.1

If information displayed on a screen is cleared before further information is displayed, this avoids information from being *scrolled* off the screen.

Readers are advised to consult their computer manual for details about clearing the screen of a V.D.U., however, there are essentially two methods available.

i. By using specific BASIC statements such as *CLEAR* and *HOME.* (Dialect dependent)

ii. Printing those ASCII characters that clear the screen and/or move the cursor to the home position.

FORMAT OF RECORDS.

3. a. In designing the format of a record for a file the following points should be considered.

    i. Are the records of fixed or variable length?

    ii. What are realistic sizes for fields?

    iii. Can certain information be represented in a coded form rather than being stored in full?

b. If the nature of the data to be stored varies considerably in length between records and file space is at a premium owing to either a large number of records, or limited file space or both factors then it would be wise to store variable length records. However, using variable length records may well dictate the mode of organisation of the file. Many computer systems do **not** allow indexed sequential or random access files to have variable length records.

c. If fixed length records are used then there is a problem of deciding what are the optimum field sizes for storing data that is variable in length. This is best achieved by investigating extreme sizes for data and choosing an optimum size that will accommodate the majority of date having that attribute.

Those items of data that are too large to be stored in a fixed length field will normally have the right-hand part of the datum truncated so that it will fit into the fixed length field.

Example. If a field width of fifteen characters is thought to be the optimum size for storing a surname then the datum MASSINGBERG-MUNDY is truncated to MASSINGBERG-MUN.

d. When data between records can only be of a number of fixed values then numeric or alphabetic codes should be used to represent data values. (See figure 17.1). This has the following advantages.

    i. The size of each field is reduced to a minimum.

    ii. The amount of wasted space (when using fixed length records) is considerably reduced.

    iii. The position of a field indicates the attribute a code relates to.

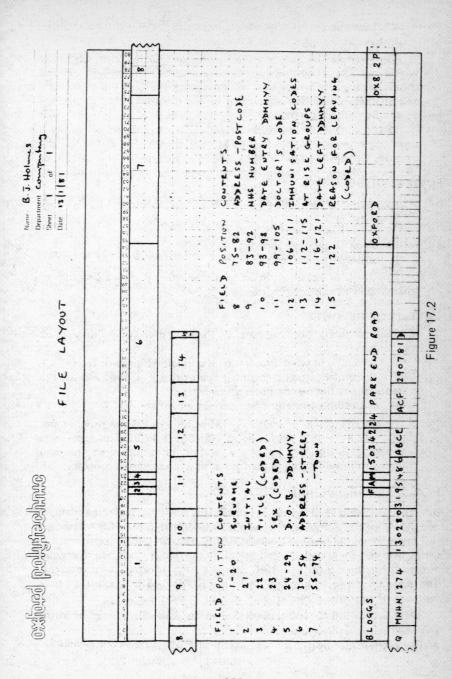

Figure 17.2

iv. Sensitive data is pre-coded thus helping to improve the security of that data.

For example the data required in figure 17.1 is coded. Clearly it would have been sheer folly not to code since the largest field required should be the sum of the four largest words describing the risk groups (62 characters) and the amount of typing required at the data entry stage would be unacceptable.

Thus the field size is reduced to four characters (fixed length fields have spaces inserted if four codes are not applicable), and unless the meaning of those characters is known to an unauthorised system user, the data cannot be interpreted and, therefore, becomes reasonably secure.

e. The layout of fields in a record should be documented (see figure 17.2) regarding:
i. Size of each field.
ii. Type of data associated with each field.
iii. Example of a record.

This form of documentation is useful when coding a program or maintaining an existing program.

LAYOUT OF REPORTS.

4. a. Reports should be meaningful and comprehensive, they must **not** contain:
i. A jumble of what appears to be unrelated figures or facts.
ii. Computer jargon (remember the people who read and use the reports may not be computer specialists).
iii. Misleading, irrelevant or incorrect information.

b. To aid the design of computer generated reports the programmer should use an output report form (see figure 17.3). This represents one page of lineprinter stationery, and contains numbered lines and columns to simplify coding the format of a report into a program.

NON-STANDARD VERB FOR OUTPUT.

5. The following verb is used to specify the format for printing numeric and string values. Although the verb is **not** defined in the ECMA standard it is implemented in many dialects of BASIC. However, the implementation varies between these dialects and therefore the reader is advised to consult a manual for the dialect of BASIC they are using if formatting is required. The dialect used in this section is from PRIME BASIC, since it is representative of the other dialects.

The syntax of the output verb used to format numeric or string values is:

PRINT USING format string, $\left\{ \begin{matrix} \text{literal--1} \\ \text{variable--1} \end{matrix} \right\}$ [, $\begin{matrix} \text{literal--2 . . . .} \\ \text{variable--2} \end{matrix}$]

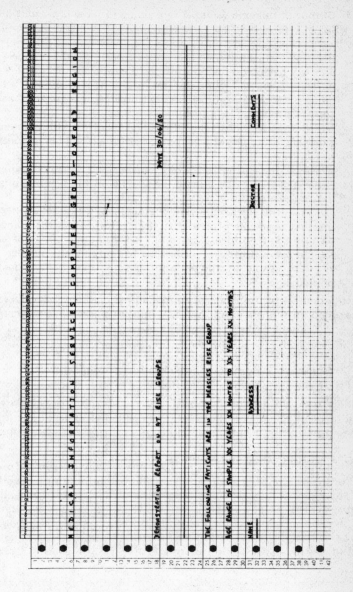

MEDICAL INFORMATION SERVICES COMPUTER GROUP - OXFORD REGION

DEMONSTRATION REPORT NO AT RISK GROUPS

DATE 30/06/80

THE FOLLOWING PATIENTS ARE IN THE MEASLES RISK GROUP

AGE RANGE OF SAMPLE XX YEARS XX MONTHS TO XX YEARS XX MONTHS

NAME

ADDRESS

DOCTOR

COMMENTS

Figure 17.3

Format string can be a literal, variable or line number.

a. **Output of numeric values.** There are up to seven characters used in defining a format string for the output of numeric values. Those characters are:

i.   A # character is used to represent each digit of a number.

ii.   A . character represents the position of a decimal point.

iii. A , character represents the position of a comma between groups of digits. If all digits prior to the comma are zero then the comma is replaced by a space.

iv.   A ↑ or △ character is used in sets of four to represent the exponent of a number in exponential format — ↑↑↑↑ corresponds to E ± nn.

v.   A ± character as the first character of a format string causes either a ± or − to be printed, depending on the sign of a number, in front of a number.

vi.   A − character has a similar effect to a ± character when it is the first character of a format string. However, if the number to be printed is positive a space will price the number, whereas, if the number is negative a − character will precede the number.

vii. A $ character represents the position of a dollar sign to be printed.

b. Examples of the effect of format strings on numerical values to be printed. In all these examples a ▽ symbol represents a space character.

i.   **The # character.**

Numeric Value	Format String	Printed Result	Comments
25	##	25	Each # represents a digit position.
25	####	▽▽25	Digits become right-hand justified.
1.95	##	▽2	Only integers are printed; the number is rounded.
73468	###	***	Number too large for specified field so * is printed for each # character present.

ii. The . character (decimal point).

Number Value	Format String	Printed Result	Comment
37.24	##.##	37.24	Value represented as specified in format string.
20	####.##	∇∇ 20.00	An alignment takes place about the decimal point of the number and format string, leading digit positions are replaced by spaces, trailing digit positions by zeros.
29.347	###.##	∇ 29.35	Number is rounded.
784.21	##.###	**	Number is too large to print using format specified.

iii. The , character.

Numeric Value	Format String	Printed Result	Comments
2000	#,###	2,000	Comma printed in indicated position.
14793.721	##,###.###	14,793.721	
37.9	##,###.##	∇∇∇∇37.90	When leading digits are blank the comma is substituted for a space.

iv. The ↑ character.

Numeric Value	Format String	Printed Result	Comments
170.35	##.###↑↑↑↑	17.035E+01	Position of decimal point shifted.
1.2	####↑↑↑↑	1200E−03	
6004.7	#.###↑↑↑↑	6.005E+02	Number rounded.

v. **The + character.**

Numeric Value	Format String	Printed Result	Comments
20.5	+##.#	+20.5	Sign appears before number.
7.36	+###.##	+▽▽7.36	Leading digit positions replaced by spaces.
10.40	++##.##	▽+10.40	Plus signs can be used to replace #. The effect is to print sign to immediate left of leading digit.
15.90	++++.##	▽+15.90	

vi. **The − character.**

Numeric Value	Format String	Printed Result	Comments
−20.5	−##.#	−20.5	Sign appears before number.
20.5	−##.#	▽20.5	If number positive sign replaced by space.
−7.36	−−−−.##	▽▽−7.36	Minus signs can be used to replace #.
0.47	−−−.#	▽▽0.5	Leading zero printed, number rounded.

vii. **The $ character.**

Numeric Value	Format String	Printed Result	Comments
30.512	$###.##	$▽30.51	Dollar printed in position shown in format.
−30.512	+$###.##	−$▽30.51	Both sign and dollar printed.
13.20	+$$$$#.##	+▽▽$13.20	Dollar signs can be used to replace #. $ printed immediately to left of leading digit.

Note. Some dialects use a £ character.

c. **Worked example.** The design document shows part of the layout of a sales invoice for motor-car spares.

QTY	DESCRIPTION	UNIT COST (PENCE)	COST
3	LIGHT BULBS	76	2.28
4	SPARK PLUGS	50	2.00
1	OIL FILTER	325	3.25
1	AIR FILTER	175	1.75
1	CONTACT POINTS	254	2.54
		SUB-TOTAL	11.82
		VAT @ 15%	1.77
		TOTAL	£ 13.59

Assume the quantity of spares N, description of spares D$ and unit cost in pence C of spares is read from a serial file.

The quantity, description, unit cost and cost for each item is output as shown in the design document.

When the quantity is input as zero the sub-total, VAT and total are calculated and output as illustrated.

Write a program segment to perform this task, assume that the file is opened, tested for not being empty and finally closed in another subroutine.

i. **Flowchart.**

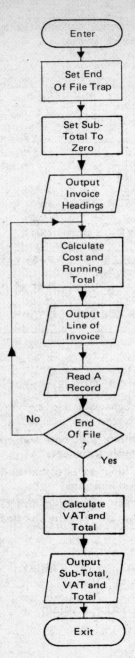

ii.

Glossary.	
Quantity Sold	N
Description of spares	Q$
Unit cost	C
Cost	X
Sub-total	S
VAT	V
Total	T

iii. Program Segment.

```
500     REM ·· SET EOF TRAP
502     ON END#1 GOTO 680
509     REM ·· INITIALISE SUB-TOTAL
510     LET S = 0
520     REM ·· OUTPUT INVOICE HEADINGS
530     PRINT "QTY"; TAB(7); "DESCRIPTION"; TAB(29); "UNIT COST";
540     PRINT TAB(43); "COST"
550     PRINT TAB(29); "(PENCE)"
560     PRINT
565     PRINT
590        REM ·· CALCULATE COST
600        LET X = N * C
610        REM ·· ACCUMULATE A RUNNING TOTAL FOR COSTS
620        LET S = S + X
630        REM ·· OUTPUT LINE OF INVOICE
640        PRINT N; TAB(7); Q$; TAB(29); C; TAB(41);
650        PRINT USING "###.##", X
652        REM ·· READ A RECORD
653        READ *#1, N, Q$, C
660     GOTO 600
670     REM ·· CALCULATE VAT AND TOTAL
680     LET V = 0.15 * S
690     LET T = S + V
700     REM ·· OUTPUT SUB-TOTAL, VAT AND TOTAL
710     PRINT
720     PRINT TAB(29); "SUB-TOTAL"; TAB(41);
730     PRINT USING "###.##", S
740     PRINT
750     PRINT TAB(29); "VAT @ 15%"; TAB(41);
760     PRINT USING "###.##", V
770     PRINT
780     PRINT TAB(29); "TOTAL"; TAB(40); "£";
790     PRINT USING "###.##", T
800  RETURN
```

d. **Notes.**

   i.   **PRINT USING** and **PRINT** should not be mixed on the same line.

   ii.   A **PRINT USING** normally generates a carriage-return line feed after the value is printed, suppression is **not** usually possible by including a semi-colon after the **PRINT USING** statement.

   iii.   From the previous example it is clear that the same format string has been used in four areas of the program (lines 650, 730, 760 and 790). Some dialects will permit the format string to be defined on a separate line, and the format string in the PRINT USING statement is replaced by a line number.

   eg. **505** **"###.##"**
         650 **PRINT USING 505, X**
         730 **PRINT USING 505, S**
           —
           —

This can also be expressed as:

         505 **LET A$ = "###.##"**
         650 **PRINT USING A$, X**
         730 **PRINT USING A$, S**
           —
           —

   iv.   In the last example the use of a dollar sign for currency was **not** desirable, thus, a £ sign was printed separately (line 780) from the format string of line 790.

e. **Output of string values.** Three characters are used to define the format for string output (PRIME dialect).

   i.   A # character is used to represent each character of a string.

   ii.   A < character is used for the left-justification of a string when printed.

   iii.   A > character is used for the right-justification of a string when printed.

f. **Examples of format strings used to output string values.**

String Value	Format String	Printed Result	Comments
Computing	####	COMP	Only the left four characters are output.
FROG	<######	FROG ▽▽	Left-justified space filled to right.
NO	>######	▽▽▽▽NO	Right-justified space filled to left.

The PRINT USING statement is used in the same way as illustrated earlier.

eg.   **PRINT USING ">##########", N$**

If **N$** is "UNITED" the output would be ▽ ▽ ▽ ▽   UNITED.

CHANGING THE WIDTH OF A PAGE.

6.   The number of characters that can be printed on one line of a page can be changed by using a non-standard BASIC command. The command varies between dialects of BASIC but the general syntax is:

Command number of characters per line.

For example on the PRIME system this would be:

   MARGIN 120

alternatively on an MSI system it could be: **LINE = 120** and using Microsoft BASIC **WIDTH 120**.

The command is extremely useful if output is to be directed to a lineprinter that uses standard width paper (143 character positions per line).

There is normally a command to revert back to the default number of characters per line (usually 80). For example on the PRIME the command is:

   MARGIN OFF

18 Program Structure

INTRODUCTION.

1. This chapter is written to demonstrate to readers that the design of programs is necessary if program writing is to be kept as simple as possible and that programs which are written can be easily read, understood and hence maintained.

a. In Part One program design was based on a single flowchart for a solution to a simple problem, and progressed to the use of several flowcharts when the solution to a problem became more complex. In the latter case each flowchart represented a specific task or a group of simple tasks. (Refer to chapter 10 para. 6). This theme is expanded under the heading of *modular programming*.

b. Throughout the book great emphasis has been placed on the use of the constructs sequencing, selection and repetition when designing programs. The majority of the flowcharts drawn have incorporated these constructs.

However, the representation of these constructs in the BASIC language does not conform to a standard. Many BASIC dialects do implement the constructs, but use ad hoc statements in doing so.

An extension of the BASIC language known as COMAL was designed in 1974 to enable programmers to use structured statements within their programs. COMAL is defined by a standard, and is the only extension of the BASIC language that has been implemented using a standard. (Refer to appendix iv).

The implementation of the three constructs will be considered through the language COMAL—80, and compared with techniques in the BASIC language for representing the same constructs.

c. The last part of this Chapter demonstrates using worked examples a *top-down* approach to program design and structured programming with COMAL—80.

MODULAR PROGRAMMING.

2. Modular programming is a term used to describe dividing a program into areas of code or modules that perform specific tasks.

a. The programmer designs the program in **levels**, where a level consists of one or more **modules**. The first level is a complete main program, and modules at successive levels consist of submodules referenced, in the prior levels. Figure 18.1 illustrates a typical *top-down* structure for a program.

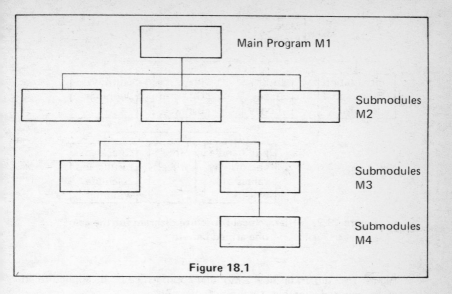

Figure 18.1

b. A **module** is a set of program statements which, when acting together, complete a specific task, and must have only one entrance and one exit point. In practice a module can be a subroutine, and the main program can consist of a sequence of calls to the subroutines that represent the modules at the next level down.

c. The order in which the modules are executed by the computer is controlled by the main program. This describes fully the procedures required in the solution to a problem. The procedures being written in the order of machine execution.

d. Modules should be structured within themselves by incorporating the constructs of sequencing, selection and repetition. This should ensure that each module has only one entry and one exit point. However, it is possible for modules to call other modules since the control of program flow will always return to the *calling* module.

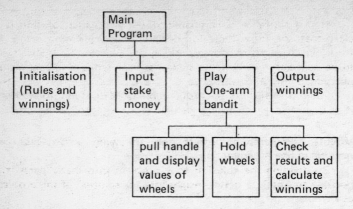

Figure 18.2. A Hierarchical Structure diagram for the game one-armed bandit.

Figure 18.2 illustrates how a modular approach could be applied to an earlier worked example. Chapter 10, para 6b.

The main program or control program should consist of calls to modules at the next level down.

The reader will observe that in the original solution to the problem this was not always the case.

The *initialisation* module should declare the arrays, store the names of the fruits and output the rules of the game.

The *input stake money* module should invite the player to input a value between 10p and 50p then validate the amount.

The *play one-armed bandit* module consists of three modules at a lower level as described in figure 18.2. The play one-arm bandit module is repeated until the stake money is zero.

Finally the *output winnings* module should display the amount the player has won during the game.

The main program could now be coded as:

```
10   REM ·· PROGRAM TO SIMULATE PLAY ON A ONE-ARMED BANDIT
20   REM ·· INITIALISE — DECLARE ARRAYS, STORE FRUITS, OUTPUT RULES
30   GOSUB 900
40   REM ·· INPUT AND VALIDATE STAKE MONEY
50   GOSUB 1230
60   REM ·· PLAY ONE-ARMED BANDIT UNTIL STAKE = 0
70   GOSUB 1300
80   REM ·· OUTPUT TOTAL WINNINGS
90   GOSUB 1900
100  STOP
110  END
```

Notes.

i. If this approach is compared with the original solution it is clear that the procedures for declaring arrays, storing names of fruits, input of stake money, asking the player which wheels are to be held and testing if the stake has been reduced to zero are all postponed until a lower level.

ii. When the solution to a problem has been divided into modules, it is then that each module can be represented by a flowchart if necessary.

f. Modular programming offers the following advantages over *monolithic* in-line programming.

i. By dividing the solution to a problem into many parts it is possible to obtain a better insight into the solution of the problem as a whole.

ii. Because it is often for easier and quicker to document specific tasks related to subroutines than document a complete unstructured program, standards of documentation must improve.

iii. Program maintenance (inserting new modules, amending code and deleting code from existing modules) is simpler for individual modules than for an entire program.

BASIC STATEMENTS THAT SUPPORT MODULARITY.

3. Two BASIC statements enable a program to be divided into modules.

a. The first statement is **GOSUB,** however, there are limitations associated with subroutines in BASIC.

i. BASIC uses **global** variable names. Thus a data-name in one subroutine will have the same value as the same data-name in a **different** subroutine.

ii. Since variable names are global there is no separate list of parameters to define, that communicate between the *calling* program module and the *called* program module. Although this can be an advantage it somewhat hinders the development of subroutines in isolation of other modules.

b. The second statement is **CHAIN.** This loads another program into the memory of a computer, overwriting the original program that was stored in the main memory, and runs the *chained* program usually from a line-number stated by the programmer in the CHAIN instruction.

i. The syntax of the **CHAIN** statement will vary between the dialects of BASIC. However, a common format is:

CHAIN filename [line-number]

where filename is the name given to a program stored on disc, and line-number (optional) is the position on the chained program from which program execution is to start.

313

ii. **Example.** Three program modules called **INDATA**, **SORT-DATA** and **PRINTDATA** are used to solve a problem. The **CHAIN** statement would be used in the following context.

```
10 ──────────
   ──────────
   ──────────
   ──────────
500 CHAIN SORTDATA
```
PROGRAM INDATA

The program **INDATA** is loaded and run, since it contains **CHAIN SORTDATA**; the computer upon reaching line 500 will load and run **SORTDATA**

```
10 ──────────
   ──────────
   ──────────
750 CHAIN PRINTDATA 300
```
PROGRAM SORTDATA

When line 750 of **SORTDATA** is executed, **PRINTDATA** will be loaded and run from line 300.

```
   ──────
300 ──────────
   ──────
   ──────
```
PROGRAM PRINTDATA

c. **Notes on the use of CHAIN.**

i. With many dialects of BASIC chaining a program will cause all the variables in the *chained* program to be initialised.

ii. The initialisation of variables in a chained program causes a parameter passing problem between related modules. This can be overcome by storing values associated with variable names on a *datafile,* in which case chaining becomes of use towards modular programming.

iii. Chaining would normally only be used if a program is too large to fit into the memory of a computer.

THE CONSTRUCTS THAT SUPPORT STRUCTURED PROGRAMMING.

4. a. **Sequencing.** This is the simplest type of structure and represents a series of *non-branching* statements. Figure 18.3 shows a schematic representation of a sequence of instructions.

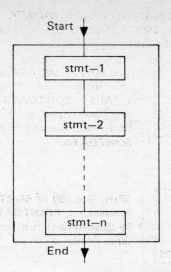

Start

stmt—1

stmt—2

stmt—n

End

Figure 18.3. Procedure X.

i.　Procedure X has **one** entry and **one** exit point and could be described in COMAL—80 by:

PROC X
　　stmt—1
　　stmt—2
　　—
　　—
　　—
　　stmt—n
ENDPROC X

ii.　This would be equivalent to any sequence of *non-branching* or *non-looping* BASIC statements.

```
110  stmt—1
120  stmt—2
130  —
     —
     —
160  stmt—n
```

b. **Selection.** This construct is also known as alternation or branching, and deals with the situation where a selection of one procedure is to be made from a series of two or more mutually exclusive procedures.

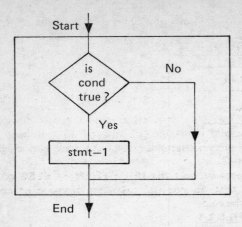

Figure 18.4. Simple Binary Selection.

i.   This construct can be described in COMAL—80 by:

IF condition **THEN**
    stmt—1
ENDIF

If the condition (cond) is true then the program statement (stmt —1) is obeyed, then control passes to the next executable statement. If the condition (cond) is false control will pass to the next executable statement.

ii.   The BASIC language supports this statement.

eg.   **50   IF A > B THEN LET X = 3 * Y**
      60 —

This construct does **not** allow for stmt—1 being a **GOTO**, this would **destroy** the construct since two exit points would then be possible.

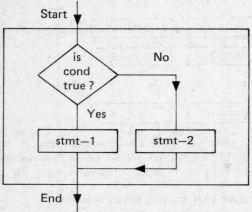

Figure 18.5. Binary Selection.

316

iii. The construct shown in figure 18.5 can be described in COMAL—80 by:

IF condition **THEN**
>   stmt —1

ELSE
>   stmt —2

ENDIF

If the condition is true then statement—1 (stmt—1) is obeyed, otherwise statement—2 (stmt—2) is obeyed. In both cases control moves to the next executable statement having obeyed either stmt—1 or stmt—2.

iv. Many dialects support the **IF ·· THEN ·· ELSE** construct, but for those that do not the following segment of code will simulate the construct.

L1 **IF cond THEN L4**
L2   stmt —2
L3 **GOTO L5**
L4   stmt -1
L5 —

Despite the use of **GOTO'S** the segment of code only has **one** entry point (L1) and **one** exit point (L5). L1, L2 . . . . represent linenumbers.

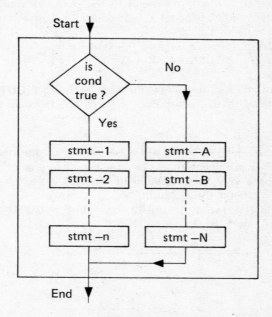

Figure 18.6. Further Binary Selection.

317

v.   The construct of figure 18.6 can be described in COMAL—80 by:

IF condition **THEN**

    stmt—1

    stmt—2

    —

    —

    stmt—n

ELSE

    stmt—A

    stmt—B

    —

    —

    stmt—N

ENDIF

vii. Some dialects of BASIC support this structure, but for those readers who do not have such features available the following program segment will simulate the construct without violating the rules of structure.

```
L1   IF cond THEN L6
L2     stmt—A
L3     stmt—B
       —
       —
L4     stmt—N
L5   GOTO L9
L6     stmt—1
L7     stmt—2
       —
       —
L8     stmt—n
L9
```

viii. A few dialects of BASIC will allow more than one statement on a line. Each statement usually being separated by a colon (:).

This can be a very useful feature for deriving code to simulate binary alternation in this last form.

```
L1   IF cond THEN stmt—1: stmt—2 · · · ·: stmt—n: GOTO L3
L2   stmt—A: stmt—B: · · · ·: stmt—N
L3
```

318

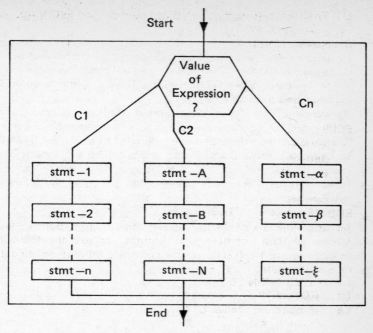

Figure 18.7. N—ARY Selection or Case Structure

ix. The construct shown in figure 18.7 can be described in COMAL—80 by:

CASE expression **OF**
WHEN C1
    stmt—1
    stmt—2
    —
    —
    stint—n
WHEN C2
    stmt—A
    stmt—B
    —
    —
    stmt—N
—
—
WHEN Cn
    stmt—α
    stmt—β
    —
    —
    stmt—ξ

OTHERWISE
   (error statement)
ENDCASE
In the implementation of the **CASE** statement if the value of the expression is not C1, C2 $\cdots$ Cn, then the computer will execute the statement(s) after **OTHERWISE**. These statements could be used to trap a possible error.

Very few dialects of BASIC support the case structure. The **ON** $\cdot\cdot$ **GOTO** $\cdot\cdot$ statement is not general enough since control is dependent upon the expression evaluating to an integer. The case structure will cause branching on any specified value numeric or string.

However, such a construct can be simulated using the following BASIC code:

```
L1    IF not cond c1 THEN L6
L2        stmt—1
L3        stmt—2
          —
          —
L4        stmt—n
L5    GOTO L18
L6    IF not cond c2 then L11
L7        stmt -A
L8        stmt -B
          —
          —
L9        stmt—n
L10   GOTO L18
L11   IF not cond c3 THEN ··
          —
          —
          —
          —
L12   IF not cond cn THEN L17
L13       stmt—α
L14       stmt—β
          —
          —
L15       stmt—ξ
L16   GOTO L18
L17   (error)
L18
```

Again the use of **GOTO** serves the purpose of simulating the construct, there, still remains only **one** entry point L1 and **one** exit point L18.

c. **Repetition.** This form of construct is also known as a loop. The reader may think that such a construct is adequately catered for in BASIC with the FOR/NEXT statements. Well it is adequate if the construct takes the form:

FOR index = initial   TO final   STEP incremental
            value   value   value
      stmt—1
      stmt—2
      —
      —
      stmt—n
NEXT index

However, this construct lacks adequate control regarding an exit from the loop based upon a condition not involving the index.

Two further constructs are available for iteration.

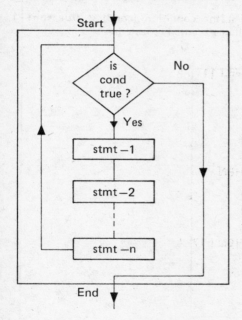

Figure 18.8. Repetition (Test for exit condition at top of loop).

i. The first of these shown in figure 18.8 can be described in COMAL—80 by:

321

WHILE condition **DO**

 stmt—1

 stmt—2

 —

 —

 stmt—n

ENDWHILE

The following BASIC code could be used to simulate this structure:

L2 **IF** not cond **THEN L1**

  stmt –1

  stmt –2

  —

  —

  stmt –n

  GOTO L2

L1 —

  —

In both examples whilst the condition (cond) is true stmt—1, stmt—2 . . . . stmt—n will be executed repeatedly.

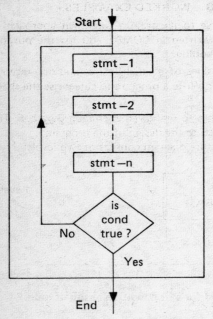

Figure 18.9. Repetition (Test for exit condition at bottom of loop).

ii.   The second form of the construct (figure 18.9) can be described using COMAL—80 by:

REPEAT
    stmt—1
    stmt—2
    —
    —
    stmt—3
UNTIL condition

The structure can be simulated using the BASIC code:

L1   stmt —1
        stmt —2
        —
        —
        stmt —n
    IF not cond **THEN L1**
L2   —

STRUCTURED PROGRAMMING — WORKED EXAMPLES.

5.   The following examples serve to illustrate a top-down approach to program design, with programs written in COMAL—80 for the purpose of demonstrating well structured coding.

a. The lengths of the four sides of a quadrilateral and one internal angle are input to a computer. Write a program to categorise the shape of the quadrilateral.

Note. This is a similar problem to that given in chapter 3 para. 5. The only difference is the approach to the design of the program.

i.   The hierarchical structure diagram consists of two levels:

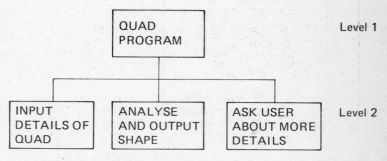

The first level (Quad program) can be represented by the following flowchart.

ii. **Flowchart.**

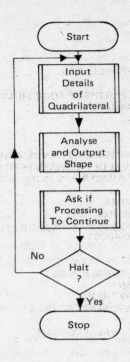

Notice that structure can exist between the modules — in this example the three modules are **repeated until** there is no more data to be input at the keyboard of a V.D.U.

The flowcharts for inputting the details of the quadrilateral and asking the user if the processing is to continue are so trivial they will not be considered here.

The flowchart to analyse and output the shape of the quadrilateral is a *subset* of the flowchart given in Chapter 3 para. 5.

324

iii. Program.

```
5     DIM REPLY$ OF 1
10    // FIRST LEVEL PROGRAM
20    REPEAT
30      EXEC DETAILS
40      EXEC ANALYSIS
50      EXEC QUESTION
60    UNTIL HALT
70    STOP
80    // SECOND LEVEL PROCEDURES
90    PROC DETAILS
100     INPUT "ENTER LENGTHS OF FOUR SIDES": A, B, C, D
110     INPUT "ENTER ANGLE" : ANG
120   ENDPROC DETAILS
130   //
140   PROC ANALYSIS
150   // CONDITIONAL EXPRESSIONS CAN BE ASSIGNED A VARIABLE NAME
160   // SUCH THAT THE VALUE REPRESENTS EITHER TRUE OR FALSE
170     COND1 : = (A = B AND B = C AND C = D)
180     IF COND1 THEN
190       IF ANG = 90 THEN
200         PRINT "SQUARE"
210       ELSE
220         PRINT "RHOMBUS"
230       ENDIF
240     ELSE
250     COND2 : = (A = C AND B = D)
260       IF COND2 THEN
270         IF ANG = 90 THEN
280           PRINT "RECTANGLE"
290         ELSE
300           PRINT "PARALLELOGRAM"
310         ENDIF
320       ELSE
330         PRINT "IRREGULAR QUADRILATERAL"
340       ENDIF
345     ENDIF
350   ENDPROC ANALYSIS
360   //
370   PROC QUESTION
380     INPUT "MORE QUADRILATERALS ANSWER Y (YES) N (NO)?" : REPLY$
390     HALT : = (REPLY $ = "N")
400   ENDPROC QUESTION
410   //
```

vi. **Notes.**

Despite this being a simple problem it has been possible to apply a top-down design to the program. The three procedures that are required in the solution being input of data (DETAILS), processing and output of information (ANALYSIS) and asking the user if the program is to be repeated (QUESTION).

The EXEC statement functions in the same way as GOSUB in BASIC, the only difference being the name of a procedure is given and not a line number.

There are three examples in the program where conditional expressions have been assigned a variable name:

COND1 : = (A = B AND B = C AND C = D)
COND2 : = (A = C AND B = D)
HALT : = (REPLY $ = "N")

The value assigned to a *conditional* variable name would represent either true or false.

Thus in the **REPEAT · · UNTIL HALT** construct the first level program will be repeated until **HALT** becomes true.

b. **Problem.** Write a computer program to simulate dealing a pack of 52 playing cards to four players. The cards should be arranged into suits and within each suit arranged into ascending order. The cards dealt to each player should then be output in their ordered form.

In the solution to this problem three arrays will be used:

A one dimensional array SUITNAME$ containing the names of the four suits; *clubs, diamonds, hearts, spades.*

A one dimensional array NAME$ containing the value of each card; *two, three, · · · · · jack, queen, king, ace.*

A two dimensional array containing the numbers of the four players showing which player has a particular card. The row value of the array represents a suit number and the column value represents the value of a card in a particular suit.

	1	2	3	4	· · · · · ·	12	13
1	2	3	1	4		4	1
2	4	4	1	2		1	2
3	3	1	1	4		2	3
4	3	3	2	2		3	2

The row subscripts 1 to 4 correspond to the suitnames *clubs, diamonds, hearts and spades* respectively.

The column subscripts 1 to 13 correspond to the value of each card in a suit, *two, three,······jack, queen, king, ace* respectively.

Thus in the first row player 2 has the two of clubs; player 3 has the three of clubs; player 1 has the four of clubs, etc.

In the second row player 4 has the two of diamonds, player 4 has the three of diamonds, player 1 has the four of diamonds, etc.

In dealing a player a card two random numbers are generated, the first number describes the suit, whilst the second describes the value of a card. These two numbers correspond to the row and column subscripts of the two-dimensional array. However, it is possible to generate the same pair of random numbers several times, therefore, it is necessary to check if a player has already been dealt a card. To this end the two-dimensional array is initialised to zero before dealing commences. If a cell of the array contains zero it implies that a player has not been dealt that card represented by the row and column subscripts.

    i.   The hierarchical structure diagram consists of three levels.

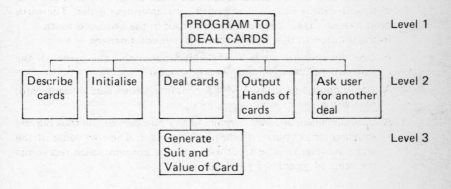

At this stage in the book the reader should have gained sufficient expertise in programming not to require flowcharts for trivial procedures.

For this reason the only flowcharts to be included show the overall structure of the program and the procedure to deal cards to the players.

ii. **Flowchart.** This illustrates the first level program showing the procedures that are necessary to solve the problem.

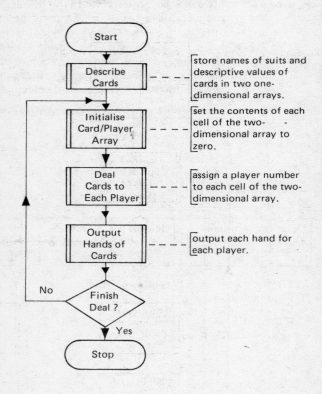

iii. **Flowchart of procedure to deal cards to players.**

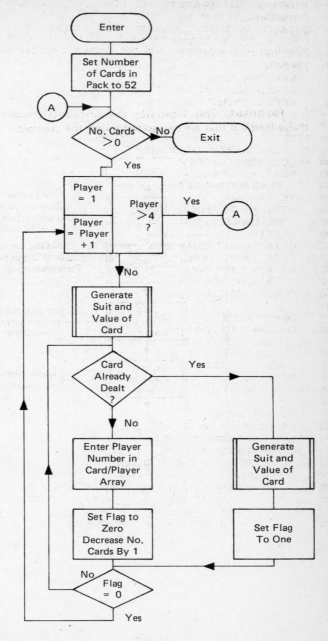

329

iv. **Program.**

```
10      // DECLARE SIZE OF ARRAYS
20      DIM CARDMATRIX (4, 13)
30      DIM SUITNAME$(4) OF 8, NAME$(13) OF 5, REPLAY$ OF 1
40      // FIRST LEVEL PROGRAM
50      EXEC DESCRIBECARDS
60      REPEAT
70        EXEC INITIALISE
80        EXEC DEALCARDS
90        EXEC OUTPUTHANDS
100       EXEC DEALAGAIN
110     UNTIL HALT
120     STOP
130     // SECOND LEVEL PROCEDURES
140     PROC DESCRIBECARDS
150       FOR I: = 1 TO 4 DO
160         READ SUITNAME$ (I)
170       NEXT I
180       FOR I: = 1 TO 13 DO
190         READ NAME$ (I)
200       NEXT I
210       DATA "CLUBS", "DIAMONDS", "HEARTS", "SPADES"
220       DATA "TWO", "THREE", "FOUR", "FIVE", "SIX", "SEVEN"
230       DATA "EIGHT", "NINE", "TEN", "JACK", "QUEEN"
240       DATA "KING", "ACE"
250     ENDPROC DESCRIBECARDS
260     //
270     PROC INITIALISE
280       FOR I: = 1 TO 4 DO
290         FOR J: = 1 TO 13 DO
300           CARDMATRIX (I, J): = 0
310         NEXT J
320       NEXT I
330     ENDPROC INITIALISE
340     //
350     PROC DEALCARDS
360       CARDSINPACK : = 52
370       WHILE CARDSINPACK > 0 DO
380         FOR PLAYERNUMBER : = 1 TO 4 DO
390           EXEC SIMCARD (SUIT, NUMBER)
400           REPEAT
410             IF CARDMATRIX (SUIT, NUMBER) = 0 THEN
420               CARDMATRIX (SUIT, NUMBER) : = PLAYERNUMBER
430               FLAG: = 0
440               CARDSINPACK : = CARDSINPACK−1
```

```
450            ELSE
460              EXEC SIMCARD (SUIT, NUMBER)
470              FLAG : = 1
480            ENDIF
490          UNTIL FLAG = 0
500        NEXT PLAYERNUMBER
510      ENDWHILE
520   ENDPROC DEALCARDS
530   //
540   PROC OUTPUTHANDS
550     FOR PLAYERNUMBER : = 1 TO 4 DO
560       PRINT "PLAYER"; PLAYERNUMBER
570       FOR SUIT : = 1 TO 4 DO
580         FOR NUMBER : = 1 TO 13 DO
590           IF CARDMATRIX (SUIT, NUMBER) = PLAYERNUMBER THEN
600             PRINT NAME$ (NUMBER); "OF"; SUITNAME$ (SUIT)
610           ENDIF
620         NEXT NUMBER
630       NEXT SUIT
640     NEXT PLAYERNUMBER
650   ENDPROC OUTPUTHANDS
660   //
670   PROC DEALAGAIN
680     INPUT "ANOTHER DEAL ANSWER Y (YES) N (NO)?" : REPLY$
690     HALT : = (REPLY$ = "N")
700   ENDPROC DEALAGAIN
710   //
720   // THIRD LEVEL PROCEDURE
730   PROC SIMCARD (SUIT, NUMBER)
740     SUIT : = RND (1, 4)
750     NUMBER : = RND (1, 13)
760   ENDPROC SIMCARD
```

c. **Problem.** A *wheel of fortune* game at a fun-fair consists of a wheel which can spin freely about a fixed axis through the centre of the wheel. The wheel is painted in different coloured sectors. The rules of the game are as follows:

A player places a bet from 10p to £1 in multiples of 10p.

The wheel is set spinning and the player throws one dart at the wheel.

A winning payout depends upon the coloured sector the dart lands on a black sector loses.

The following table shows the winning colours and the amount paid back to the player.

Winning colour	Multiple of stake money paid back in winnings
RED	20x
BLUE	10x
GREEN	5x
YELLOW	1x

Write a computer program to simulate the game, using the following random number distribution to represent a dart hitting a coloured sector.

Random numbers	Coloured Sectors
1	RED
2, 3, 4, 5, 6	BLACK
7, 8	BLUE
9, 10, 11	BLACK
12, 13, 14	GREEN
15, 16, 17, 18	BLACK
19, 20, 21, 22	YELLOW
23, 24, 25, 26	BLACK

i.   The hierarchical structure chart is:

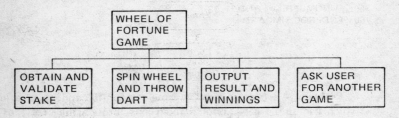

332

ii.   **Flowchart.**

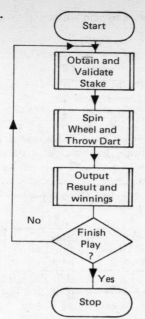

iii.   **Flowchart of Procedure to Input and Validate Stake.**

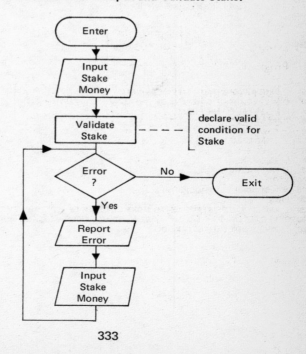

333

iv. **Flowchart of procedure to spin wheel and throw dart.**

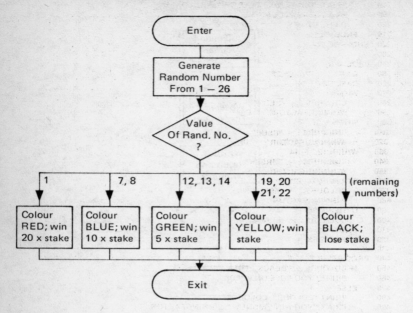

v. **Program.**

```
10    // DECLARE MAXIMUM SIZE OF STRING
20    DIM COLOUR$ OF 6, REPLY$ OF 1
30    // FIRST LEVEL PROGRAM
40    REPEAT
50       EXEC STAKE
60       EXEC SPIN
70       EXEC RESULT
80       EXEC ANSWER
90    UNTIL HALT
100   STOP
110   // SECOND LEVEL PROCEDURES
120   PROC STAKE
130      INPUT "ENTER STAKE 10P TO 100P MULTIPLES OF 10P" : MONEY
140      LEGALSTAKE : = (10 < = MONEY AND MONEY < = 100 AND MONEY—INT (MONEY)=0)
150      WHILE NOT LEGALSTAKE DO
```

```
160       PRINT "ILLEGAL QUANTITY"
170       PRINT "STAKE FROM 10P to 100P"
180       PRINT "ONLY MULTIPLES OF 10P ALLOWED"
190       PRINT "EXAMPLE 40P"
200       INPUT MONEY
210    ENDWHILE
220  ENDPROC STAKE
230  //
240  PROC SPIN
250    DART : = RND (1, 26)
260    CASE DART OF
270    WHEN 1
280       COLOUR$ : = "RED"
290       WINNINGFACTOR : = 20
300    WHEN 7, 8
310       COLOUR$ : = "BLUE"
320       WINNINGFACTOR : = 10
330    WHEN 12, 13, 14
340       COLOUR$ : = "GREEN"
350       WINNINGFACTOR : = 5
360    WHEN 19, 20, 21, 22
370       COLOUR$ : = "YELLOW"
380       WINNINGFACTOR : = 1
390    OTHERWISE
400       COLOUR$ : = "BLACK"
410    ENDCASE
420  ENDPROC SPIN
430  //
440  PROC RESULT
450    IF COLOUR$ = "BLACK" THEN
460       PRINT "YOU LOSE ON BLACK"
470    ELSE
480       PRINT "COLOUR"; COLOUR$;
490       PRINT "YOU WIN"; MONEY * WINNINGFACTOR
500    ENDIF
510  ENDPROC RESULT
520  //
530  PROC ANSWER
540    INPUT "FINISHED PLAY ANSWER Y (YES) N (NO)" : REPLY$
550    HALT : = (REPLY$ = "Y")
560  ENDPROC ANSWER
570  //
```

EXERCISE.

Use the worked examples in this chapter and appendix iv the definition of the COMAL—80 programming language in order to answer the following questions.

1. Explain the following features in the COMAL—80 language.

    a. How many characters can be used in composing a variable name?

    b. How are string variables declared?

    i.   As a single string.

    ii. As strings stored in an array.

c. Contrast the use of the characters : = and =.

d. What is the function of the IN operator?

Use LEGAL $: = ''.RED.YELLOW.GREEN.BLUE.'' and .GUESS $. IN LEGAL $ to explain your answer.

e. What is the purpose of // on a line? What is the equivalent in BASIC?

f. Explain the function of RND (X, Y).

2. Re-write the following segments of BASIC code in the COMAL—80 language.

```
a. 10    INPUT I
   15    IF I = 0 THEN 70
   20    IF I > 100 THEN 50
   30    PRINT "VALUE OF I TOO LOW"
   40    GOTO 60
   50    PRINT "VALUE OF I TOO HIGH"
   60    GOTO 10
   70    STOP
```

```
b. 5     PRINT "ENTER CHOICE FROM MENU"
   10    INPUT C$
   20    IF C$ <> "ADD" THEN 50
   30    GOSUB 1000
   40    GOTO 160
   50    IF C$ <> "SUB" THEN 80
   60    GOSUB 2000
   70    GOTO 160
   80    IF C$ <> "MLT" THEN 110
   90    GOSUB 3000
   100   GOTO 160
   110   IF C$ <> "DIV" THEN 140
   120   GOSUB 4000
   130   GOTO 160
   140   PRINT "ERROR"
   150   GOTO 5
   160
```

```
c. 10    INPUT A
   20    INPUT B
   30    INPUT C
   40    LET D = B * B — 4 * A * C
   50    IF D < 0 THEN 110
   60    IF D = 0  THEN 90
   70    PRINT "REAL DISTINCT"
   80    GOTO 120
   90    PRINT "REAL EQUAL"
  100    GOTO 120
  110    PRINT "IMAGINERY"
  120
d. 10    LET A = 1
   20    LET B = 1
   30    PRINT A, B
   40    LET A = A + B
   50    LET B = B + A
   60    IF B > 1000 THEN 80
   70    GOTO 30
   80
```

3. Write computer programs in COMAL—80 for the following questions to be found earlier in the book.

* a. Chapter 3.   Exercise question 7.

* b. Chapter 6.   Exercise questions 6 and 7.

  c. Chapter 7.   Exercise question 7b.

  d. Chapter 10.   *Para. 6b. Use the structure diagram in figure 18.2 as the basis of your program structure.

                  Exercise question 10.

* Having written the programs in a structured form, re-code them using your dialect of BASIC. If your computer does not support the three constructs then use the techniques described in this chapter to simulate those constructs.

19 Case Studies

INTRODUCTION.

1.   This chapter represents a culmination of many of the techniques in programming dealt with in the previous chapters.

   a. The chapter covers two case studies; the first of these is designed to include much of the material presented in part one and does not include the use of files. The second case study incorporates many of the techniques covered in both parts of the book, and includes the use of sequential files.

   b. Both case studies are written where possible using E.C.M.A. BASIC.

   c. The case studies will include:
   i.   A full description of the problem.
   ii.   A narrative of the method of solution including the data structures to be used.
   iii. Input/output and file design documentation.
   iv.   A series of flowcharts representing a top-down approach to program design.
   v.   Glossary of terms.
   vi.   Source listing of the computer program.
   vii. Results of a computer run.

CASE STUDY ONE.

2.   a. **Problem.** A popular restaurant will take table reservations one day in advance only, for lunches and evening meals.

   There are twenty tables in the restaurant with a distribution of seating as follows.

Table Number	Seats per table
1, 2, 7, 14, 20	2
3, 4, 5, 6, 10, 11, 12, 13	4
8, 15, 17, 18, 19	6
9, 16	8

The restaurant proprietor has purchased a cheap microcomputer that includes a teleprinter for input of data and for the output of information. The machine has no secondary storage devices (ie. no backing store other than a cassette unit for loading the program).

The proprietor wishes to use the micro computer for a table reservation system. He plans to use the computer between 9.00 a.m.

to 12.00 midnight to take table reservations for the next day. At midnight he will obtain from the computer a complete listing of all the tables that have been reserved, and then switch the machine off.

The proprietor is not worried if the computer breaks down or is accidently switched off during the day since the system prints the details of every transaction as it occurs. In the event of the computer breaking down he would resort to a manual system for table reservations; alternatively if only the power had been switched off, he would switch the power back on and re-build the contents of memory from the print out of transactions prior to the failure.

The computer system should cater for the following features.

i. Allow an enquiry whether a table is vacant and reserve that table.

ii. Cancel a reservation.

iii. Obtain a printed listing of table reservations and vacant tables.

The proprietor wishes to impose certain restrictions on the computer reservations system, as follows.

iv. The restaurant will not cater for parties that exceed fourteen persons.

v. The computer system, in order to cater for parties of different numbers, will combine two **adjacent** tables when necessary.

vi. If as the result of combining tables more than one seat will not be occupied then the proprietor will refuse the reservation.

b. **Method of Solution.** The choice of facilities available on the computer system will be listed in a *menu* so that the proprietor can take the appropriate course of action. (See figure 19.1).

The following details will need to be input to the system.

i. To make an enquiry the meal time (luncheon or dinner) and size of party will be entered. Luncheon and dinner could be coded as 1 and 2 respectively, and the size of a party would range between 1 and 14. If a table or tables are vacant then the name of the client needs to be input — assume a maximum of 20 alphanumeric characters. Confirmation of a table reservation is made by informing the client of the table number reserved. (See figures 19.2 and 19.3).

To cancel a reservation the meal-time and table number are input. The table number being provided in case there are different reservations made by clients having the same name. (See figure 19.4).

ii. The reports to be output are a printed listing of table reservations for both lunch and dinner. This should include the table number, maximum number of seats available at that table and name of client. At the end of each listing the table numbers of vacant tables should be printed. (See figure 19.5).

Minor reports would be confirmation of booking and error reports.

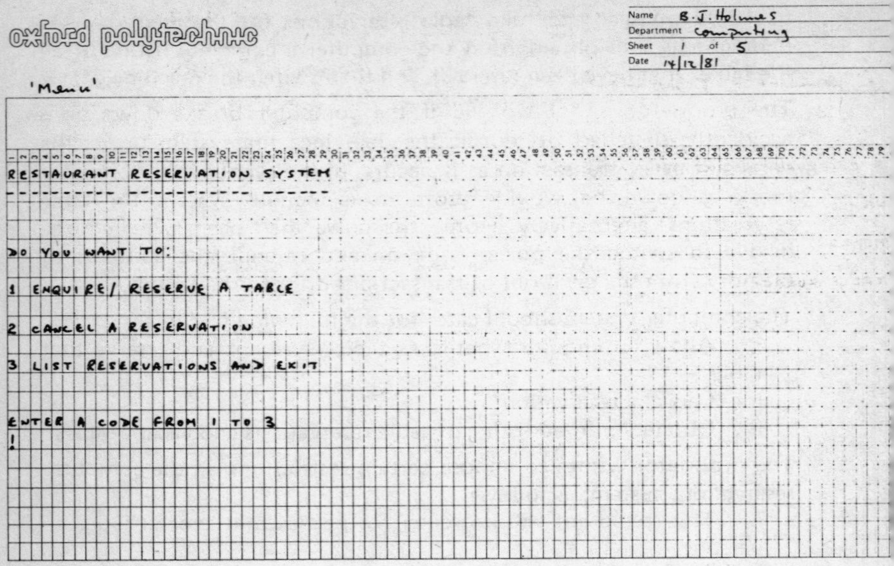

oxford polytechnic

Name   B. J. Holmes
Department Computing
Sheet   1   of 5
Date   14/12/81

'Menu'

```
RESTAURANT RESERVATION SYSTEM
--------- ----------- -----

DO YOU WANT TO:

1 ENQUIRE/ RESERVE A TABLE

2 CANCEL A RESERVATION

3 LIST RESERVATIONS AND EXIT

ENTER A CODE FROM 1 TO 3
!
```

Figure 19.1.

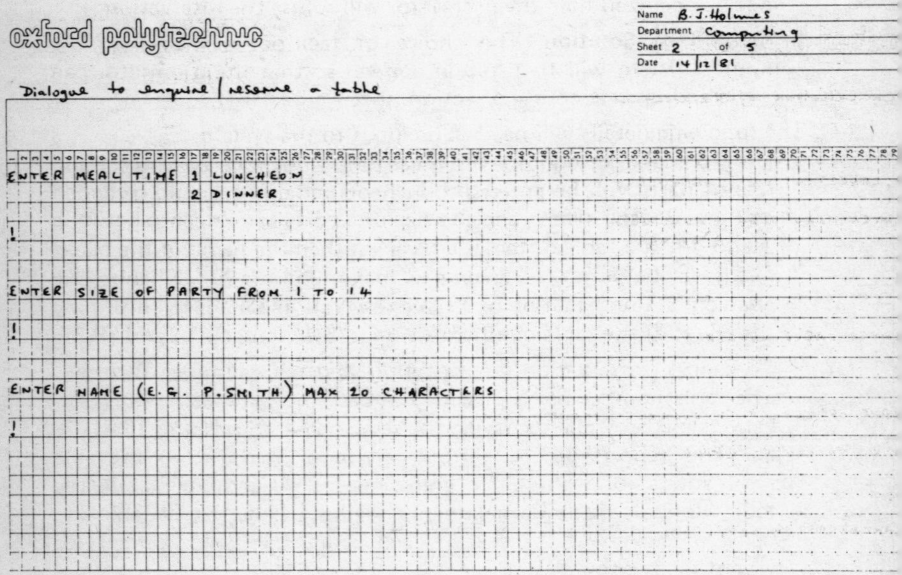

oxford polytechnic

Name   B. J. Holmes
Department Computing
Sheet   2   of 5
Date   14/12/81

Dialogue to enquire/reserve a table

```
ENTER MEAL TIME 1 LUNCHEON
               2 DINNER

!

ENTER SIZE OF PARTY FROM 1 TO 14

!

ENTER NAME (E.G. P.SMITH) MAX 20 CHARACTERS

!
```

Figure 19.2.

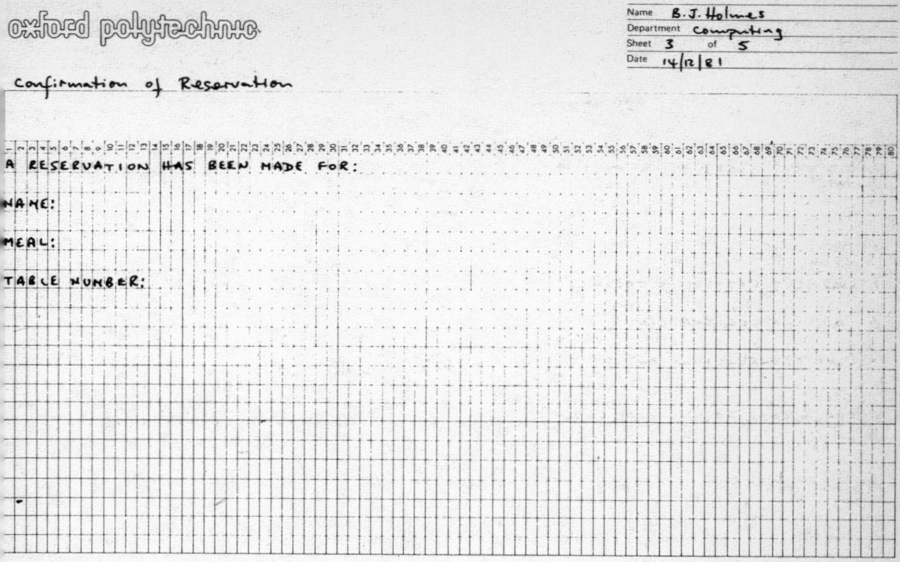

oxford polytechnic

Name	B. J. Holmes
Department	Computing
Sheet	3 of 5
Date	14/12/81

Confirmation of Reservation

```
A RESERVATION HAS BEEN MADE FOR:

NAME:

MEAL:

TABLE NUMBER:




-
```

Figure 19.3.

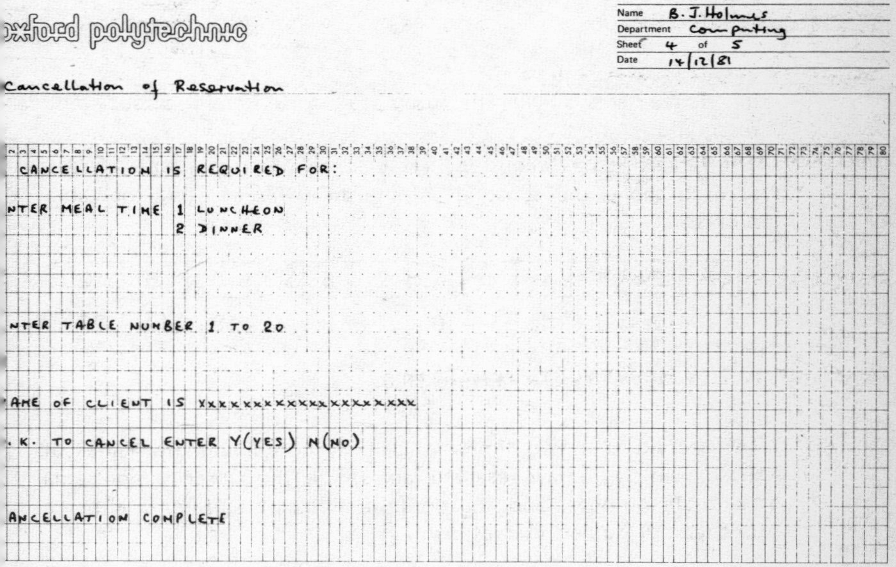

oxford polytechnic

Name	B. J. Holmes
Department	Computing
Sheet	4 of 5
Date	14/12/81

Cancellation of Reservation

```
CANCELLATION IS REQUIRED FOR:

ENTER MEAL TIME 1 LUNCHEON
                2 DINNER



ENTER TABLE NUMBER 1 TO 20



NAME OF CLIENT IS XXXXXXXXXXXXXXXXXXXX

O.K. TO CANCEL ENTER Y(YES) N(NO)



CANCELLATION COMPLETE
```

Figure 19.4.

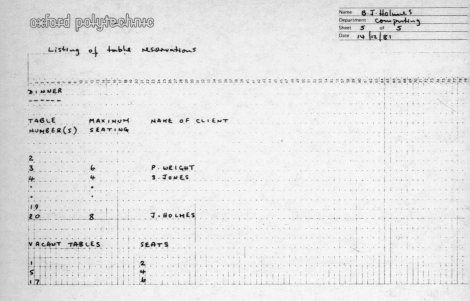

Figure 19.5.

iii. Three arrays will be used to store details about table reservations.

The first is a one-dimensional array containing the number of seats at each table, the subscript of the array representing the table-number.

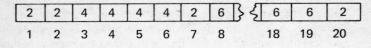

Figure 19.6.

The second is a two-dimensional array containing the names of those clients who have reserved tables. The row subscript represents the table number, and the column subscript represents either a luncheon or dinner reservation.

342

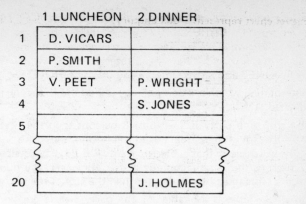

	1 LUNCHEON	2 DINNER
1	D. VICARS	
2	P. SMITH	
3	V. PEET	P. WRIGHT
4		S. JONES
5		
⋮		
20		J. HOLMES

Figure 19.7.

The third is a two-dimensional array showing which tables have been booked, and those tables that are combined for the same client. The code 99 indicates that a table is vacant, whilst 0 indicates that a table has been reserved. A number 1 — 19 inclusive is used to point to the next table reserved if a pair of tables have been combined for a client. A zero is stored in the second table for each pair. When a reservation requires more than one table the name of the client need only be entered once, preferably against the table number whose pointer has been coded as zero.

	1	2
1	0	99
2	0	3
3	0	0
4	99	0
5	99	99
⋮		
19	0	20
20	99	0

Figure 19.8.

343

The last two arrays show that for luncheons table 1 has been reserved for D. VICARS, table 2 for P. SMITH, table 3 for V. PEET, table 4 is vacant, table 5 is vacant, etc. However, for dinner table 1 is vacant, table 2 and 3 have been reserved for P. WRIGHT, table 4 for S. JONES and lastly table 19 and 20 for J. HOLMES.

In determining whether a party can be seated the following method is adopted.

If the size of a party is 2, 4, 6 or 8 persons then the first vector is scanned for the correct sized table and the third vector is referenced to see if that table is vacant. For a party of size 1, 3, 5 or 7 persons the same technique is used, however, the number of seats at a table must be one greater than the size of the party.

If no single table is available, or the party size is greater than 8 persons then the first and third arrays are scanned for a pair of tables that will give the correct number of seats or one extra seat when combined.

c. **Flowcharts.**

    i.   **First level chart representing main program.**

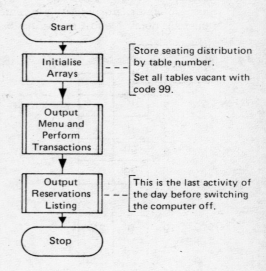

ii. **Second level chart representing menu subroutine.**

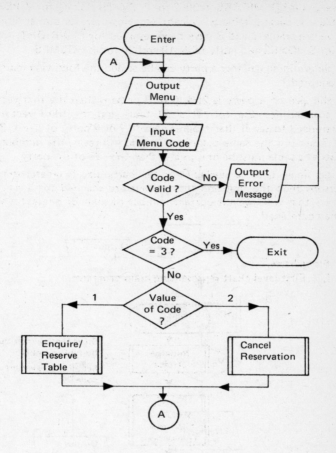

345

iii. **Third level chart representing enquire/reserve table.**

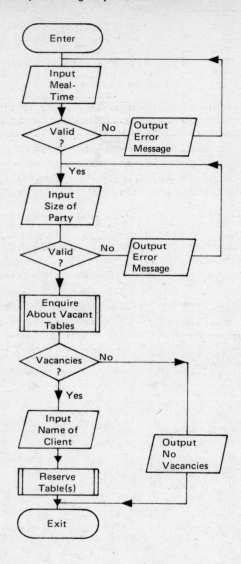

iv. **Third level chart representing a cancellation.**

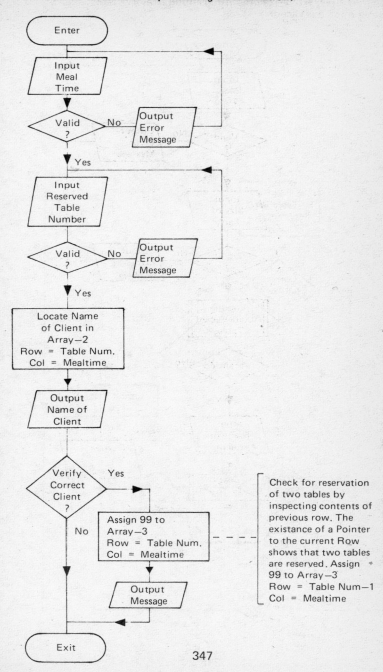

Check for reservation
of two tables by
inspecting contents of
previous row. The
existance of a Pointer
to the current Row
shows that two tables
are reserved. Assign
99 to Array—3
Row = Table Num—1
Col = Mealtime

v. Fourth Level Flowchart representing subroutine to enquire whether a table is vacant.

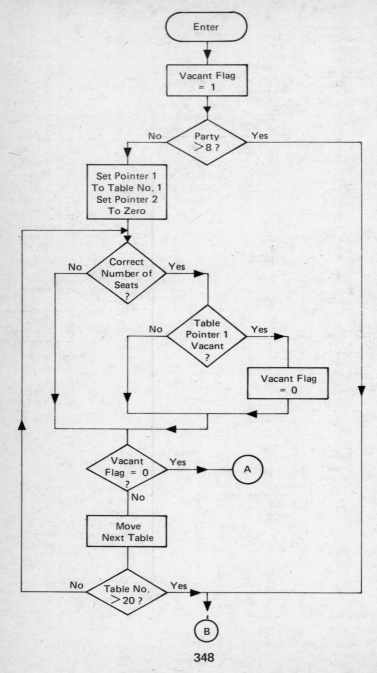

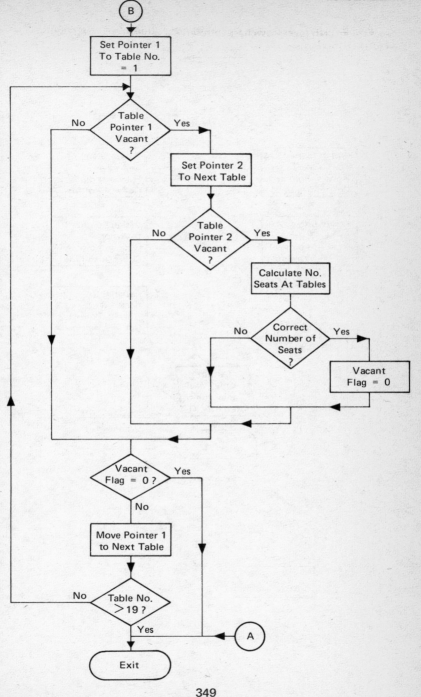

vi. **Fourth level flowchart to reserve a table.**

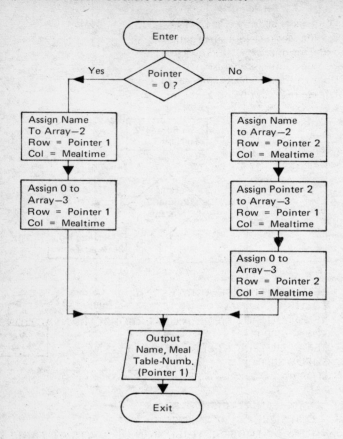

d. **Glossary.**

One dimensional array (Figure 19.6) containing seat distribution at tables	S
Two dimensional array (Figure 19.7) containing names of clients	C$
Two dimensional array (Figure 19.8) containing reservation codes.	R
Menu Code	M
Meal time	T
Size of party	P
Name of client	N$
Reply to question	A$
Vacancy flag	F
Table Number	X
Pointer1	P1
Pointer2	P2
Number of seats	Y

e. **Program.**

```
10      REM ·· INITIALISE ARRAYS
20      GOSUB 1000
30      REM ·· OUTPUT MENU AND PERFORM TRANSACTIONS
40      GOSUB 2000
50      REM ·· OUTPUT RESERVATIONS LISTING
60      GOSUB 3000
70      STOP
80      REM ··
90        REM ·· INITIALISE ARRAYS
1000    DIM S(20), C$(20, 2), R(20, 2)
1010    REM ·· STORE DISTRIBUTION OF SEATS AT TABLES
1020    FOR X = 1 TO 20
1030      READ S(X)
1040      DATA 2, 2, 4, 4, 4, 4, 2, 6, 8, 4, 4, 4, 4, 2, 6, 8, 6, 6, 6, 2
1050    NEXT X
1060    REM ·· SET ALL TABLES TO VACANT FOR LUNCHEON AND
1070    REM ·· DINNER WITH CODE 99
1080    FOR X = 1 TO 20
1090      LET R(X, 1) = 99
1100      LET R(X, 2) = 99
1110    NEXT X
1120    RETURN
1130    REM ··
1140    REM ·· OUTPUT MENU AND PERFORM TRANSACTIONS
```

```
2000    PRINT "RESTAURANT RESERVATION SYSTEM"
2010    PRINT "———————— ———————————— —————"
2020    PRINT
2030    PRINT
2040    PRINT "DO YOU WANT TO:"
2050    PRINT
2060    PRINT "1 ENQUIRE/RESERVE A TABLE"
2070    PRINT
2080    PRINT "2 CANCEL A RESERVATION"
2090    PRINT
2100    PRINT "3 LIST RESERVATIONS AND EXIT"
2110    PRINT
2120    PRINT
2130    PRINT "ENTER A CODE FROM 1 TO 3"
2140    INPUT M
2150    REM ·· VALIDATE CODE
2160    IF M = 1 OR M = 2 OR M = 3 THEN 2190
2170       PRINT "ERROR — INCORRECT CODE"
2180    GOTO 2130
2190    IF M = 3 THEN 2250
2200    ON M GOTO 2210, 2230
2210       GOSUB 2300
2220    GOTO 2000
2230       GOSUB 2800
2240    GOTO 2000
2250 RETURN
2260    REM ··
2270    REM ·· SUBROUTINE TO ENQUIRE/RESERVE A TABLE
2300    PRINT "ENTER MEAL TIME 1 LUNCHEON"
2310    PRINT "                    2 DINNER"
2320    PRINT
2330    INPUT T
2340    REM ·· VALIDATE MEAL TIME
2350    IF T = 1 OR T = 2 THEN 2380
2360       PRINT "ERROR — INCORRECT CODE"
2370    GOTO 2300
2380    PRINT
2390    PRINT
2400    PRINT "ENTER SIZE OF PARTY FROM 1 TO 14"
2410    PRINT
2420    INPUT P
2425    REM ·· VALIDATE SIZE OF PARTY
2430    IF INT(P) — P = 0 AND P > = 1 AND P < = 14 THEN 2465
2440       PRINT "ERROR — INCORRECT SIZE"
2450    GOTO 2400
```

```
2460    REM ·· ENQUIRE ABOUT VACANT TABLES
2465    GOSUB 2600
2470    IF F = 1 THEN 2550
2480       PRINT
2490       PRINT
2500       PRINT "ENTER NAME (E.G. P. SMITH) MAX 20 CHARACTERS"
2505       PRINT
2510       INPUT N$
2520       IF LEN (N$) > 20 THEN N$ = LEFT$ (N$, 20)
2530          GOSUB 2700
2540       GOTO 2560
2550    PRINT "NO VACANT TABLES"
2560    RETURN
2570    REM ··
2580    REM ·· SUBROUTINE TO ENQUIRE ABOUT VACANT TABLES
2600    LET F = 1
2602    IF P > 8 THEN 2622
2604       LET P1 = 1
2606       LET P2 = 0
2608       IF S(P1) = P OR S(P1) = P + 1 THEN 2612
2610          GOTO 2614
2612          IF R(P1, T) = 99 THEN LET F = 0
2614       IF F = 0 THEN 2648
2616          LET P1 = P1 + 1
2618       IF P1 > 20 THEN 2622
2620          GOTO 2608
2622    LET P1 = 1
2624    IF R (P1, T) = 99 THEN 2628
2626       GOTO 2642
2628       LET P2 = P1 + 1
2630       IF R (P2, T) = 99 THEN 2634
2632          GOTO 2642
2634          LET Y = S(P1) + S(P2)
2636       IF Y = P OR Y = P + 1 THEN 2640
2638          GOTO 2642
2640          LET F = 0
2642    IF F = 0 THEN 2648
2644       LET P1 = P1 + 1
2646       IF P1 > 19 THEN 2648
2647       GOTO 2624
2648 RETURN
2650    REM ··
2652    REM ·· SUBROUTINE TO RESERVE TABLES
2700    IF P2 = 0 THEN 2710
2702       LET C$(P2, T) = N$
```

```
2704        LET R(P1, T) = P2
2706        LET R(P2, T) = 0
2708     GOTO 2714
2710        LET C$(P1, T) = N$
2712        LET R(P1, T) = 0
2714     PRINT "A RESERVATION HAS BEEN MADE FOR:"
2716     PRINT
2718     PRINT "NAME:"; N$
2720     PRINT
2722     PRINT "MEAL:";
2724     IF T = 1 PRINT "LUNCHEON"
2726     IF T = 2 PRINT "DINNER"
2728     PRINT
2730     PRINT "TABLE NUMBER:";
2732     IF P2 = 0 THEN PRINT P1
2734     IF P2 > 0 THEN PRINT P2
2736 RETURN
2738     REM ··
2740     REM ·· SUBROUTINE TO CANCEL RESERVATION
2800     PRINT "A CANCELLATION IS REQUIRED FOR:"
2802     PRINT
2804     PRINT "ENTER MEAL TIME 1 LUNCHEON"
2806     PRINT "                     2 DINNER"
2808     PRINT
2810     INPUT T
2812     REM ·· VALIDATE MEAL TIME
2814     IF T = 1 OR T = 2 THEN 2820
2816        PRINT "ERROR — INCORRECT CODE"
2818        GOTO 2804
2820     PRINT
2822     PRINT
2824     PRINT "ENTER TABLE NUMBER 1 TO 20"
2826     PRINT
2828     INPUT X
2830     REM ·· VALIDATE TABLE NUMBER
2832     IF INT(X) — X = 0  AND X > = 1 AND X < = 20 THEN 2838
2834        PRINT "ERROR — INCORRECT TABLE NUMBER"
2836        GOTO 2824
2838     PRINT
2840     PRINT "NAME OF CLIENT IS"; C$ (X, T)
2842     PRINT
2844     PRINT "O.K. TO CANCEL ENTER Y(YES) N(NO)"
2846     PRINT
2848     INPUT A$
2850     IF A$ = "Y" THEN 2854
```

```
2852        GOTO 2864
2854        LET R(X, T) = 99
2856        IF X = 1 THEN 2860
2858          IF R(X - 1, T) = X THEN LET R(X - 1, T) = 99
2860        PRINT
2862        PRINT "CANCELLATION COMPLETE"
2864 RETURN
2866     REM · ·
2868     REM · · SUBROUTINE TO OUTPUT RESERVATIONS
3000     FOR T = 1 TO 2
3010       IF T = 1 THEN 3050
3020          PRINT "DINNER"
3030          PRINT "————— "
3040        GOTO 3070
3050          PRINT "LUNCHEON"
3060          PRINT " —————— "
3070        PRINT
3080        PRINT "TABLE MAXIMUM NAME OF CLIENT"
3100        PRINT "NUMBER(S) SEATING"
3110        PRINT
3120        PRINT
3130        LET Y = 0
3140        FOR X = 1 TO 20
3150          IF R(X, T) = 99 THEN 3230
3160            IF R(X, T) = 0 THEN 3200
3170              PRINT X
3180              LET Y = Y + S(X)
3190            GOTO 3230
3200              LET Y = Y + S(X)
3210              PRINT X; TAB(12); Y; TAB(23); C$(X, T)
3220              LET Y = 0
3230        NEXT X
3240        PRINT
3250        PRINT
3260        PRINT "VACANT TABLES"
3270        PRINT
3280        FOR X = 1 TO 20
3290          IF R(X, T) = 99 THEN PRINT X
3300        NEXT X
3310        PRINT
3320        PRINT
3330     NEXT T
3340 RETURN
3350 END
```

f. Extracts from a computer run.

```
RESTAURANT RESERVATION SYSTEM
---------- ----------- ------


DO YOU WANT TO:

1 ENQUIRE/ RESERVE A TABLE

2 CANCEL A RESERVATION

3 LIST RESERVATIONS AND EXIT


ENTER A CODE FROM 1 TO 3
!1
ENTER MEAL TIME 1 LUNCHEON
                2 DINNER

!1


ENTER SIZE OF PARTY FROM 1 TO 14

!7


ENTER NAME (E.G. P.SMITH) MAX 20 CHARACTERS

!J WRIGHT
A RESERVATION HAS BEEN MADE FOR:

NAME:J WRIGHT

MEAL:LUNCHEON

TABLE NUMBER:11
```

RESTAURANT RESERVATION SYSTEM
---------- ----------- ------

DO YOU WANT TO:

1 ENQUIRE/ RESERVE A TABLE

2 CANCEL A RESERVATION

3 LIST RESERVATIONS AND EXIT

ENTER A CODE FROM 1 TO 3
!1
ENTER MEAL TIME 1 LUNCHEON
                2 DINNER

!2

ENTER SIZE OF PARTY FROM 1 TO 14

!7

ENTER NAME (E.G. P.SMITH) MAX 20 CHARACTERS

!J COLLINS
A RESERVATION HAS BEEN MADE FOR:

NAME:J COLLINS

MEAL:DINNER

TABLE NUMBER:4

```
RESTAURANT RESERVATION SYSTEM
---------- ----------- ------


DO YOU WANT TO:

1 ENQUIRE/ RESERVE A TABLE

2 CANCEL A RESERVATION

3 LIST RESERVATIONS AND EXIT


ENTER A CODE FROM 1 TO 3
!2
A CANCELLATION IS REQUIRED FOR:

ENTER MEAL TIME 1 LUNCHEON
                2 DINNER

!1

ENTER TABLE NUMBER 1 TO 20

!6

NAME OF CLIENT IS:P JONES

O.K. TO CANCEL ENTER Y(YES) N(NO)

!Y

CANCELLATION COMPLETE
```

```
RESTAURANT RESERVATION SYSTEM
---------- ----------- ------


DO YOU WANT TO:

1 ENQUIRE/ RESERVE A TABLE

2 CANCEL A RESERVATION

3 LIST RESERVATIONS AND EXIT


ENTER A CODE FROM 1 TO 3
!3
LUNCHEON
--------
```

TABLE NUMBER(S)	MAXIMUM SEATING	NAME OF CLIENT
1	2	M SMYTHE
3		
4	8	G HENRY
8		
9	14	P ADAMS
10		
11	8	J WRIGHT
15	6	D CARTER
16	8	G DAVIS
17		
18	12	B BAXTER

VACANT TABLES	SEATS
2	2
5	4
6	4
7	2
12	4
13	4
14	2
19	6
20	2

```
DINNER
------

TABLE          MAXIMUM      NAME OF CLIENT
NUMBER(S)      SEATING


3
4              8         -  J COLLINS
5
6              8            H BAKER
8
9              14           T JONES
10
11             8            P WEST
15

16             14           L HAMBLE
18             6            G HOLT



VACANT TABLES             SEATS

1                         2
2                         2
7                         2
12                        4
13                        4
14                        2
17                        6
19                        6
20                        2


STOP AT LINE 70
```

g. **Notes:** Further testing of this program will reveal that:

i.   There is no data type validation on the input of data. This has been omitted from the program for demonstration purposes only. In practice if an alphabetic quantity is entered in place of a numeric quantity the program will halt and a BASIC system error message will be output.

ii.   It is possible to cancel a table booking that has **not** been made. The system does not generate an error message. Despite this being an undesirable feature of the system, it does **not** cause an error to be introduced into the booking system.

CASE STUDY TWO.

3.   a. **Problem.** A wine merchant has been advised to purchase a small microcomputer which comprises, a self contained V.D.U., keyboard and C.P.U., one floppy disc drive unit and a matrix printer in order to develop a computerised stock control and invoicing system.

The wine merchant wants to be able to use the computer to:

i.   Enquire how much stock is available for a particular brand of wine.

ii.   Reduce stock levels from customer orders.

iii.   Print sales invoices from each customer's order.

iv.   Increase stock levels as new stock arrives to replenish stocks. (**Not** to introduce new stock lines).

v.   Print a report of those items of stock that have fallen below a re-order level.

Note: At the early stage in the development of such a system the wine merchant does **not** want to keep a file of his customers. For every sale a copy of the sales invoice is sent to his finance section to be dealt with as manual office practice demands.

The number of different brands of wine in stock is not normally more than 200.

b. **Method of Solution.**

i.   **Files.** Since the number of different types of wine held in stock is relatively small it is feasible to hold the stock details in an array in the main memory of the computer. If the subscript for a particular brand of wine is known then using an array one has direct access to the details of that wine. It is necessary to store the details for each wine on a sequential file, the format of a record being shown in figure 19.10. The key to a record being the brand of wine, and the sequence of records are ordered alphabetically. (Readers note that this last detail will not be used in the solution to the problem, but will be required in chapter 20, project 8).

361

At the beginning of each days trading the contents of the stock file is read and stored in the stock array.

Every time a stock transaction is made the event is written onto a transaction file by the computer. The details of a transaction file record are shown in figure 19.11.

The precaution is taken in the event of a system crash (computer malfunction).

To re-build a system that had crashed, assuming the fault had been rectified the stock file would be read and stored in the stock array, then the transaction file would be read and used to change the contents of the stock array. The contents of the stock array would then reflect the situation just prior to the system crash.

At the end of a days trading the contents of the stock array is written to a new stock file.

Figure 19.9 illustrates the number of files being used by the system.

The security of data held on the stock file is adequate, since at the end of a days trading three files exist; the original stock file (father), the latest stock file (son) and the transaction file.

On the next day of trading the son stock file can be used to initialise the array, yesterdays transaction file can be overwritten by the new transaction file, and at the end of a days trading the grandfather stock file can be overwritten by the new son stock file. The *son* stock file used to initialise the system now becomes a *father* stock file.

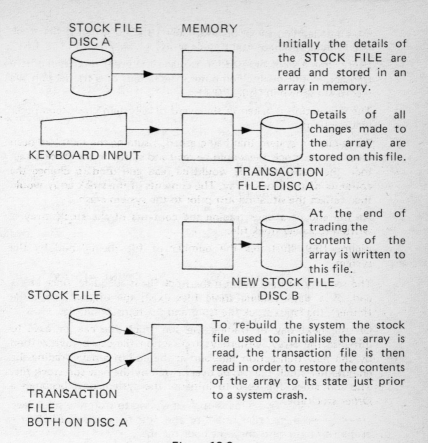

Initially the details of the STOCK FILE are read and stored in an array in memory.

Details of all changes made to the array are stored on this file.

At the end of trading the content of the array is written to this file.

To re-build the system the stock file used to initialise the array is read, the transaction file is then read in order to restore the contents of the array to its state just prior to a system crash.

STOCK FILE DISC A

MEMORY

KEYBOARD INPUT

TRANSACTION FILE. DISC A

NEW STOCK FILE DISC B

STOCK FILE

TRANSACTION FILE BOTH ON DISC A

Figure 19.9.

Notice that the proposed system only requires one disc drive unit, and two floppy discs for storing data files. A third floppy disc would be used to store the program. For the purpose of this problem assume that the original stock file for use on the first day of trading has been created. Assume also that the wine merchant has a computer generated listing of the name of each brand of wine and its associated wine code number. **The code number happens to be the row subscript of the array in which the details of the wine can be found.**

ii.   **Keyboard Input.** The system is *menu* driven with the user being given a choice as to which data processing activity to pursue. (See figure 19.12).

The various input formats required are for stock enquiry (figure 19.13); increasing stock levels for selected items (figure 19.14), and details of customer orders (figure 19.15).

iii. **Reports.** There are three reports to be printed. The first is displayed on the screen of a V.D.U., and gives the details related to an enquiry regarding a particular wine (figure 19.16). The second report involves printing sales invoices (if the printer is loaded with *two-part* stationery an invoice need only be printed once — one part can be despatched with the order to the customer and the second part passed on to the finance office). Figure 19.17 illustrates a layout for the sales invoice.

The third report is a list of those brands of wine that are below the respective re-order levels together with the quantities of wine to be re-ordered (figure 19.18).

iv. **Data Structures.** Three arrays will be used. The first is a one dimensional array capable of storing up to 200 different names of wines held in stock. The subscript represents the wine code number.

1	ANJOU — ROSE	**WINE ARRAY**
2	ANJOU — WHITE	
3	BORDEAUX	
200		

The second is a two dimensional array used to store the stock level, re-order level, re-order quantity and cost for each wine. The row subscript represents the wine code number.

	STOCK LEVEL	RE-ORDER LEVEL	RE-ORDER QUANTITY	COST
1	250	40	200	1.80
2	175	50	150	1.95
3	168	25	100	2.45
200				

STOCK ARRAY

A third array is used to store a customer order, each row is used to store an item from the order, the first column the wine code and the second column the quantity ordered.

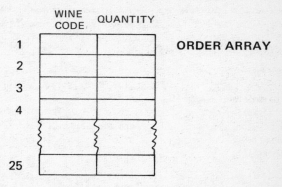

ORDER ARRAY

Assume an order does not contain more than 25 different wines.

oxford polytechnic

Name	B. J. Holmes
Department	Computing
Sheet	1 of 2
Date	11/1/82

Format of stock file record

```
                    1                2   3   4   5

          STOCK    FILE

FIELD  POSITION  CONTENTS
1       1-25      DESCRIPTION OF WINE
2       26-29     QUANTITY IN STOCK (STOCK LEVEL)
3       30-32     RE-ORDER LEVEL
4       33-36     RE-ORDER QUANTITY
5       37-40     COST IN PENCE


EXAMPLE RECORD

BORDEAUX CLARET          0512050050000205
```

Figure 19.10.

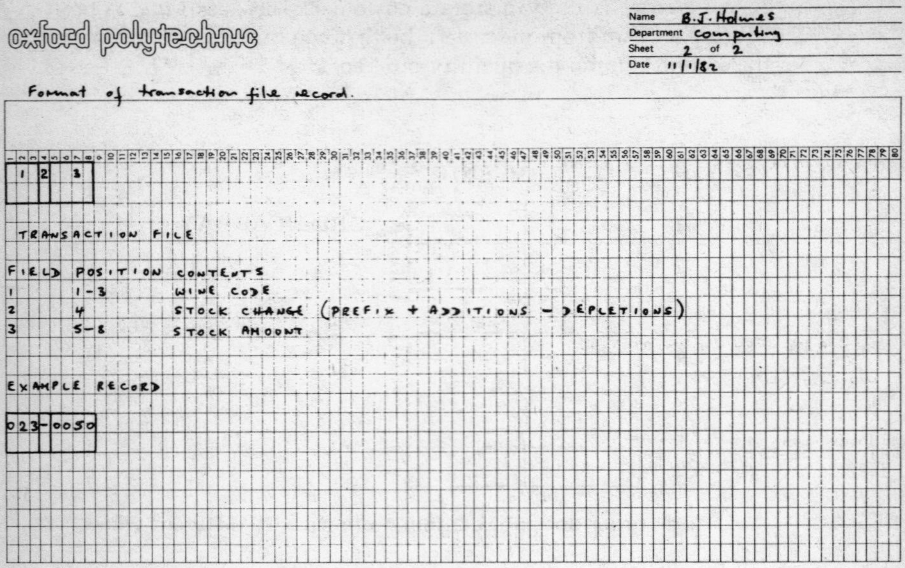

oxford polytechnic

Name	B.J. Holmes
Department	Computing
Sheet	2 of 2
Date	11/1/82

Format of transaction file record.

```
 1  2  3
```

TRANSACTION FILE

FIELD POSITION CONTENTS
1   1-3   WINE CODE
2   4   STOCK CHANGE (PREFIX + ADDITIONS - DEPLETIONS)
3   5-8   STOCK AMOUNT

EXAMPLE RECORD

```
023-0050
```

Figure 19.11.

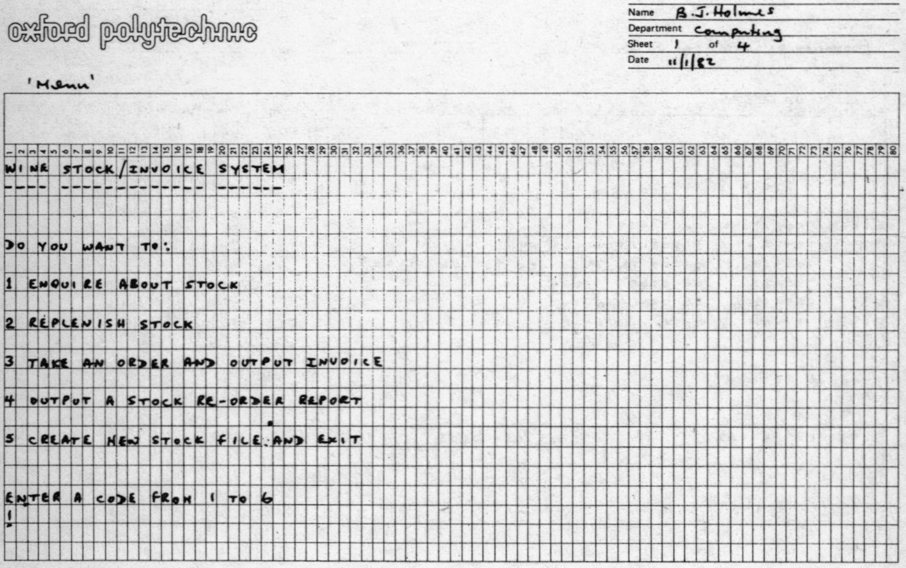

oxford polytechnic

Name	B.J. Holmes
Department	Computing
Sheet	1 of 4
Date	11/1/82

'Menu'

WINE STOCK/INVOICE SYSTEM
--- ---------------- ------

DO YOU WANT TO:

1 ENQUIRE ABOUT STOCK

2 REPLENISH STOCK

3 TAKE AN ORDER AND OUTPUT INVOICE

4 OUTPUT A STOCK RE-ORDER REPORT

5 CREATE NEW STOCK FILE AND EXIT

ENTER A CODE FROM 1 TO 6

Figure 19.12.

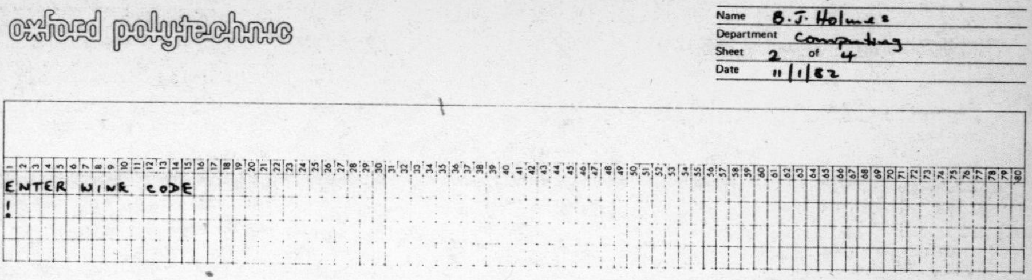

oxford polytechnic

Name B. J. Holmes
Department Computing
Sheet 2 of 4
Date 11/1/82

```
ENTER WINE CODE
!
```

Figure 19.13

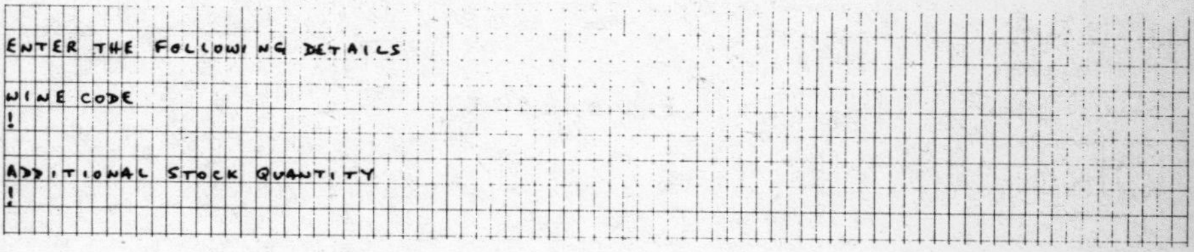

```
ENTER THE FOLLOWING DETAILS

WINE CODE
!

ADDITIONAL STOCK QUANTITY
!
```

Figure 19.14

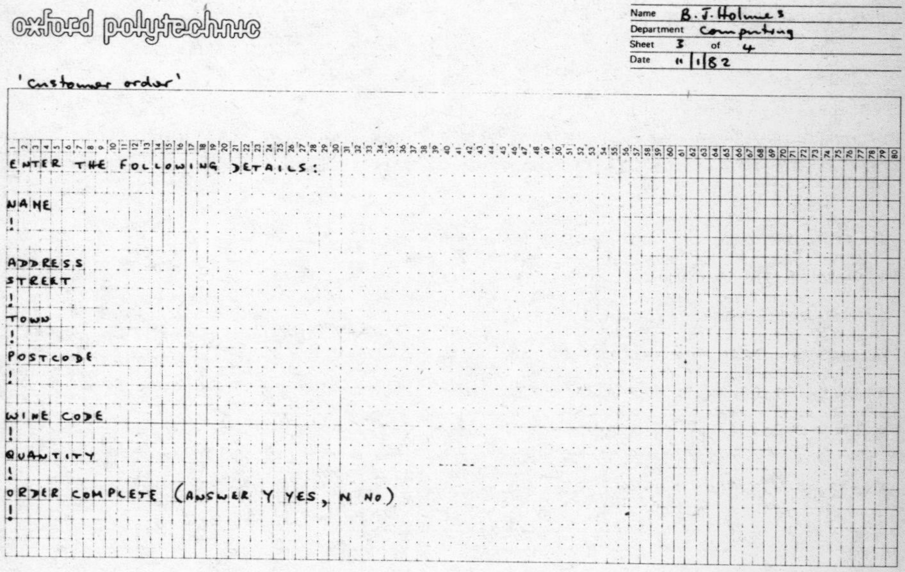

oxford polytechnic

Name B. J. Holmes
Department Computing
Sheet 3 of 4
Date 11/1/82

'customer order'

```
ENTER THE FOLLOWING DETAILS:

NAME
!

ADDRESS
STREET
!
TOWN
!
POSTCODE
!

WINE CODE
!
QUANTITY
!
ORDER COMPLETE (ANSWER Y YES, N NO)
!
```

Figure 19.15.

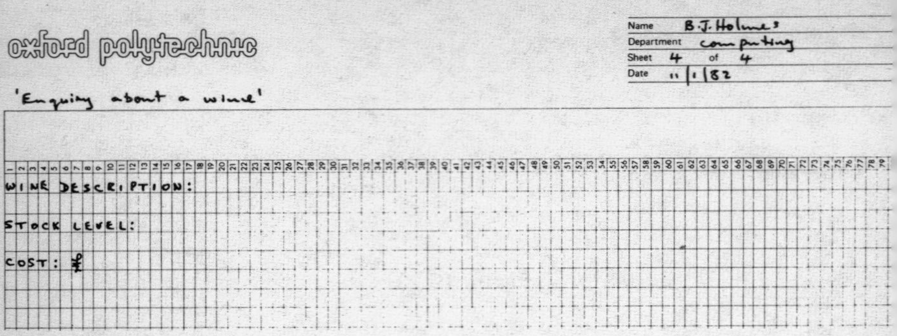

oxford polytechnic

Name   B.J. Holmes

Department   computing

Sheet   4   of   4

Date   11 | 1 |82

'Enquiry about a wine'

WINE DESCRIPTION:

STOCK LEVEL:

COST: £

Figure 19.16.

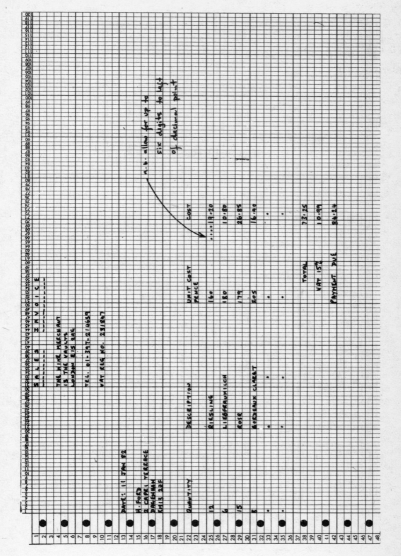

Figure 19.17.

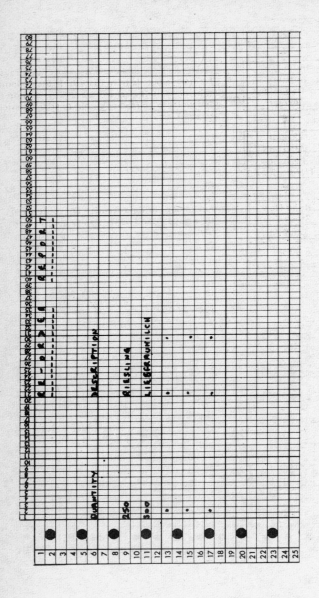

Figure 19.18.

c. **Flowcharts.**

   i.   **First level chart representing the main program.**

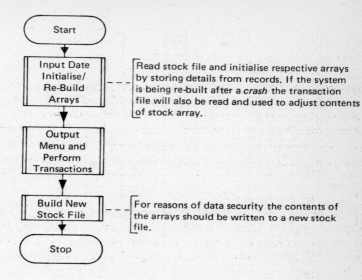

ii.   **Second level chart representing initialisation.**

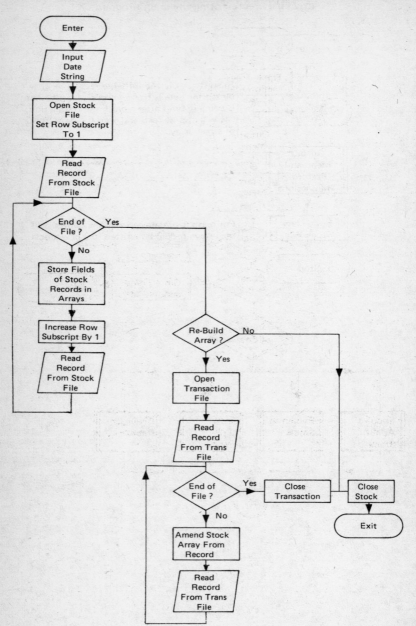

372

iii. **Second level chart representing menu subroutine.**

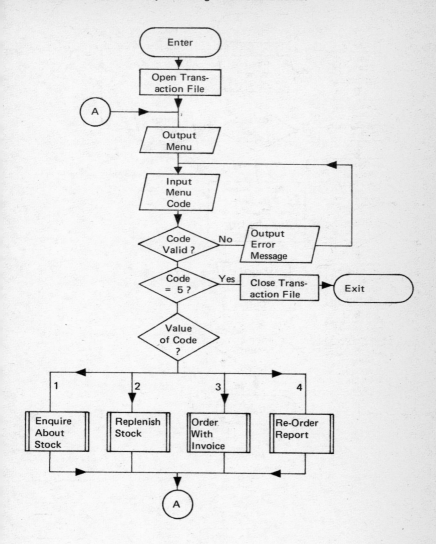

iv. **Third level chart represent stock enquiry.**

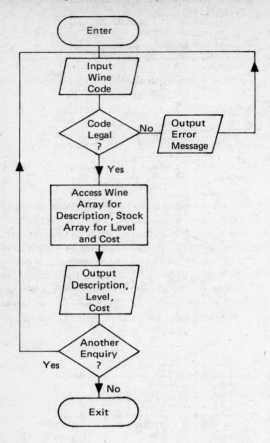

v. **Third level chart representing replenish stock.**

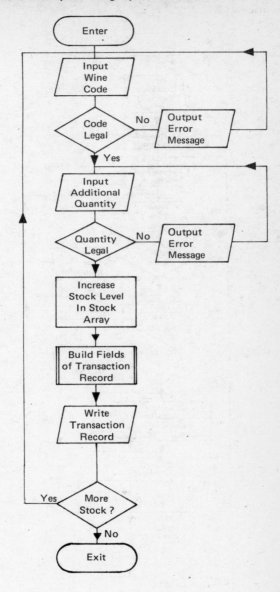

375

vi. **Third level chart representing an order and production of a sales invoice**

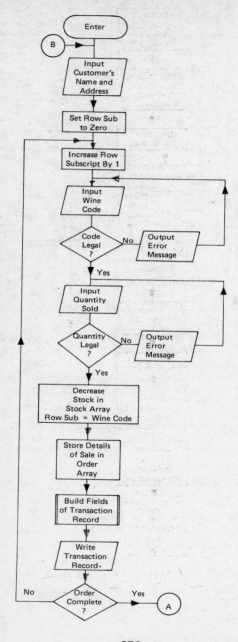

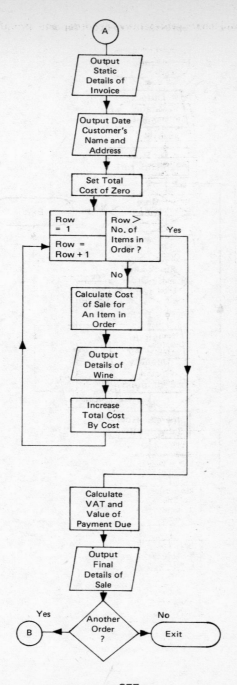

vii. Third level chart representing re-order report.

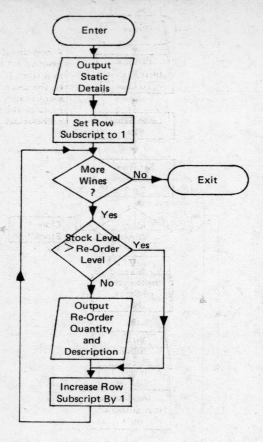

viii. Second level chart to build new stock master file.

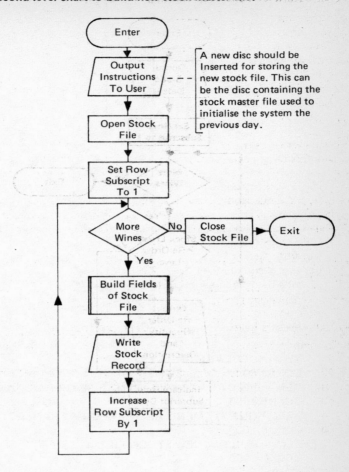

d. **Glossary.**

Stock array	S
Wine array	W$
Order array	O
Row Subscripts	I, I1
Stock level	L
Re-order level	R
Re-order quantity	Q
Cost	C
Wine code	X
Name of customer	N$
Address — street	A$
town	T$
postcode	P$
Reply to a question	K$
Menu code	M
Date string	J$
Record stock file	X$
Record transaction file	Y$
Total cost excluding VAT	T1
Wine code field Transaction file	C$
Quantity field	Q$
Length of field	F
Contents of a field	Z$

e. **Program.**

```
10      REM ·· DECLARE ARRAYS
20      DIM S(200, 4), O(25, 2), W$(200)
30      REM ·· INPUT DATE AND INITIALISE OR RE-BUILD ARRAYS
40      GOSUB 1000
50      REM ·· OUTPUT MENU AND PERFORM TRANSACTIONS
60      GOSUB 2000
70      REM ·· BUILD A NEW STOCK FILE
80      GOSUB 4000
90      STOP
100     REM
110         REM ·· SUBROUTINE TO INPUT DATE AND INITIALISE
120         REM ·· OR RE-BUILD ARRAYS
1000        PRINT "INPUT DATE STRING E.G. 14 JAN 82"
1010        INPUT J$
1020        REM ·· OPEN STOCK FILE AND SET EOF TRAP
1030        DEFINE FILE#1 = "STOCK"
1035        ON END#1 GOTO 1180
1036        REM ·· SET ROW SUBSCRIPT
1040        LET I = 1
1050        REM ·· READ RECORD FROM STOCK FILE
1060        READ#1, X$
```

```
1080      REM ·· STORE FIELDS OF STOCK RECORD IN STOCK ARRAY
1090      LET S(I, 1) = VAL (MID$ (X$, 26, 4))
1100      LET S(I, 2) = VAL (MID$ (X$, 30, 3))
1110      LET S(I, 3) = VAL (MID$ (X$, 33, 4))
1120      LET S(I, 4) = VAL (RIGHT$ (X$, 4))
1130      LET W$(I) = LEFT$ (X$, 25)
1140      REM ·· INCREASE ROW SUBSCRIPT
1150      LET I = I + 1
1155      READ #1, X$
1060    GOTO 1090
1170    REM ·· REBUILD STOCK ARRAY AFTER SYSTEM CRASH
1180    PRINT "RE-BUILD SYSTEM, ANSWER Y(YES) N(NO)"
1190    INPUT R$
1200    IF R$ = "N" THEN 1340
1210      REM ·· OPEN TRANSACTION FILE SET EOF TRAP, READ FILE
1220      DEFINE FILE#2 = "TRANS"
1225      ON END#2 GOTO 1330
1230      READ#2, Y$

1250      REM ·· AMEND STOCK ARRAY FROM TRANSACTION RECORD
1260      LET X = VAL (LEFT$ (Y$, 3))
1270      LET L = VAL (RIGHT$ (Y$, 4))
1280      IF MID$ (Y$, 4, 1) = "+" THEN 1310
1290         LET S(X, 1) = S(X, 1) − L
1300      GOTO 1230
1310         LET S(X, 1) = S(X, 1) + L
1315      READ #2, Y$
1320      GOTO 1260
1330      CLOSE#2
1340      CLOSE#1
1350 RETURN
1360    REM
1370    REM ·· OUTPUT MENU AND PERFORM TRANSACTIONS
2000    DEFINE FILE#2 = "TRANS"
2010    PRINT "WINE STOCK/INVOICE SYSTEM"
2020    PRINT "——— ——————————— ————— "
2030    PRINT
2040    PRINT
2050    PRINT "DO YOU WANT TO:"
2060    PRINT
2070    PRINT "1 ENQUIRE ABOUT STOCK"
2080    PRINT
2090    PRINT "2 REPLENISH STOCK"
2100    PRINT
2110    PRINT "3 TAKE AN ORDER AND OUTPUT INVOICE"
2120    PRINT
2130    PRINT "4 OUTPUT A STOCK RE-ORDER REPORT"
```

```
2140     PRINT
2150     PRINT "5 CREATE NEW STOCK FILE AND EXIT"
2160     PRINT
2170     PRINT
2180       PRINT "ENTER A CODE FROM 1 TO 5"
2190       INPUT M
2200       IF INT(M) — M = 0 AND M > = 1 AND M < = 5 THEN 2230
2210       PRINT "ERROR — INCORRECT CODE"
2220     GOTO 2180
2230     IF M = 5 THEN 2330
2240       ON M GOTO 2250, 2270, 2290, 2310
2250       GOSUB 3000
2260     GOTO 2010
2270       GOSUB 3200
2280     GOTO 2010
2290       GOSUB 3500
2300     GOTO 2010
2310       GOSUB 3910
2320     GOTO 2010
2330     CLOSE #2
2340 RETURN
2350     REM
2360     REM · · SUBROUTINE TO ENQUIRE ABOUT STOCK
3000       PRINT "ENTER WINE CODE"
3010       INPUT X
3020       IF INT(X) — X = 0  AND X > = 1 AND X < = 200 THEN 30
3030       PRINT "ERROR — INCORRECT CODE"
3040       GOTO 3000
3050       PRINT "WINE DESCRIPTION:" ; W$(X)
3060       PRINT
3070       PRINT "STOCK LEVEL:" ; S(X, 1)
3080       PRINT
3090       PRINT "COST: £" ;
3100       LET C = S(X, 4) / 100
3110       PRINT C
3120       PRINT "ANOTHER ENQUIRY ANSWER Y(YES) N(NO)"
3130       INPUT R$
3140     IF R$ = "Y" THEN 3000
3150 RETURN
3160     REM
3170     REM · · SUBROUTINE TO REPLENISH STOCK
3200     PRINT "ENTER THE FOLLOWING DETAILS"
3210     PRINT
3220       PRINT "WINE CODE"
3230       INPUT X
```

```
3240       IF INT(X) — X = 0 AND X > = 1 AND X < = 200 THEN 3270
3250       PRINT "ERROR — INCORRECT CODE"
3260     GOTO 3220
3270     PRINT
3280       PRINT "ADDITIONAL STOCK QUANTITY"
3290       INPUT Q
3300       IF INT(Q) — Q = 0 AND Q > = 0 AND Q < = 9999 THEN 3330
3310       PRINT "ERROR — ILLEGAL QUANTITY"
3320     GOTO 3280
3330     LET S(X, 1) = S(X, 1) + Q
3340     LET Z$ = STR$ (X)
3350     LET F = 3
3360     GOSUB 4160
3370     LET Y$ = Z$ + "+"
3380     LET Z$ = STR$ (Q)
3390     LET F = 4
3400     GOSUB 4160
3410     LET Y$ = Y$ + Z$
3420     WRITE#2, Y$
3430     PRINT "MORE STOCK ANSWER Y(YES) N(NO)"
3440     INPUT R$
3450     IF R$ = "Y" THEN 3200
3460 RETURN
3470     REM
3480     REM · · SUBROUTINE TO PLACE ORDER AND PRINT INVOICE
3500     PRINT "ENTER THE FOLLOWING DETAILS:"
3510     PRINT
3515     PRINT "NAME"
3520     INPUT N$
3525     PRINT
3530     PRINT "ADDRESS"
3535     PRINT "STREET"
3540     INPUT A$
3545     PRINT "TOWN"
3550     INPUT T$
3555     PRINT "POSTCODE"
3560     INPUT P$
3565     PRINT
3570     LET I = 0
3575     LET I = I + 1
3580       PRINT "WINE CODE"
3585       INPUT X
3590       IF INT(X) — X = 0  AND X > = 1 AND X < = 200 THEN 3605
3595       PRINT "ERROR — INCORRECT CODE"
3600     GOTO 3580
```

```
3605      PRINT "QUANTITY"
3610      INPUT Q
3615      IF INT(Q) – Q = 0  AND Q > = 0 AND Q < = S(X, 1) THEN 36
3620      PRINT "ERROR – ILLEGAL QUANTITY"
3625      GOTO 3605
2630      LET S(X, 1) = S(X, 1) – Q
3635      LET O(I, 1) = X
3640      LET O(I, 2) = Q
3645      LET Z$ = STR$ (X)
3650      LET F = 3
3655      GOSUB 4160
3660      LET Y$ = Z$ + "–"
3665      LET Z$ = STR$ (Q)
3670      LET F = 4
3675      GOSUB 4160
3680      LET Y$ = Y$ + Z$
3685      WRITE#2, Y$
3690      PRINT "ORDER COMPLETE ANSWER Y(YES) N(NO)"
3695      INPUT R$
3700      IF R$ = "N" THEN 3575
3705      PRINT TAB(31); "SALES INVOICE"
3710      PRINT TAB(31); "–––– –––––––"
3715      PRINT
3720      PRINT TAB(31); "THE WINE MERCHANT"
3725      PRINT TAB(31); "13 THE VAULTS"
3730      PRINT TAB(31); "LONDON E15 2AG"
3735      PRINT
3740      PRINT TAB(31); "TEL. 01–397–214639"
3745      PRINT
3750      PRINT TAB(31); "VAT REG NO. 231847"
3755      PRINT
3760      PRINT
3765      PRINT "DATE:" ; J$
3770      PRINT
3775      PRINT N$
3780      PRINT A$
3785      PRINT T$
3790      PRINT P$
3795      PRINT
3800      PRINT
3805      PRINT
3810      PRINT "QUANTITY"; TAB(21); "DESCRIPTION"; TAB(51);
3815      PRINT "UNIT COST"; TAB (71); "COST"
3820      PRINT TAB(51); "PENCE"
3825      PRINT
```

```
3830      LET T1 = 0
3835      FOR I1 = 1 TO I
3840      LET C = O(I1, 2) * S(O(I1, 1), 4) / 100
3845      PRINT O(I1, 2); TAB(21); W$ (O(I1, 1)); TAB (51);
3850      PRINT S(O(I1, 1), 4); TAB (66);
3852      PRINT USING " ——————.##", C
3855      LET T1 = T1 + C
3860      NEXT I1
3865      PRINT
3870      LET V = INT (T1 * 15) / 100
3875      PRINT TAB(56); "TOTAL"; TAB(66);
3877      PRINT USING "——————.##", T1
3880      PRINT
3885      PRINT TAB(54); "VAT 15%"; TAB(66);
3887      PRINT USING "——————.##", V
3890      PRINT
3891      PRINT TAB(51); "PAYMENT DUE"; TAB(66);
3892      PRINT USING "——————.##", T1 + V
3895      PRINT "ANOTHER ORDER ANSWER Y(YES) N(NO)"
3897      INPUT R$
3898      IF R$ = "Y" THEN 3500
3899 RETURN
3900      REM
3901      REM ·· SUBROUTINE TO PRINT RE-ORDER REPORT
3910      PRINT TAB(21); "RE-ORDER REPORT"
3915      PRINT TAB(21); "———————  ————— "
3816      PRINT
3917      PRINT
2918      PRINT
3920      PRINT "QUANTITY"; TAB(21); "DESCRIPTION"
3921      PRINT
3922      PRINT
3925      LET I = 1
3930      IF W$(I) = " " THEN RETURN
3935      IF S(I, 1) > S(I, 2) THEN 3945
3940      PRINT S(I, 3); TAB(21); W$(I)
3945      LET I = I + 1
3950      GOTO 3930
3955      REM
3960      REM ·· SUBROUTINE TO BUILD NEW STOCK FILE
4000      PRINT "INSERT NEW DISC — PRESS SPACE RETURN WHEN READY"
4005      INPUT R$
4010      DEFINE FILE#1 = "STOCK"
4015      LET I = 1
4020         IF W$(I) = " " THEN 4130
```

385

```
4025      FOR I1 = LEN(W$(I)) + 1 TO 25
4030         LET W$(I) = W$(I) + " "
4035      NEXT I1
4040      LET Z$ = STR$(S(I, 1))
4045      LET F = 4
4050      GOSUB 4160
4055      LET X$ = W$(I) + Z$
4060      LET Z$ = STR$(S(I, 2))
4065      LET F = 3
4070      GOSUB 4160
4075      LET X$ = X$ + Z$
4080      LET Z$ = STR$(S(I, 3))
4085      LET F = 4
4090      GOSUB 4160
4095      LET X$ = X$ + Z$
4100      LET Z$ = STR$(S(I, 4))
4105      GOSUB 4160
4110      LET X$ = X$ + Z$
4115      WRITE#1, X$
4120      LET I = I + 1
4125   GOTO 4020
4130   CLOSE#1
4135 RETURN
4140   REM
4150   REM ·· SUBROUTINE TO RIGHT JUSTIFY DATA FOR FILES
4160   IF LEN(Z$) = F THEN 4200
4170      FOR I1 = LEN(Z$) + 1 TO F
4180         LET Z$ = "O" + Z$
4190      NEXT I1
4200 RETURN
4210 END
```

f. **Extracts from a computer run.**

```
INPUT DATE STRING E.G. 14 JAN 82
!10 MARCH 1982
RE-BUILD SYSTEM, ANSWER Y(YES) N(NO)
!N
WINE STOCK/INVOICE SYSTEM
---- ------------- ------


DO YOU WANT TO:

1 ENQUIRE ABOUT STOCK

2 REPLENISH STOCK

3 TAKE AN ORDER AND OUTPUT INVOICE

4 OUTPUT A STOCK RE-ORDER REPORT

5 CREATE NEW STOCK FILE AND EXIT


ENTER A CODE FROM 1 TO 5
!1
ENTER WINE CODE
!1
WINE DESCRIPTION:ANJOU ROUGE

STOCK LEVEL:870

COST: £2.25
ANOTHER ENQUIRY ANSWER Y(YES) N(NO)
!Y
ENTER WINE CODE
!6
WINE DESCRIPTION:CHABLIS

STOCK LEVEL:230

COST: £3.85
ANOTHER ENQUIRY ANSWER Y(YES) N(NO)
!Y
ENTER WINE CODE
!8
WINE DESCRIPTION:CHATEAU GRAMET

STOCK LEVEL:170

COST: £2.65
ANOTHER ENQUIRY ANSWER Y(YES) N(NO)
!N
```

```
WINE STOCK/INVOICE SYSTEM
---- --------------- ------

DO YOU WANT TO:

1 ENQUIRE ABOUT STOCK

2 REPLENISH STOCK

3 TAKE AN ORDER AND OUTPUT INVOICE

4 OUTPUT A STOCK RE-ORDER REPORT

5 CREATE NEW STOCK FILE AND EXIT


ENTER A CODE FROM 1 TO 5
!3
ENTER THE FOLLOWING DETAILS:

NAME
!B JENKINS

ADDRESS
STREET
!2 HIGH ST
TOWN
!WATFORD
POSTCODE
!UX2 5TR

WINE CODE
!2
QUANTITY
!10
ORDER COMPLETE ANSWER Y(YES) N(NO)
!N
WINE CODE
!4
QUANTITY
!20
ORDER COMPLETE ANSWER Y(YES) N(NO)
!N
WINE CODE
!8
QUANTITY
!25
ORDER COMPLETE ANSWER Y(YES) N(NO)
!N
WINE CODE
!15
QUANTITY
!100
ORDER COMPLETE ANSWER Y(YES) N(NO)
!N
WINE CODE
!13
QUANTITY
!45
ORDER COMPLETE ANSWER Y(YES) N(NO)
!Y
```

```
                    S A L E S   I N V O I C E
                    ---------   -------------

                    THE WINE MERCHANT
                    13 THE VAULTS
                    LONDON E15 2AG

                    TEL. 01-397-214539

                    VAT REG NO. 231847


DATE:10 MARCH 1982

B JENKINS
2 HIGH ST
WATFORD
UX2 5TR


QUANTITY              DESCRIPTION                UNIT COST          COST
                                                 PENCE

10                    BEAUJOLAIS NOUVEAU         255              25.50
20                    BORDEAUX ROUGE             199              39.80
25                    CHATEAU GRANET             265              66.25
100                   SAUTERNES                  295             295.00
45                    MEDOC                      259             116.55

                                                 TOTAL           543.10

                                                 VAT 15%          81.46

                                                 PAYMENT DUE     624.56
ANOTHER ORDER ANSWER Y(YES) N(NO)
IN
WINE STOCK/INVOICE SYSTEM
----- --------------- ------


DO YOU WANT TO:

1 ENQUIRE ABOUT STOCK

2 REPLENISH STOCK

3 TAKE AN ORDER AND OUTPUT INVOICE

4 OUTPUT A STOCK RE-ORDER REPORT

5 CREATE NEW STOCK FILE AND EXIT


ENTER A CODE FROM 1 TO 5
14
                      R E - O R D E R   R E P O R T
                      ---------------   -----------


QUANTITY              DESCRIPTION

200                   BORDEAUX ROUGE
50                    CHATEAU BARON
200                   MACON ROUGE
200                   MEDOC
```

```
WINE STOCK/INVOICE SYSTEM
---- ------------- ------

DO YOU WANT TO:

1 ENQUIRE ABOUT STOCK

2 REPLENISH STOCK

3 TAKE AN ORDER AND OUTPUT INVOICE

4 OUTPUT A STOCK RE-ORDER REPORT

5 CREATE NEW STOCK FILE AND EXIT


ENTER A CODE FROM 1 TO 5
!2
ENTER THE FOLLOWING DETAILS

WINE CODE
!3

ADDITIONAL STOCK QUANTITY
!100
MORE STOCK ANSWER Y(YES) N(NO)
!Y
ENTER THE FOLLOWING DETAILS

WINE CODE
!5

ADDITIONAL STOCK QUANTITY
!260
MORE STOCK ANSWER Y(YES) N(NO)
!Y
ENTER THE FOLLOWING DETAILS

WINE CODE
!15

ADDITIONAL STOCK QUANTITY
!200
MORE STOCK ANSWER Y(YES) N(NO)
!N
```

Original Stock File

```
ANJOU ROUGE            0 870 250 05 000 225
BEAUJOLAIS NOUVEAU     0 075 025 01 000 255
BLANC ANJOU            0 480 250 03 000 179
BORDEAUX ROUGE         0 050 050 02 000 199
BOURGOGNE HAUTES       0 175 100 01 000 575
CHABLIS                0 230 100 02 000 385
CHATEAU BARON          0 040 050 00 500 295
CHATEAU GRAMET         0 170 080 01 000 265
CHIANTI                0 650 250 05 000 185
COTES-DU-RHONE         0 110 100 03 000 199
LIEBFRAUMILCH          0 690 250 05 000 205
MACON ROUGE            0 200 150 02 000 199
MEDOC                  0 100 080 02 000 259
RIOJA                  0 380 250 04 000 245
SAUTERNES              0 450 250 05 000 295
```

Transaction File

```
002-0010
004-0020
008-0025
015-0100
013-0045
003-0010
005-0045

003-0040
005-0020
006-0030
013-0050
012-0100
001-0250
003+0100
005+0200
015+0200
```

Son Stock File Created at End of Computer Run.

```
ANJOU ROUGE              0620250050000225
BEAUJOLAIS NOUVEAU       0065025010000255
BLANC ANJOU              0530250030000179
BORDEAUX ROUGE           0030005002000199
BOURGOGNE HAUTES         0310100010000575
CHABLIS                  0200100020000385
CHATEAU BARON            0040050005000295
CHATEAU GRAMET           0145080010000265
CHIANTI                  0650250050000185
COTES-DU-RHONE           0110100030000199
LIEBFRAUMILCH            0690250050000205
MACON ROUGE              0100150020000199
MEDOC                    0005080020000259
RIOJA                    0380250040000245
SAUTERNES               0550250050000295
```

g. **Notes:** Further testing of this program will reveal that:

i. As with the first case study there is no data type validation on the input of data. Hence it is possible for the program to be terminated by the computer if data of the wrong type is entered.

ii. It is possible to place an order for a stock item that is not contained in the stock file. In such an event the name of the stock item is a null string, stock level, re-order level, re-order quantity and price are all zero. Although this is clearly an undesirable feature it does **not** cause an error to be introduced into the stock file, or stock array.

20 Projects

INTRODUCTION.

The following problems are designed to test the knowledge and skills the reader has gained from studying the chapters within part two of the text.

Each programming solution should contain:

a. Analysis of the problem.

b. Flowcharts.

c. Glossary of terms.

d. Annotated computer program.

e. Test data.

f. Dry-run of either the flowchart or the program.

g. The results from the program being run on a computer.

QUESTIONS.

1. Store a passage of text in a serial file such that each line of text represents a record. Records will be of variable length since words will **not** be split between two lines.

Analyse the text line by line such that each **new** word on a line is stored in an array and the frequency of occurences of each word in the passage is also stored. For example:

TO	2
BE	2
OR	1
NOT	1
THAT	1
IS	1
THE	1
QUESTION	1

At the end of the passage the arrays should be sorted into descending order of usage of the words, and then the contents of the two arrays output.

Repeat the procedure for different passages of text.

2. Store a BASIC program in a serial file such that each line of the program represents a variable length record. The BASIC lines should **not** be indented initially. Re-format the BASIC program such that lines are indented according to the following rules.

a. The body of a FOR/NEXT is indented three spaces from the words FOR and NEXT.

```
FOR | I = 1 TO N
        FOR K = − − −
         |
        |NEXT K
NEXT I
```

b. Statements of a selection process are indented three spaces, L1 and L2 are line numbers.

```
IF cond THEN L1
     | statements
   GOTO
L1
     |
     | statements
L2
```

c. i. Repetition using an IF statement, the body of the loop is indented by three spaces.

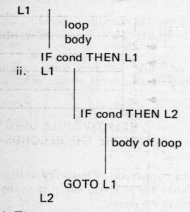

```
   L1  |
       |   loop
       |   body
      IF cond THEN L1
ii.  L1  |
```

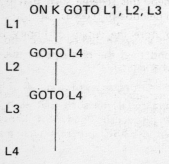

```
          | IF cond THEN L2
          |
          |  body of loop
          |
       GOTO L1
   L2
```

d. The program statements of an ON GOTO segment are indented three spaces.

```
          ON K GOTO L1, L2, L3
      L1  |
          |
          GOTO L4
      L2  |
          |
          GOTO L4
      L3  |
          |
          |
      L4  |
```

e. The body of a subroutine is indented three spaces.

REM ·· SUBROUTINE — — — —

statements

RETURN

Build the re-formatted program in a different file and output the contents of this file when the entire program has been changed.

3. Write a program to implement the Merge Sort described in Chapter 15 para 6b.

4. The following scheme can be used to simulate the organisation of an indexed sequential file. The index is represented by a two-dimensional array. The keys to records are stored in either ascending or descending order in the first column of the array. The second column contains the positions of the respective records held in a relative file. These record positions are numeric keys to the records.

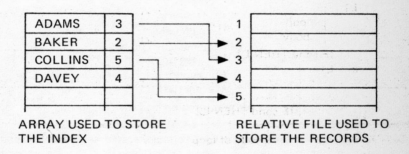

ADAMS	3
BAKER	2
COLLINS	5
DAVEY	4

ARRAY USED TO STORE
THE INDEX

RELATIVE FILE USED TO
STORE THE RECORDS

To retrieve a record a binary search is made of the array until a key match is found. The respective relative file numeric key is then used to access the relative file and hence retrieve the record.

The index must also be stored as an entry in a sequential file.

Write a program to implement this scheme such that it is suitable for the insertion, amendment and deletion of records.

5. A sequential file is used to store the details of library books. The format of a record on the file is:

book title	(30 characters)
catalogue index	(8 digits)
author(s)	(40 characters)
publisher	(20 characters)
status code	(1 character)
price	(4 digits)

where status code is

    A for active
    L for lost
    D for damaged
    E for external loan.

Design and write a program which will enable a librarian to up-date the file through amendment, deletion and insertion or replacement of a complete record. The librarian should be able to obtain complete lists of old and new records.

6. An estate agent wants to keep on file the following details about properties.

Vendor code	(4 digits)
Address	(50 characters)
Details of	Price (6 digits)
Property	Type of dwelling (1 character)
	Number of bedrooms (2 digits)
	Freehold or Leasehold (1 character).

where:

Type of dwelling   A Detached house.
                             B Semi-detached house.
                             C Terraced house.
                             D Bungalow.
                             E Maisonette/Flat.

Assume that the records are stored on a relative file having the vendor code as a key to a record.

Design and write a program for an enquiry system such that the estate agents can obtain a complete listing of the specification of a property knowing the vendor's code.

Extend the system to incorporate a file maintenance scheme.

7. A builders merchants sells ballast at a flat rate of £2 per cubic metre. Two forms of discount are allowed:

a. A discount on bulk purchases according to the following table.

Ballast m^3	Discount %
< 5	0
5 to < 10	5
10 to < 20	10
20 to < 50	15
50 to < 100	20
100 and over	25

b. A discount for prompt payment.

> 7% if payment is within one month.
> 3% if payment is within three months.

Design and write a program which will accept dated orders and produce invoices showing the discounts illustrated above.

Charge VAT at the current rate.

8. With reference to chapter 19 case study two write routines to allow new brands of wine to be added to the existing stock. The routine should store the new wine details in the wine and stock arrays — remember the wine array contains the wines in alphabetical order.

Include a routine to output the new list of wines together with their code numbers.

Modify case study two to store the details of orders in an order file having the following format for a single record.

customer account number	(4 digits)
stock quantity	(4 digits)
stock number	(3 digits)

Customer details are stored in a separate relative file using customer account number as a key. The format of a record in the customer file is:

Name	(30 characters)
Address	(50 characters)
Balance outstanding	(6 digits)

Re-write part of the case study two program that produces sales invoices to include the order and customer files.

9. A teaching machine is used to test a student's ability at arithmetic — addition, subtraction multiplication and division. However, the machine is to cater for a student's level of development in this subject by introducing levels of difficulty.

Level 1 (simple) uses integers in the range 1 — 10, except for division when the division is an integer in the range 1 — 5.

Level 2 (harder) uses integers in the range 10 — 19 except for divisors which are integers in the range 1 — 10.

Level 3 (difficult) uses integers in the range 20, 99 and divisors in the range 10, 19.

A random number generator should be used to generate numbers for different arithmetic problems.

Design and write a program in the COMAL—80 language to implement the teaching machine.

10. A college lecturer wants to hold on file the following details about his students.

Student number	(3 digits)
Surname	(20 characters)
Initial	(1 character)
Date of Birth	(6 digits)

Percentage examination marks for:

English language
Mathematics
Computer Studies
General Science
Geography
History.

The organisation of the file is relative using student number as the key.

The college lecturer wants to be able to manipulate the contents of the file to:

a. Enrol students (enter surname, initial and date of birth), the student number should be generated by the system as the next available relative key.

b. Enter individual examination marks by subject.

c. Print out a list of all the students on the file together with their performance in each subject area.

d. Display records.

e. Amend and delete records.

The COMAL—80 language offers the following verbs for relative file processing (these will not be found in appendix IV).

OPEN file, "filename", RANDOM length of record
      number

file number — an integer 1 — 255.
length of record — number of bytes in a record (to calculate bytes count the number of characters in a record string).

e.g. OPEN 1, "MARKS", RANDOM 54.

READ FILE file , key : variable names representing fields
              number variable

Key variable — represents a positive integer.

e.g. READ FILE 1, X: R$

R$ represents the record string.

e.g. READ FILE 1, X: A$, B$, C, D
       A$, B$, C, D represent fields within the record.

  WRITE FILE file , key : variable names representing fields
        number variable

e.g. WRITE FILE 1, X: A$, B$, C, D

  CLOSE closes all files.

  Design and write a program in the COMAL—80 language to implement
the system required by the college lecturer.

Appendix 1

Answers To Questions Set at End of Chapters

CHAPTER 2.
1.

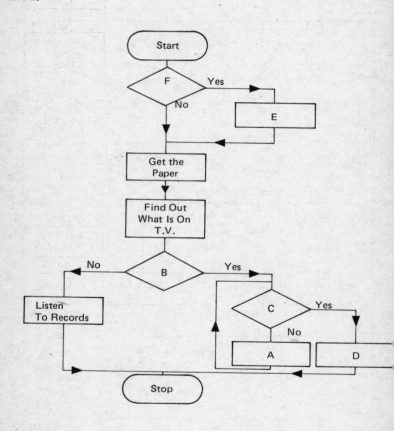

2.

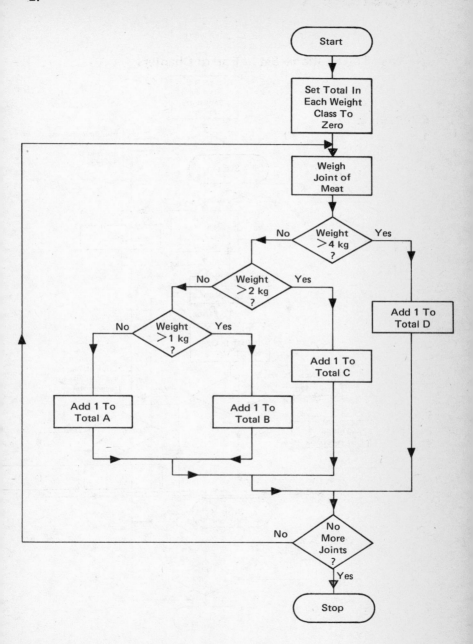

5.

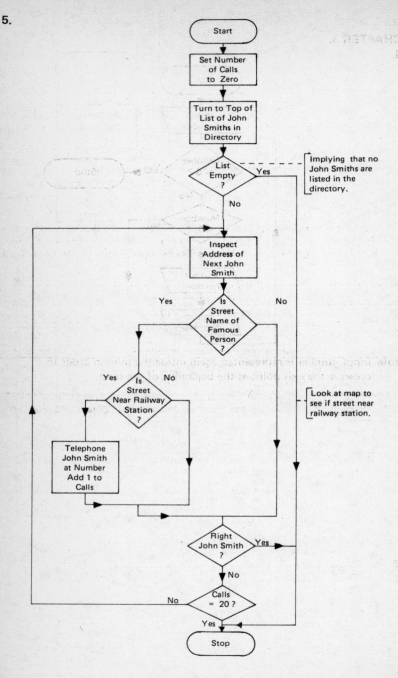

CHAPTER 3.
1.

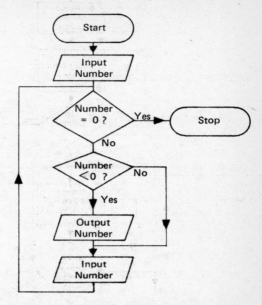

Note: Input number is represented again inside the loop in order to preserve the exit point at the beginning of the loop.

2.

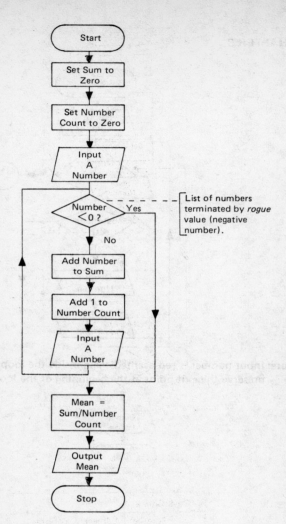

Test data   4 8 3 7 3 −2

Desk check

Sum	Number Count	Number	Mean
0	0	4·	
4	1	8	
12	2	3	
15	3	7	
22	4	3	
25	5	−2	
			5

3.

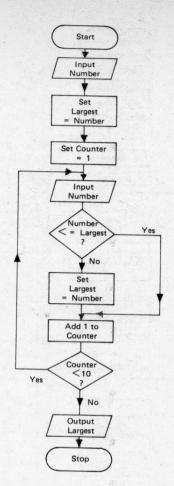

Desk Check		
Number	Largest	Counter
7	7	1
3		2
19	19	3
41	41	4
26		5
5		6
17		7
8		8
0		9
23		10
Largest = 41		

405

4.

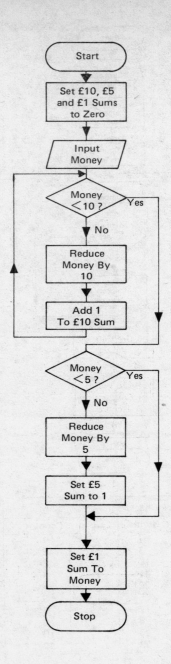

5.

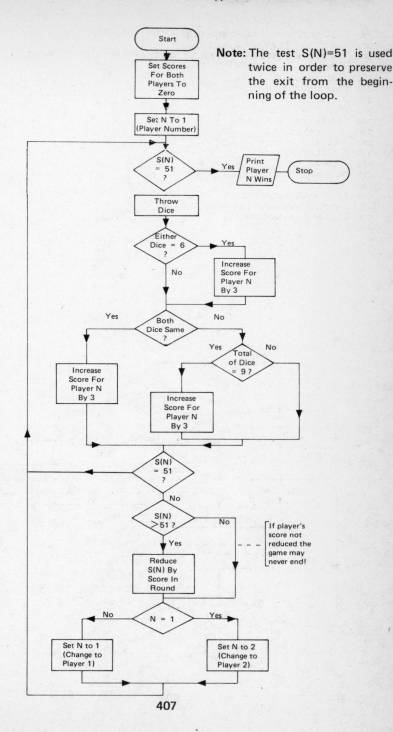

Note: The test S(N)=51 is used twice in order to preserve the exit from the beginning of the loop.

6.

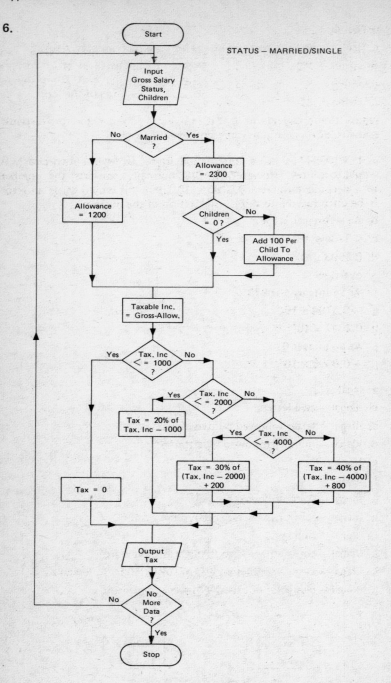

STATUS – MARRIED/SINGLE

CHAPTER 4.

1. a. real   A   b. integer   N   c. real   A1
d. string   X\$ e. string   Y\$ f. integer   B
g. integer   K   h. string   G\$ i. integer   C
j. string   Z\$

   Note: Some dialects of BASIC append a % character to a variable name to distinguish it as representing an integer.

2. a. If 6195847 is to be stored explicitly as an integer then clearly it would overflow. However, BASIC normally converts the number to a decimal form: eg. 0.6195×10^7, but this would cause an error to be introduced into the representation of the number.

   b. As an integer —156

   c. 0.3764×10^3

   d. 0.2593×10^0

   e. overflow

   f. As an integer +16973

   g. $- 0.3794 \times 10^{-43}$

   h. 0.2347×10^{49}

   i. As an integer 0

   j. $- 0.9999 \times 10^0$

3. a. legal
   b. illegal — two letters
   c. illegal — letter followed by two digits
   d. illegal — number followed by letter
   e. legal
   f. legal
   g. illegal — name followed by digit
   h. illegal — lower case letter and hyphen
   i. illegal — number
   j. illegal — three letters (also BASIC reserved word)
   k. illegal — string variables consist of single letters followed by \$
   l. illegal — character not used in name composition

4. a. legal — numeric
    b. legal — numeric
    c. legal — string
    d. illegal missing right-hand delimiter
    e. illegal — variable name
    f. legal — but be careful about embedded commas in your dialect
    g. legal — numeric
    h. legal — string
    i. legal — string
    j. illegal — % character not part of numeric constant

5. a. ASCII 48
    b. ASCII
       i.   65
       ii. 66
       iii. 59
       iv. 51
       v.   57
       vi. 33

6. a. A + B / C   b. X / (Y + Z)   c. (U * V) / (W * X)
    d. A ↑ B   e. (D − B) / (2 * A)   f. (A * A + B * B) / 2
    g. (A − B) * (C + D) ↑ 2   h. B * B − 4 * A * C
    i. Q1 * Q2 / (4 * P * E * R * R)   P represents 3.14159 . . . . .
    j. 2 * P * ((A * A + B * B) / 2) ↑ 0.5   an approximation to Π in
                                                 i and j.

7. a. missing *
    b. two operators together
    c. two operators together
    d. illegal variable name Z60 or missing operator
    e. missing right parenthesis
    f. no error
    g. missing operator between (A − B) and (A + B)
    h. two operators together
    i. illegal operators
    j. variable names illegal — capital letters required.

8. a. $x + y^3$ b. $x + \dfrac{2}{y} + 4$ c. $\dfrac{a.b}{c + 2}$

   d. $\left(\dfrac{x}{y}\right)^{n-1}$ e. $\dfrac{a}{b} + \dfrac{c.d}{(f.g.h)}$

   f. $\dfrac{-1}{2p} + \dfrac{q^2}{4\,r^2}$ g. $\sqrt{a^2 + b^2}$

   h. $\dfrac{1}{(x + y)^2}$ i. $\dfrac{a}{b} + \dfrac{c}{d} + \dfrac{e}{f}$ j. $\dfrac{U_3 \cdot U_1}{U_2 \cdot U_0}$

CHAPTER 5.

1. a. **INPUT H**   b. **PRINT Q**   c. **PRINT Z3**
   d. **IF A $<>$ B THEN 40**   e. **LET Z = X $\uparrow$ 2 + Y $\uparrow$ 2**
   f. **LET H = I**   g. **LET X = 36 + Y / Z**
      LET J = I
   h. **IF A$ $>$ B$ THEN STOP**   note: this is not a syntax error but a matter of style.

   i. **EXIT** is not a legal verb

   j. **IF P $>$ Q THEN 510**   note: mixed data types in condition as well as negative line number in statement.

2. Does not detect negative integers, only prints positive numbers (real or integer) or zero.

   Continuous loop created — no method of exit from the loop.

3.

Line Number(s)	A	B	C
10, 20, 30, 40, 50 60	1	1	2
70, 80, 90, 100, 40, 50 60	2	3	4
70, 80, 90, 100, 40, 50 60	5	8	6
70, 80, 90, 100, 40, 50 60	13	21	8
70, 80, 90, 100, 40, 50 60	34	55	10
70, 80, 90, 100, 40, 50 60	89	144	12

4. In the line **10 LET S = T**, the value of T has not been defined. T would be assumed to be zero, hence line 20 is redundant.

Line 30 **LET A = S / T** implies that the numerator and denominator are both zero — hence the answer cannot be determined.

Line 40 **LET B = 2.8 / T** implies dividing a value by zero, and hence causing overflow.

5.

Line numbers(s)	X	C	S	Y	A
10, 20, 30, 40	5	0	0	7	
50, 60, 70		1	7		
40, 50, 60, 70		2	10	3	
40, 50, 60, 70		3	18	8	
40, 50, 60, 70		4	22	4	
40, 50, 60, 70		5	25	3	
80, 90, 100					5

6.

Line number(s)	T
10	Data type mismatch
20	DOVER has missing delimiters
30, 40, 50, 60	Population of more than one town output
10	No method of controlling an exit from the loop

CHAPTER 6.

2.

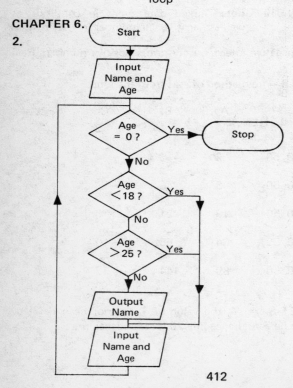

412

Glossary.

Name	N$
Age	A

Program.
```
10    INPUT N$
20    INPUT A
30    IF A = 0 THEN STOP
40    IF A < 18 THEN 70
50    IF A > 25 THEN 70
60    PRINT N$
65    INPUT N$
66    INPUT A
70    GOTO 30
80    END
```

3. a. Glossary.

Number	N
Sum	S
Count	C
Mean	M

Program.
```
10    LET S = 0
20    LET C = 0
30      INPUT N
40      IF N < 0 THEN 80
50        LET S = S + N
60        LET C = C + 1
65    INPUT N
70    GOTO 40
80    LET M = S / C
90    PRINT M
100   STOP
110   END
```

b. Glossary.

Number	H
Largest Number	L
Counter	C

413

Program.

```
10    INPUT N
20    LET L = N
30    LET C = 1
40       INPUT N
50       IF N = < L THEN 70
60       LET L = N
70       LET C = C + 1
80    IF C < 10 THEN 40
90    PRINT L
100   STOP
110   END
```

4.

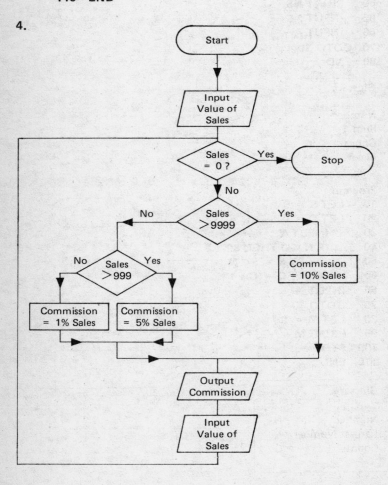

414

Glossary

Value of Sales   S
Commission   C

```
10      INPUT S
20      IF S = 0 THEN STOP
30      IF S > 9999 THEN 90
40      IF S > 999 THEN 70
50        LET C = 0.01 * S
60      GOTO 100
70        LET C = 0.05 * S
80      GOTO 100
90        LET C = 0.1 * S
100     PRINT C
105       INPUT S
110    GOTO 20
120    END
```

5.

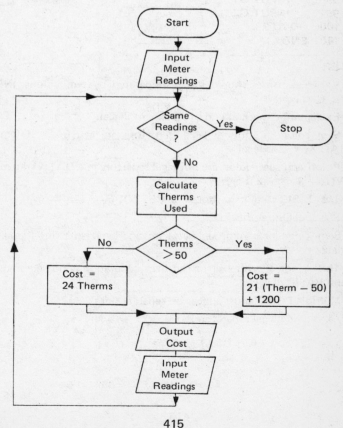

Glossary

First Meter Reading	Q1
Second Meter Reading	Q2
Therms used	T
Cost	C

Program.
```
10      INPUT Q1
20      INPUT Q2
30      IF Q1 = Q2 THEN STOP
40         LET T = 1.04 * (Q2 - Q1)
50      IF T > 50 THEN 80
60         LET C = 24 * T
70      GOTO 90
80         LET C = 21 * (T - 50) + 1200
90      PRINT C
95      INPUT Q1
96      INPUT Q2
100  GOTO 30
110  END
```

CHAPTER 7.

1. a. Variables names should not be separated by semi-colons. INPUT A, B, C is legal.

b. Exclamation mark at end of statement illegal.

c. Semi-colon is not a legal separtors in a READ statement. READ X, Y, Z is legal.

d. Colon and semi-colon are not legal separtors in a DATA statement. DATA - 6, 14, 32 is legal.

e. The BASIC statement should be RESTORE.

f. String delimiter missing.

g. Semi-colon or comma separator missing between string literal and variable.

h. This is not a syntax error but back tabulation is not common to many BASIC dialects.

i. Multiple PRINT must appear on separate lines.

j. / and ; are illegal separators.

2.

Line Number	A	B	C	D$	E$	F$	X	Y	Z
10	8	16	32						
30				EIGHT	SIXTEEN	THIRTY-TWO			
50							8	16	32

3.

Line Number	A	B	X$	Y$	Z$
10	Error data type mismatch				
40			SALARY	TAX	out of data

4.

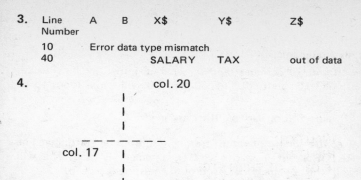

col. 20

col. 17

Flowcharts are omitted in the answers that follow since the computer program illustrates the procedures required in the solution to a problem.

5. Glossary

Pounds Sterling	P
French Francs	F
German Marks	M
Italian Lire	L
Exchange rate Francs	R1
Marks	R2
Lire	R3

```
10      REM · · INPUT EXCHANGE RATES
20      PRINT "INPUT RATES FOR FRANCS, MARKS AND LIRE"
30      INPUT R1, R2, R3
40      PRINT
50      REM · · OUTPUT HEADINGS
60      PRINT TAB (25); "CURRENCY CONVERSION TABLE"
70      PRINT
80      PRINT "POUNDS", "FRANCS", "MARKS", "LIRE"
90      PRINT
100     REM · · SET POUNDS TO INITIAL VALUE
110     LET P = 5
120     REM · · COMPUTE CURRENCIES
130       LET F = P * R1
140       LET M = P * R2
150       LET L = P * R3
160     REM · · OUTPUT CONVERSIONS
170       PRINT P, F, M, L
180     REM · · INCREASE POUNDS
190       LET P = P + 5
200     REM · · TEST FOR UPPER LIMIT OF TABLE
210     IF P < = 50 THEN 130
220     STOP
230     END
```

CHAPTER 8

1. a. line 10 STEP—1 omitted
    line 40 should be NEXT I

    b. lines 10 and 20 commas used to separate initial and final values of loops. (ie. TO omitted) line 50 and 60 will cause loops to be crossed.

    c. line 20 value of loop variable (I) re-assigned.

3. Program control does not return from the subroutine starting at line 600 via a RETURN but instead a GOTO statement is used. This will cause an error of the possible type — subroutine nesting too deep.

4. a.
```
10    FOR I = 1 TO 49 STEP 2
20       PRINT I
30    NEXT I
40    STOP
50    END
```

    b.
```
10    FOR I = 2 TO 50 STEP 2
20       LET S = I * I
30       PRINT S
40    NEXT I
50    STOP
60    END
```

    c.
```
10    LET S = 0
20    FOR I = 11 TO 19 STEP 2
30       LET S = S + I ↑ 3
40    NEXT I
50    PRINT S
60    STOP
70    END
```

5.

Glossary.	
Employee counter	E
Hours worked per week	H
Overtime pay	P

Program

```
10      FOR E = 1 TO 10
20        READ H
30        DATA 50, 45, 39, 40, 52, 43, 44, 49, 55, 53
40        IF H > 40 THEN 70
50          LET P = 0
60        GO TO 80
70        LET P = 12 * (H − 40)
80        PRINT "OVERTIME PAY EMPLOYEE NUMBER"; E; "IS £"; P
90      NEXT E
100     STOP
110     END
```

6.

Glossary.	
Month counter	M
Cars sold	C
Car counter	F

Program

```
10      REM · · PRINT HORIZONTAL AXIS
20      PRINT "▽0 ▽▽▽▽ 5 ▽▽▽▽ 10▽ SALES"
30      PRINT "▽———————————"
40      REM · · PRINT BAR CHART
50      FOR M = 1 TO 6
60        READ C
70        DATA 5, 4, 7, 9, 8, 6
80        PRINT M; "I";
90        FOR F = 1 TO C
100         PRINT "*";
110       NEXT F
120       PRINT " "
130     NEXT M
140     PRINT "MONTHS"
150     STOP
160     END
```

Note: The scale of this chart will be small, the program should be modified to give an output at least four times the size of that already obtained.

419

9.
Glossary	
First number of pair	A
Second number of pair	B
Counter	C

Program

```
10      LET A = 1
20      LET B = 1
30      FOR C = 1 TO 10
40        PRINT A; " "; B; " ";
50        LET A = A + B
60        LET B = B + A
70      NEXT C
80      STOP
90      END
```

CHAPTER 9

1. a. The declaration of the size of the array A is too small, should be DIM A (50).

b. The intentional error is missing parenthesis around the subscripts for X1, X2 and X3. The use of a variable to declare the size of an array is dialect dependent.

c. If $M > 15$ and $N > 10$ then $B (I + N, J + M)$ will be outside the range of the declared array DIM B (20, 30).

d. Line 10 should be DIM V (10).

If $N > 10$ then the declaration for the size of the array is too small.

However, if $N > 5$ then the program will be out of data. There exists a type mismatch between $V(I)$ and the data.

e. Line 40 there exists a type mismatch between $T(I, J)$ and the first five items of data.

2.
```
10      DIM T (6, 9)
20      FOR I = 1 TO 6
30        FOR J = 1 TO 9
40          LET T (I, J) = 100
50        NEXT J
60      NEXT I
70
```

3.
```
10      DIM X(8), Y(8)
20      FOR I = 1 TO 8
30        LET J = 9 − I
40        LET Y(J) = X(I)
50      NEXT I
60
```

```
4.  10    DIM A(10), B(10)
    20    REM ·· PROCEDURE TO INPUT NUMBERS
    30    FOR I = 1 TO 10
    40      INPUT A(I), B(I)
    50    NEXT I
    60    REM ·· TO OUTPUT THOSE NUMBERS THAT ARE COMMON (a)
    70    FOR I = 1 TO 10
    80      FOR J = 1 TO 10
    90        IF A(I) <> B(J) THEN 120
    100         PRINT A(I)
    110       GOTO 130
    120     NEXT J
    130   NEXT I
    140   REM ·· FIND SUMS OF CORRESPONDING ELEMENTS (b)
    150   FOR I = 1 TO 10
    160     LET S = A(I) + B(I)
    170     PRINT S
    180   NEXT I
    190   REM ·· FIND SMALLEST OF CORRESPONDING ELEMENTS (c)
    200   FOR I = 1 TO 10
    210     IF A(I) < B(I) THEN 240
    220       PRINT B(I)
    230     GOTO 250
    240     PRINT A(I)
    250   NEXT I
    260   STOP
    270   END
```

5.
> **Glossary.**
>
> | | |
> |---|---|
> | One dimensional array to hold word | A$ |
> | One dimensional array to hold vowels | V$ |
> | One dimensional array to hold number of vowels | S |
> | Letters of word | X$ |
> | Subscripts | I, J, K |

Assume the end of a word is terminated by a space, and a word contains no more than twenty letters.

```
10      DIM A$(20), V$(5), S(5)
20      REM · · STORE VOWELS IN ARRAY V
30      FOR I = 1 TO 5
40       READ V$(I)
50       DATA "A", "E", "I", "O", "U"
60      NEXT I
70      REM · · INITIALISE ARRAY S
80      FOR I = 1 TO 5
90       LET S(I) = 0
100     NEXT I
110     REM · · INPUT AND STORE LETTERS OF WORD
120     REM · · TERMINATE WORD WITH A SPACE
130     LET I = 1
140      INPUT X$
150      IF X$ = " " THEN 200
160      LET A$(I) = X$
170      LET I = I + 1
180     GOTO 140
190     REM · · COUNT NUMBER OF VOWELS IN WORD
200     FOR J = 1 TO I − 1
210      FOR K = 1 TO 5
220       IF A$(J) < > V$(K) THEN 250
230        LET S(K) = S(K) + 1
240       GOTO 260
250      NEXT K
260     NEXT J
270     REM · · OUTPUT CLASSIFIED VOWEL COUNT
280     FOR I = 1 TO 5
290      PRINT V$(I); TAB(10); S(I)
300     NEXT I
310     STOP
320     END
```

6. Assume that the set of numbers contains no more than 50 entries, and the number of entries is known in advance.

a. Median for an odd number of entries.

> **Glossary.**
>
> | | |
> |---|---|
> | One dimensional array to store numbers | V |
> | One dimensional array to store number of entries **less** than a selected entry | A |
> | One dimensional array to store number of entries **greater** than a selected entry | B |
> | Subscript | I, P |
> | Number of entries in set | N |

```
10      DIM V(50), A(49), B(49)
20      REM ·· INPUT NUMBER OF ENTRIES IN SET
30      INPUT N
40      REM ·· STORE NUMBERS IN ARRAY V
50      FOR I = 1 TO N
60       INPUT V(I)
70      NEXT I
80      REM ·· STORE NUMBER OF ENTRIES THAT ARE LESS
90      REM ·· THAN A SINGLE ENTRY IN ARRAY A, AND
100     REM ·· THE NUMBER OF ENTRIES THAT ARE GREATER
110     REM ·· THAN A SINGLE ENTRY IN ARRAY B
120     LET P = 1
130     FOR I = 1 TO N
140      IF V(I) > V(P) THEN A(P) = A(P) + 1
150     NEXT I
160     LET B(P) = N − A(P) − 1
170     LET P = P + 1
180     IF P < N + 1 THEN 130
190     REM ·· SELECT MEDIAN
200     FOR I = 1 TO N
210      IF A(I) = B(I) THEN 230
220     NEXT I
230     PRINT "MEDIAN IS"; V(I)
240     STOP
250     END
```

7.

> **Glossary.**
>
> | | |
> |---|---|
> | Two dimensional 4 x 5 array | M |
> | Largest value of row/column | B |
> | Smallest value of row/column | S |
> | Subscripts | I, J |

```
5       DIM M(4, 5)
10      REM · · STORE VALUES IN ARRAY M
20      FOR I = 1 TO 4
30       FOR J = 1 TO 5
40         INPUT M(I, J)
50       NEXT J
60      NEXT I
70      REM · · SEARCH ROWS FOR HIGHEST AND LOWEST VALUES
80      FOR I = 1 TO 4
90       LET B = M(I, 1)
100      LET S = M(I, 1)
110      FOR J = 2 TO 5
120         IF B < M(I, J) THEN B = M(I, J)
130         IF S > M(I, J) THEN S = M(I, J)
140      NEXT J
150      PRINT "ROW"; I; "MAX"; B; "MIN"; S
160     NEXT I
170     REM · · SEARCH COLUMNS FOR HIGHEST AND LOWEST VALU
180     FOR J = 1 TO 5
190      LET B = M(I, J)
200      LET S = M(I, J)
210      FOR I = 2 TO 4
220         IF B < M(I, J) THEN B = M(I, J)
230         IF S > M(I, J) THEN S = M(I, J)
240      NEXT I
250      PRINT "COLUMN"; J; "MAX"; B; "MIN"; S
260     NEXT J
270     STOP
280     END
```

CHAPTER 10

1.

a. 4817.395	b. -0.0001942
c. $0.1784318E + 38$	d. 129.74
e. 183796219	f. $-0.2684715E - 06$
g. $0.1493786E - 14$	h. $0.274647941E + 35$
i. overflow	j. $0.7927194E - 36$

2. a. 4.29   b. − 5   c. − 1

   d. 1.3090   e. 0.5774   f. 1.6094

   g. 7.3891   h. error negative argument.

   i. + 1.0   j. + 1

3.
```
10     DEF FNL(A) = LOG(A) / LOG(B)
20     PRINT "NUMBERS", "BASES"
30     PRINT TAB(10); "2"; TAB(25); "4"; TAB(40); "6"; TAB(55);
40     PRINT "8"; TAB(70); "10"
50     FOR A = 2 TO 10 STEP 0.5
60       PRINT A;
70       FOR B = 2 TO 10 STEP 2
80         PRINT TAB(10 + 15 * (B − 2) / 2); FNL(A);
90       NEXT B
100      PRINT
110    NEXT A
120    STOP
130    END
```

6. a.
```
10     FOR X = 0 TO 1 STEP 0.05
20       LET Y = (SQR (X)) ↑ 2 − X
30       PRINT X, Y
40     NEXT X
50     STOP
60     END
```

   b.
```
10     FOR X = 1 TO 10
20       LET Y = EXP(LOG(X)) − X
30       PRINT X, Y
40     NEXT X
50     STOP
60     END
```

   c.
```
10     FOR X = − 100 TO 100 STEP 10
20       LET Y = TAN (ATN(X)) − X
30       PRINT X, Y
40     NEXT X
50     STOP
60     END
```

```
8.   10       INPUT X, Y
     20       REM ·· CALCULATE ORDINATE OF Y = 2X + 3
     30       LET Y1 = 2 * X + 3
     40       REM ·· FIND POSITION OF POINT RELATIVE TO LINE
     50       LET D = Y − Y1
     60       PRINT "CO-ORDINATES"; X; " "; Y;
     70       IF D < 0 THEN PRINT "BELOW LINE"
     80       IF D = 0 THEN PRINT "ON LINE"
     90       IF D > 0 THEN PRINT "ABOVE LINE"
     100      STOP
     110      END


10.  10       DIM S(2)
     20       REM ·· SET SCORES TO ZERO
     30       LET S(1) = 0
     40       LET S(2) = 0
     50       REM ·· SELECT FIRST PLAYER
     60       LET N = 1
     65       IF S(N) = 51 THEN 290
     70       REM ·· THROW DICE
     80        LET D1 = INT(6 * RND(0) + 1)
     90        LET D2 = INT(6 * RND(0) + 1)
     100      REM ·· TEST EITHER DIE FOR 6
     110      IF D1 = 6 THEN 130
     120         IF D2 <> 6 THEN 150
     130         LET S(N) = S(N) + 3
     140      REM ·· TEST FOR BOTH DICE SAME
     150      IF D1 = D2 THEN 190
     160         REM ·· TEST FOR TOTAL = 9
     170         IF D1 + D2 = 9 THEN LET S(N) = S(N) + 3
     180      GOTO 210
     190      LET S(N) = S(N) + 3
     200      REM ·· TEST SCORE FOR END OF GAME
     210      IF S(N) = 51 THEN 65
     220         IF S(N) > 51 THEN S(N) = S(N) − 6
     230      REM ·· CHANGE PLAYER
     240      IF N = 1 THEN 270
     250         LET N = 1
     260      GOTO 280
     270         LET N = 2
     280      GOTO 65
     290      PRINT "PLAYER"; N; "WINS"
     300      STOP
     310      END
```

CHAPTER 11

2. a. Flowchart.

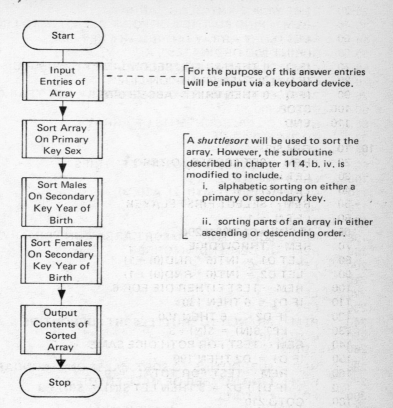

For the purpose of this answer entries will be input via a keyboard device.

A *shuttlesort* will be used to sort the array. However, the subroutine described in chapter 11 4. b. iv. is modified to include.

    i.   alphabetic sorting on either a primary or secondary key.

    ii. sorting parts of an array in either ascending or descending order.

b. **Glossary.**

Two dimensional array	A$
Maximum number of entries to be sorted	N
Position of first entry in sort	X
Key used in sorting (primary = 1 secondary = 2)	K
Sort in order (ascending = 0 descending = 1)	S
Subscripts	I, J
Tempary storage array — one dimensional	T$
Pointers (as described in chapter 11 4. b. iv.)	P1, P2, P3, P4

c. Program.

```
10      DIM A$(20, 3), T$(3)
20      REM · · INPUT ENTRIES OF ARRAY
30      GOSUB 100
40      REM · · SORT ARRAY ON PRIMARY KEY SEX
50      GOSUB 200
60      REM · · SORT MALES ON SECONDARY KEY YEAR OF BIRTH
70      GOSUB 300
75      REM · · SORT FEMALES ON SECONDARY KEY YEAR OF BIRTH
80      GOSUB 400
85      REM · · OUTPUT CONTENTS OF ARRAY
90      GOSUB 500
95      STOP
99      REM · · SUBROUTINE TO INPUT ENTRIES
100     FOR I = 1 TO 20
110        INPUT A$(I, 1), A$(I, 2), A$(I, 3)
120     NEXT I
130   RETURN
198     REM · · SUBROUTINE TO SORT ARRAY ON PRIMARY KEY
199     REM · · IN DESCENDING ORDER
200     LET N = 20
210     LET X = 1
220     LET K = 1
230     LET S = 1
240     REM · · BRANCH TO SHUTTLESORT SUBROUTINE
250     GOSUB 1010
260   RETURN
298     REM · · SUBROUTINE TO SORT MALES ON SECONDARY KEY
299     REM · · FIND NUMBER OF MALE ENTRIES
300     FOR I = 1 TO 19
310        IF A$(I, 1) <> A$(I + 1, 1) THEN 340
320     NEXT I
330     REM · · SET PARAMETERS FOR SORTING MALES ON
335     REM · · ASCENDING SECONDARY KEY
340     LET N = I
350     LET X = 1
360     LET K = 2
370     LET S = 0
380     GOSUB 1010
390   RETURN
398     REM · · SUBROUTINE TO SORT FEMALES ON SECONDARY KEY
399     REM · · SET PARAMETERS
400     LET N = 20
410     LET X = I + 1
420     LET K = 2
```

```
430      LET S = 0
440      GOSUB 1010
450   RETURN

499      REM · · SUBROUTINE TO OUTPUT CONTENTS OF ARRAY
500      FOR I = 1 TO 20
510         PRINT A$(I, 1); " "; A$(I, 2); " "; A$(I, 3)
520      NEXT I
530   RETURN

1000     REM · · SUBROUTINE TO SORT CONTENTS OF ARRAY
1010     LET P1 = X
1015     LET P2 = X + 1
1020     IF S = 0 THEN 1040
1030         IF A$(P1, K) < A$(P2, K) THEN GOSUB 2000
1035     GOTO 1045
1040         IF A$(P1, K) > A$(P2, K) THEN GOSUB 2000
1045         LET P1 = P1 + 1
1050         LET P2 = P2 + 1
1070     IF P1 < N THEN 1020
1080 RETURN

1999     REM · · SUBROUTINE TO SWAP ENTRIES
2000     FOR J = 1 TO 3
2010        LET T$(J) = A$(P1, J)
2020     NEXT J
2030     FOR J = 1 TO 3
2040        LET A$(P1, J) = A$(P2, J)
2050        LET A$(P2, J) = T$(J)
2060     NEXT J
2070     IF P1 = X THEN RETURN
2080     LET P3 = P1
2090     LET P4 = P3 − 1
2100        IF S = 0 THEN 2130
2110           IF A$(P4, K) > = A$(P3, K) THEN RETURN
2120        GOTO 2140
2130           IF A$(P4, K) < = A$(P3, K) THEN RETURN
2140        FOR J = 1 TO 3
2150           LET T$(J) = A$(P3, J)
2160        NEXT J
2170        FOR J = 1 TO 3
2180           LET A$(P3, J) = A$(P4, J)
2190           LET A$(P4, J) = T$(J)
2200        NEXT J
2210        LET P3 = P3 − 1
2220        LET P4 = P4 − 1
2230     IF P3 > X THEN 2100
2240 RETURN
```

5. **Flowchart.**

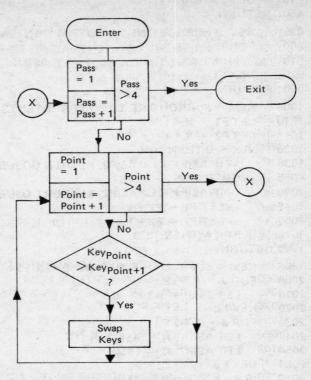

Glossary.

One dimensional array used to store keys	V
Pass value	P
Pointer to key (Point)	K
Temporary store	T

Note: Since the method of sorting the keys is described in a subroutine it can be assumed that the keys are already stored in a one dimensional array.

Program

```
999     REM ·· SUBROUTINE TO BUBBLE SORT KEYS
1000    FOR P = 1 TO 4
1010      FOR K = 1 TO 4
1020        REM ·· COMPARE ADJACENT KEYS
1030        IF V(K) < V(K + 1) THEN 1080
1040          REM ·· SWAP KEYS
1050          LET T = V(K)
1060          LET V(K) = V(K + 1)
1070          LET V(K + 1) = T
1080      NEXT K
1090    NEXT P
1100    RETURN
```

Program refinement.

```
999     REM ·· IMPROVED BUBBLE SORT SUBROUTINE
1000    FOR P = 1 TO 99
1010      REM ·· RESET FLAG (F) TO SHOW KEYS NOT SWAPPED
1020      LET F = 0
1030      FOR K = 1 TO 100 − P
1040        REM ·· COMPARE ADJACENT KEYS
1050        IF V(K) < V(K + 1) THEN 1110
1060          REM ·· SET FLAG TO SHOW SWAP
1070          LET F = 1
1080          LET T = V(K)
1090          LET V(K) = V(K + 1)
1100          LET V(K + 1) = T
1110      NEXT K
1120      REM ·· TEST FLAG FOR SWAP − NO SWAP EXIT
1130      IF F = 0 THEN 1150
1140    NEXT P
1150    RETURN
```

a. The introduction of a flag will ensure that on a pass through the list of keys if no swap is made, the keys are sorted and an exit can be made from the subroutine.

b. On the first pass through the list of keys the largest key will be moved to the bottom of the list; on the second pass the second largest key will be moved to the penultimate end position, etc.

Thus the number of comparisons each pass is reduced by using the BASIC statement 1030 for K = 1 TO 100 − P.

Therefore on pass 1, 99 comparisons are made; pass 2, 98 comparisons; pass 3, 97 comparisons; etc.

CHAPTER 13

1. a. The function ASC returns a numeric value, hence K$ causes a mismatch of data types.

   b. The function CHR$ requires a numeric argument **not** a string argument. The function returns a single character, hence K causes a mismatch of data types.

   c. The function RIGHT only requires two arguments.

   d. A string **literal** has been used as an argument that only contains two characters X$. Yet the second argument 3 suggests the third character of X$ should be printed.

   e. The function VAL requires a string argument. The function returns a numeric value, hence Y$ will cause a mismatch of data types.

   f. The argument of VAL should be a string consisting of or at least beginning with digits.

   g. The function is LEN not LEN$.

   h. The GET verb requires a string variable name.

   i. The CHANGE statement must contain one string variable and one numeric variable.

   j. The minus sign is **not** defined in string manipulation.

2.
```
10    READ A$
20    DATA "ABCDEFGHIJKLMNOPQRSTUVWXYZ"
30    REM ·· PRINT ALPHABET
40    PRINT A$
50    REM ·· PRINT FIRST SIX CHARACTERS
60    PRINT LEFT$ (A$, 6)
70    REM ·· PRINT LAST TEN CHARACTERS
80    PRINT RIGHT$ (A$, 10)
90    REM ·· PRINT TENTH CHARACTER
100   PRINT MID$ (A$, 10, 1)
110   STOP
120   END
```

```
3.  5       LET X$ = ""
    10      READ A$
    20      DATA "ABCDEFGHIJKLMNOPQRSTUVWXYZ"
    30      FOR I = 1 TO 25 STEP 2
    40        LET X$ = X$ + MID$ (A$, I, 1)
    50      NEXT I
    60      REM ·· PRINT LENGTH OF STRING X$
    70      PRINT LEN(X$)
    80      REM ·· SEARCH FOR POSITION OF SUBSTRING QSU
    90      FOR I = 1 TO 13
    100       IF MID$ (X$, I, 1) = "Q" THEN 120
    110     NEXT I
    120     PRINT "SUBSTRING STARTS AT POSITION"; I
    130     STOP
    140     END

4.  10      DIM V(26)
    20      READ A$
    30      DATA "ABCDEFGHIJKLMNOPQRSTUVWXYZ"
    40      REM ·· INITIALISE V TO ZERO
    50      FOR I = 1 TO 26
    60        LET V(I) = 0
    70      NEXT I
    80      REM ·· INPUT POEM CHARACTER BY CHARACTER, TERMINATED
    90      REM ·· BY A FULL STOP
    100     REM ·· THE POEM IS NOT STORED
    110       GET C$
    120     IF C$ = "." THEN 200
    130       REM ·· INCREASE FREQUENCY COUNT
    140     FOR I = 1 TO 26
    150         IF C$ = MID$(A$, I, 1) THEN 180
    160     NEXT I
    170       GOTO 190
    180       LET V(I) = V(I) + 1
    190     GOTO 110
    195     REM ·· OUTPUT FREQUENCY OF LETTERS
    200     PRINT "LETTER", "FREQUENCY"
    210     FOR I = 1 TO 26
    220       PRINT MID$(A$, I, 1), V(I)
    230     NEXT I
    240     STOP
    250     END
```

433

6. Assume the words are separated by spaces and the sentence is terminated by a full stop.

```
5     REM · · SET WORD COUNT  = 0
10    LET T = 0
20    REM · · INPUT SINGLE CHARACTERS DO NOT STORE
30    REM · · THE SENTENCE
40     GET C$
50     REM · · TEST FOR END OF SENTENCE
60     IF C$ = "." THEN 120
70     REM · · TEST FOR END OF WORD
80     IF C$ = " " THEN 100
90    GOTO 40
100    LET T = T + 1
110   GOTO 40
120   LET T = T + 1
130   REM · · OUTPUT NUMBER OF WORDS IN SENTENCE
140   PRINT "NUMBER OF WORDS"; T
150   STOP
160   END
```

CHAPTER 18

1. a. 16 (see Appendix IV — page 518).

b. All string variables must be declared in a DIM statement (see Appendix IV — page 517).

i.   For a single string the maximum length of the string must be specified.

ii.   For strings in an array both the number of strings and the maximum length of a string must be given.

c. The composite character : = is used for assigning a value to a variable, whereas the character = is used to define a logical operator.

d. The IN operator gives the index of the first occurrence of the first string expression .GUESS$. in the second string expression LEGAL$.

e. // Allows comments to be written on a line, similar to a REM statement in BASIC.

f. The function RND(X, Y) generates a random number as an integer in the range X to Y inclusive.

2. a.
```
    10    PROC SEGA
    20       INPUT I
    30       WHILE I <> 0 DO
    40         IF I > 100 THEN
    50           PRINT "VALUE OF I TOO HIGH"
    60         ELSE
    70           PRINT "VALUE OF I TOO LOW"
    80         ENDIF
    90         INPUT I
    100      ENDWHILE
    110      STOP
    120   ENDPROC SEGA
```

b.
```
    10    PROC SEGB
    20       INPUT "ENTER CHOICE FROM MENU": C$
    30       CODE: = (C$ = "ADD" OR C$ = "SUB" OR C$ = "MLT" OR C$ = "DIV")
    40       WHILE NOT CODE DO
    50         PRINT "ERROR"
    60         INPUT C$
    70       ENDWHILE
    80       CASE C$ OF
    90       WHEN "ADD"
    100        EXEC ONE
    110      WHEN "SUB"
    120        EXEC TWO
    130      WHEN "MLT"
    140        EXEC THREE
    150      WHEN "DIV"
    160        EXEC FOUR
    170      ENDCASE
    180   ENDPROC SEGB
```

c.
```
    10    PROC SEGC
    20       INPUT A, B, C
    30       D: = B * B - 4 * A * C
    40       X: = ABS(D)
    50       CASE X OF
    60       WHEN -1
    70         PRINT "IMAGINERY"
    80       WHEN 0
    90         PRINT "REAL EQUAL"
    100      WHEN I
    110        PRINT "REAL DISTINCT"
    120      ENDCASE
    130   ENDPROC SEGC
```

435

```
       d. 10    PROC SEGD
          20       A : = 1
          30       B : = 1
          40       WHILE B < = 1000 DO
          50          PRINT A, B
          60          A : = A + B
          70          B : = B + A
          80       ENDWHILE
          90    ENDPROC SEGD

3.  c. 10    DIM REPLY$ OF 1, TAXSTATUS$ OF 1
       20    // FIRST LEVEL PROGRAM
       30    REPEAT
       40       EXEC DETAILS
       50       EXEC ALLOWANCES
       60       EXEC TAXCALC
       70       EXEC ANSWER
       80    UNTIL HALT
       90    STOP
      100    //
      110    // SECOND LEVEL PROCEDURES
      120    PROC DETAILS
      130       INPUT "GROSS SALARY" : GROSS
      140       INPUT "TAX STATUS M OR S": TAXSTATUS $
      150       INPUT "NUMBER OF CHILDREN": CHILDREN
      160    ENDPROC DETAILS
      170    //
      180    PROC ALLOWANCES
      190       IF TAXSTATUS $ = "M" THEN
      200          ALLOW: = 2300
      210          IF CHILDREN < > 0 THEN
      220             ALLOW: = ALLOW + 100 * CHILDREN
      230          ENDIF
      240       ELSE
      250          ALLOW: = 1200
      260       ENDIF
      270       TAXINC: = GROSS − ALLOW
      280    ENDPROC ALLOWANCES
      290    //
      300    PROC TAXCALC
      310       IF TAXINC < = 1000 THEN
      320          TAX: = 0
      330       ELSE
      340          IF TAXINC < = 2000 THEN
      350             TAX: = 0.2 * (TAXINC − 1000)
```

```
360      ELSE
370        IF TAXINC < = 4000 THEN
380          TAX: = 0.3 * (TAX INC − 2000) + 200
390        ELSE
400          TAX: = 0.4 * (TAXINC − 4000) + 800
410        ENDIF
420      ENDIF
430    ENDIF
440    PRINT "TAX TO PAY = "; TAX
450  ENDPROC TAXCALC
460  //
470  PROC ANSWER
480  INPUT "NO MORE DATA ANSWER Y OR N": REPLY $
490  HALT: = (REPLY$ = "Y")
500  ENDPROC ANSWER
510  //

d. 10   DIM SCORE (2)
20   //
30   EXEC INITIALISE
40   REPEAT
50     EXEC PLAYGAME
60     EXEC CHANGEPLAYER
70   UNTIL GAMEOVER
80   EXEC WINNERNUMBER
90   STOP
100  PROC INITIALISE
110    SCORE (1): = 0
120    SCORE (2): = 0
130    PLAYER: = 1
140  ENDPROC INITIALISE
150  //
160  PROC PLAYGAME
170    DIE 1: = RND(1, 6)
180    DIE 2: = RND(1, 6)
190    IF DIE 1 = 6 OR DIE 2 = 6 THEN
200      SCORE (PLAYER): = SCORE (PLAYER) + 3
210    ENDIF
220    IF DIE 1 = DIE 2 THEN
230      SCORE (PLAYER): = SCORE (PLAYER) + 3
240    ELSE
250      IF DIE 1 + DIE 2 = 9 THEN
260        SCORE (PLAYER): = SCORE (PLAYER) + 3
270      ENDIF
280    ENDIF
```

437

```
290    GAMEOVER: = (SCORE (PLAYER) = 51)
300    IF SCORE (PLAYER) > 51 THEN
310       SCORE (PLAYER): = SCORE (PLAYER) – 6
320    ENDIF
330    WINNER: = PLAYER
340 ENDPROC PLAYGAME
345 //
350 PROC CHANGEPLAYER
360    IF PLAYER = 1 THEN
370       PLAYER: = 2
380    ELSE
390       PLAYER: = 1
395    ENDIF
400 ENDPROC CHANGEPLAYER
410 //
420 PROC WINNERNUMBER
430    PRINT "WINNING PLAYER IS"; WINNER
440 ENDPROC WINNERNUMBER
450 //
```

Appendix 2

ORDINARY LEVEL G.C.E. COMPUTER STUDIES.

1.   The following computer print-out, listing the numbers of the houses to which each paper is to be delivered, is designed to assist a newsagent in sorting his morning papers.

```
ROSE GARDENS
    FULCHESTER

MAIL 3,6,8,9
SUN 2,5,6,7,11
TELEGRAPH 1,4,9
GUARDIAN 3,8,12
EXPRESS 7,10


PRIMROSE WALK
    FULCHESTER

MAIL 2,3,5,6
SUN 4,7,9
TELEGRAPH 5,6,7
GUARDIAN 1,2,9,10
EXPRESS 1,8,9,12
```

a. Give two reasons why this information in this format is not very helpful to the paper boy.

b. Redraw the print-out in a format more useful to the paper boy explaining why you have used that format.

c. Using the data above describe an algorithm to convert the data into the new format suitable for the paper boy.

[A.E.B.]

2.   Your school introduces a new assessment scheme. For each subject studied the procedure is:

   i.   3 assessments per term are given and a mark out of 10 awarded to each assessment

   ii.   each term the 3 assessments are averaged

   iii.   at the end of the year the best average over the three terms is printed on the pupil's report.

Consider a class of 20 pupils, studying several subjects. During one year each pupil will have 9 assessment marks for each subject. Draw that part of a flowchart (which must be language independent) that will read in the 9 marks for each pupil for one subject and will output.

    i.   the three termly averages for each pupil;

    ii. the best average for each pupil in this subject.

[A.E.B.]

3.   Draw a flowchart to read in a series of positive and negative numbers, ending in the rogue value − 999, and to count and print out the number of positive and the number of negative numbers read in (0 (zeros) are counted as positive numbers).

[A.E.B.]

4.   During the construction and running of a computer program the following types of error may occur;

        Coding,   Syntax,   Logical,   Execution (Runtime)

For **each** of the above,

    a. explain the nature of the error

    b. give a suitable example

    c. describe how each particular error can be dealt with so that the final program is correct.

[A.E.B.]

5.   Using any high level language write a program,

    i.   to read in a piece of prose,

    ii. to count how often the letter "a", and the word "the" occurs in the piece of prose,

    iii. to print out the respective totals.

[A.E.B.]

6.   The following sequence of BASIC statements forms part of a larger program. (A is an array of dimension 20.)

```
70      IF I > 20 THEN 120
80      IF I < 1 THEN 120
90        LET A (I) = N
100       LET I = I + 1
110       GOTO 130
120     PRINT "                              "
130     REM · · CONTINUATION OF PROGRAM
```

Suppose, in each case below, that the statement numbered 70 is about to be executed. For each of the three sets of values of I and N at the time of commencement of execution, state the effect of the above sequence of statements.

i.   I contains   14 N contains   − 7
ii. I contains   21 N contains   10
iii. I contains   − 3 N contains   5

Complete statement 120 by adding a suitable message.

[University of Cambridge Local Examinations Syndicate]

7. a. State what you understand by *program documentation*.

b.

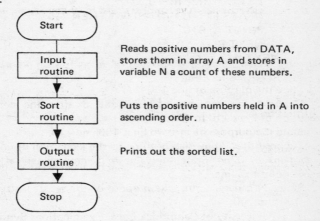

An outline flowchart is given above for arranging in ascending order a set of positive numbers, terminated by a negative number.

    i.   Draw a program flowchart for the *sort routine* which puts the numbers, which have been stored in an array A, into ascending order.

    ii. Dry run your flowchart using the sequence of numbers 1, 5, 3, 2, 6, −1.

[University of Cambridge Local Examinations Syndicate]

8. The following program is designed to find sets of positive whole numbers a, b, c such that $a^2 + b^2 = c^2$ with a and b both less than 100.

```
100     DIM S (100)
110      FOR A = 1 TO 100
120      LET S (A) = A * A
130      NEXT A
140        FOR A = 1 TO 100
150           FOR B = A TO 100
160              LET T = S (A) + S (B)
170              LET C = SQR (T)
180              LET C = INT (C + 0.001)
190              IF ABS (T – C * C) > 0.001 THEN 210
200              PRINT A; B; C
210           NEXT B
220        NEXT A
230     END
```

   i.   State the purpose of line 100.

   ii.   Describe the contents of the array S after the complete execution of lines 110 to 130.

   iii.   State the purpose of the two lines 160 and 170.

   iv.   Suppose that, immediately prior to the execution of line 180, C contains 47.6254. State the value of C immediately after the execution of this line.

   v.   State, in general terms, the purpose of the set of instructions 180, 190 and 200.

   [University of Cambridge Local Examinations Syndicate]

9.   The statements below are part of a BASIC program.

```
100     DIM A (3)
110     FOR J = 1 TO 3
120      LET A (J) = J
130     NEXT J
140     IF N = 1 THEN 180
150     LET T = A (1)
160     LET A (1) = A (2)
170     LET A (2) = T
180     PRINT A (1); A (2); A (3)
```

   a.   What is the purpose of statement 130?

   b.   Write down the output from the program if
   i.   the value contained in N is 1,
   ii.   the value contained in N is 3.

   [University of Cambridge Local Examinations Syndicate]

10. JENNIFER ANDERSON   4C   14   5 STATION ROAD
      PETER AVERY   2L   13   18 HIGH STREET
      DAVID BELLAMY   5A   15   32 ESTELLE ROAD
      CATHERINE BEST   4S   15   154 LOWER ROAD

The data shown above is taken from a file containing data about all the pupils attending a certain school. The data shown gives each pupil's name, class, age and address.

a. With reference to the data above, or otherwise, explain what are meant by the terms *record* and *field*.

b. Describe a validation check which might reasonably be made on the data in the file.

c. Why is it inadvisable to include each pupil's age in the file if the data is to be used for a period of time?

What would be better to use instead of the *age* of each pupil?
      [University of Cambridge Local Examinations Syndicate]

11. a. Draw a flowchart for an algorithm to read in a sequence of characters, character by character, ending with an asterisk ($*$), and then to print out
    i.   the number of vowels (A, E, I, O, U),
    ii.   the number of consonants,
    iii. the number of characters which are not letters,
    iv. the number of occurrences of the letter P.

b. When a program is written for this algorithm a number of variables will be used.

List the variables you would use, stating the purpose of each.

c. Dry run your flowchart for the following data: PETER PAN*
      [University of Cambridge Local Examinations Syndicate]

12. The algebraic expression $x = a + b \times c$ means that the values expressed by b and c are first multiplied together **before** the value of a is added to their product. Programming languages must also make provision for this so-called *precedence of arithmetic operators* (ie. of the symbols for addition, subtraction, multiplication, division and raising to a power).

For a **named** high level language with which you are familiar:

a. give the equivalent symbols for the algebraic (arithmetic) symbols;

b. explain the rules for creating an arithmetic statement and the rules for the arithmetic operator precedence.

c. Convert the following algebraic expressions into arithmetic statements in the high level language which you have named:
    i. $x = (a + b)c$;

ii. $x = \dfrac{a^{3\ 4}b}{c \times d}$

d. Explain with an example the purpose of built-in library functions.

[Oxford Local Examinations]

13. a. Explain what is meant in programming by a *loop* and a *subroutine,* showing clearly the differences between them, and explain why the use of loops and subroutines is advantageous.

b. What types of documentation should be provided for a program written by a candidate as project work for this examination?

[Oxford Local Examinations]

14. For a named high level language explain as clearly as you can:
   i.   the character set;
   ii. the rules for naming variables;
   iii. a statement that enables a decision to be made;
   iv. the statements for printing the value of a simple variable, with suitable headings and layout.

[Oxford Local Examinations]

15. Draw a flowchart and write a program to work out and print how much money a customer owes for a quarter's gas bill. The input to your program is the customer's code number and the number of units of gas used in the quarter. The output, which should be self-explanatory and printed at the top of a page, should include the customer's code number, the number of units used, and the cost. The cost is worked out as follows:

   there is a standing charge of £1.50,
   the first 52 units cost 19.3 p each,
   the remaining units cost 15.3 p each.

[Oxford Local Examinations]

16. Explain clearly and in detail, in the correct sequence, the stages in the preparation of a program, from the first idea to the production of useful results; in your explanation show where errors may occur, what their effects would be on the subsequent stages, and how you would detect them.

[Oxford Local Examinations]

17. a. What is a *subroutine?* State with reasons what advantages there are in using subroutines.

b. i. Explain what is meant by the term *array*.
   ii. In a named high level language describe the facilities for using arrays.

c. Convert the box shown in Figure 1 from a flow diagram into a statement in a named high level language. Explain your variable names and the rules for forming them, and the grammatical rules of your statement.

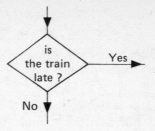

Figure 1.

[Oxford Local Examinations]

18. a. Explain why high level languages are used for programming.

b. Name a high level language, and use it to write a program, including explanatory remarks (comments), which reads a value for each of the variables a and b, and calculates and prints a headed table of the function

$$y = b\sqrt{(1 + \frac{x^2}{a^2})},$$

for values of x from 0 to 10 in steps of 0.5.

[Oxford Local Examinations]

19. A comparison is being made of the relative popularity of two television programmes. A number of viewers complete questionnaires in which they state whether they are male or female, and give marks, from 1 (meaning very bad) to 9 (meaning very good), for each of the two programmes. If a viewer misses a programme its mark is entered as 0.

Draw a flowchart to work out from these questionnaires:

  i.   the number of men and the number of women in the sample;

  ii.   the total number of viewers who watched the first programme, the total number who watched the second programme, and the number who watched neither;

  iii. the average score for those men who watched each programme, and the corresponding average score for the women;

  iv. which programme was preferred by the men, and which was preferred by the women.

[Oxford Local Examinations]

ALTERNATIVE ORDINARY LEVEL G.C.E. COMPUTER STUDIES.

[Oxford and Cambridge Schools Examination Board]

20. Give an algorithm written in English for sorting a sequence of positive integers into ascending or descending order.

Apply your algorithm to the sequence

| 3 | 9 | 1 | 5 | 2 | 7 | 10 | 4 | 8 | 6 |

21. Write down some high-level language statements that will cause the instructions contained within them to be repeated a specified number of times. Give also a flowchart that explains the action arising from your statements.

22. When writing a computer program, why is accompanying document-ation considered important? Describe the components you think ought to be part of the documentation for a large program.

23. For three different backing store devices, compare how each could be used, firstly, for serial access and, secondly, for random access of the data contained within them.

24. Give two algorithms for the control of a number of data items, firstly, where the number of items is given as part of the data and, secondly, where the items are terminated by a rogue. (Do not produce programming code as your answer.)

25. Write down a section of high-level language code that will add together the numbers stored in corresponding location of two arrays A(m,n) and B(m,n) and store the result in the first array. Also give a flowchart to explain the action of your code.

ADVANCED LEVEL G.C.E. COMPUTER SCIENCE.

26. a. Construct a flow diagram for a sorting algorithm which uses as little storage space as possible but which may require n^2 comparisons to sort n numbers into ascending order.

b. For sorting large quantities of information (n large) which are initially in random sequence, it is desirable to have more efficient algorithms. Give an account (which need **not** include a flow diagram) of one such algorithm.

c. Explain how you estimate the number of comparisons needed for each of the algorithms you have described and what penalties are paid for the efficiency of the faster algorithm.

[Oxford Local Examinations]

27. a. Describe the structure of a file designed to hold the names, addresses and accounts of the users of electricity supplied by an area board. Your description should indicate the items held and the way in which they would be arranged.

b. Construct flow diagrams for routines designed to process such a file, held on magnetic tape, so as to (i) insert a set of new users into the file, (ii) record a set of payments made by the majority of the users, (iii) scan the file to produce demand notes for overdue accounts.

[Oxford Local Examinations]

28. a. Three bus routes run from A to B, B to C and A to C respectively. Construct a flow diagram for a program which stores the time tables for the three routes, accepts a time by which a traveller is ready to leave A and produces a statement of his arrivals and departures on his way to C **by the fastest route.**

b. Explain what additional problems would arise if your program were to be generalized for any two points in a network of routes covering a country.

[Oxford Local Examinations]

29. Each of five supermarket check-out desks can scan an item number for a computer which returns the cost of the item and adds this cost to the total for the bill which is printed on demand.

i.   Construct a flow diagram, and write a program in a high level language for this purpose. The program should also provide totals of the day's takings for each desk and takings for the super-market as a whole.

ii.   Explain one further calculation which could usefully be added to this program.

[Oxford Local Examinations]

30. a. Construct a flow diagram for a routine designed to place a file of 100 000 items from a magnetic tape into a sequential order defined by *keys* within the items. Your answer should make clear what types of storage are to be used.

b. Described the documentation which should be provided:

i.   to users of such a routine;

ii.   to a programmer maintaining it. [Explain what is meant by program maintenance.]

c. To sort n items into sequence, some routines make a number of comparisons of order n^2, while others make a number of order n log n. Give an example of a method of each type and explain how the difference between them arises.

[Oxford Local Examinations]

31. a. Some methods of data preparation employ an external medium such as paper tape or punched cards, while others involve direct input to a computer store. Describe how each type of method could be used in the preparation of data for electricity bills and discuss their relative advantages for this purpose.

b. Why is it desirable that programs for calculating electricity bills should contain a number of checks on the data? Discuss the various types of error that can arise and explain what action can be taken in a program when they are detected.

[Oxford Local Examinations]

32. a. Construct a flow diagram for a program to display month, day, hour, minute and second, assuming that a device is available which sets an indicator once each second. The indicator can be cleared by the program.

b. How would you arrage for the user of such a display to set it to the correct time?

[Oxford Local Examinations]

33. Construct a flow diagram, and write a program in a high level language, to take as data the weights and prices of a series of grocery items, and to produce as results the price per gram weight of each item, suitably identified. It should also produce a table showing the numbers of items with prices per gram weight not exceeding 10p, 20p, 30p, and 40p.

Credit will be given for comments in your program text which relate it to the flow diagram.

[Oxford Local Examinations]

34. Describe how each of the following steps is carried out when developing a program in a high-level language:

a. flowcharting

b. allocation of data areas to hold program variables and constants

c. coding

d. detection of syntax errors

e. detection of logic errors.

Indicate any differences in the steps for programs written in a low-level language.

[A.E.B.]

35. A company holds on magnetic tape information relating to sales of items. Each record contains the fields:

Item number
Description
Number sold in 1978
Number sold in 1979
Number currently in stock.

These records are sequenced in ascending order on item number.

The file is to be processed to produce separate listings of

    i.   specific records whose item numbers are held in ascending sequence on paper-tape,

    ii. records of items for which the sales have fallen from 1978 to 1979:

The file is very long and should only be read once; the company has two printers one of which is dedicated to error messages.

Explain how you would overcome the problem of producing separate listings, and draw a flowchart for a procedure to carry out the required processing of the file.

[A.E.B.]

36. A professional society keeps, on magnetic tape, records relating to its members, and each record contains the following fields:

Membership Number
Name
Address
Grade
Subscription
Code

The code is "P" if subscription has been paid, "space" otherwise and these records are sequenced on membership number.

From this file, invoices are prepared and despatched to members. Two months later, cards are prepared for those members who have paid their subscription or resigned. The record on the card contains the fields:

Membership Number
Code

The code is "P" if paid and "R" if resigned.

These cards are also sequenced on membership number, and are to be used to update the master file, by deleting resignations and changing the code of those members who have paid. It is also required to produce a list of members who have not paid and have not resigned.

Draw a flowchart for a program to update the master file.

[A.E.B.]

37. A construction company uses a computer to calculate weekly bonus payments to its fifty workers.

A magnetic tape file contains information relating to the various jobs on which workers may be employed. Each record contains the following fields:

Job number
Description
Target hours per worker (an integer value).

The records are sequenced in ascending job number order.

At the end of every week a card is punched for each job on which each worker has been employed.

The cards contain the following fields:

Job number
Works number (in the range 1 to 50)
Hours taken to complete the job (an integer value)

The cards have not been validated, but are in ascending job number order.

Note that each worker may have been employed on several jobs and many workers may work on the same job.

Each worker receives a bonus of 50p per hour for each hour by which the target hours exceed the hours taken to complete the job. Bonuses may not be negative.

Draw a flowchart for a procedure to calculate and output the total bonus payable to each worker, in ascending works number order.

You may assume, if you wish, that each file is terminated by a dummy record containing a high value job number.

[A.E.B.]

CITY & GUILDS OF LONDON INSTITUTE BASIC CERTIFICATE IN COMPUTER PROGRAMMING.

38. A manufacturing organisation runs a stock control and costing system for its retail outlets. The details of the sale are forwarded to the data processing department at the head office.

The details of a sale are as follows:

branch code   (3 digits)
product code   (3 digits, 1 letter)
quantity   (less than 1000)

The cost of each product is held on a file.

Write a program which will

a. read the file of costs into the main store (ie. IAS) of the computer (which is assumed to be big enough)

b. read the sale details from a suitable computer input medium, checking their validity

c. using a *table look-up* method, find the cost of the product

d. print out any invalid input record indicating whether the input is in incorrect format or the product code is not listed in the cost table

e. write the original input data plus the cost to a file, in readiness for further processing.

39. The record on a personnel file is as follows:

surname	20 characters
forename	10 characters
other initials	4 letters
date of birth — day	2 digits
month	2 digits
year	2 digits
sex	M or F (for Male or Female)
marital status	M or S (for Married or Single)
Works number	4 digits

Write a program to print out or display a histogram which illustrates the percentage of male employees in each age group.

The histogram should be laid out as follows

```
         Percentage of Male Employees for Each Age
          0  1  2  3  4  5  6  7  8  9  10 .....
Age  15         x
     16         x
     17            x
     18               x
     19               x
     20                  x
      —
      —
      —
      —
     65               x
     66         x
over 66      x
```

40. A file is stored on magnetic tape in ascending sequence. Write a program to produce a magnetic tape file which is the reverse order of the original file, ie. with the same key item, the order of the file is in descending sequence.

451

The following restrictions apply.

No sort subroutine or program should be used.

The working store (IAS) of the computer will only hold a small proportion of the total number of records in the file.

No random access backing store is available.

Two additional magnetic tape decks are available for intermediate storage.

Only forward-reading magnetic tape decks are available.

41. The record in a file in a pay system contains the following items necessary to print the pay slip.

Gross pay and additions to pay	Deductions from pay	Name
Basic pay	P.A.Y.E.	Works number
Overtime pay	National Insurance	Bank code
Bonus	Pension contribution	Account number
Holiday pay	Car Park	Tax Code
	Sports Club	National Insurance number
	Union dues	Taxable pay this year
		Tax paid this year

Write a program to read the file, defining suitable formats for the items, and print out the pay slips as illustrated in the following example.

Gross pay & additions	Deductions		
BASIC PAY 200.67 OVERTIME 10.50 BONUS 50.00	PAYE 26.65 NAT. INSURANCE 8.44 PENSION 10.00 CAR PARK 40	*Taxable pay this month* 261.17	
		Taxable pay this year 2050.50	*Schnerde Frankfurter Company Ltd. Pay statement for period ending*
		Tax paid this year 240.45	31 Dec. 76
		nett pay 215.68	
Total 261.17	*Total* 45.49		

Bank Code	Account No.	Tax Code	NI Number	Works Number	
22-75-11	12345678	223H	AB 98 76 41 B	0123	D.C. Smith

NOTE: Italic letters are preprinted on form.

Capital letters and numbers are printed by the Computer.

If any of the additions to or deductions from pay are nil, they should not be listed on the pay slip.

The taxable pay this month is the sum of gross pay and additions. The nett pay is the taxable pay less deductions. The date has been input as a parameter at the beginning of the print program.

CITY & GUILDS OF LONDON INSTITUTE.
COMPUTER PROGRAMMING AND INFORMATION PROCESSING.

42. A student record file contains the following information on each student attending a course

surname	20 characters
initials	5 characters
course code	6 characters
student reference number	6 digits
personal tutor's surname	20 characters
personal tutor's initials	5 characters.

The file medium is magnetic tape, sequentially organised in ascending order of student reference number.

Write a program which reads in a list of personal tutors' names and prints for each a list of the names and course codes of those students for whom he is responsible. Appropriate documentation should be provided.

43. Write a subroutine which, given a position in a standard (3 x 3) game of noughts and crosses with 'X' to play, determines the best position in which to place the 'X'. If faced with a lost position, the message *YOU WIN* should be printed. Design your own data structures, and provide suitable documentation.

44. The present value, A, of an amount of money, P, invested for N years at an interest rate of R% is given by the formula

$$A = P (1 + .01R)^N$$

Write an interactive program with a suitable input routine which, given any THREE of the variables (A, P, R, N,) computes and prints the value of the other variable. Document your program fully.

45. Write a program for the marking of multiple-choice examination answers, to the following specification.

Each examination paper has up to 60 questions, and there are exactly five possible answers to each question. At the data preparation stage, these answers are coded as 1, 2, 3, 4 or 5, and a 0 is used to indicate that a question was not attempted. Data input is organised into batches, one for each examination, consisting of:

the examination number, range 0—20
the number of questions on the paper, range 20—60
the set of correct answers, coded as described above
for each candidate: candidate number, range 0-9999
candidate's answers, coded as described above.

For each correct answer, 1 point is scored; for each wrong answer ¼ point is deducted. If a question is not attempted, no penalty is incurred.

The final output for each examination should be a list of the number and the score for each candidate, the latter expressed as a percentage. Document your work fully.

46. Write a subroutine which, given a crossword skeleton in the form of a two-dimensional array in which white squares are represented by the value 'O' and black squares by '—1', will put the number of the clues into the appropriate positions.

For example,

```
 0   -1    0    0    0                1   -1    2    3    0
 0    0    0    0   -1                4    5    0    0   -1
 0    0   -1    0    0  will become   6    0   -1    7    8
-1    0    0    0    0               -1    9   10    0    0
 0    0    0   -1    0               11    0    0   -1    0
```

which represents the following crossword skeleton

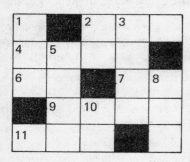

Figure iii.

In figure iii (above), it can be seen that not all the white squares are numbered. A square receives a number if
EITHER

a. it is in column 1 or has a black square to its immediate left, and has a white square to its immediate right,

454

OR

b. it is in row 1 or has a black square immediately above it, and has a white square immediately below. The clue numbers are allocated starting at one and increasing in steps of one, on a row by row basis.

47. A trainee typist requires sets of practice material based on those characters which she has currently learnt. Write an interactive program which will generate groups of randomly selected characters chosen from a given list. Assume that there exists a library routine for the generation of a random real number, r, in the range $0.0 < r < 1.0$, and that each time the routine is called a new value of r is obtained.

The program should

a. ask for a list of the characters it is to use

b. output the list and ask whether it is correct

c. if the response at step (b) is *NO,* return to step (a), and after three successive *NO* responses abort the program with an appropriate message to the user.

d. if the response at step (b) is *YES,* generate and output 50 groups of five characters, randomly selected from the list input at step (a). Five groups should be output on each line

e. regard any other response at step (b) as though it were *NO*

f. return to step (a).

Step (a) should include allowance for terminating the session when the user has finished.

THE BRITISH COMPUTER SOCIETY PART I EXAMINATIONS. OPTION B: PROGRAMMING.

48. In documenting a program, what information would you include to describe how the program was tested? How could this information be used during program maintenance?

49. An array of keys K_1, K_2 ... K_n is held in ascending order. A routine is to be provided which searches for a given key and returns its index if found, or 0 otherwise.

Describe, by means of flowcharts or otherwise, algorithms for the routine which use

    i.   a linear search

and ii.   a binary search.

Under what conditions would you choose a linear rather than a binary search algorithm?

50. A program is required to compute the mean and variance of an array of numbers x_i, $i = 1$ to N.

The formulae required are

$$\text{mean} = \sum_{i=1}^{N} x_i/N$$

$$\text{variance} = \sum_{i=1}^{N} (x_i - \text{mean})^2/N \quad \text{or} \quad \sum_{i=1}^{N} x_i^2/N - \text{mean}^2$$

State, with reasons, which formula you would use to compute the variance
   i.   to improve program efficiency and
   ii. to improve the accuracy of the results.

51. Discuss this statement.

"All programs should be completely tested".

A subroutine SORT(N, A) sorts N integers stored in A_1 to A_N into non-decreasing order in A. Describe in detail how you would test such a routine.

52. Specify the documentation necessary for a program.

Indicate the special requirements for a program which is a member of a suite of programs.

How is documentation continued when the program is maintained?

53. Discuss the errors in
   i.   syntax
   ii.   semantics
   iii. execution

which occur during the development of a program. Illustrate each situation with at least one example from a standard high level language.

54. Explain what is meant by *modularity* when it is used to refer to the structure of a program. State the advantages and disadvantages of modularity when used in the design of a suite of programs for a commercial application.

Appendix 3

ECMA
EUROPEAN COMPUTER MANUFACTURERS ASSOCIATION

STANDARD ECMA-55

Minimal BASIC

January 1978

BRIEF HISTORY

The first version of the language BASIC, acronym for Beginner's All-purpose Symbolic Instruction Code, was produced in 1964 at the Dartmouth College in the USA. This version of the language was oriented towards interactive use. Subsequently, a number of implementations of the language were prepared, that differed in part from the original one.

In 1974, the ECMA General Assembly recognized the need for a standardized version of the language, and in September 1974 the first meeting of the ECMA Committee TC 21, BASIC, took place. In January 1974, a corresponding committee, X3J2, had been founded in the USA.

Through a strict co-operation it was possible to maintain full compatibility between the ANSI and ECMA draft standards. The ANSI one was distributed for public comments in January 1976, and a number of comments were presented by ECMA.

A final version of the ECMA Standard was prepared at the meeting of June 1977 and adopted by the General Assembly of ECMA on Dec. 14, 1977 as Standard ECMA—55.

Table of Contents.

1. SCOPE

This Standard ECMA—55 is designed to promote the interchangeability of BASIC programs among a variety of automatic data processing systems. Subsequent Standards for the same purpose will describe extensions and enhancements to this Standard. Programs conforming to this Standard, as opposed to extensions or enhancements of this Standard, will be said to be written in "Minimal BASIC".

This Standard establishes:

— the syntax of a program written in Minimal BASIC.

— The formats of data and the precision and range of numeric representations which are acceptable as input to an automatic data processing system being controlled by a program written in Minimal BASIC.

— The formats of data and the precision and range of numeric representations which can be generated as output by an automatic data processing system being controlled by a program written in Minimal BASIC.

— The semantic rules for interpreting the meaning of a program written in Minimal BASIC.

— The errors and exceptional circumstances which shall be detected and also the manner in which such errors and exceptional circumstances shall be handled.

Although the BASIC language was originally designed primarily for interactive use, this Standard describes a language that is not so restricted.

The organization of the Standard is outlined in Appendix 1. The method of syntax specification used is explained in Appendix 2.

2. REFERENCES

ECMA—6   :   7-Bit Input/Output Coded Character Set, 4th Edition
ECMA—53   :   Representation of Source Programs

3. DEFINITIONS.

For the purposes of this Standard, the following terms have the meanings indicated.

3.1   BASIC

A term applied as a name to members of a special class of languages which possess similar syntaxes and semantic meanings; acronym for Beginner's All-purpose Symbolic Instruction Code.

3.2   Batch-mode

The processing of programs in an environment where no provision is made for user interaction.

461

3.3   End-of-line

The character(s) or indicator which identifies the termination of a line. Lines of three kinds may be identified in Minimal BASIC: program lines, print lines and input reply lines. End-of-line may vary between the three cases and may also vary depending upon context. Thus, for example, an end of input line may vary on a given system depending on the terminal being used in interactive or batch mode.

Typical examples of end-of-line are carriage-return, carriage-return line-feed, and end of record (such as end of card).

3.4   Error

A flaw in the syntax of a program which causes the program to be incorrect.

3.5   Exception

A circumstance arising in the course of executing a program which results from faulty data or computations or from exceeding some resource constraint. Where indicated certain exceptions (non-fatal exceptions) may be handled by the specified procedures; if no procedure is given (fatal exceptions) or if restrictions imposed by the hardware or operating environment make it impossible to follow the given procedure, then the exception shall be handled by terminating the program.

3.6   Identifier

A character string used to name a variable or a function.

3.7   Interactive mode

The processing of programs in an environment which permits the user to respond directly to the actions of individual programs and to control the commencement and termination of these programs.

3.8   Keyword

A character string, usually with the spelling of a commonly used or mnemonic word, which provides a distinctive identification of a statement or a component of a statement of a programming language.

The keywords in Minimal BASIC are: BASE, DATA, DEF, DIM, END, FOR, GO, GOSUB, GOTO, IF, INPUT, LET, NEXT, ON, OPTION, PRINT, RANDOMIZE, READ, REM, RESTORE, RETURN, STEP, STOP, SUB, THEN and TO.

3.9   Line

A single transmission of characters which terminates with an end-of-line.

3.10 Nesting

A set of statements is nested within another set of statements when:

— the nested set is physically contiguous, and

— the nesting set (divided by the nested set) is non-null.

3.11 Print zone

A contiguous set of character positions in a printed output line which may contain an evaluated print statement element.

3.12 Rounding

The process by which the representation of a value with lower precision is generated from a representation of higher precision taking into account the value of that portion of the original number which is to be omitted.

3.13 Significant digits

The contiguous sequence of digits between the high-order non-zero digit and the low-order non-zero digit, without regard for the location of the radix point. Commonly, in a normalized floating point internal representation, only the significant digits of a representation are maintained in the significance.

NOTE: The Standard requires that the ability of a conforming implementation to accept numeric representations be measured in terms of significant digits rather than the actual number of digits (that is including leading or trailing zeroes) in the representation.

3.14 Truncation

The process by which the representation of a value with lower precision is generated from a representation of higher precision by merely deleting the unwanted low order digits of the original representation.

4. CHARACTERS AND STRINGS

4.1 General Description

The character set for BASIC is contained in the ECMA 7-bit coded character set. Strings are sequences of characters and are used in BASIC programs as comments (see 19), as strings constants (see 6), or as data (see 15).

4.2 Syntax

1.	letter	=	A/B/C/D/E/F/G/H/I/J/K/L/M/N/O/P/Q/ R/S/T/U/V/W/X/Y/Z
2.	digit	=	0/1/2/3/4/5/6/7/8/9
3.	string-character	=	quotation-mark / quoted-string-character
4.	quoted-string-	=	exclamation-mark / number-sign / dollar-sign / percent-sign / ampersand / apostrophe left-parenthesis / right-parenthesis / asterisk / comma / solidus / colon / semi-colon / less-than-sign / equals-sign / greater-than-sign / question-mark / circumflex-accent / underline / unquoted -string-character
5.	unquoted-string character	=	space / plain-string-character
6.	plain-string-character	=	plus-sign / minus-sign / full-stop / digit / letter
7.	remark-string	=	string-character*
8.	quoted-string	=	quotation-mark quoted-string-character* quotation-mark
9.	unquoted-string	=	plain-string-character / plain-string-character unquoted-string-character* plain-string-character

4.3 Examples

ANY CHARACTERS AT ALL (?!*!!) CAN BE USED IN A "REMARK".
"SPACES AND COMMAS CAN OCCUR IN QUOTED STRINGS."
COMMAS CANNOT OCCUR IN UNQUOTED STRINGS.

4.4 Semantics

The letters shall be the set of upper-case Roman letters contained in the ECMA 7-bit coded character set in positions 4/1 to 5/10.

The digits shall be the set of arabic digits contained in the ECMA 7-bit coded character set in positions 3/0 to 3/9.

The remaining string-characters shall correspond to the remaining graphic characters in position 2/0 to 2/15, 3/10 to 3/15 and in positions 5/14, 5/15 of the ECMA 7-bit coded character set.

The names of characters are specified in Table 1.

The coding of characters is specified in Table 2; however, this coding applies only when programs and/or input/output data are exchanged by means of coded media.

4.5 Exceptions

None.

4.6   Remarks

Other characters from the ECMA 7-bit coded character set (including control characters) may be accepted by an implementation and may have a meaning to some other processor (such as an editor but have no prescribed meaning within this Standard. Programs containing characters other than the string-characters described above are not standard-conforming programs.

The several kinds of characters and strings described by the syntax correspond to the various uses of strings in a BASIC program. Remark-strings may be used in remark-statements (see 19). Quoted-strings may be used as string-constants (see 6). Unquoted-strings may be used in addition to quoted-strings as data elements (see 17) without being enclosed in quotation marks; unquoted-strings cannot contain leading or trailing spaces.

5.   PROGRAMS

5.1   General Description

BASIC is a line-oriented language. A BASIC program is a sequence of lines, the last of which shall be an end-line and each of which contains a keyword. Each line shall contain a unique line-number which serves as a label for the statement contained in that line.

5.2   Syntax

1. program   = block* end-line
2. block   = (line/for-block)*
3. line   = line-number statement end-of-line
4. line-number   = digit digit? digit? digit?
5. end-of-line   = [implementation-defined]
6. end-line   = line-number end-statement end-of-line
7. end-statement = END
8. statement   = data-statement / def-statement /
                     dimension-statement / gosub-statement /
                     goto-statement / if-then-statement /
                     input-statement / let-statement /
                     on-goto-statement / option-statement /
                     print-statement / randomize-statement /
                     read-statement / remark-statement /
                     restore-statement / return-statement /
                     stop-statement

5.3   Examples
999 END

5.4 Semantics

A BASIC program shall be composed of a sequence of lines ordered by line-numbers, the last of which contains an end-statement. Program lines shall be executed in sequential order, starting with the first line, until

— some other action is dictated by a control statement, or
— an exception condition occurs, which results in a termination of the program, or
— a stop-statement or end-statement is executed.

Special conventions shall be observed regarding spaces. With the following exceptions, spaces may occur anywhere in a BASIC program without affecting the execution of that program and may be used to improve the appearance and readability of the program.

Spaces shall not appear:

— at the beginning of a line
— within keywords
— within numeric constants
— within line numbers
— within function or variable names
— within two-character relation symbols

All keywords in a program shall be preceded by at least one space and, if not at the end of a line, shall be followed by at least one space.

Each line shall begin with a line-number. The values of the integers represented by the line-numbers shall be positive nonzero; leading zeroes shall have no effect. Statements shall occur in ascending line-number order.

The manner in which the end of a statement line is detected is determined by the implementation; e.g. the end-of-line may be a carriage-return character, a carriage-return character followed by a line-feed character, or the end of a physical record.

Lines in a standard-conforming program may contain up to 72 characters; the end-of-line indicator is not included within this 72 character limit.

The end-statement serves both to mark the physical end of the main body of a program and to terminate the execution of the program when encountered.

5.5 Exceptions
None.

5.6 Remarks

Local editing facilities may allow for the entry of statement lines in any order and also allow for duplicate line-numbers and lines containing only a line-number. Such editing facilities usually sort the program into the proper order and in the case of duplicate line-numbers, the last line entered with that line-number is retained. In many implementations, a line containing only a line-number (without trailing spaces) is usually deleted from the program.

6. CONSTANTS

6.1 General Description

Constants can denote both scalar numeric values and string values.

A numeric-constant is a decimal representation in positional notation of a number. There are four general syntactic forms of (optionally signed) numeric constants:

—	implicit point representation	sd . . . d
—	explicit point unscaled representation	sd . . drd . . d
—	explicit point scaled representation	sd . . drd . . dEsd . . d
—	implicit point scaled representation	sd . . dEsd . . d

where:

- d   is a decimal digit,
- r   is a full-stop
- s   is an optional sign, and
- E   is the explicit character E.

A string-constant is a character string enclosed in quotation marks (see 4).

6.2 Syntax

1. numeric-constant = sign? numeric-rep
2. sign   = plus-sign / minus-sign
3. numeric-rep   = significand exrad?
4. significand   = integer full-stop? / integer? fraction
5. integer   = digit digit*
6. fraction   = full-stop digit digit*
7. exrad   = E sign? integer
8. string-constant = quoted-string

6.3 Examples

1	500	−21.	.255	1E10
5E−1	.4E+1			
"XYZ"		"X − 3B2"		"1E10"

6.4 Semantics

The value of a numeric-constant is the number represented by that constant. "E" stands for "times ten to the power"; if no sign follows the symbol "E", then a plus sign is understood. Spaces shall not occur in numeric-constants.

A program may contain numeric representations which have an arbitrary number of digits, though implementations may round the values of such representations to an implementation-defined precision of not less than six significant decimal digits. Numeric constants can also have an arbitrary number of digits in the exrad, though nonzero constants whose magnitude is outside an implementation-defined range will be treated as exceptions. The implementation-defined range shall be at least 1E−38 to 1E+38. Constants whose magnitudes are less than machine infinitesimal shall be replaced by zero, while constants whose magnitudes are larger than machine infinity shall be diagnosed as causing an overflow.

A string-constant has as its value the string of all characters between the quotation marks; spaces shall not be ignored. The length of a string-constant, i.e. the number of characters contained between the quotation-marks, is limited only by the length of a line.

6.5 Exceptions

The evaluation of a numeric constant causes an overflow (non-fatal, the recommended recovery procedure is to supply machine infinity with the appropriate sign and continue).

6.6 Remarks

Since this Standard does not require that strings with more than 18 characters be assignable to string variables (see 7), conforming programs can use string constants with more than 18 characters only as elements in a print-list.

It is recommended that implementations report constants whose magnitudes are less than machine infinitesimal as underflows and continue.

7. VARIABLES

7.1 General Description

Variables in BASIC are associated with either numeric or string values and, in the case of numeric variables, may be either simple variables or references to elements of one or two dimensional arrays; such references are called subscripted variables.

Simple numeric variables shall be named by a letter followed by an optional digit.

Subscripted numeric variables shall be named by a letter followed by one or two numeric expressions enclosed within parentheses.

String variables shall be named by a letter followed by a dollar sign.

Explicit declarations of variable types are not required; a dollar-sign serves to distinguish string from numeric variables, and the presence of a subscript distinguishes a sub-scripted variable from a simple one.

7.2 Syntax

1. variable = numeric-variable / string-variable
2. numeric-variable = simple-numeric-variable / numeric-array-element
3. simple-numeric-variable = letter digit?
4. numeric-array-element = numeric-array- name subscript
5. numeric-array-name = letter
6. subscript = left-parenthesis numeric-expression (comma numeric-expression)? right-parenthesis
7. string-variable = letter dollar-sign

7.3 Examples

X	A5	V(3)	W(X,X+Y/2)
S$	C$		

7.4 Semantics

At any instant in the execution of a program, a numeric-variable is associated with a single numeric value and a string-variable is associated with a single string value. The value associated with a variable may be changed by the execution of statements in the program.

The length of the character string associated with a string-variable can vary during the execution of a program from a length of zero characters (signifying the null or empty string) to 18 characters.
Simple-numeric-variables and string-variables are declared implicitly through their appearance in a program.

A subscripted variable refers to the element in the one or two dimensional array selected by the value(s) of the subscript(s). The value of each subscript is rounded to the nearest integer. Unless explicitly declared in a dimension statement, subscripted variables are implicly declared by their first appearance in a program. In this case the range of each subscript is from zero to ten inclusive, unless the presence of an option-statement indicates that the range is from one to ten inclusive. Subscript expressions shall have values within the appropriate range (see 18).

The same letter shall not be the name of both a simple variable and an array, nor the name of both a one-dimensional and a two-dimensional array.

There is no relationship between a numeric-variable and a string-variable whose names agree except for the dollar-sign.

At the initiation of execution the values associated with all variables shall be implementation-defined.

7.5   Exceptions
A subscript is not in the range of the explicit or implicit dimensioning bounds (fatal).

7.6   Remarks
Since initialization of variables is not specified, and hence may vary from implementation to implementation, programs that are intended to be transportable should explicitly assign a value to each variable before any expression involving that variable is evaluated.

There are many commonly used alternatives for associating implementation-defined initial values with variables; it is recommended that all variables are recognizably undefined in the sense that an exception will result from any attempt to access the value of any variable before that variable is explicitly assigned a value.

8.   EXPRESSIONS

8.1   General Description
Expressions shall be either numeric-expressions or string-expressions.

Numeric-expressions may be constructed from variables, constants, and function references using the operations of addition, subtraction, multiplication, division and involution.

String-expressions are composed of either a string-variable or a string-constant.

8.2   Syntax

1.	expression	=	numeric-expression / string-expression
2.	numeric-expression	=	sign? term (sign term)*
3.	term	=	factor (multiplier factor)*
4.	factor	=	primary (circumflex-accent primary)*
5.	multiplier	=	asterisk / solidus
6.	primary	=	numeric-variable / numeric-rep / numeric-function-ref / left-parenthesis numeric-expression right-parenthesis
7.	numeric-function-ref	=	numeric-function-name argument-list?
8.	numeric-function-name	=	numeric-defined-function / numeric-supplied-function

9.   argument-list   = left-parenthesis argument / right-parenthesis
10. argument   = numeric-expression
11. string-expression = string-variable / string-constant

8.3   Examples

$3*X - Y^2$ $A(1) + A(2) + A(3)$ $2^{(-X)}$

$-X/Y$ $SQR(X^2 + Y^2)$

8.4   Semantics

The formation and evaluation of numeric-expressions follows the normal algebraic rules. The symbols circumflex-accent, asterisk, solidus, plus-sign and minus-sign represent the operations of involution, multiplication, division, addition and subtraction, respectively. Unless parentheses dictate otherwise, involutions are performed first, then multiplications and divisions, and finally additions and subtractions. In the absence of parentheses, operations of the same precedence are associated to the left.

$A-B-C$ is interpreted as $(A-B)-C$, A^B^C as $(A^B)^C$, $A/B/C$ as $(A/B)/C$ and $-A^B$ as $-(A^B)$.

If an underflow occurs in the evaluation of a numeric expression, then the value generated by the operation which resulted in the underflow shall be replaced by zero.

0^0 is defined to be 1, as in ordinary mathematical usage.

When the order of evaluation of an expression is not constrained by the use of parentheses, and if the mathematical use of operators is associative, commutative, or both, then full use of these properties may be made in order to revise the order of evaluation of the expression.

In a function reference, the number of arguments supplied shall be equal to the number of parameters required by the definition of the function.

A function reference is a notation for the invocation of a predefined algorithm, into which the argument value, if any, is substituted for the parameter (see 9 and 10) which is used in the function definition. All functions referenced in an expression shall either be implementation-supplied or be defined in a def-statement. The result of the evaluation of the function, achieved by the execution of the defining algorithm, is a scalar numeric value which replaces the function reference in the expression.

8.5   Exceptions

— Evaluation of an expression results in division by zero (nonfatal, the recommended recovery procedure is to supply machine infinity with the sign of the numerator and continue).

471

- Evaluation of an expression results in an overflow (nonfatal, the recommended recovery procedure is to supply machine infinity with the algebraically correct sign and continue).
- Evaluation of the operation of involution results in a negative number being raised to a non-integral power (fatal).
- Evaluation of the operation of involution results in zero being raised to a negative value (nonfatal, the recommended recovery procedure is to supply positive machine infinity and continue).

8.6   Remarks

The accuracy with which the evaluation of an expression takes place will vary from implementation to implementation. While no minimum accuracy is specified for the evaluation of numeric-expressions, it is recommended that implementations maintain at least six significant decimal digits of precision.

The method of evaluation of the operation of involution may depend upon whether or not the exponent is an integer. If it is, then the indicated number of multiplications may be performed; if it is not, then the expression may be evaluated using the LOG and EXP functions (see 9).

It is recommended that implementations report underflow as an exception and continue.

9.   IMPLEMENTATION SUPPLIED FUNCTIONS

9.1   General Description

Predefined algorithms are supplied by the implementation for the evaluation of commonly used numeric functions.

9.2   Syntax

1.   numeric-supplied-= ABS / ATN / COS / EXP / INT / LOG /
     function   RND / SGN / SIN / SQR / TAN

9.3   Examples

None.

9.4   Semantics

The values of the implementation-supplied functions, as well as the number of arguments required for each function, are described below. In all cases, X stands for a numeric expression.

Function	Function value
ABS(X)	The absolute value of X.
ATN(X)	The arctangent of X in radians, i.e. the angle whose tangent is X. The range of the function is

$$-(pi/2) < ATN(X) < (pi/2)$$

where pi is the ratio of the circumference of a circle to its diameter.

COS(X)	The cosine of X, where X is in radians.
EXP(X)	The exponential of X, i.e. the value of the base of natural logarithms (e = 2,71828 . . .) raised to the power X; if EXP(X) is less than machine infinitesimal, then its value shall be replaced by zero.
INT(X)	The largest integer not greater than X; e.g. INT(1.3) = 1 and INT(−1.3) = −2.
LOG(X)	The natural logarithm of X; X must be greater than zero.
RND	The next pseudo-random number in an implementation-supplied sequence of pseudo-random numbers uniformly distributed in the range $0 <= RND < 1$ (see also 20).
SGN(X)	The sign of X: −1 if $X < 0$, 0 if X = 0 and +1 if $X > 0$.
SIN(X)	The sine of X, where X is in radians.
SQR(X)	The nonnegative square root of X; X must be nonnegative.
TAN(X)	The tangent of X, where X is in radians.

9.5 Exceptions

— The value of the argument of the LOG function is zero or negative (fatal).

— The value of the argument of the SQR function is negative (fatal).

— The magnitude of the value of the exponential or tangent function is larger than machine infinity (nonfatal, the recommended recovery procedure is to supply machine infinity with the appropriate sign and continue).

9.6 Remarks

The RND function in the absence of a randomize-statement (see 20) will generate the same sequence of pseudo-random numbers each time a program is run. This convention is chosen so that programs employing pseudo-random numbers can be executed several times with the same result.

It is recommended that, if the value of the exponential function is less than machine infinitesimal, implementations report this as an underflow and continue.

10. USER DEFINED FUNCTIONS

10.1 General Description

In addition to the implementation supplied functions provided for the convenience of the programmer (see 9), BASIC allows the programmer to define new functions within a program.

The general form of statements for defining functions is

DEF FNx = expression

or   DEF FNx (parameter) = expression

where x is a single letter and a parameter is a simple numeric-variable.

10.2 Syntax

1. def-statement   = DEF numeric-defined-function parameter-list? equals-sign numeric-expression
2. numeric-defined-function   = FN letter
3. parameter-list   = left-parenthesis parameter right-parenthesis
4. parameter   = simple-numeric-variable

10.3 Examples

DEF FNF(X) = X^4 − 1   DEF FNP = 3.14159
DEF FNA(X) = A*X + B

10.4 Semantics

A function definition specifies the means of evaluating the function in terms of the value of an expression involving the parameter appearing in the parameter-list and possibly other variables or constants. When the function is referenced, i.e. when an expression involving the function is evaluated, then the expression in the argument list for the function reference, if any, is evaluated and its value is assigned to the parameter in the parameter-list for the function definition (the number of arguments shall correspond exactly to the number of parameters). The expression in the function definition is then evaluated, and this value is assigned as the value of the function.

The parameter appearing in the parameter-list of a function definition is local to that definition, i.e. it is distinct from any variable with the same name outside of the function definition. Variables which do not appear in the parameter-list are the variables of the same name outside the function definition.

A function definition shall occur in a lower numbered line than that of the first reference to the function. The expression in a def-statement is not evaluated unless the defined function is referenced.

If the execution of a program reaches a line containing a def-statement, then it shall proceed to the next line with no other effect.

A function definition may refer to other defined functions, but not to the function being defined. A function shall be defined at most once in a program.

10.5   Exceptions
None.

11. LET STATEMENT

11.1   General Description
A let-statement provides for the assignment of the value of an expression to a variable. The general syntactic form of the let-statement shall be

LET variable = expression

11.2   Syntax
1. let-statement   = numeric-let-statement / string-let-statement
2. numeric-let-statement   = LET numeric-variable equals-sign numeric-expression
3. string-let-statement   = LET string-variable equals-sign string-expression

11.3   Examples
LET P = 3.14159
LET A(X, 3) = SIN(X)*Y + 1
LET A\$ = "ABC"
LET A\$ = B\$

11.4   Semantics
The expression is evaluated (see 8) and its value is assigned to the variable to the left of the equals sign.

11.5   Exceptions
A string datum contains too many characters (fatal).

12. CONTROL STATEMENTS

12.1   General Description
Control statements allow for the interruption of the normal sequence of execution of statements by causing execution to continue at a specified line, rather than at the one with the next higher line number.

The goto-statement
    GO TO line-number
allows for an unconditional transfer.

The if-then-statement
    IF exp1 rel exp2 THEN line-number
where "exp1" and "exp2" are expressions and "rel" is a relational operator, allows for a conditional transfer.

The gosub and return statements
    GO SUB line-number
    RETURN
allow for subroutine calls.

The on-goto-statement
    ON expression GOTO line-number, . . ., line-number
allows control to be transferred to a selected line.

The stop-statement
    STOP
allows for program termination.

12.2 Syntax

1. goto-statement   = GO space* TO line-number
2. if-then-statement = IF   relational-expression   THEN   line-number
3. relational-   = numeric-expression   relation   numeric-expression / string-expression   equality-relation string-expression
    expression
4. relation   = equality-relation / less-than-sign / greater-than-sign / not-less / not-greater
5. equality-relation = equals-sign / not-equals
6. not-less   = greater-than-sign equals-sign
7. not-greater   = less-than-sign equals-sign
8. not-equals   = less-than-sign greater-than-sign
9. gosub-statement = GO space* SUB line-number
10. return-statement = RETURN
11. on-goto-   = ON numeric-expression GO space* TO line-number (comma line-number)*
    statement
12. stop-statement   = STOP

12.3 Examples

GO TO 999   IF X > Y + 83 then 200
IF A$ < > B$ THEN 550   ON L + 1 GO TO 300, 400, 500

12.4 Semantics

A goto-statement indicates that execution of the program is to be continued at the specified line-number.

If the value of the relational-expression in an if-then-statement is true, then execution of the program shall continue from the specified line-number; if the value of the relational-expression is false, then execution shall be continued in sequence i.e. with the statement on the line following that containing the if-then-statement.

The relation "less than or equal to" shall be denoted by < =. Similarly, "greater than or equal to" shall be denoted by > =, while "not equal to" shall be denoted by < >.

The relation of equality holds between two strings if and only if the two strings have the same length and contain identical sequences of characters.

The execution of the gosub-statement and the return-statement can be described in terms of a stack of line-numbers (but may be implemented in some other fashion). Prior to execution of the first gosub-statement by the program, this stack is empty. Each time a gosub-statement is executed, the line-number of the gosub-statement is placed on top of the stack and execution of the program is continued at the line specified in the gosub-statement. Each time a return-statement is executed, the line-number on top of the stack is removed from the stack and execution of the program is continued at the line following the one with that line-number.

It is not necessary that equal numbers of gosub-statements and return-statements be executed before termination of the program.

The expression in an on-goto-statement shall be evaluated and rounded to obtain an integer, whose value is then used to select a line-number from the list following the GOTO (the line-numbers in the list are indexed from left to right, starting with 1). Execution of the program shall continue at the statement with the selected line-number.

All line-numbers in control-statements shall refer to lines in the program.

The stop-statement causes termination of the program.

12.5 Exceptions
— An attempt is made to execute a return-statement without having executed a corresponding gosub-statement (fatal).
— The integer obtained as the value of an expression in an on-goto-statement is less than one or greater than the numbers in the list (fatal).

13. FOR AND NEXT STATEMENTS

13.1 General Description
The for-statement and next-statement provide for the construction of loops. The general syntactic form of the for-statement and next-statement is

    FOR v = initial-value TO limit STEP increment
    NEXT v

where "v" is a simple numeric variable and the "initial-value", "limit" and "increment" are numeric expressions; the clause "STEP increment" is optional.

13.2 Syntax

1.	for-block	=	for-line for-body
2.	for-body	=	block next-line
3.	for-line	=	line-number for-statement end-of-line
4.	next-line	=	line-number next-statement end-of-line
5.	for-statement	=	FOR control-variable equals-sign initial-value TO limit (STEP increment)?
6.	control-variable	=	simple-numeric-variable
7.	initial-value	=	numeric-expression
8.	limit	=	numeric-expression
9.	increment	=	numeric-expression
10.	next-statement	=	NEXT control-variable

13.3 Examples

```
FOR I = 1 TO 10      FOR I = A TO B STEP −1
NEXT I               NEXT I
```

13.4 Semantics

The for-statement and the next-statement are defined in conjunction with each other. The physical sequence of statements beginning with a for-statement and continuing up to and including the first next-statement with the same control variable is termed a "for-block". For-blocks can be physically nested, i.e. one can contain another, but they shall not be interleaved, i.e. a for-block which contains a for-statement or a next-statement shall contain the entire for-block begun or ended by that statement.

Furthermore, physically nested for-blocks shall not use the same control variable.

In the absence of a STEP clause in a for-statement, the increment is assumed to be +1.

The action of the for-statement and the next-statement is defined in terms of other statements, as follows:

```
    FOR v = initial-value TO limit STEP increment
    (block)
    NEXT v
is equivalent to:
    LET own1 = limit
    LET own2 = increment
    LET v = initial-value
line1 IF (v-own1) * SGN (own2) > 0 THEN Line2
    (block)
    LET v = v + own2
    GOTO line1
line2 REM continued in sequence
```

Here v is any simple-numeric-variable, own1 and own2 are variables associated with the particular for-block and not accessible to the programmer, and line1 and line2 are line-numbers associated with the particular for-block and not accessible to the programmer. The variables own1 and own2 are distinct from similar variables associated with other for-blocks. A program shall not transfer control into a for-body by any statement other than a return statement (see 12).

13.5 Exceptions
None.

13.6 Remarks
Where arithmetic is approximate (as with decimal fractions in a binary machine), the loop will be executed within the limits of machine arithmetic. No presumptions about approximate achievement of the end test are made. It is noted that in most ordinary situations where machine arithmetic is truncated (rather than rounded), such constructions as

FOR X = 0 TO 1 STEP 0.1

will work as the user expects, even though 0.1 is not representable exactly in a binary machine. If this is indeed the case, then the construction

FOR X = 1 TO 0 STEP —0.1

will probably not work as expected.

As specified above, the value of the control-variable upon exit from a for-block via its next-statement is the first value not used; if exit is via a control-statement, the control-variable retains the value it has when the control-statement is executed.

The variables "own1" and "own2" associated with a for-block are assigned values only upon entry to the for-block through its for-statement.

14. PRINT STATEMENT

14.1 General Description
The print-statement is designed for generation of tabular output in a consistent format.

The general syntactic form of the print-statement is

PRINT item p item p . . . p item

where each item is an expression, a tab-call, or null, and each punctuation mark p is either a comma or a semi-colon.

14.2   **Syntax**
   1.   print-statement   =   PRINT print-list?
   2.   print-list   =   (print-item? print-separator)* print-item?
   3.   print-item   =   expression / tab-call
   4.   tab-call   =   TAB left-parenthesis numeric-expression right-parenthesis
   5.   print-separator   =   comma / semi-colon

14.3   **Examples**
PRINT X   PRINT "X" EQUALS", 10
PRINT X; (Y + Z)/2   PRINT X, Y
PRINT   PRINT , , , X
PRINT TAB(10); A$; "IS DONE."

14.4   **Semantics**
The execution of a print-statement generates a string of characters for transmission to an external device. This string of characters is determined by the successive evaluation of each print-item and print-separator in the print-list.

Numeric-expressions shall be evaluated to produce a string of characters consisting of a leading space if the number is positive or a leading minus-sign if the number is negative followed by the decimal representation of the absolute value of the number and a trailing space. The possible formats for the decimal representation of a number are the same as those described for numeric-constants in 6 and are used as follows.

Each implementation shall define two quantities, a significance-width d to control the number of significant decimal digits printed in numeric representations, and an exrad-width e to control the number of digits printed in the exrad component of a numeric representation. The value of d shall be at least six and the value of e shall be at least two.

Each number that can be represented exactly as an integer with d or fewer decimal digits is output using the implicit point unscaled representation.

All other numbers shall be output using either explicit point unscaled notation or explicit point scaled notation. Numbers which can be represented with d or fewer digits in the unscaled format no less accurately than they can be represented in the scaled format shall be output using the unscaled format. For example, if $d = 6$, then 10^{-6} is output as .000001 and 10^{-7} is output as 1.E−7.

Numbers represented in the explicit point unscaled notation shall be output with up to d significant decimal digits and a full-stop; trailing zeroes in the fractional part may be omitted. A number with magnitude less than 1 shall be represented with no digits to the left of the full-stop. This form requires up to d+3 characters counting the sign, the full-stop and the trailing space.

Numbers represented in the explicit point scaled notation shall be output in the format

significand E sign integer

where the value x of the significand is in the range $1 <= x < 10$ and is to be represented with exactly d digits of precision, and where the exrad component has one to e digits. Trailing zeroes may be omitted in the fractional part of the significand and leading zeroes may be omitted from the exrad. This form requires up to d+e+5 characters counting the two signs, the fullstop, the "E" and a trailing space.

String-expressions shall be evaluated to generate a string of characters.

The evaluation of the semi-colon separator shall generate the null string, i.e. a string of zero length.

The evaluation of a tab-call or a comma separator depends upon the string of characters already generated by the current or previous print-statements. The "current line" is the (possibly empty) string of characters generated since the last end-of-line was generated. The "margin" is the number of characters, excluding the end-of-line character, that can be output on one line and is defined by the implementation. The "columnar position" of the current line is the print position that will be occupied by the next character output to that line; print positions are numbered consecutively from the left, starting with position one.

Each print-line is divided into a fixed number of print zones, where the number of zones and the length of each zone is implementation defined. All print zones, except possibly the last one on a line, shall have the same length. This length shall be at least d+e +6 characters in order to accomodate the printing of numbers in explicit point scaled notation as described above and to allow the comma separator to move the printing mechanism to the next zone as described below.

The purpose of the tab-call is to set the columnar position of the current line to the specified value prior to printing the next print-item. More precisely, the argument of the tab-call is evaluated and rounded to the nearest integer n. If n is less than one, an exception occurs. If n is greater than the margin m, then n is reduced by an integral multiple of m so that it is in the range $1 <= n <= m$; i.e. n is set equal to

$$n - m * INT ((n - 1)/m).$$

If the columnar position of the current line is less than or equal to n, then spaces are generated, if necessary, to set the columnar position to n; if the columnar position of the current line is greater than n, then an end-of-line is generated followed by enough spaces to set the columnar position of the new current line to n.

The evaluation of the comma-separator generates one or more spaces to set the columnar position to the beginning of the next print zone, unless the current print zone is the last on the line, in which case an end-of-line is generated.

If the print list does not end in a print-separator, then an end-of-line is generated and added to the characters generated by the evaluation of the print-list.

If the evaluation of any print-item in a print-list would cause the length of a nonempty line to exceed the margin, then an end-of-line is generated prior to the characters generated by that print-item. Subsequently, if the evaluation of a print-item generates a string whose length is greater than the margin, then end-of-lines are inserted after every m characters in the string, where m is the margin value.

14.5 Exceptions

The evaluation of a tab-call argument generates a value less than one (nonfatal: the recommended recovery procedure is to supply one and continue).

14.6 Remarks

The comma-separator allows the programmer to tabulate the printing mechanism to fixed tab settings at the end of each print zone.

A completely empty print-list will generate an end-of-line, thereby completing the current line of output. If this line contained no characters, then a blank line results.

A print line on a typical terminal might be divided into five print zones of fifteen print positions each.

15. INPUT STATEMENT

15.1 General Description

Input-statements provide for user interaction with a running program by allowing variables to be assigned values that are supplied by a user. The input-statement enables the entry of mixed string and numeric data, with data items being separated by commas. The general syntactic form of the input-statement is

    INPUT variable, . . . , variable

15.2   Syntax

1.   input-statement   =   INPUT variable-list
2.   variable-list   =   variable (comma variable)*
3.   input-prompt   =   [implementation-defined]
4.   input-reply   =   input-list end-of-line
5.   input-list   =   padded-datum (comma padded-datum)*
6.   padded-datum   =   space* datum space*
7.   datum   =   quoted-string / unquoted-string

15.3   Examples

INPUT X   INPUT X, A$, Y(2)   INPUT A, B, C
3.14159   2, SMITH, −3   25, 0, −15

15.4   Semantics

An input-statement causes the variables in the variable-list to be assigned, in order, values from the input-reply. In the interactive mode, the user of the program is informed of the need to supply data by the output of an input-prompt. In batch mode, the input-reply is requested from the external source by an implementation-defined means. Execution of the program is suspended until a valid input-reply has been supplied.

The type of each datum in the input-reply shall correspond to the type of the variable to which it is to be assigned; i.e., numeric-constants shall be supplied as input for numeric-variables, and either quoted-strings or unquoted-strings shall be supplied as input for string-variables. If the response to input for a string-variable is an unquoted-string, leading and trailing spaces shall be ignored (see 4).

If the evaluation of a numeric datum causes an underflow, then its value shall be replaced by zero.

Subscript expressions in the variable-list are evaluated after values have been assigned to the variables preceding them (i.e. to the left of them) in the variable-list.

No assignment of values in the input-reply shall take place until the input-reply has been validated with respect to the type of each datum, the number of input items, and the allowable range for each datum.

15.5   Exceptions

—   The type of datum does not match the type of the variable to which it is to be assigned (nonfatal, the recommended recovery procedure is to request that the input-reply be re-supplied).

—   There is insufficient data in the input-list (nonfatal, the recommended recovery procedure is to request that the input-reply be resupplied).

—   There is too much data in the input-list (nonfatal, the recommended recovery procedure is to request that the input-reply be resupplied).

> — The evaluation of a numeric datum causes an overflow (non-fatal, the recommended recovery procedure is to request that the input-reply be resupplied).
> — A string datum contains too many characters (nonfatal, the recommended recovery procedure is to request that the input-reply be resupplied).

15.6 Remarks

This Standard does not require an implementation to perform any editing of the input-reply, though such editing may be performed by the operating environment.

It is recommended that the input-prompt consists of a question-mark followed by a single space.

This Standard does not require an implementation to output the input-reply.

It is recommended that implementations report an underflow as an exception and allow the input-reply to be resupplied.

16. READ AND RESTORE STATEMENTS

16.1 General Description

The read-statement provides for the assignment of values to variables from a sequence of data created from data-statements (see 17). The restore-statement allows the data in the program to be reread. The general syntactic forms of the read and restore statements are

    READ variable, . . . , variable
    RESTORE

16.2 Syntax

1. read-statement = READ variable-list
2. restore-statement = RESTORE

16.3 Examples

    READ X, Y, Z   READ X(1), A$, C

16.4 Semantics

The read-statement causes variables in the variable-list to be assigned values, in order, from the sequence of data (see 17). A conceptual pointer is associated with the data sequence. At the initiation of execution of a program, this pointer points to the first datum in the data sequence. Each time a read-statement is executed, each variable in the variable-list in sequence is assigned the value of the datum indicated by the pointer and the pointer is advanced to point beyond that datum.

The restore-statement resets the pointer for the data sequence to the beginning of the sequence, so that the next read-statement executed will read data from the beginning of the sequence once again.

The type of a datum in the data sequence shall correspond to the type of the variable to which it is to be assigned; i.e., numeric-variables require unquoted-strings which are numeric-constants as data and string-variables require quoted-strings or unquoted-strings as data. An unquoted-string which is a valid numeric representation may be assigned to either a string-variable or a numeric-variable by a read-statement.

If the evaluation of a numeric datum causes an underflow, then its value shall be replaced by zero.

Subscript expressions in the variable-list are evaluated after values have been assigned to the variables preceding them (i.e. to the left of them) in the list.

16.5 Exceptions

— The variable-list in a read-statement requires more data than are present in the remainder of the data-sequence (fatal).

— An attempt is made to assign a string datum to a numeric variable (fatal).

— The evaluation of a numeric datum causes an overflow (non-fatal, the recommended recovery procedure is to supply machine infinity with the appropriate sign and continue).

— A string datum contains too many characters (fatal).

16.6 Remarks

It is recommended that implementations report an underflow as exception and continue.

17. DATA STATEMENT

17.1 General Description

The data-statement provides for the creation of a sequence of representations for data elements for use by the read-statement. The general syntactic form of the data-statement is

    DATA datum, . . . , datum

where each datum is either a numeric constant, a string-constant or an unquoted string.

17.2 Syntax

1. data-statement = DATA data-list
2. data-list = datum (comma datum)*

17.3 Examples

DATA 3.14159, PI, 5E−10, '',''

17.4 Semantics

Data from the totality of data-statements in the program are collected into a single data sequence. The order in which data appear textually in the totality of all data-statements determines the order of the data in the data sequence.

If the execution of a program reaches a line containing a data-statement, then it shall proceed to the next line with no other effect.

17.5 Exceptions
None.

18. ARRAY DECLARATIONS

18.1 General Description
The dimension-statement is used to reserve space for arrays. Unless declared otherwise, all array subscripts shall have a lower bound of zero and an upper bound of ten. Thus the default space allocation reserves space for 11 elements in one-dimensional arrays and 121 elements in two-dimensional arrays. By use of a dimension-statement, the subscript(s) of an array may be declared to have an upper bound other than ten. By use of an option-statement, the subscripts of all arrays may be declared to have a lower bound of one.

The general syntactic form of the dimension-statement is
> DIM declaration, . . . , declaration

where each declaration has the form
> letter (integer)

or letter (integer , integer)

The general syntactic form of the option-statement is
> OPTION BASE n

where n is either 0 or 1.

18.2 Syntax
1. dimension-statement = DIM array declaration (comma array-declaration)*
2. array-declaration = numeric-array-name left-parenthesis bounds right-parenthesis
3. bounds = integer (comma integer)?
4. option-statement = OPTION BASE (0/1)

18.3 Examples
DIM A (6), B(10, 10)

18.4 Semantics
Each array-declaration occurring in a dimension-statement declares the array named to be either one or two dimensional according to whether one or two bounds are listed for the array. In addition, the bounds specify the maximum values that subscript expressions for the array can have.

The declaration for an array, if present at all, shall occur in a lower numbered line than any reference to an element of that array. Arrays that are not declared in any dimension-statement are declared implicitly to be one or two dimensional according to their use in the program, and to have subscripts with a maximum value of ten (see 7).

The option-statement declares the minimum value for all array subscripts; if no option-statement occurs in a program, this minimum is zero. An option-statement, if present at all, must occur in a lower-numbered line than any dimension-statement or any reference to an element of an array. If an option-statement specifies that the lower bound for array subscripts is one, then no dimension-statement in the program may specify an upper bound of zero. A program may contain at most one option-statement.

If the execution of a program reaches a line containing a dimension-statement or an option-statement, then it shall proceed to the next line with no other effect.

An array can be explicitly dimensioned only once.

18.5 **Exceptions**
None.

19. REMARK STATEMENT

19.1 **General Description**
The remark-statement allows program annotation.

19.2 **Syntax**
1.   remark-statement =   REM remark-string

19.3 **Examples**
REM FINAL CHECK

19.4 **Semantics**
If the execution of a program reaches a line containing a remark-statement, then it shall proceed to the next line with no other effect.

19.5 **Exceptions**
None.

20. RANDOMIZE STATEMENT

20.1 **General Description**
The randomize-statement overrides the implementation-predefined sequence of pseudo-random numbers as values for the RND function, allowing different (and unpredictable) sequences each time a given program is executed.

20.2 **Syntax**
1.   randomize-   =   RANDOMIZE
     statement

20.3 **Examples**
RANDOMIZE

20.4 Semantics

Execution of the randomize-statement shall generate a new un-predictable starting point for the list of pseudo-random numbers used by the RND function (see 9).

20.5 Exceptions

None.

20.6 Remarks

In the case of implementations which do not have access to a rand-omizing device such as a real-time clock, the randomize-statement may be implemented by means of an interaction with the user.

NAME	GRAPHIC
Space	
Exclamation-mark	!
Quotation-mark	"
Number-sign	#
Dollar-sign	$
Percent-sign	%
Ampersand	&
Apostrophe	'
Left-parenthesis	(
Right-parenthesis	)
Asterisk	*
Plus-sign	+
Comma	,
Minus-sign	—
Full-stop	.
Solidus	/
Digits	0 – 9
Colon	:
Semi-colon	;
Less-than-sign	<
Equals-sign	=
Greater-than-sign	>
Question-mark	?
Letters	A – Z
Circumflex-accent	^
Underline	—

TABLE 1

b₇	0	0	0	0	1	1	1	1
b₆	0	0	1	1	0	0	1	1
b₅	0	1	0	1	0	1	0	1

b₄ b₃ b₂ b₁				0	1	2	3	4	5	6	7
0	0	0	0	0	NUL	TC₇ (DLE)	SP	0	@	P	`	p
0	0	0	1	1	TC₁ (SOH)	DC₁	!	1	A	Q	a	q
0	0	1	0	2	TC₂ (STX)	DC₂	"	2	B	R	b	r
0	0	1	1	3	TC₃ (ETX)	DC₃	#	3	C	S	c	s
0	1	0	0	4	TC₄ (EOT)	DC₄	¤	4	D	T	d	t
0	1	0	1	5	TC₅ (ENQ)	TC₈ (NAK)	%	5	E	U	e	u
0	1	1	0	6	TC₆ (ACK)	TC₉ (SYN)	&	6	F	V	f	v
0	1	1	1	7	BEL	TC₁₀ (ETB)	'	7	G	W	g	w
1	0	0	0	8	FE₀ (BS)	CAN	(	8	H	X	h	x
1	0	0	1	9	FE₁ (HT)	EM	)	9	I	Y	i	y
1	0	1	0	10	FE₂ (LF)	SUB	*	:	J	Z	j	z
1	0	1	1	11	FE₃ (VT)	ESC	+	;	K	[	k	{
1	1	0	0	12	FE₄ (FF)	IS₄ (FS)	,	<	L	\	l		
1	1	0	1	13	FE₅ (CR)	IS₃ (GS)	−	=	M	]	m	}
1	1	1	0	14	SO	IS₂ (RS)	.	>	N	^	n	‾
1	1	1	1	15	SI	IS₁ (US)	/	?	O	_	o	DEL

TABLE 2

NOTE: *In the 7-bit and in the 8-bit code tables two characters are allocated to pos. 2/4, namely $ and ¤ . In any version of the codes a single character is to be allocated to this position. The character of the 7-bit or of the 8-bit coded character set, which corresponds to the character $ of the Minimal BASIC character set is either $ or ¤ (¤ in the International Reference Version).*

The same applies to pos. 2/3 for the characters £ and #, the latter being the character of the International Reference Version.

APPENDIX 1

Organization of the Standard

This Standard is organized into a number of sections, each of which covers a particular feature of BASIC. Sections 4 to 20 are divided into sub-sections, as follows.

Sub-section 1. General Description
This sub-section briefly describes the features of BASIC to be treated and indicates the general syntactic form of these features.

Sub-section 2. Syntax
The exact syntax of features of the language is described in a modified context-free grammar or Backus-Naur Form. The details of this method of syntax specification are described in Appendix 2.

In order to keep the syntax reasonably simple the syntax specification will allow it to describe some constructions which, strictly speaking, are not legal according to this Standard, e.g. it will allow the generation of the statement

        100 LET X = A(1) + A(1, 2)

in which the array A occurs with differing numbers of subscripts. Rather than ruling such constructions out by a more complicated syntax, this Standard shall instead rule them out in the semantics.

Sub-section 3. Examples
A short list of valid examples that can be generated by certain of the syntax equations in sub-section 2 is given.

Sub-section 4. Semantics
The semantic rules in this Standard serve two purposes. First, they rule out certain constructions which are permitted by the syntax, but which have no valid meaning according to this Standard. Second, they assign a meaning to the remaining constructions.

Sub-section 5. Exceptions
An exception occurs when an implementation recognizes that a program may not perform or is not performing in accordance with this Standard. All exceptions described in this section shall be reported unless some mechanism is provided in an enhancement to this Standard that has been invoked by the user to handle exceptions.

Where indicated, certain exceptions may be handled by the specified procedures; if no procedure is given, or if restrictions imposed by the hardware or the operating environment make it impossible to follow the given procedures, then the exception must be handled by terminating the program. Enhancements to this Standard may describe mechanisms for controlling the manner in which exceptions are reported and handled, but no such mechanisms are specified in this Standard.

This Standard does not specify an order in which exceptions shall be detected or processed.

Sub-section 6. Remarks
This sub-section contains remarks which point out certain features of this Standard as well as remarks which make recommendations concerning the implementation of a BASIC language processor in an operating environment.

APPENDIX 2

Method of Syntax Specification

The syntax, through a series of rewriting rules known as "productions", defines syntactic objects of various types, such as "program" or "expression", and describes which strings of symbols are objects of these types.

In the syntax, upper-case letters, digits, and (possibly hyphenated) lower-case words are used as "metanames", i.e. as names of syntactic objects. Most of these metanames are defined by rewriting rules in terms of other metanames. In order that this process terminate, certain metanames are designated as "terminal" metanames, and rewriting rules for them are not included in the syntax. All terminal metanames occur for the first time and are defined in Section 4. It should be noted in particular that all upper-case letters are terminal metanames which denote themselves.

We illustrate further details of the syntax by considering some examples. In Section 12 we find the production

        gosub-statement = GO space* SUB line-number

which indicates that a "gosub-statement" consists of the letters G, O, any number of spaces, S, U, and B followed by a line number.

What is a "line number"? In Section 5, the production

        line-number = digit digit? digit? digit?

indicates that a "line-number" is a "digit" followed by up to three other "digits" (the question mark is a syntactic operator indicating that the object it follows may or may not be present).

What is a "digit"? In Section 4, the production

        digit = 0 / 1 / 2 / 3 / 4 / 5 / 6 / 7 / 8 / 9

indicates that a "digit" is either a "0", a "1", . . . or a "9" (the solidus is a syntactic operator meaning "or" and is used to indicate that a metaname can be rewritten in one of several ways). Since the digits are terminal metanames (i.e. they do not occur on the left-hand side of any production), our decipherment of the syntax for the "gosub-statement" comes to an end. The semantics in Section 4 identify the digits in terms of the characters they represent.

An asterisk is a syntactic operator like the question-mark, and it indicates that the object it follows may occur any number of times, including zero times, in the production.

For example

        integer = digit digit*

indicates that an "integer" is a "digit" followed by an arbitrary number of other "digits".

Parentheses may be used to group sequences of metanames together. For example

variable-list = variable (comma variable)*

defines a "variable-list" to consist of a "variable" followed by an arbitrary number of other "variables" separated by "commas".

When several syntactic-operators occur in the same production, the operators "?" and "*" take precedence over the operator "/".

Spaces in the syntax are used to separate hyphenated lower-case words from each other. Special conventions are observed regarding spaces in BASIC programs (see Section 5). The syntax as described generates programs which contain no spaces other than those occurring in remarks, in certain string constants, or where the presence of a space is explicitly indicated by the metaname "space".

Additional spaces may be inserted to improve readability provided that the restrictions imposed in Section 5 are observed.

APPENDIX 3

Conformance

There are two aspects of conformance to this language Standard : conformance by a program written in the language, and conformance by an implementation which processes such programs.

A program is said to conform to this Standard only when

— each statement contained therein is a syntactically valid instance of a statement specified in this Standard,
— each statement has an explicitly valid meaning specified herein, and
— the totality of statements compose an instance of a valid program which has an explicitly valid meaning specified herein.

An implementation is said to conform to this Standard only when

— it accepts and processes programs conforming to this Standard,
— it reports reasons for rejecting any program which does not conform to this Standard,
— it interprets errors and exceptional circumstances according to the specifications of this Standard,
— its interpretation of the semantics of each statement of a standard-conforming program conforms to the specification in this Standard,
— its interpretation of the semantics of a standard-conforming program as a whole conforms to the specifications in this Standard,
— it accepts as input, manipulates, and can generate as output numbers of at least the precision and range specified in this Standard, and
— it is accompanied by a reference manual which clearly defines the actions taken in regard to features which are called "undefined" or "implementation-defined" in this Standard.

This Standard does not include requirements for reporting specific syntactic errors in the text of a program. Implementations conforming to this Standard may accept programs written in an enhanced language without having to report all constructs not conforming to this Standard. However, whenever a statement or other program element does not conform to the syntactic rules given herein, either an error shall be reported or the statement or other program element shall have an implementation-defined meaning.

494

APPENDIX 4

Implementation-defined Features

A number of the features defined in this Standard have been left for definition by the implementor. However, this will not affect portability, provided that the limits recommended in the various sections are respected. The way these features are implemented shall be defined in the user- or system-manual of the specific implementation.

The following is a list of implementation-defined features:

— accuracy of evaluation of numeric expressions (see 8)
— end-of-line (see 5, 14 and 15)
— exrad-width for printing numeric representations (see 14)
— initial value of variables (see 7)
— input-prompt (see 15)
— longest string that can be retained (see 11)
— value of machine infinitesimal (see 6)
— value of machine infinity (see 6)
— margin for output lines (see 14)
— precision for numeric values (see 6)
— print-zone length (see 14)
— pseudo-random number sequence (see 9 and 20)
— significance width for printing numeric representations (see 15)
— means of requesting the input-reply in batch mode (see 15)

Appendix 4

COMAL 80 PROGRAMMING LANGUAGE.

proposal

COMAL 80 (NUCLEUS) DEFINITION
MARCH, 1980.

Background.

The first COMAL language was designed in 1974 by Børge R. Christensen, State Teachers' College, Tønder, Denmark, and Benedict Løfstedt, Department of Computer Science, University of Aarhus.

COMAL (COMmon Algorithmic Language) was constructed as an extension to BASIC, reflecting developments in programming languages and techniques, such as structured programming.

COMAL was intended primarily for use in public schools, but the language has found broader applications.

Since 1974 the language has been extended with additional facilities. Today several different versions of the language exist, supplied by a number of manufacturers.

In October 1979 a group interested in COMAL, including manufacturers, school teachers, and university people, concluded that a standardization of COMAL, in the form of COMAL 80, was needed. A working group was formed to write a proposal for the COMAL 80 language.

The standardization was to contain a nucleus forming the COMAL 80 language and recommendations for extending the language.

This report, written by the working group, is the proposal for the nucleus of the COMAL 80 language. Recommendations for extending the language will appear later.

The members of the working group included:

Arne Christensen, International Computers Limited A/S
Borge R. Christensen, Tonder State Teachers' College
Steffen Dhyrberg, International Computers Limited A/S
H. B. Hansen, Roskilde University Center
Rolf Molich, Dansk Data Elektronik Aps.
Jorgen Olsen, RC Computer A/S
Jesper Barfod, Digitek Data og Instrumentering
Tom Osterby (editor), Technical University of Denmark.

Other manufacturers, companies, and groups have followed the work with great interest.

The group grants free permission to reproduce this report for using the COMAL 80 language.

General Information.

COMAL 80 is a general purpose programming language intended for use by non-export programmers.

COMAL 80 has facilities for writing structured programs.

The COMAL 80 language system is designed to operate in an interactive environment. COMAL statements are entered directly from the user's terminal and checked immediately for syntactical errors.

Execution of programs is also done in interactive mode. Normally the system will include facilities for debugging. These facilities are not part of the standard.

Description of the COMAL 80 Language.

The language is described in the following order — program, statements, expressions, variables, constants, and characters. The description of each construction includes a general introduction, the syntactical format, the effect, and notes.

The syntax is specified by means of Backus-Naur notation, extended with the following notation:

{ } : meaning zero, one, or more occurrences
[ ] : meaning zero or one occurrences.

Notes contain remarks concerning use of the construction, including rules, precautions, operation, etc.

Space characters may be included where it is not specifically forbidden.

In the description of the language there are some places where the effect or result is undefined. An implementation might choose to give an error reaction here.

COMAL programs.

Format

⟨comal program⟩ : : = ⟨statement list⟩
⟨statement list⟩ : : =   { ⟨statement⟩ }
⟨statement⟩ : : = ⟨unstructured statement⟩ ¦ ⟨structured statement⟩
⟨unstructured statement⟩ : : = ⟨simple statement⟩ ¦
                    ⟨simple declaration statement⟩
⟨structured statement⟩ : : = ⟨compound statement⟩ ¦
                    ⟨structured declaration statement⟩
⟨simple statement⟩ : : = ⟨assignment statement⟩ ¦ ⟨io statement⟩
                    ⟨goto statement⟩ ¦
                    ⟨procedure call statement⟩ ¦
                    ⟨end statement⟩ ¦ ⟨stop statement⟩
⟨io statement⟩ : : = ⟨read statement⟩ ¦ ⟨restore statement⟩
                    ⟨input statement⟩ ¦
                    ⟨print statement⟩ ¦ ⟨print-using statement⟩
                    ⟨select output statement⟩ ¦
⟨compound statement⟩ : : = ⟨conditional statement⟩
                    ⟨repetitive statement⟩
⟨conditional statement⟩ : : = ⟨if statement⟩ ¦ ⟨case statement⟩
⟨repetitive statement⟩ : : = ⟨for statement⟩ ¦ ⟨while statement⟩ ¦
                    ⟨repeat statement⟩
⟨simple declaration statement⟩ : : = ⟨data declaration⟩
                    ⟨label statement⟩
⟨data declaration⟩ : : = ⟨dim statement⟩ ¦ ⟨data statement⟩
⟨structured declaration statement⟩ : : = ⟨procedure declaration⟩

Input format.

A COMAL program consists of a number of statements. A statement is written on one or more program lines depending on the type of statement.

A program line may begin with a line number and may end with a comment.

If line number is present, then it must be an integer in the range 1 to 9999. The line numbers determine the order in which statements are stored in the program. The line number must be followed by at least one space character. A program line may consist of a line number only. Execution of such a program line has no effect.

A program line may end with a comment. The comment begins with two consecutive slashes (//), and may be followed by any sequence of displayable ASCII characters. A comment is stored, but has no effect on statement execution. Consecutive program lines in a structured statement must have increasing line numbers.

A ⟨simple statement⟩ must be contained within one program line. A program line must contain only one ⟨simple statement⟩.

A ⟨structured statement⟩ may extend over one or more program lines. In the Backus-Naur description of a structured statement each line must correspond to a separate program line.

When a program is run the statements in the program are normally executed in the order in which they are stored. Certain statements can alter the sequence of execution.

Assignment statement.

A statement to assign values to numeric and string variables.

Format

⟨assignment statement⟩ : : = ⟨assignment list⟩
⟨assignment list⟩ : : =⟨assignment⟩ { ; ⟨assignment⟩ }
⟨assignment⟩ : : = ⟨numeric assignment⟩ | ⟨string assignment⟩
⟨numeric assignment⟩ : : =
        ⟨left side⟩ : = ⟨arithmetic expression⟩
⟨left side⟩ : : = ⟨numeric variable⟩ | ⟨procedure identifier⟩
⟨string assignment⟩ : : =
     ⟨string variable⟩ : = ⟨string expression⟩

Statement execution.

a.   The reference to the variable on the left side of ":=" is computed.

b.   The expression, string or numeric, is evaluated.

c.   The result of step b is assigned to the variable on the left side of ':='.

d.   Steps a, b, and c are repeated for all assignments in the assignment list.

Notes.

1.   In an assignment the type of variable and expression must be the same, either numeric or string.

2.   If ⟨string expression⟩ is longer than the string variable, the string expression is right truncated to the length of the variable. If the string expression is shorter than the string variable, the string expression is placed left justified in the string variable or the substring. If the string variable is not a substring, the rest of the string variable is filled with characters indicating 'null' values. If the string variable is a substring, and the string expression is shorter than the substring, the rest of the substring is filled with blanks.

3.   If the string variable is a substring, the start position of the substring must be less than or equal to the length of the string plus one (start

position ⟨ = LEN (string variable) + 1), otherwise the result is unde-fined.

READ statement.

A statement, applied to read values from the list defined by one or more DATA statements, to assign values to string and numeric variables listed in the READ statement.

Format

⟨read statement⟩ : : = READ ⟨variable⟩   { , ⟨variable⟩ }
⟨variable⟩ : : = ⟨numeric variable⟩   ⟨string variable⟩

Notes.

1. READ statements are always used in conjunction with DATA state-ments.
2. The variables listed in the READ statement may be subscripted or simple numeric or string variables.
3. A data element pointer is moved to the next available value in the DATA statement list as values are retrieved for variables in the READ statement. If the number of variables in the READ statement exceeds the number of values in the DATA statement list, a run-time error occurs.
4. The type (numeric or string) of a READ statement variable must match the type of the corresponding data element value; otherwise a run-time error occurs.
5. Reading a value to a string variable follows the same rules as described in the assignment statement.

RESTORE statement.

A statement to reset the data element pointer to the beginning of the DATA statement list.

Format

⟨restore⟩ : : = RESTORE

INPUT statement.

A statement to assign values entered from the user's terminal during program execution to a list of string and/or numeric variables.

Format

⟨input statement⟩ : : =
 INPUT [⟨string constant⟩ :] ⟨variable⟩ { , ⟨variable⟩ } [⟨cont⟩]
⟨variable⟩ : : = ⟨numeric variable⟩   ⟨string variable⟩
⟨cont⟩ : : =   ;

500

Statement execution.

a. A prompt character is output unless a string constant is included, in which case the value of the string constant is output. The standard prompt is a colon (:).

b. The user responds by typing a list of data items, which are assigned to the variables listed in the INPUT statement. The user ends the list of data items by activating the 'end-of-input' key.

c. If ⟨cont⟩ is specified, the printing position is left unchanged; otherwise the printing position will be the first position on the next line.

Notes.

1. Data entered must be of the same type (numeric or string) as the variable in the argument list for which the data is being supplied. Variables in the argument list may be subscripted or unsubscripted.

2. A data item supplied for a numeric variable can be typed in the following form:

   [+ ¦ −] ⟨real number⟩

   One or more spaces can be typed before a numeric value.

3. A separator between two numeric values may be any character not part of a real number. The separator between a numeric value and a string is the first character not included in a real number.

4. If the data entered does not match the type of the current variable, an error will take place; the user can then enter data of the correct type.

5. If the 'end-of-input' key is activated before values have been assigned to all of the variables in the argument list, a prompt character will be output, indicating that further items are expected.

6. Entering a value for a string variable follows the same rules as described in the assignment statement.

7. 'End-of-input' is the only possible separator between two string values.

PRINT statement.

A statement to output values on the user's terminal.

Format

⟨print statement⟩ : : = PRINT [⟨print list⟩ [⟨print end⟩]]
⟨print list⟩ : : = ⟨print element⟩
                     { ⟨print separator⟩ ⟨print element⟩ }
⟨print element⟩ : : = ⟨arithmetic expression⟩ ¦
                     ⟨string expression⟩ ¦ ⟨tab function⟩
⟨print end⟩ : : = ⟨print separator⟩
⟨print separator⟩ : : = , ¦ ;
⟨tab function⟩ : : = TAB (⟨arithmetic expression⟩)

Notes.

1. The print line on a terminal is divided into print zones. The width of a print zone is not part of the standard.

2. If ⟨print separator⟩ is a comma (,) the output of the next element starts from the leftmost position of the next zone. If there are no more zones on the current line, printing continues in the first zone on the next line. If a print element requires more than one zone, the next element is printed in the next free zone. A print element is always printed on one line.

3. If ⟨print separator⟩ is a semicolon (;), the output of the next print element starts from the next character position. A space is printed after a number.

4. The effect of a ⟨print end⟩ is the same as a ⟨print separator⟩ (note 2 and 3). If no ⟨print end⟩ is specified, printing is continued on the first position on the next line.

5. A PRINT statement with no ⟨print list⟩ causes output of an empty line.

6. TAB(exp) is a function to tabulate the printing position for an item in the print list to the column number evaluated from 'exp'. Columns on the print line are numbered 1, 2, ... If ⟨arithmetic expression⟩ evaluates to a column number greater than or equal to the current column number and less than or equal the length of the print line, the value of the expression indicates the new column position. If the equations are not satisfied, the effect of the function is undefined.

PRINT-USING statement.

A statement to output values of items using a specified format.

Format

⟨print-using statement⟩ : : =
    PRINT USING ⟨string expression⟩ : ⟨using list⟩ [⟨using end⟩]
⟨using list⟩ : : = ⟨using element⟩ { , ⟨using element⟩ }
⟨using element⟩ : : = ⟨arithmetic expression⟩
⟨using end⟩ : : = ;

Notes.

1. ⟨string expression⟩ is used as a format string. The characters in this string are treated in the following way:
    #   digit position and sign (sign position required only for negative numbers)
    .   decimal point (only if surrounded by #)

All other characters in the format string are output directly.

2. The effect of ⟨using end⟩ is the same as described in note 4 for the PRINT statement.

3. String variables must not appear in the using list. However the value of a string variable can be output by concatenating it with the string expression.

SELECT OUTPUT statement.

A statement to control the device to which results from a program (PRINT or PRINT USING statement) shall be directed.

Format.

⟨select output statement⟩ : : = SELECT OUTPUT ⟨unit⟩
⟨unit⟩ : : = ⟨string expression⟩

Notes.

1. ⟨string expression⟩ specifies the output device. The names of output devices are not part of the standard.

2. All output from PRINT and PRINT USING will be directed to the unit specified until a new SELECT OUTPUT statement is executed.

GOTO statement.

A statement to transfer control unconditionally to another part of the program.

Format

⟨goto statement⟩ : : = GOTO ⟨label name⟩
⟨label name⟩ : : = ⟨identifier⟩

Notes.

1. A GOTO statement must not transfer control to a statement which is part of another structured statement or a procedure declaration.

2. A GOTO statement transferring control out of one or more structured statements will terminate these statements.

3. Execution of a GOTO statement out of a procedure will cause an error.

EXEC statement.

A statement to activate a procedure defined in a procedure declaration.

Format

⟨procedure call⟩ : : =
     EXEC ⟨procedure identifier⟩ [(⟨actual parameter list⟩)]
⟨actual parameter list⟩ : : =
               ⟨actual parameter⟩ { , ⟨actual parameter⟩ }
⟨actual parameter⟩ : : = ⟨simple variable⟩ |
                         ⟨simple string name⟩ |
                         ⟨numeric array name⟩ |
                         ⟨string vector name⟩ |
                         ⟨arithmetic expression⟩ |
                         ⟨string expression⟩

Statement execution.

a. The procedure designated by ⟨procedure identifier⟩ is activated. Execution is started with the statement after PROC.

b. Execution is continued until an ENDPROC statement is encountered. Then execution is continued with the statement immediately following the EXEC statement.

Notes.

1. The number of actual parameters must be the same as the number of formal parameters in the procedure declaration.

2. The rules for substitution of the formal parameters by actual parameters are the following:

Formal parameter spec.	Actual parameter allowed
⟨simple variable⟩	⟨arithmetic expression⟩
REF ⟨simple variable⟩	⟨simple variable⟩
⟨simple string name⟩	⟨string expression⟩
REF ⟨simple string name⟩	⟨simple string name⟩
REF ⟨numeric array name⟩	⟨numeric array name⟩
REF ⟨string vector name⟩	⟨string vector name⟩

3. An actual parameter which is a ⟨numeric array name⟩ must have the same number of indices as specified for the formal parameter.

END statement.

A statement to terminate execution of the program and to return control to interactive mode.

Format

⟨end statement⟩ : : = END

Note.

1. An END statement will terminate execution of the program. In an interactive environment a prompt is output on the user's terminal.

STOP statement.

A statement to stop execution of the program and to return control to the terminal in interactive mode.

Format

⟨stop statement⟩ : : = STOP

Notes.

1. A STOP statement will terminate execution of the program. A stop indication, including the line number of the stop statement, will be output on the user's terminal.
2. In an interactive environment program execution may be resumed after a STOP statement.
3. In a batch environment execution of a STOP statement has the same effect as the END statement.

IF statement.

A statement to execute one of two blocks of statements depending on whether the value of a logical expression is true or false.

Format

⟨if statement⟩ : : =
       IF ⟨logical expression⟩ THEN ⟨simple statement⟩ ¦
       IF ⟨logical expression⟩ THEN
       ⟨statement list⟩
       [⟨else part⟩]
       ENDIF
⟨else part⟩ : : = ELSE
        ⟨statement list⟩

Statement execution.

a. ⟨logical expression⟩ is evaluated.

b1. If the value is true, the ⟨simple statement⟩ after THEN is executed, otherwise the statement is skipped.

b2. If the value is true, the ⟨statement list⟩ between THEN and ELSE/ ENDIF is executed.

    If the value is false, the ⟨statement list⟩ after ELSE will be executed. If ELSE is not specified, execution will continue at the first statement following ENDIF.

    If none of the executed statements cause transfer of control to another part of the program, execution will continue at the first statement following ENDIF.

CASE statement.

A statement to execute one of several blocks of statements depending on the value of an expression.

Format

⟨case statement⟩ : : = CASE ⟨expression⟩ OF
           ⟨case list element⟩
           { ⟨case list element⟩ }
           [⟨otherwise part⟩]
           ENDCASE
⟨case list element⟩ : : = WHEN ⟨case expression list⟩
           ⟨statement list⟩
⟨case expression list⟩ : : = ⟨expression⟩   , ⟨expression⟩
⟨otherwise part⟩ : : = OTHERWISE
           ⟨statement list⟩

Statement execution

a. The expression after CASE is evaluated.

b. The expressions after WHEN are evaluated one by one until a value is found which is equal to the value obtained in step a.

c. If a matching value is found, the following statement list is executed until the next WHEN, OTHERWISE, or ENDCASE. After this, control is transferred to the first statement following ENDCASE, provided none of the executed statements caused transfer of control to another part of the program.

d. If a matching value is not found, the statement list after OTHERWISE is executed; if OTHERWISE is not present, the CASE statement has no effect, and execution continues with the statement following ENDCASE.

Note.

1. All ⟨expression⟩'s in ⟨case expression list⟩ must be of the same type as ⟨expression⟩ in ⟨case statement⟩.

FOR statement.

A statement to establish the initial, terminating, and incremental values of a control variable, which is used to determine the number of times a statement or a statement list contained in a loop is to be executed. The loop is repeated until the value of the control variable meets the termination condition or until a statement causes transfer of control from the loop.

Format

⟨for statement⟩ : : =
    FOR ⟨control variable⟩ : = ⟨for list⟩ DO ⟨simple statement⟩ ¦
    FOR ⟨control variable⟩ : = ⟨for list⟩ DO
    ⟨statement list⟩
    NEXT ⟨control variable⟩
⟨control variable⟩ : : = ⟨simple numeric variable⟩
⟨for list⟩ : : = ⟨initial value⟩ TO ⟨final value⟩ { STEP ⟨step value⟩ }
⟨initial value⟩ : : = ⟨arithmetic expression⟩
⟨final value⟩ : : = ⟨arithmetic expression⟩
⟨step value⟩ : : = ⟨arithmetic expression⟩

Statement execution.

a.   ⟨initial value⟩, ⟨final value⟩ and ⟨step value⟩ are evaluated. If ⟨step value⟩ is not specified, it is assumed to be +1.

b.   ⟨control variable⟩ is set equal to ⟨initial value⟩.

c.   If ⟨step value⟩ is positive (negative) and ⟨control variable⟩ is greater than (less than) ⟨final value⟩, the termination condition is satisfied, and control passes to the first statement following the corresponding NEXT; otherwise step d is performed.

d1. The statement after DO is executed.

d2. The statement list after DO is executed.

e.   ⟨control variable⟩ is set equal to
    ⟨control variable⟩ + ⟨step value⟩

f.   Step c is executed.

Notes.

1. After the execution of a FOR statement without transfer of control from the loop, the value of ⟨control variable⟩ is the first value satisfying the termination condition.

2. The ⟨control variable⟩ after NEXT is checked against the ⟨control variable⟩ after FOR; if they are not identical, an error occurs.

WHILE statement.

A statement to execute a statement or a statement list repetitively while the value of a logical expression is true.

Format

⟨while statement⟩ : : =
        WHILE ⟨logical expression⟩ DO ⟨simple statement⟩ ¦
        WHILE ⟨logical expression⟩ DO
        ⟨statement list⟩
        ENDWHILE

Statement execution.

a. 〈logical expression〉 is evaluated.

b. If the value of 〈logical expression〉 is false, the termination condition is satisfied and step e is performed.

c1. The statement after DO is executed.

c2. The statement list after DO is executed.

d. Step a is repeated.

e. Control passes to the first statement following the corresponding ENDWHILE, provided no statement caused transfer of control from the WHILE statement during step c2.

REPEAT statement.

A statement to execute a statement list repetitively until the value of a logical expression is true.

Format

〈repeat statement〉 : : = REPEAT
                       〈statement list〉
                       UNTIL 〈logical expression〉

Statement execution.

a. 〈statement list〉 is executed.

b. 〈logical expression〉 is evaluated, provided no statement caused transfer of control from the REPEAT statement during step a.

c. If the value of 〈logical expression〉 is false, step a is repeated.

d. If the value is true, the termination condition is satisfied and control passes to the first statement following UNTIL.

DATA statement.

A statement to provide values to be read to variables appearing in READ statements.

Format

〈data statement〉 : : = DATA 〈value〉 { , 〈value〉 }
〈value〉 : : = [+ —] 〈real number〉 | 〈string constant〉

Notes.

1. The DATA statement is non-executable.

2. The values appearing in the DATA statement(s) form a single list. The first element in this list is the first value in the first DATA statement in the program. The last element in the list is the last value in the last DATA statement.

PROC — ENDPROC statement.

A statement to define a procedure or a function which can be called by means of an EXEC statement or in an arithmetic expression.

Format

⟨procedure declaration⟩ : : =
        ⟨procedure head⟩
        ⟨statement list⟩
        ⟨ENDPROC part⟩
⟨procedure head⟩ : : =
    PROC ⟨procedure identifier⟩ [(⟨formal parameter list⟩)]
⟨ENDPROC part⟩ : : = ENDPROC ⟨procedure identifier⟩
⟨procedure identifier⟩ : : = ⟨dentifier⟩
⟨formal parameter list⟩ : : =
   ⟨formal parameter specification⟩
     { , ⟨formal parameter specification⟩ }
⟨formal parameter specification⟩ : : =
        [REF] ⟨simple variable⟩ ¦
        [REF] ⟨simple string name⟩ ¦
        REF ⟨numeric array name⟩ ([,]) ¦
        REF ⟨string vector name⟩ ( ) ¦

Notes.

1. A procedure declaration specifies that ⟨statement list⟩ is treated as a unit named ⟨procedure identifier⟩.

2. A procedure can be activated only by an EXEC statement or by a function call in an arithmetic expression. Return from the procedure occurs when an ENDPROC statement is executed.

3. Transfer of data between the calling program and the procedure or vice versa can be done using parameters. The transfer of data can also be done using global variables.

4. Formal parameters can be used in ⟨statement list⟩ as simple or sub-scripted variables, simple or subscripted string variables, or actual parameters.

   Formal parameters used as numeric array names or string vector names must specify the dimension of the array in the following way:
       ( ) : one-dimensional array
       (,) : two-dimensional array

5. Whenever the procedure is activated, formal parameters in ⟨statement list⟩ will be assigned the values of (call by value) or replaced by (call by reference) corresponding actual parameters.

Formal specification in the procedure head determines the choice based on the following rules:

⟨formal parameter spec.⟩	equal to
⟨simple variable⟩	call by value
REF ⟨simple variable⟩	call by reference
⟨simple string name⟩	call by value
REF ⟨simple string name⟩	call by reference
REF ⟨numeric array name⟩	call by reference
REF ⟨string vector name⟩	call by reference

The REF before ⟨numeric array name⟩ and ⟨string vector name⟩ must be specified to allow for possible future extensions.

6. Activation of a procedure can take place as a function call in an arithmetic expression. A procedure used in this way should contain at least one assignment statement with the procedure identifier on the left side of ':='.

7. ⟨procedure identifier⟩ after ENDPROC must be the same as ⟨procedure identifier⟩ after PROC, otherwise an error will occur.

8. If the procedure was activated by an EXEC statement, execution of an ENDPROC statement will cause execution to continue with the statement after the EXEC statement. If the procedure was activated by a function call, the value of the function will be used in evaluation of the expression in which the call occurred.

9. Procedures may be called recursively.

Label statement.

A statement to define a label to which control can be transferred by a GOTO statement.

Format

⟨label statement⟩ : : = ⟨label name⟩ :
⟨label name⟩ : : = ⟨identifier⟩

Note.

1. The label statement is non-executable.

DIM statement.

A statement to define storage for one or more numeric array variables or string variables.

Format

⟨dim statement⟩ : : = DIM ⟨declaration⟩ { , ⟨declaration⟩ }
⟨declaration⟩ : : = ⟨numeric array declaration⟩ ¦
            ⟨string variable declaration⟩
⟨numeric array declaration⟩ : : =
  ⟨numeric array name⟩ (⟨max row index⟩ [,⟨max column index⟩])
⟨string variable declaration⟩ : : =
  ⟨simple string name⟩ OF ⟨string length⟩ ¦
  ⟨string vector name⟩ (⟨max subscript⟩) OF ⟨string length⟩
⟨max row index⟩ : : = ⟨simple numeric variable⟩ ¦ ⟨real number⟩
⟨max column index⟩ : : = ⟨simple numeric variable⟩ ¦ ⟨real number⟩
⟨max subscript⟩ : : = ⟨simple numeric variable⟩ ¦ ⟨real number⟩
⟨string length⟩ : : = ⟨simple numeric variable⟩ ¦ ⟨real number⟩

Statement execution.

a.   Storage space is allocated for the numeric array or the string variable for each declaration.

Notes.

1.   A declaration of an array or a string must be executed before it is used in the program.

2.   A numeric array or a string variable may be declared only once. Redimensioning of arrays or strings is not allowed.

3.   If the value for ⟨max row index⟩, ⟨max column index⟩, ⟨max subscript⟩, or ⟨string length⟩ does not evaluate to an integer, rounding is applied.

4.   All of the elements in a declared numeric array are set to a value indicating undefined. A declared string variable is set to null ('''').

Expressions.

Expressions are used in a number of different statements and constructions. An expression may be composed of parentheses, constants, variables (numeric or string), and functions, linked together by operators.

Format

⟨expression⟩ : : = ⟨logical expression⟩ ¦
            ⟨arithmetic expression⟩ ¦
            ⟨string expression⟩

Logical expressions.

A logical expression is used primarily for making the execution of a statement or a statement list conditional, but may also be used in assignment statements or as actual procedure parameters.

511

Format

⟨logical expression⟩ : : = [NOT] ⟨l-expression⟩

⟨l-expression⟩ : : = ⟨logical term⟩ ¦
                  ⟨l-expression⟩ OR ⟨logical term⟩

⟨logical term⟩ : : = ⟨logical operand⟩ ¦
                ⟨logical term⟩ AND ⟨logical operatnd⟩

⟨logical operand⟩ : : = ⟨relation⟩ ¦ (⟨logical expression⟩)

⟨relation⟩ : : = ⟨string relation⟩ ¦ ⟨arithmetic relation⟩

⟨string relation⟩ : : =
    ⟨string expression⟩ ⟨relational operator⟩ ⟨string expression⟩
    ⟨string expression⟩ IN ⟨string expression⟩

⟨arithmetic relation⟩ : : =
    ⟨arithmetic expression⟩
      [⟨relational operator⟩ ⟨arithmetic expression⟩]

⟨relational operator⟩ : : = ⟩ ¦)= ¦ = ¦ ◊ ¦)= ¦)

Notes.

1. The logical operators have the following meaning:

NOT:	A		NOT A
	FALSE	¦	TRUE
	TRUE	¦	FALSE

OR :	A		B		A OR B
	FALSE	¦	FALSE	¦	FALSE
	FALSE	¦	TRUE	¦	TRUE
	TRUE	¦	FALSE	¦	TRUE
	TRUE	¦	TRUE	¦	TRUE

AND:	A		B		A AND B
	FALSE	¦	FALSE	¦	FALSE
	FALSE	¦	TRUE	¦	FALSE
	TRUE	¦	FALSE	¦	FALSE
	TRUE	¦	TRUE	¦	TRUE

2. The relational operators have the following meaning:

    ⟩   : greater than
)= : greater than or equal to
    =   : equal to
    ◊   : not equal to
    ⟨= : less than or equal to
    ⟨   : less than

3. If the relation between the two expressions is satisfied, the value of the relation is TRUE, otherwise FALSE.

4. If ⟨relation⟩ contains only an ⟨arithmetic expression⟩, the relation has the value TRUE, if the value of the expression is not equal to zero, otherwise FALSE.

5. In a ⟨string relation⟩ the two string expressions are compared character by character (from lower towards higher subscripts) on the basis of their ASCII decimal values. If a character in a given position in one string expression has a higher decimal value than the character in the corresponding position in the other string expression, the first string expression is the greater of the two. If the characters in corresponding positions are identical, but one string expression contains more characters than the other, the shorter string expression is the lesser of the two.

6. The IN operator (A\$ IN B\$) gives the index of the first occurrence of the first string expression in the second string expression. If the first string expression is not a substring in the second, the value of IN is 0. If the length of the first string expression is zero (LEN(A\$) = 0), then IN = LEN (B\$) +1.

7. The priorities of logical and relational operators are:

    First   : Relational operators, IN
    Second : NOT
    Third   : AND
    Fourth : OR

    Where two operators have the same priority, evaluation proceeds strictly from left to right. Parentheses can be used to change the priority of logical and relational operators.

Arithmetic expression.

An arithmetic expression is a rule for computing a value of the numeric type. It is primarily used in assignment statements, but may also be used in logical expressions, PRINT statements, CASE statements and FOR statements.

Format

⟨arithmetic expression⟩ : : =   { ⟨monadic operator⟩ } ⟨a-expression⟩
⟨monadic operator⟩ : : = + ¦ —
⟨a-expression⟩ : : = ⟨term⟩ ¦ ⟨a-expression⟩ + ⟨term⟩ ¦
            ⟨a-expression⟩ — ⟨term⟩
⟨term⟩ : : = ⟨factor⟩ ¦ ⟨term⟩ * ⟨factor⟩ ¦
        ⟨term⟩ / ⟨factor⟩ ¦ ⟨term⟩ DIV ⟨factor⟩ ¦
        ⟨term⟩ MOD ⟨factor⟩
⟨factor⟩ : : = ⟨operand⟩ ¦ ⟨factor⟩ ↑ ⟨operand⟩
⟨operand⟩ : : = (⟨arithmetic expression⟩) ¦ ⟨real number⟩ ¦
        ⟨numeric variable⟩ ¦ ⟨system numeric function⟩ ¦
        ⟨numeric function⟩ ¦ (⟨logical expression⟩)
⟨numeric function⟩ : : =
        ⟨procedure identifier⟩ [(⟨actual parameter list⟩)]

Notes.

1. The arithmetic operators have the following meaning:

+	: monadic +	(+A)
—	: monadic —	(—A)
↑	: exponentiation	(A ↑ B)
*	: multiplication	(A * B)
/	: division	(A / B)
DIV	: integer division	(A DIV B)
MOD	: modulus calculation	(A MOD B)
+	: addition	(A + B)
—	: subtraction	(A — B)

    Exponentiation is standardized only for positive A. The result of an integer division (DIV) is standardized only for A $\rangle$ = 0 and B $\rangle$ 0.

    The result of modulus calculation (MOD) is standardized only for A $\rangle$ = 0 and B $\rangle$ 0 (remainder).

2. During evaluation of floating point underflow may occur. In this case the result is set to zero. A floating point overflow will cause a run-time error.

3. A value must be assigned to a numeric variable before it may be used as an operand in an arithmetic expression. If this condition is not satisfied, a run-time error may occur.

4. The priorities of arithmetic operators are:

First	:	monadic + and —
Second	:	↑
Third	:	*, /, DIV, MOD
Fourth	:	+, —

    Where two operators have the same priority, evaluation proceeds strictly from left to right. Parentheses may be used to change the priority of arithmetic operators.

5. If a logical expression is used as an operand, the value TRUE is equivalent to 1 and the value FALSE to 0.

6. In a call of a ⟨numeric function⟩, actual parameters are treated in the same way as actual parameters in an EXEC statement.

System numeric functions.

System numeric functions may be used as operands in arithmetic expression.

The following numeric functions exist:

ABS(X)	Absolute value of X.
ATN(X)	Arctangent of X, result in radians.
COS(X)	Cosine of X, where X is in radians.
EXP(X)	e to the power of X.
LOG(X)	Natural logarithm of X (X > 0).
SIN(X)	Sine of X, where X is in radians.
SQR(X)	Square root of X (X > 0).
TAN(X)	Tangent of X, where X is in radians.
INT(X)	Integer value of X. The largest integer less than or equal to X.
ORD(S$)	The ordinal number of the first character in S$.
LEN(S$)	The current length of S$.

Note.

1. Identifiers must not be the same as names of numeric functions.

Numeric variables.

COMAL includes two types of numeric (real) variables: simple variables and subscripted variables.

Format

⟨numeric variable⟩ : : = ⟨simple variable⟩ ¦
                           ⟨subscripted variable⟩
⟨simple variable⟩ : : = ⟨identifier⟩
⟨subscripted variable⟩ : : =
    ⟨numeric array name⟩ (⟨row index⟩ [, ⟨column index⟩])
⟨numeric array name⟩ : : = ⟨identifier⟩
⟨row index⟩ : : = ⟨arithmetic expression⟩
⟨column index⟩ : : = ⟨arithmetic expression⟩

Notes.

1. A simple variable is referred to by using the identifier.

2. A simple variable may not be declared explicitly. The declaration is made automatically.

3. Subscripted variables are elements in arrays having either one or two dimensions.

4. Array variables must be declared in a DIM statement before they are used. Such a declaration contains the name of the array, its dimension, and the upper bounds for each index.

5. A subscripted variable must satisfy the following:
    1 <= row index <= upper bound for first index
    1 <= column index <= upper bound for second index
    If not, a run-time error occurs.

6. If the arithmetic expression for ⟨row index⟩ or ⟨column index⟩ does not evaluate to an integer, rounding is applied.

7. The value of a ⟨numeric variable⟩ is undefined before a value has been explicitly assigned to it.

String expression.

String expressions are used for assigning values to string variables (in assignment statements), for output (in PRINT statements), CASE statement and in relations.

Format

⟨string expression⟩ : : = ⟨string operand⟩ { + ⟨string operand⟩ }
⟨string operand⟩ : : = ⟨string variable⟩ ¦ ⟨string constant⟩ ¦
                    ⟨system string function⟩
⟨string constant⟩ : : = " " ¦ "⟨sequence of ASCII characters⟩"

Notes.

1. ⟨string constant⟩ can be empty or a sequence of characters, which may include letters, digits, spaces, and special characters except " and non-printable characters.

2. The string operator '+' denotes concatenation.

System string function.

System string functions may be used as operands in string expressions. The following system string function exists:

CHR$(X)   The ASCII character corresponding to the ordinal number X.

String variables.

COMAL 80 contains a type of variable called a string variable. The value of a string variable is a sequence of ASCII characters. There are two types of string variables: simple string variable and string array variable.

Format

⟨string variable⟩ : : = ⟨simple string variable⟩ ¦
⟨subscripted string variable⟩

⟨simple string variable⟩ : : =
⟨simple string name⟩ [(⟨selector⟩)]

⟨subscripted string variable⟩ : : =
⟨string vector name⟩ (⟨index⟩ [, ⟨selector⟩])

⟨simple string name⟩ : : = ⟨simple string identifier⟩$

⟨string vector name⟩ : : = ⟨string vector identifier⟩$

⟨index⟩ : : = ⟨arithmetic expression⟩

⟨selector⟩ : : = ⟨start position⟩ [: ⟨substring length⟩]

⟨start position⟩ : : = ⟨arithmetic expression⟩

⟨substring length⟩ : : = ⟨arithmetic expression⟩

⟨simple string identifier⟩ : : = ⟨identifier⟩

⟨string vector identifier⟩ : : = ⟨identifier⟩

Notes.

1. All string variables contain a dollar sign ($) after the identifier.

2. Substrings may be specified using a selector, containing the start position and length of the substring. If the length of the substring is not specified, it is assumed to be one.

3. All string variables must be declared in a DIM statement. For simple string variables, the maximum length of the string must be specified. For subscripted string variables, the number of strings and maximum length of a string must be given.

4. The following must be satisfied:
   1 ⟨= subscript ⟨= maximum number of strings
   1 ⟨= start position ⟨= string length
   1 ⟨= start position + substring length − 1 ⟨ = string length
   0 ⟨= substring length
   If not, a run-time error takes place.

5. If the arithmetic expression for ⟨index⟩, ⟨start position⟩ or ⟨substring length⟩ does not evaluate to an integer, rounding is applied.

6. The value of a string variable is zero ("") before a value has been assigned to it. The value of a substring with a substring length equal to zero is zero ("").

Real numbers.

Real numbers may be used as operands in arithmetic expressions. Real numbers may be expressed as integers, decimal numbers, or in exponential form.

Format

⟨real number⟩ : : = ⟨decimal number⟩ [⟨exponent part⟩]
⟨decimal number⟩ : : = ⟨integer⟩ ¦ ⟨integer⟩ . ⟨integer⟩
⟨integer⟩. ¦ .⟨integer⟩
⟨exponent part⟩ : : = E [+ ¦—] ⟨integer⟩
⟨integer⟩ : : = ⟨digit⟩   ⟨digit⟩
⟨digit⟩ : : = 0 ¦ 1 ¦ 2 ¦ 3 ¦ 4 ¦ 5 ¦ 6 ¦ 7 ¦ 8 ¦ 9

Notes.

1. A real number may not contain space characters.
2. The range of real numbers is not part of the standard.

Identifiers.

Identifiers are used to designate entities in a COMAL 80 program.

Format

⟨identifier⟩ : : = ⟨letter⟩ { ⟨letter⟩ ¦ ⟨digit⟩ ¦ _ }
⟨letter⟩ : : = ⟨ ASCII letters plus national characters ⟩

Notes.

1. Identifiers may contain at least 16 characters.
2. Both capital and small letters may be used. No distinction is made between a capital and a small letter.
3. Space characters are not allowed within an identifier.
4. The character just before and after an identifier must neither be a letter nor a digit.
5. Identifiers must not be the same as the reserved keywords or names of system functions.
6. Identifiers designate entities in a program. The following types exist:
   - simple variables
   - subscripted variables
   - simple string variables
   - subscripted string variables
   - label names
   - procedure names
   - formal parameters.
7. An identifier may designate only one entity in a program.

Keywords.

COMAL 80 contains a number of keywords with a fixed meaning.

Format

⟨keyword⟩ : : = AND | CASE | DATA | DIM | DIV | DO |
ELSE | END | ENDCASE | ENDIF | ENDPROC |
ENDWHILE | EXEC | FOR | GOTO | IF | IN |
INPUT | LET | MOD | NEXT | NOT | OF |
OR | OTHERWISE | OUTPUT | PRINT | PROC |
READ | REF | REPEAT | RESTORE | SELECT |
STEP | STOP | TAB | THEN | TO | UNTIL |
USING | WHEN | WHILE

Notes.

1. Keywords may be typed using both capital and small letters.
2. A keyword must not be used as an identifier for other entities.
3. Space characters are not allowed in a keyword.
4. The character just before and after a keyword must neither be a letter nor a digit.

Appendix 5

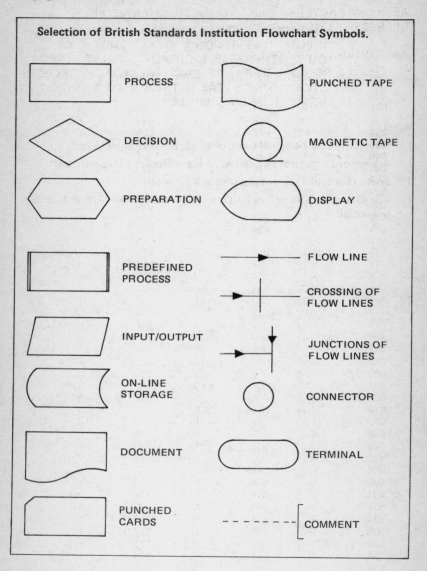

Selection of British Standards Institution Flowchart Symbols.

	PROCESS		PUNCHED TAPE
	DECISION		MAGNETIC TAPE
	PREPARATION		DISPLAY
	PREDEFINED PROCESS		FLOW LINE
			CROSSING OF FLOW LINES
	INPUT/OUTPUT		JUNCTIONS OF FLOW LINES
	ON-LINE STORAGE		CONNECTOR
	DOCUMENT		TERMINAL
	PUNCHED CARDS		COMMENT

Appendix 6

ASCII CHARACTER CODES AND EBCDIC CHARACTER
REPRESENTATION.

ASCII CHARACTER CODES.

DECIMAL	CHAR.	DECIMAL	CHAR.	DECIMAL	CHAR.
000	NUL	043	+	086	V
001	SOH	044	,	087	W
002	STX	045	—	088	X
003	ETX	046	.	089	Y
004	EOT	047	/	090	Z
005	ENQ	048	0	091	[
006	ACK	049	1	092	\
007	BEL	050	2	093	]
008	BS	051	3	094	↑
009	HT	052	4	095	↓
010	LF	053	5	096	@
011	VT	054	6	097	a
012	FF	055	7	098	b
013	CR	056	8	099	c
014	SO	057	9	100	d
015	SI	058	:	101	e
016	DLE	059	;	102	f
017	DC1	060	<	103	g
018	DC2	061	=	104	h
019	DC3	062	>	105	i
020	DC4	063	?	106	j
021	NAK	064	'	107	k
022	SYN	065	A	108	l
023	ETB	066	B	109	m
024	CAN	067	C	110	n
025	EM	068	D	111	o
026	SUB	069	E	112	p
027	ESC	070	F	113	q
028	S	071	G	114	r
029	GS	072	H	115	s
030	RS	073	I	116	t
031	US	074	J	117	u
032	SP	075	K	118	v
033	!	076	L	119	w
034	"	077	M	120	x
035	#	078	N	121	y
036	$	079	O	122	z
037	%	080	P	123	{
038	&	081	Q	124	¦
039	'	082	R	125	}
040	(	083	S	126	~
041	)	084	T	127	DEL
042	*	085	U		

ASCII CHARACTER SET (7-BIT CODE)

$b_3 b_2 b_1 b_0$ $b_6 b_5 b_4$

$b_3 b_2 b_1 b_0$	000	001	010	011	100	101	110	111
0000	NUL	DLE	SP	0	'	P	@	p
0001	SOH	DC1	!	1	A	Q	a	g
0010	STX	DC2	''	2	B	R	b	r
0011	ETX	DC3	#	3	C	S	c	s
0100	EOT	DC4	$	4	D	T	d	t
0101	ENQ	NAK	%	5	E	U	e	u
0110	ACK	SYN	&	6	F	V	f	v
0111	BEL	ETB	'	7	G	W	g	w
1000	BS	CAN	(	8	H	X	h	x
1001	HT	EM	)	9	I	Y	i	y
1010	LF	SUB	*	:	J	Z	j	z
1011	VT	ESC	+	;	K	[	k	{
1100	FF	S	,	<	L	\	l	:
1101	CR	GS	—	=	M	]	m	}
1110	SO	RS	•	>	N	↑	n	~
1111	SI	US	/	?	O	↓	o	DEL

Control characters:

NULL	— Null/idle	DLE	— Data link escape (CC)
SOH	— Start of heading (CC)	DC1	
STX	— Start of text (CC)	DC2	— Device controls
ETX	— End of text (CC)	DC3	
EOT	— End of transmission (CC)	DC4	— Device control (stop)
ENQ	— Enquiry (CC)	NAK	— Negative acknowledge (CC)
ACK	— Acknowledge (CC)	SYN	— Synchronous idle CC
BEL	— Audible or attention signal	ETB	— End of transmission block (CC)
BS	— Backspace (FE)		
HT	— Horizontal tabulation (punch card skip) (FE)	C	— Cancel
		EM	— End of medium
LF	— Line feed (FE)	SS	— Start of special sequence
VT	— Vertical tabulation (FE)	ESC	— Escape
FF	— Form feed (FE)	FS	— File separator (IS)
CR	— Carriage return (FE)	GS	— Group separator (IS)
SO	— Shift out	RS	— Record separator (IS)
SI	— Shift in	US	— Unit separator (IS)
		DEL	— Delete

Note: b_i represents the *ith* bit position.

EBCDIC CHARACTER REPRESENTATION.

EBCDIC	BIT CONFIGURATION	EBCDIC	BIT CONFIGURATION
NUL	0000 0000	PN	0011 0100
SOH	0000 0001	RS	0011 0101
STX	0000 0010	UC	0011 0110
ETX	0000 0011	EOT	0011 0111
PF	0000 0100		0011 1000
HT	0000 0101		0011 1001
LC	0000 0110		0011 1010
DEL	0000 0111	CU3	0011 1011
	0000 1000	DC4	0011 1100
RLF	0000 1001	NAK	0011 1101
SMM	0000 1010		0011 1110
VT	0000 1011	SUB	0011 1111
FF	0000 1100	SP	0100 0000
CR	0000 1101		0100 0001
SO	0000 1110		0100 0010
SI	0000 1111		0100 0011
DLE	0001 0000		0100 0100
DC1	0001 0001		0100 0101
DC2	0001 0010		0100 0110
TM	0001 0011		0100 0111
RES	0001 0100		0100 1000
NL	0001 0101		0100 1001
BS	0001 0110	c [	0100 1010
IL	0001 0111	.	0100 1011
CAN	0001 1000	<	0100 1100
EM	0001 1001	(	0100 1101
CC	0001 1010	+	0100 1110
CU1	0001 1011	I	0100 1111
IFS	0001 1100	&	0101 0000
IGS	0001 1101		0101 0001
IRS	0001 1110		0101 0010
IUS	0001 1111		0101 0011
DS	0010 0000		0101 0100
SOS	0010 0001		0101 0101
FS	0010 0010		0101 0110
	0010 0011		0101 0111
BYP	0010 0100		0101 1000
LF	0010 0101		0101 1001
ETB	0010 0110	!]	0101 1010
ESC	0010 0111	$	0101 1011
	0010 1000	*	0101 1100
	0010 1001	)	0101 1101
SM	0010 1010	;	0101 1110
CU2	0010 1011	¬	0101 1111
	0010 1100	−	0110 0000
ENQ	0010 1101	/	0110 0001
ACK	0010 1110		0110 0010
BEL	0010 1111		0110 0011
	0011 0000		0110 0100
	0011 0001		0110 0101
SYN	0011 0010		0110 0110
	0011 0011		0110 0111

EBCDIC	BIT CONFIGURATION
	0110 1000
	0110 1001
7/12	0110 1010
,	0110 1011
%	0110 1100
—	0110 1101
>	0110 1110
?	0110 1111
	0111 0000
	0111 0001
	0111 0010
	0111 0011
	0111 0100
	0111 0101
	0111 0110
	0111 0111
	0111 1000
6/0	0111 1001
:	0111 1010
#	0111 1011
@	0111 1100
	0111 1101
=	0111 1110
''	0111 1111
	1000 0000
a	1000 0001
b	1000 0010
c	1000 0011
d	1000 0100
e	1000 0101
f	1000 0110
g	1000 0111
h	1000 1000
i	1000 1001
	1000 1010
	1000 1011
	1000 1100
	1000 1101
	1000 1110
	1000 1111
	1001 0000
j	1001 0001
k	1001 0010
l	1001 0011
m	1001 0100
n	1001 0101
o	1001 0110
p	1001 0111
q	1001 1000
r	1001 1001
	1001 1010
	1001 1011
	1001 1100

EBCDIC	BIT CONFIGURATION
	1001 1101
	1001 1110
	1001 1111
	1010 0000
—	1010 0001
s	1010 0010
t	1010 0011
u	1010 0100
v	1010 0101
w	1010 0110
x	1010 0111
y	1010 1000
z	1010 1001
	1010 1010
	1010 1011
	1010 1100
	1010 1101
	1010 1110
	1010 1111
	1011 0000
	1011 0001
	1011 0010
	1011 0011
	1011 0100
	1011 0101
	1011 0110
	1011 0111
	1011 1000
	1011 1001
	1011 1010
	1011 1011
	1011 1100
	1011 1101
	1011 1110
	1011 1111
PZ 7/11	1100 0000
A	1100 0001
B	1100 0010
C	1100 0011
D	1100 0100
E	1100 0101
F	1100 0110
G	1100 0111
H	1100 1000
I	1100 1001
	1100 1010
	1100 1011
⌐	1100 1100
	1100 1101
⊔	1100 1110
	1100 1111
MZ 7/13	1101 0000
J	1101 0001

K	1101 0010		W	1110 0110
L	1101 0011		X	1110 0111
M	1101 0100		Y	1110 1000
N	1101 0101		Z	1110 1001
O	1101 0110			1110 1010
P	1101 0111			1110 1011
Q	1101 1000		H	1110 1100
R	1101 1001			1110 1101
	1101 1010			1110 1110
	1101 1011			1110 1111
⊢	1101 1100		0	1111 0000
	1101 1101		1	1111 0001
	1101 1110		2	1111 0010
	1101 1111		3	1111 0011
RM 5/12	1110 0000		4	1111 0100
	1110 0001		5	1111 0101
S	1110 0010		6	1111 0110
T	1110 0011		7	1111 0111
U	1110 0100		8	1111 1000
V	1110 0101		9	1111 1001
W	1110 0110		⇌	1111 1010
X	1110 0111			1111 1011
Y	1110 1000			1111 1100
Z	1110 1001			1111 1101
	1110 1010			1111 1110
	1110 1011		EO	1111 1111

Appendix 7

SCHEMES OF WORK

The reader will probably be aware that BASIC Programming is one of the most comprehensive texts on the market today. Since the book covers the programming requirements for many computing examinations the following tables are a guide to those readers who wish to abstract from the text the material relevant to their particular level of study or tuition.

The schemes that are suggested should also be supplemented by the appropriate examination questions found in Appendix II.

1. *BASIC Programming as a suitable text for the preparation of C.S.E. in Computer Studies — Recommended scheme of work.*

CHAPTER	QUESTIONS 1	2	3	4	5	6	7	8
2	X	X						
3	X	X		X				
4	X		X	X	X		X	
5	X	X	X	X	X	X	X	X
6	X	X	X(a)	X	X			
7	X	X	X	X	X	X		
8	X	X	X	X	X	X		
12	X		X		X			

2. *BASIC Programming as a suitable text for the preparation of 'O' level G.C.E. Computer Studies. Recommended scheme of work.*

| CHAPTER | \multicolumn{10}{c}{Q U E S T I O N S} |
	1	2	3	4	5	6	7	8	9	10
1										
2	X	X	X	X	X					
3	X	X	X	X	X	X	X	X		
4	X	X	X	X	X	X	X	X		
5	X	X	X	X	X	X	X	X		
6	X	X	X	X	X	X	X			
7	X	X	X	X	X	X	X			
8	X	X	X	X	X	X	X	X		
9	X	X	X	X	X	X	X	X		
10	X	X		X			X	X	X	X
11					X					
12	X	X	X	X	X	X	X			

3. *BASIC Programming as a suitable text for a typical college course in programming for non-mathematicians to a standard adequate for 'A' G.C.E., OND/C in business studies, City and Guilds 746/746 programming papers and first year undergraduate level.*

CHAPTERS	\multicolumn{9}{c}{QUESTIONS}

CHAPTERS	1	2	3	4	5	6	7	8	9
1									
2	X			X	X				
3				X		X	X		
4	X		X	X	X				
5	X	X	X	X		X			
6		X		X	X	X			
7	X	X	X	X	X	X	X		
8	X	X	X		X	X	X	X	
9	X	X	X		X			X	
10									
11	X	X	X		X				
12	X	X	X	X	X	X	X		
13	X	X	X	X	X				
14									
15									
16	X	X	X	X	X				
17									
18									
19									
20			X		X	X	X	X	X

4. *BASIC Programming as a suitable text for the preparation of 'A' level G.C.E. Computer Science for the student with a mathematical bias. Recommended scheme of work.*

CHAPTERS	QUESTIONS													
	1	2	3	4	5	6	7	8	9	10	11	12	13	14
1														
2	X	X	X		X									
3	X	X	X		X		X	X						
4	X	X	X	X	X	X	X	X						
5	X	X	X	X	X	X	X	X						
6	X		X		X		X							
7	X	X	X	X	X		X(a)							
8	X	X	X	X		X			X	X				
9	X	X	X	X		X	X		X					
10	X	X	X	X	X	X	X	X	X	X				
11		X		X	X									
12		X						X	X	X	X	X	X	X
13	X	X	X		X			X						
14														
15														
16			X		X									
17														
18														
19														
20	X	X	X	X										

Index

Computer Science

C.S. French

This manual is now in use as text for courses leading to the examination of GCE 'A' level Computer Science, BCS Part 1, City and Guilds and for BEC/TEC.

"... the coverage is excellent, with plenty of examples and questions ... a good buy".

Review extract NATFE.

"Data Processing and Computer Science have a great deal in common, but also possess their exclusive areas of knowledge. A reader wishing to find an introductory work on data processing is well served by the number of excellent texts available, including one from this publisher. Hitherto the same had not been true of computer science, a situation now remedied by this publication ... the text is eminently readable and is supplemented by useful illustrations, charts, tables and graphs. Each chapter has a helpful selection of self-testing questions to which answers are provided at the end of the book ... highly recommended".

Review extract AUTA

"May I congratulate your company and the Author on the publication of 'Computer Science'. At last a down to earth yet authorative summary of GCE and City and Guilds topics".

Lecturer

"I have recently been informed that I have passed the British Computer Society Part 1 examinations. My success was undoubtedly due to the fact that I used your publication 'Computer Science' during my course of study.

Before I read your book many aspects of computing remained quite vague. However, your treatment of the subject matter and style of writing helped to clear up all the 'hazy' points.

May I congratulate you on what is an excellent piece of work and is without doubt the most useful textbook I have ever used".

Student

Contents

The author is a Senior Lecturer at Hatfield Polytechnic and has spent a number of years teaching on a wide variety of computer courses. He is also the author of "Computer Studies".

448 pages: 1980: ISBN 0 905435 13 3

Computer Studies

C.S. French

This manual aims to satisfy the 'O' level, and equivalent Computer Studies text book requirement, and follows the style of Carl French's highly successful 'A' level Computer Science text first published in 1980.

Apart from GCE 'O' level "Computer Studies" the text is eminently suitable for CSE "Computer Studies", BEC General Option "Elements of Data Processing", BEC National Option "Computer Studies", RSA examinations in Computer Studies and TEC units in computer technology.

Included are many examination questions and answers and assignments for course work.

Contents

Introduction
  Modern Computers, their General
  Characteristics
  Computer types and their origins
  Computer elements and operation
Data, Information. Language and
Communication
  Data Types and Data Representation
  Number Bases
  Data Structures and Files
  Flowcharts and Program Design
  Operations (Arithmetic and Logic)
Hardware Features and Use
  From Manual Methods to Modern Systems
  Input devices, media, methods and uses
  Output devices, media, methods and uses
  Storage devices, media, methods and uses
  Choice of methods and media
The CPU and its Operation
  Elements of the CPU
  Program writing and execution
  Arithmetic
  Logic and Control
  Modern system architecture

Software and Programming
  Software Types
  Program development
  Low Level Languages (Features and
  Programming)
  Computational Methods (Programming
  Techniques)
  High Level Languages (Program Structure)
  Operating Systems (Purpose and Facilities)
Practical Data Processing
  Batch Processing by example
  Interactive Systems by example
Applications
  Batch, Real-Time, Time Sharing, Bureaux
  Application Areas (Science, Dp, Engineering etc)
  Organisation and Control Resources
The Social Aspects
  Privacy, Jobs etc.
  Computers and Society
Appendices
  Revision Test Questions, with and without
  answers
  Answers to questions at chapter ends and
  revision test questions
  Course Work and Projects
  Details omitted from the text for the sake of
  clarity
  Assignments — suitable for BEC courses

The author is a Senior Lecturer at Hatfield Polytechnic and is also author of "Computer Science".

Note to Lecturers — Answer Supplement available which contains answers to questions at end of Chapters, answers to revision tests and Assignments (see inside front cover of catalogue).

400 pages (approx): June 1982: ISBN 0 905435 24 9